Exploring Natural Language
Working with the British Component of the International Corpus of English

Varieties of English Around the World

General Series

Volume G29

Exploring Natural Language: Working with the British Component of the International Corpus of English
Gerald Nelson, Sean Wallis and Bas Aarts

Exploring Natural Language

Working with the British Component of the International Corpus of English

Gerald Nelson
University of Hong Kong

Sean Wallis
University College London

Bas Aarts
University College London

John Benjamins Publishing Company
Amsterdam / Philadelphia

∞ ™ The paper used in this publication meets the minimum requirements of American National Standard for Information Sciences – Permanence of Paper for Printed Library Materials, ANSI Z39.48-1984.

CIP-data for this book is available from the Library of Congress

ISBN 90 272 4888 5 (Eur.) / 1 58811 270 5 (US) (Hb; alk. paper)
ISBN 90 272 4889 3 (Eur.) / 1 58811 271 3 (US) (Pb; alk. paper)

John Benjamins Publishing Co. · P.O. Box 36224 · 1020 ME Amsterdam · The Netherlands
John Benjamins North America · P.O. Box 27519 · Philadelphia PA 19118-0519 · USA

CONTENTS

SERIES EDITOR'S INTRODUCTION

With this volume, a new sub-series is being launched within the *Varieties of English Around the World* series, consisting of volumes that serve as handbooks for the various corpora in the International Corpus of English (ICE) project. As is well known, ICE is a large-scale collaborative research effort, the aim of which is to provide comparable machine-readable corpora of spoken and written English from countries which count as "English-speaking" in some sense but which in fact are culturally and linguistically as diverse as Great Britain, Australia, India, Singapore, Hong Kong, Nigeria, or Fiji, to name but a few. It has been shown repeatedly that structural differences between various national varieties of English, the linguistic correlates of the nativization of the language, as it were, are largely of a highly inconspicuous nature, with alternative preferences for subtle syntactic choices (*e.g.*, varying verb complementation patterns) gradually evolving. Obviously, a set of comparable text databases like the ones envisioned in the ICE project will be a first-rate research tool for the documentation and investigations of emerging differences in usage, the evolution of New Varieties of English in a strictly linguistic perspective.

Given this overlap in their subject matter, there should be an intrinsic affinity between the concerns of ICE as an international research effort and *VEAW* as a book series devoted to the scholarly study of varieties of English. Thus, in a letter to all ICE regional project directors, dated 17 February 1998, I proposed that descriptive handbooks on individual projects might be published in *VEAW* (subject to the usual reviewing process, of course). I suggested that these volumes should contain some background information on the nature and the compilation process of a given corpus in the light of its respective cultural context; technical information required by future corpus users in investigations of their own; possibly sample texts; and sample analyses, providing insights into the nature of the varieties concerned and illustrating possible uses of the corpus. Responses have been extremely supportive, and it is anticipated that some such volumes will be submitted and published in due course, as more ICE subcorpora are becoming available. The present volume, covering the British component of ICE, the first one to be completed and thus a model case for all later ones, is the first product resulting from these contacts.

Given this background, the present volume differs from earlier *VEAW* volumes in some respects. It is both a handbook of ICE-GB as the first finished corpus and a manual to the software that has been written specifically to facilitate complex syntactic analyses in this corpus environment — currently to investigate spoken and written British English as represented in ICE-GB; some day, hopefully, allowing applications to corpora of New Varieties of English and, on that basis, comparative research into grammatical variation from one variety of English to another. While also teaching us something about British English, especially the grammar of spoken BrE, this volume primarily introduces ICECUP, an exciting, remarkably sophisticated software tool to make novel qualitative and quantitative analyses of syntactic patterns possible. It is to be hoped that the tagging and parsing procedures described in this book will be applied to future ICE corpora as well to allow comparative analyses of grammar — a strategy which should open up an enormous research potential.

Edgar W. Schneider

Editor, *VEAW*

University of Regensburg

FOREWORD

This volume will be an essential companion for all linguists using the International Corpus of English (ICE). But as well as a companion, a welcome introduction.

It directly relates, of course, only to the British component: five hundred 2000-word samples ("texts") of British educated speech and writing of the 1990s. But the researchers in UCL's Survey of English Usage had always envisaged the British element of the 21-nation enterprise as not just a "pilot project" (p.2) but as the model and pace setter. Even so, it is far from being a solely London-led achievement: there has been a very great deal of productive international collaboration in the planning, design, execution, and analysis – most notably through the contribution of the TOSCA Research Group in Nijmegen.

The book provides a history of the project, itemises (in Appendix 2) the sources of the language samples, and presents alphabetic lists (in Chapter 2) of the 21 word-classes and 68 grammatical categories (each carefully explained and illustrated) to which the analysis relates. But the heart of the book is Chapters 3 through 7, which is a step-by-step exposition of the "Utility Program" (ICECUP): no easy read, in all conscience, but made accessible and attractive by direct address to the users, with sympathetic anticipation of any difficulties they may have.

All in all, a major milestone in the development not only of ICE but of computational linguistics itself.

Randolph Quirk

February 2002
University College London

PREFACE

This book represents the culmination of a major research effort initiated in the early 1990s by the late Sidney Greenbaum at the Survey of English Usage, University College London. In this book we describe the structure and grammatical annotation of the *British Component of the International Corpus of English* (ICE-GB). One of the major strengths of this corpus is that it contains some 600,000 words of spoken English which are fully tagged and parsed.

ICE-GB is proving to be a popular research tool. Even before it was released in 1998, the ICE-GB corpus was extensively used in linguistic research. Most notably, the *Oxford English Grammar* (Greenbaum 1996b) drew heavily on the grammatically tagged version of ICE-GB, and used many citations from the corpus to exemplify grammatical points. ICE-GB was also used, though to a lesser extent, in the writing of the *Internet Grammar of English* (IGE), an on-line undergraduate course in English grammar which was constructed at the Survey of English Usage in 1996-8 (Aarts, Nelson and Buckley 1999). (IGE is available from http://www.ucl.ac.uk/internet-grammar/, and was funded by the Joint Information Systems Committee, grant JTAP 2/247.)

In 1994-6, a subcorpus of 42 texts from ICE-GB was used in research to investigate the patterns of clause relationships in spoken and written English. An important aspect of that research was the notion of clause complexity itself, an issue on which there has been some dispute in recent years (Greenbaum and Nelson 1995a, 1995b, 1996; 1998; Greenbaum, Nelson and Weitzman 1996).

In 1999, a research project entitled *Subordination in Spoken and Written English: A Corpus-based Study* began at the Survey of English Usage which used the parsed ICE-GB corpus as its main dataset.

In 2000, the Survey received funding to conduct large-scale corpus-based research into the grammar and usage of English Noun Phrases. (This project was funded by the Economic and Social Research Council (ESRC); grant number R000271083. The project home page is at http://www.ucl.ac.uk/english-usage/subord/.)

ICE-GB has been used to explore a wide range of issues in grammar. Here we mention a selection of studies: Fang (1995) on infinitives, García-Gonzálvez (1996) on complex-transitive complementation, Ljung (1996) on adverbial clauses, Nelson (1997a) on cleft constructions, Nelson (1997b) on lexical differences between speech and writing, Kaltenböck (1998) on extraposition in English discourse, Nelson and Greenbaum (1999) on elliptical clauses, Depraetere and Reed (2000) on the present progressive, Declerck and Reed (2000, 2001) on conditional clauses, Lavelle (2000) on nominalisations and related constructions, Meunier (2000) on NP complexity in advanced learner writing, Spinillo (2000) on determiners, Capelle (2001) on *out of* as a preposition, Denison (2001) on gradience and linguistic change, Holmes (2001) on sexism in language, and Taglicht (2001) on the adverb *actually*. Among the first studies using ICE-GB's sound material is Wichmann (2001). For a complete listing of studies using the 'SEU Corpus' (the Spoken part of the London-Lund Corpus, LLC) and ICE-GB please consult the on-line *SEU Bibliography*.[1]

The real value of the ICE corpora lies in their mutual compatibility, as the title of the series in which this book appears makes clear, and the overall aim of ICE has always been to enable researchers to compare varieties of English with each other. Many of the component corpora are not yet generally available for research, but already the ICE project has generated a number of comparative studies. Collins (1996) looked at *get*-passives in ICE-GB and ICE-Australia, as well as in several other datasets. Peters (1996) used the same two ICE components to examine comparative structures. In Meyer (1996), data from ICE-GB and ICE-USA were compared in a study of coordination ellipsis.

Comparative studies may of course be pursued with non-ICE corpora. Leech (2000) contrasted ICE-GB diachronically with the LLC in a paper on recent language change. The SEU received funding in 2002 to construct a parallel corpus of spoken English containing selected material from the LLC and ICE-GB which will be parsed in a directly comparable way. (This project is funded by the ESRC; grant no R000239643, with a home page at http://www.ucl.ac.uk/english-usage/diachronic/.) This corpus will be a benchmark for studies of recent grammatical change in spoken English, and will be distributed with ICECUP.

We hope that in the coming years a great deal of new research will be carried out using ICE-GB and the other ICE components as they become available. We would be grateful if you could notify us of any your publications based on ICE-GB, so that we can regularly update our on-line Bibliography. We also welcome users' comments on any aspect of ICE-GB or ICECUP.[2]

It would not have been possible to get to where we are now without a great deal of assistance from a number of organizations and people.

We gratefully acknowledge support for the initial part of the ICE-GB project from the ESRC (grant number R000232077), The Leverhulme Trust (grant number F134BG) and the Sasakawa Foundation. The development of the corpus query system was also funded by the ESRC (grant number

[1] The Survey Bibliography can be found at http://www.ucl.ac.uk/english-usage/archives/seu-biblio.htm. Contributions to the Bibliography, and other comments may be emailed to ucleseu@ucl.ac. uk, or mailed to the Survey of English Usage, University College London, Gower St., London WC1E 6BT, UK.

[2] There is an electronic feedback form for ICE-GB and ICECUP on the web at http://www. ucl.ac.uk/english-usage/ice-gb/feedback.htm, or you can simply email icecup@ucl.ac.uk.

R000222598). The final stages of parsing were carried out using the Survey Parser, which was developed by Alex Fang and supported by the Engineering and Physical Sciences Research Council (EPSRC; grant number GR/K75033). Thanks are also due to the British Academy for a small research grant (grant number SG-AN25308/APN28749) that provided financial assistance for the writing of this book.

We are especially indebted to the TOSCA Research Group at the University of Nijmegen, under the directorship of Jan Aarts, who provided tagging and parsing software. In particular, we wish to thank Nelleke Oostdijk and Hans van Halteren.

We are indebted to the following people who worked on the annotation of the corpus at various stages: Celine Bijleveld, Judith Broadbent, Justin Buckley, Brian Davies, Ken Fletcher, Yanka Gavin, Marie Gibney, Howard Gregory, Jasper Holmes, Gunther Kaltenböck, Ine Mortelmans, Yibin Ni, the late René Quinault (who passed away just before we sent this book to press), And Rosta, the late Oonagh Sayce, Laura Tollfree, Ian Warner, Jonathan White and Vlad Zegarac. We owe a particular debt of gratitude to Marie Gibney for her administrative support, to Jonathan White for his work in preparing Chapter 2, and to Evelien Keizer for comments on draft chapters of the book.

For advice and assistance in collecting the corpus, we thank Brian Bennett, Mark Huckvale, Robert Ilson and Sue Peppe. For technical support, we thank Professor John Campbell, Tony Dodd, David Elkan, Isaac Hallegua, Neil Morgenstern, Richard Wilson, and especially Nick Porter and Akiva Quinn. We would also like to thank a number of linguists who performed an essential service as beta-testers for the corpus and software. These include Chuck Meyer, Tom Lavelle, Roberta Fachinetti and Hilde Hasselgård.

The sources of individual texts in the corpus are acknowledged in Appendix 2. They can also be viewed in ICECUP's Corpus Map. Finally, we wish to thank the following organisations and institutions which made extensive contributions to the project:

Audio Visual Centre, UCL
BBC Copyright & Artists' Rights Department
British Museum Board
Careers Service, UCL
Channel 4 Television
Faculty of Arts, UCL
HMSO
Independent Television
The House of Commons
The Royal Courts of Justice, London
The Royal Society of Arts
Staff Development & Training Unit, UCL
UCL Students' Union

Gerald Nelson
Sean Wallis
Bas Aarts

February 2002
University College London

PART 1:
Introducing the corpus

1. INTRODUCING ICE-GB

1.1 Aims and background

The International Corpus of English (ICE) project was initiated in 1988 by the late Sidney Greenbaum, the then Director of the Survey of English Usage, University College London. In a brief notice in *World Englishes,* Greenbaum pointed out that grammatical studies had been greatly facilitated by the availability of two computerized corpora of printed English, the Brown Corpus of American English, and the LOB (Lancaster/Oslo-Bergen) Corpus of British English. Greenbaum continued:

> We should now be thinking of extending the scope for computerized comparative studies in three ways: (1) to sample standard varieties from other countries where English is the first language, for example Canada and Australia; (2) to sample national varieties from countries where English is an official additional language, for example India and Nigeria; and (3) to include spoken and manuscript English as well as printed English. (Greenbaum 1988)

In response, linguists from around the world came forward to discuss Greenbaum's proposal, and ultimately to put it into effect (Greenbaum 1991). The project soon became known as the International Corpus of English (ICE), and was coordinated by Greenbaum until 1996. From 1996 to 2001, ICE was coordinated by Charles Meyer, University of Massachusetts-Boston. It is now coordinated by Gerald Nelson, the University of Hong Kong. At the time of writing, the ICE project involves research teams in each of the countries or regions shown in Table 1.

Table 1: Components of the ICE project.

Australia	Malawi
Cameroon	New Zealand
Canada	Nigeria
Fiji	Philippines
Ghana	Sierra Leone
Great Britain	Singapore
Hong Kong	South Africa
India	Sri Lanka
Ireland	Tanzania
Jamaica	USA
Kenya	

Each ICE team is compiling – or has already compiled – a one million-word corpus of their own national or regional variety of English. Crucially, each team follows a common corpus design and a common annotation scheme, in order to ensure maximum comparability between the components (Nelson 1996). The long-term aim of ICE is to produce up to twenty one million-word corpora, each syntactically analysed according to a common parsing scheme, and supplied with the retrieval software, *ICECUP*.

Each ICE corpus samples the English of adults (age 18 or over) who have been educated through the medium of English to at least the end of secondary schooling. Furthermore, each component corpus is grammatically analysed using a common grammatical annotation scheme. For many of the participating countries, ICE represents the first systematic attempt to compile a corpus of the national variety, though mention should be made here of some notable earlier corpora, including the *Kolhapur Corpus of Indian English* (Shastri 1988), the *Wellington Corpus of Spoken New Zealand English* (Holmes 1995), and the *Macquarie Corpus of Written Australian English* (Green and Peters 1991).

ICE-GB is the British component of ICE.[1] It was compiled and grammatically analysed at the Survey of English Usage, University College London, between 1990 and 1998. Version 1, which is fully parsed, was released on CD-ROM in 1998, together with the dedicated retrieval software, ICECUP (the *ICE Corpus Utility Program*, see Part 2). ICE-GB may be ordered via the Survey's website (http://www.ucl.ac.uk/english-usage/), where a free sample corpus of ten texts, together with ICECUP, is available for download.

While the ICE-GB corpus is just one among many ICE components, the ICE-GB project has had a wider significance. From the start, the project was designed to serve as a pilot project for the other ICE teams. As well as compiling ICE-GB, the role of the Survey team has been to establish, implement, and document the various stages in compiling and analysing ICE corpora. These stages are:

1. Text collection
2. Optical scanning and transcription
3. Applying structural markup
4. Part-of-speech tagging
5. Tag selection
6. Syntactic marking
7. Parsing
8. Parse selection
9. Alignment of tagged and parsed versions
10. Cross-sectional checking
11. Speech digitization

During the stages of grammatical analysis – chiefly, part-of-speech tagging and parsing – the Survey collaborated with the TOSCA Research Group at the University of Nijmegen, which developed the tagging and parsing software (see Sections 1.6 and 1.7 below). The completion of ICE-GB means that each stage

[1] The initial period of the ICE-GB project was funded in part by grant R000 23 2077 from the Economic and Social Research Council.

has now been fully documented, so the other ICE teams have clear guidelines on how to proceed.

The Survey has also been involved in software development for ICE. This effort has produced, most importantly, ICECUP, the retrieval software supplied with parsed ICE corpora and is documented in Part 2. In addition, it has produced *ICETree II*, a program which allows users to view, build, and edit syntactic trees (Wallis and Nelson 1997), *TagSelect*, which assists in the selection of the correct part-of-speech tags, and *ICEMark*, which enables users to insert syntactic markers into the tagged text (Quinn and Porter 1996).

1.2 Corpus design

ICE-GB contains 500 texts of approximately 2,000 words each. Many of these texts are composite, that is, they consist of two or more different samples of the same type which have been combined to make up a 2,000-word 'text'. In the category of business letters, for instance, a total of 198 individual letters have been included. We refer to these individual samples as 'subtexts'. Table 2 provides a summary of the composition of the ICE-GB corpus. Appendix 2 provides a complete list of text sources.

With just over one million words, ICE-GB is small in comparison with the *British National Corpus* (BNC: Aston and Burnard 1998). The BNC contains 100 million words, and samples British English from approximately the same period. However, ICE-GB was designed primarily as a resource for syntactic studies, not for lexical studies. Unlike the BNC, every text unit ('sentence') in ICE-GB has been syntactically parsed at function and category level, and each unit is presented in the form of a syntactic tree. The 83,394 trees in the corpus represent an invaluable resource for studies of the syntax of contemporary British English.

The texts in ICE-GB date from 1990 to 1993 inclusive. This means that the printed texts were originally published, and the spoken texts originally recorded, during this period. The corpus does not include reprints, second or later editions, or transcripts of repeat broadcasts. For handwritten material, such as letters and essays, these dates refer to the date of composition.

All authors and speakers are British. This means that they were born in Great Britain, that is, England, Scotland, or Wales. In a small number of cases, we have relaxed this criterion to include those who were born elsewhere, but moved to Britain at an early age.

In selecting the texts for ICE-GB, we did not use the language that they contain as a criterion for inclusion. The corpus is not based on any prior notion of what constitutes "standard" or "educated" British English. Instead, we selected the informants – the speakers and the writers. We did this on the basis of the educational level that they had reached, setting a second-level education as our minimum requirement. This means that all the informants in the corpus

Table 2: The composition of ICE-GB: summary statistics.

	Spoken	Written	TOTAL
Number of words	637,562	423,702	1,061,264
Number of 2,000-word texts	300	200	500
Number of individual samples	447	554	1,001
Average number of words per text	2,125	2,118	2,122
Average number of words per sample	1,426	764	1,060
Number of syntactic trees	59,460	23,934	83,394
Average number of trees per text	198	119	166
Average number of trees per sample	133	43	83

have completed second-level schooling. This is a minimum requirement: many of the informants have received tertiary education as well. We adopted this approach because "educational level", unlike "educated English", is something which can be objectively measured. Having said that, we excluded certain types of text on other grounds: poetry, because it tends to be (consciously) syntactically idiosyncratic, and texts containing large amounts of foreign terms, quotations, mathematical formulae, tables, and diagrams.

The corpus is intended to be broadly representative of British English in the 1990s. We have therefore attempted to include as full a range as possible of the social variables which define the population. In each text category we have sampled both males and females, and included informants from a wide range of age groups. The dialogues, for instance, include male/female, female/female and male/male exchanges. Similarly, the speakers come from different age groups and from different regional backgrounds. However, we have not attempted to ensure that the proportions of these social variables are the same in the corpus as in the population as a whole. In students' writing, for instance, the vast majority of informants are in the 18-25 age group; to attempt to achieve a balance of all the age groups would seriously misrepresent this category. Similarly, the sexes are not equally represented in many professions such as technology, politics and law, so they do not produce equal amounts of discourse in these fields.

As Appendix 1 shows, the text categories are arranged in a hierarchical structure. The first major division is between the two modes of speech and writing. There are 300 spoken texts and 200 written, giving 600,000 words of speech and 400,000 words of writing. However, 50 of the spoken texts are scripted. These have some of the attributes of both spoken and written English, and as such provide an overlap between the two modes. For scripted texts, we used the spoken version as our source, not the script.

Each text in the corpus has been assigned a unique *textcode,* corresponding to its position in the hierarchy of text categories. Codes beginning with "S" (*e.g.*, S1A-001) denote spoken texts; codes beginning with

"W" (*e.g.*, W1A-001), denote written texts. Subtexts are denoted by a number following the textcode, for example, S1A-001-2 denotes the second subtext in S1A-001. The textcodes are listed in Appendix 1. For details of the source of each sample, see Appendix 2.

The spoken texts are divided into dialogues and monologues. The dialogues consist of both private and public types. This distinction is based on the settings in which the interactions take place. Private dialogues – direct conversations and telephone calls – are ones in which there is no audience. Though the exchange may be overheard, the speakers address only each other; in general they do not speak for the benefit of anyone else who may be present. The direct conversations were recorded in a wide variety of settings, including private homes, offices, and restaurants.

Public dialogues are specifically intended to be heard by others who are present and who are not participating in the exchange. Legal cross-examinations provide the clearest example of this type. In these texts, the speakers address an individual – a witness, a lawyer, or a judge – but the exchange is intended to be heard by everyone present in the courtroom. The legal cross-examinations were recorded in the Royal Courts of Justice, London, and include only proceedings which were conducted in the public arena. Other public dialogues in ICE-GB include parliamentary debates (from the House of Commons, Westminster), classroom lessons (mostly undergraduate seminars at University College London), and business transactions (business meetings, faculty meetings, and consultations with professionals).

In monologues, the chief distinction is between unscripted and scripted material. Unscripted texts include spontaneous commentaries, unscripted speeches (lectures), demonstrations and legal presentations. The spontaneous commentaries were recorded from radio and television. They are mostly commentaries on sports events – football, rugby, horse racing, snooker, boxing – though we have also included commentaries on ceremonial events, including the Trooping of the Colour (S2A-011), and various church services (S2A-019, S1A-020). In all of these texts, the commentators describe what they see as it occurs. They have no opportunity to prepare their speech, since they must react instantly to events over which they have no control.

The other unscripted monologues – lectures, demonstrations, legal presentations – permit some degree of planning. Speakers in these texts may refer from time to time to prepared notes, but the speech itself is extempore. Many of the lectures were recorded at University College London, though ICE-GB also contains lectures from the Royal Society of Arts, London (S2A-023, S2A-045), and public lectures delivered in the British Museum (S2A-022, S2A-024). In demonstrations, the speaker's objective is to demonstrate and describe an instrument, a procedure, or an object which is visible to the audience. This category includes demonstrations of a microscope (S2A-051), a laryngograph (S2A-056), and a software package (S2A-058-1). The legal presentations are monologues delivered by lawyers and judges during the course of trials at the Royal Courts of Justice, London.

Scripted texts are *fully* scripted. That is, they are lectures and talks in which the speaker reads verbatim from a prepared script. This category includes the Queen's Speech at the State Opening of Parliament (S2B-041-1), and a resignation speech by the Chancellor of the Exchequer, delivered to the House of Commons (S2B-050). Some of the scripted material was prepared specifically for broadcasting, including television documentary scripts (S2B-022, S2B-024, S2B-027), radio talks (S2B-025, S2B-028), and the Prime Minister's address to the nation at the outbreak of the Gulf War (S2B-030-1).

The written component of the corpus consists of 150 printed texts, and 50 non-printed texts. The two types differ not only in their mode of composition, but also in their intended readership. Printed material is written for a large, unrestricted audience that the writer does not know. In some cases, such as newspapers, popular writing, and fiction, this audience is the general public. The intended readership for non-printed material is considerably smaller. In the case of social letters, for instance, the readership is usually one individual who is personally known to the writer. Business letters are also addressed, usually, to one individual, though the addressee is not necessarily known personally to the writer. Student essays are generally written for one teacher, and examination scripts for one or two examiners (whose identity may not be known to the students).

In their modes of composition, the distinction between printed and non-printed material is also clear. Non-printed texts are a direct product of the individual writer. They are usually not edited by anyone else and, especially in the case of examination scripts, they afford the writer little time for revision. In contrast with this, writers of printed works are usually required to follow the house style of the publisher or newspaper for which they are writing. Printed material may have been edited by a number of different people, and the final version is often the product of several earlier revisions. Some non-printed texts, of course, are now regularly produced on wordprocessors (business letters, for example), and can benefit from the use of automatic spelling, grammar and style checkers. In all cases, these facts about the mode of composition have been recorded with each text.

The category of informational writing includes academic writing, non-academic writing, and press reportage. Academic writing is represented in ICE-GB by journal articles and extracts from academic monographs, and covers a wide variety of topics, including literary criticism, history, biology, economics, surgery, robotics, and astronomy. These texts were written by academics for academics. In contrast with this, non-academic writing has a wider and more varied readership, although the subject areas may still be quite specialised. This category includes texts on personal computers, hi-fi equipment, personal health, history, wildlife, and politics.

Press reportage includes leading articles, general domestic and foreign news, sports reports and business news. All the reports were written by staff reporters and journalists; we have been careful to exclude reports provided by international news agencies such as Reuters and Associated Press. The corpus contains a total of 84 individual press reports, taken from national, regional, and local newspapers. Sources include *The Times*, *The Guardian*, *The Daily Telegraph*, *The Yorkshire Post*, *The Western Mail*, *The Glasgow Herald*, and *The Wembley Observer*.

Instructional writing is divided into administrative/regulatory writing and publications dealing with skills and hobbies. Administrative/regulatory writing is corporate in origin. It is written on behalf of government departments or other administrative bodies and its chief aim is to convey information to the general public. In ICE-GB, this includes information about social security, health benefits, and student grants, together with instructions on how to apply for these. This category also includes printed regulations, including regulations for users of the British Library and regulations on the use of academic titles in the University of London. Texts in the skills/hobbies category also offer instruction, but these are directed towards a smaller and more specialised readership. They include car maintenance manuals, cookery books, and gardening manuals.

Press editorials have been distinguished from general news reports on the grounds that their main intention is to persuade rather than to inform. They are less directly tied to current events, and they afford the writer the opportunity to be discursive in a way that news journalism does not. In general, however, the editorials in ICE-GB have been taken from the same sources as the texts in the "press reportage" category.

The last category in the corpus is creative writing – novels and short stories. It includes a variety of fiction types, including science fiction, thrillers, and detective novels. In addition, we have included both narrative/descriptive prose and passages of dialogue.

1.3 Extra-corpus material

In spoken texts, utterances by non-British speakers have been included in the transcriptions in order to provide complete context.[2] We refer to these utterances as *extra-corpus text*. Extra-corpus text has not been analysed in any way. It has not been tagged or parsed, so no tags or syntactic trees are available for these utterances. Furthermore, in ICECUP's default view, extra-corpus text is not visible; it appears instead as one or more blank lines in the corpus text.

---

[2] In the spontaneous commentaries and broadcast news categories, extended segments of speech by non-British speakers have not been transcribed at all. Instead, these are represented simply by an editorial note in the text, such as "<O>speech by President Bush</O>".

Speakers of extra-corpus utterances are referred to throughout the transcriptions as 'speaker Z'. No biographical details have been recorded for extra-corpus speakers.

In the written part of the corpus, extra-corpus text consists for the most part of sentences which are beyond the agreed 2,000-word limit for ICE texts. Usually, extra-corpus text of this type is located after the 2,000-word text proper. Extended quotations are also treated as extra-corpus text. Again, this material has not been analysed, and is not visible in the default view.

1.4 Copyright

The text samples in ICE-GB are under copyright. Permission has been obtained from the copyright holders for their inclusion in the corpus on the strict understanding that they be used exclusively for non-commercial, academic research. Users of the corpus are bound by the conditions set out in the License Agreement.

For ethical and legal reasons, the recording of spoken texts was non-surreptitious. Permission was received from the speakers in non-broadcast material before the recordings were made. In cases where pre-recorded material was used, such as parliamentary debates and legal proceedings, permission was received afterwards, though in all cases the speakers were aware that their speech was being recorded.

In a small number of cases, names and addresses have been changed in order to preserve the anonymity of speakers and authors. Pseudonyms are identified as such in the texts themselves (see Structural Markup, Appendix 4).

1.5 Transcription and markup

The transcription of spoken texts was the subject of much debate during the planning stages of the ICE project. As far back as 1988, a meeting was held at the Survey of English Usage with phoneticians and with personnel who had previously transcribed the SEU Corpus. The idea of producing full phonetic transcriptions was very quickly ruled out, since ICE is chiefly concerned with syntax, not with pronunciation. During subsequent discussions, usually at the annual ICE meetings, various levels of prosodic annotation were suggested. At one point, it was suggested that we encode pauses, tone unit boundaries, and the location and direction of nuclear tones. In the end, however, it was agreed to produce orthographic transcriptions, and to encode only pauses, using a binary system of long and short pauses. As Greenbaum (1991) points out, that decision was made partly on the grounds of economy. Even a minimum prosodic transcription would be so costly in terms of time (and therefore of financial resources) that it would be impractical for almost all the ICE teams. Furthermore, it was felt that it would be almost impossible to enforce consistency of annotation, both within the individual corpora, and across component corpora.

The transcriptions in ICE-GB observe the usual conventions of spelling, capitalization, and word spacing. No punctuation has been included in the transcripts, but sentence-initial words have been capitalized to improve readability.

In spoken texts, numerals have been transcribed as words, not as digits (thus, *six* not *6*). This convention is necessary because speakers may refer to dates and years in a variety of ways, *e.g.*, *the fourth of May*, or *May the fourth*, *nineteen hundred and twelve* or *nineteen twelve*. In each case, these have been transcribed as they were spoken.

Standard abbreviations have been used, including *Mr* and *Mrs*, but without a period. Words which were spelled out by a speaker were transcribed as space-separated upper-case characters, *e.g., we've got sauna S A U N A*.

Contractions such as *he's*, *I'm*, *we'll*, and genitive nouns, such as *John's*, were transcribed as in writing, that is, as solid words, with no space before the apostrophe. However, during part-of-speech tagging (see Section 1.5), these items were automatically separated, since they are grammatically distinct, and must be labelled separately. So, for example, the original transcription *we'll* became *we*[space]*'ll* after splitting, and the two items were tagged as a pronoun and as a modal auxiliary verb respectively. This has an important implication for searching. If you wish to find *we'll* in the corpus, you must remember to insert a space between the two parts in your search argument.

However, the negative modals (*won't*, *wouldn't*, *can't*, *couldn't*, etc.) and the negative *do* auxiliary (*don't*) are exceptions to this rule. These have not been split, since we do not consider, for example, *won't* to consist of *won* plus *'t*. Instead, these items were treated as single units, and were given a single grammatical label (in the case of *won't*, the label is '**`AUX(modal,pres,neg)`**', that is, modal auxiliary, present tense, negative form). For details of the grammatical tagging scheme, see Section 2.2.

The printed material in the corpus was optically scanned onto computer, and handwritten material was entered manually. In all cases, both spoken and written texts were proofread on screen prior to the first annotation stage, structural markup.

Structural markup encodes features of the original texts that are lost when it is converted into a plain text file on a computer. In written texts, markup symbols are used to encode typographic features, such as boldface, italics, and underlining, as well as structural features such as sentence boundaries, paragraph boundaries, and headings. In spoken texts, markup encodes sentence boundaries, speaker turns, overlapping strings, and pauses. Markup symbols usually appear in pairs, with an opening symbol <symbol> and a corresponding closing symbol </symbol>. For instance, the start of each paragraph is marked <p>, and the end of each paragraph is marked </p>.

Similarly, words in boldface print are enclosed within <bold> and </bold> markers (Nelson 1993a, 1993b).

The markup symbols were inserted semi-automatically, using the *Markup Assistant* program, a set of WordPerfect™ macros which assigns whole markup symbols to single keys (Quinn and Porter 1996). When all the markup was applied, the sentences – marked with # at the beginning – were automatically numbered in sequence for reference purposes.

The following extract shows the structural markup and sentence numbering in a printed text. It is taken from a sample of academic writing (W2A-038 #45ff.).

<#45:1> <h> <it> 2.2 Use of Occam concurrent features </h> </it>
<#46:1> <p> One of the changes between Mascot 2 and 3 is that Mascot 3 systems are not mandated to use the standard Mascot primitives .
<#47:1> Instead , they allow <quote> the (Mascot) model to be mapped onto equivalent features in a concurrent language </quote> .
<#48:1> This approach was therefore considered and found to be far more attractive . <#49:1> It is the approach proposed by this paper . </p>

In this example, the markup encodes the heading (<h>.... </h>), italicised words (<it>... </it>), paragraph boundaries (<p>... </p>), and a quotation (<quote>... </quote>).

Non-printed texts generally contain more structural markup than printed texts. The following extract is taken from an examination script in Psychology (W1A-017 #8ff.).

<p> <#8:1> The James-Lange theory stresses the importance of the physiological effects .
<#9:1> <del> It was an in </del> It is central to the study of emotions as it was <del> one o </del> an early theory (in the nineteenth century) from which others can work .
<#10:1> It is also <del> of i </del> stimulating because it is <}> <-> counter intuitive </-> <+> counter-intuitive </+> </}> as it hypothesizes that the physiological changes are the subjective emotional experience .
<#11:1> <del> That is to say </del> For example we run and are therefore <-> affraid </-> <+> afraid </+> .

In this extract, there are four instances of text which the author has deleted. These are marked <del>... </del> in the computerized corpus version. The extract also contains two misspellings (*counter intuitive* and *affraid*). During markup, the correct form of each misspelling was added by the corpus annotators, and enclosed within <+> and </+>. The original misspellings were retained, and enclosed within <-> and </->. This markup was applied in order to ensure accurate word frequency counts, and to ensure that every instance of a word – even when it is misspelled – can be retrieved.

In spoken texts, the speaker turns are identified as <$A>, <$B>, <$C>, and so on. The following is an extract from a conversation involving three speakers (S1A-047 #1ff.).

<$A> <#1:1:A> What time is it <,>
<$B> <#2:1:B> Twenty past eight
<$A> <#3:1:A> Ah yeah
<$B> <#4:1:B> Yeah <,,>
<$C> <#5:1:C> Fancy a drink John
<#6:1:C> We've got some <[> left </[>
<$A> <#7:1:A> <[> I </[> think all the pubs are closed
<$C> <#8:1:C> No
<#9:1:C> We 've got some in the fridge some ale...

Pauses are marked using a binary system. The symbol <,> denotes a short pause, and the symbol <,,> denotes a long pause. A short pause is defined as any perceptible break in phonation equal in length to one syllable, uttered at the speaker's tempo. A long pause is any longer break in phonation. By convention, pauses occurring between speaker turns are attached to the end of the first speaker turn. The extract above also illustrates the markup for overlapping speech (<[>... </[>). In sentence 6, speaker C's *left* overlaps with speaker A's *I*, in sentence 7. Both overlapping strings are enclosed within '<[>' and '</[>' symbols (Meyer 1994). In more complex examples these symbols may be numbered to differentiate different portions of overlapping speech.

As these extracts show, a fully marked-up text can be very difficult to read. Fortunately for the user, the markup symbols do not actually appear in the default view of the corpus. Instead, ICECUP translates the markup into a less daunting representation, so that boldface in the original text, for instance, actually appears as boldface on the screen. Similarly, overlapping speech appears on the screen against a coloured background, not as strings enclosed within markup symbols (Figure 1). In order to search for markup, however, the user must know what the relevant symbols are. A complete list of these, together with ICECUP's representation of them, may be found in Appendix 4.

Figure 1: Viewing the conversational extract (S1A-047 #1ff.) in ICECUP.

s1a-047 001	A	What time is it <,>
s1a-047 002	B	Twenty past eight
s1a-047 003	A	Ah yeah
s1a-047 004	B	Yeah <,,>
s1a-047 005	C	Fancy a drink John
s1a-047 006	C	We 've got some left
s1a-047 007	A	I think all the pubs are closed
s1a-047 008	C	No
s1a-047 009	C	We 've got some in the fridge some ale

Figure 2: An example of a series of overlapping speech segments in ICE-GB (S1A-006 #143ff.). Arrows have been added for clarity.

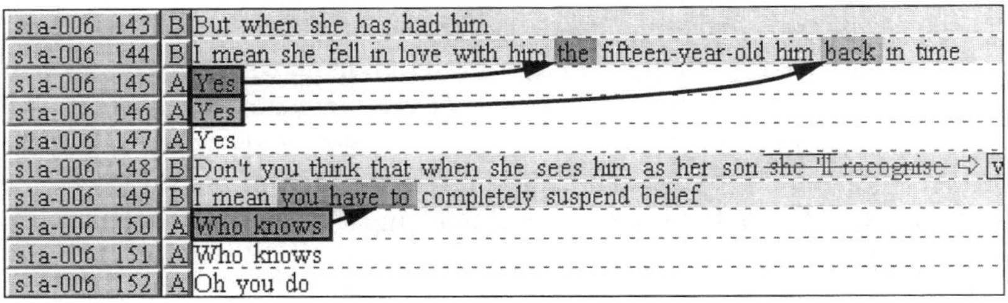

A slightly more complicated example of speaker overlap is shown in Figure 2. The sentence that starts first precedes the overlapping utterance, as we can see here.

Sometimes, several utterances overlap a single utterance, as in the first example in Figure 2 (units #144-146). The next sentence spoken (#147) may therefore appear a little further down the text. Thus, in the example, Speaker A interrupts speaker B twice and the third *Yes* follows B's utterance. This is the general pattern in the corpus. More dense patterns of overlap can arise, but these are actually quite rare.

1.6 Part-of-speech tagging

The second stage of annotation which we applied to ICE-GB was part-of-speech tagging, or word-class tagging. During this stage, each lexical item was assigned a part-of-speech label or tag, such as '**N**' for noun, or '**V**' for verb. In addition to the main label, most tags carry additional information, which appears in brackets. Thus a common, singular noun is labelled '**N(com,sing)**'. Figure 3 illustrates the tagging of an example sentence.

The repertoire of word class tags – the ICE Tagset – was devised by the Survey of English Usage, in collaboration with the TOSCA research group at the University of Nijmegen (Greenbaum and Ni 1996). With some modifica-

Figure 3: An example of word class tagging: "I think that's absolutely right"(S1B-050#33).

Sentence	**Word class tag**	**Explanation**
I	**PRON(pers, sing)**	Pronoun, personal, singular
think	**V(montr, pres)**	Verb, monotransitive, present tense
that	**PRON(dem, sing)**	Pronoun, demonstrative, singular
's	**V(cop, pres, encl)**	Verb, copular, present tense, enclitic
absolutely	**ADV(inten)**	Adverb, intensifying
right	**ADJ(ge)**	Adjective, general

tions, the tagset is based on the classifications given in Quirk *et al.* (1985). It consists of 20 main word classes, and is described in detail in Section 2.1.

The automatic word class tagging was carried out using the TOSCA tagger (Oostdijk 1991). The tagger assigned one or more tags to each lexical item, and the output was manually checked at the Survey of English Usage. The checking stage involved choosing the correct tag for each item and removing the incorrect tags. In making these decisions, the checkers used the *ICE Tagset Manual* (Greenbaum 1995) as their chief reference. The *Manual* explains and exemplifies all the ICE word classes and their associated features, and discusses problem cases in some detail.

1.7 Syntactic parsing

The tagged corpus formed the input to the next major stage, syntactic parsing. Again, we used software developed by the TOSCA group – the TOSCA parser – to automate this stage. However, the corpus required an additional stage of pre-editing before it could be submitted to the parser.

The pre-editing stage – what we call 'syntactic marking' – involved manually marking several high-frequency constructions in order to reduce the ambiguity of the input, and thereby reduce the number of decisions that the automatic parser would have to make. Some of the constructions which were manually marked are shown in Table 3.

Following syntactic marking, the corpus was submitted to the TOSCA parser for syntactic analysis. The output from the parser was a series of labelled syntactic trees, in which the nodes were labelled for function, category, and features. In many cases, the parser produced several alternative analyses, either for entire sentences, or for individual constituents. In these cases, the corpus annotators had to select the contextually correct analysis, and to eliminate the incorrect ones. Figure 4 illustrates the final, corrected analysis for the sentence "I think that's absolutely right".

The tree 'grows' from left to right, and from top to bottom. In this example, the sentence is analysed as consisting of a subject NP *I* (**SU,NP**), at the top of the figure, followed by a verb phrase *think* ('**VB,VP**'), followed by a

Table 3: Items manually marked prior to parsing.

Construction	**Example**
Conjoins	*[Jack] and [Jill]*
Noun phrase postmodifiers	*the house [on the corner]*
Noun phrases with adverbial function	*I spoke to him [last week]*
Appositive noun phrases	*The President, [Mr Smith]*
Adverb phrases premodifying a noun phrase	*the [above] diagram*
Vocatives	*What are you doing, [Sam]?*

Figure 4: The parse analysis for the sentence "I think that's absolutely right" (S1B-050 #33).

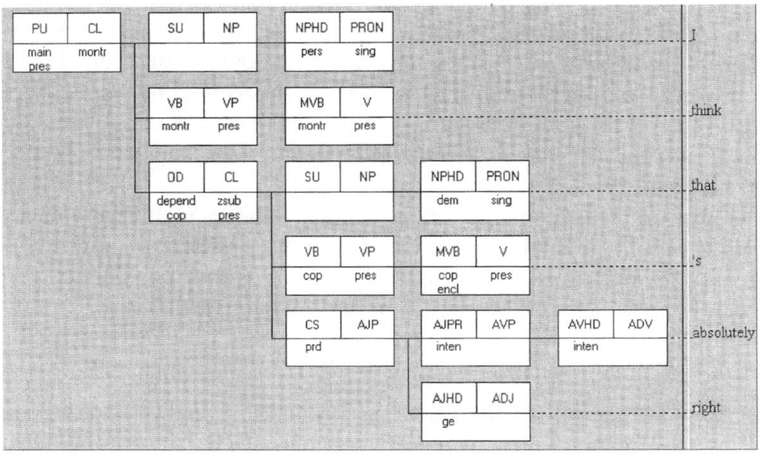

direct object clause *that's absolutely right* ('**OD,CL**'). The parsing scheme is described in detail in Chapter 2. Appendix 5 contains a Quick Reference Guide to all the parsing labels.

The syntactic parsing was by far the most difficult and time-consuming stage of the whole ICE-GB project. The TOSCA parser yielded a complete analysis for around 70% of the parsing units in the corpus. For the remainder, we used the Survey Parser, which was developed specifically for that purpose (Fang 1996). The Survey Parser produced, for the most part, *partial* analyses. These partial trees were then manually completed and corrected, using ICE Tree II, a tree editing program developed at the Survey of English Usage (Wallis and Nelson 1997). Before applying the Survey Parser, however, many of our original parsing units had to be further segmented into shorter units. This procedure was chiefly used to separate clauses in speech which are loosely connected by *and* or *but*. For example, the following utterance by a sports commentator was originally transcribed as a single unit:

> A good idea to set Barker away again but a vital interception coming in from Blackmore and now United move forward

In order to parse this, it was necessary to divide it into three separate parsing units, as shown here:

> A good idea to set Barker away again [S2A-003 #49]
> but a vital interception coming in from Blackmore [S2A-003 #50]
> and now United move forward [S2A-003 #51]

Therefore this utterance is represented in the corpus by three separate syntactic trees. In making these divisions, it was necessary to amend the part-of-speech tags which had originally been assigned to *and* and *but*. Instead of coordinating conjunctions – '**CONJUNC(coord)**' – they are now tagged as general connectives – '**CONNEC(ge)**' – since they fulfill no coordinating role. It is worth noting, however, that in the digitized version of the original recording, we have reverted to the original segmentation, so that this utterance is represented by a single sound file, not by three separate sound files (on digitization, see Section 1.9 below)

As well as the segmentation issue, the spoken texts presented other problems in automatic analysis, due largely to the presence of nonfluencies – repetitions, reformulations, and partial words. To illustrate, consider extract (1), which is a fairly typical utterance from an informal conversation.

(1) I you know I want to s hear it from from his point of view as well [S1A-005 #119]

This contains the partial word *s*, as well as repetition of the subject *I*, and of *from*. These nonfluencies presented special difficulties for the automatic parser, and had to be manually 'normalised' during the structural markup stage (see Section 1.5). This meant that the parser effectively ignored the nonfluencies, and only analysed the version shown in (2):

(2) you know I want to hear it from his point of view as well

In a final stage – *alignment* – we re-attached the ignored material to the syntactic tree which the parser produced. The result is a tree (Figure 5) in which the nonfluencies appear as 'grayed' nodes, usually without internal analysis, loosely attached to the analysis of (2).

When searching the corpus with ICECUP, the default setting is to disregard these nonfluencies, since including them in search patterns would

Figure 5: The syntactic tree for S1A-005 #119.

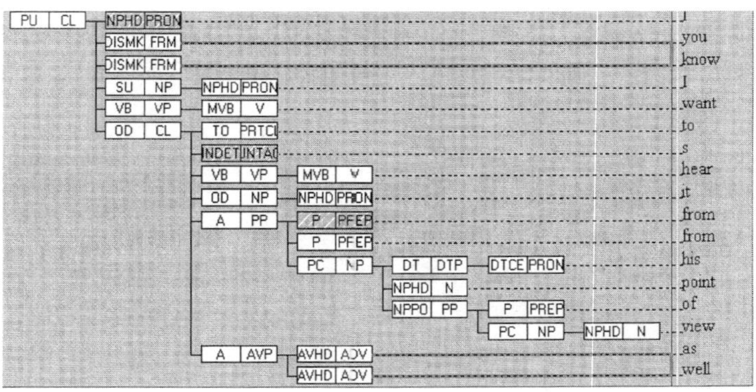

make almost every search excessively restricted. For the same reason, pauses, punctuation, and interjections are ignored during searches. However, the user can opt to include 'ignored' material by changing this default.

1.8 Cross-sectional checking

The corpus contains 83,394 syntactic trees. These were checked in two separate stages, using two very different approaches. In the first stage, we manually checked the corpus *longitudinally*, that is, sentence-by-sentence, text-by-text. However, this approach was not only very labour-intensive and time-consuming (Wallis and Nelson 1997), it also highlighted a very real problem of consistency. Working on single texts, the checkers were presented daily with a wide variety of grammatical constructions, each of which had to be analysed separately, and correctly. However, we could not guarantee that all similar constructions would always be analysed in the same way throughout the corpus.

In other words, while we could achieve accuracy in individual cases, we could not guarantee consistency across the whole corpus. Therefore we adopted a new approach, *cross-sectional checking*. We determined that the corpus as a whole should be checked and corrected on a cross-sectional, construction-by-construction basis (Wallis 1999). This allowed each checker to concentrate on just one grammatical construction at a time, checking and correcting, if necessary, each instance of the construction throughout the whole corpus. This had two advantages: it enforced greater consistency, and it greatly eased the decision-making process for the checkers. The cross-sectional approach was made possible by using ICECUP to search for constructions, with greater or lesser refinement. We did not, of course, check every type of construction in ICE-GB. Instead, we concentrated on major constructions, and on known 'problem' cases, and this 'inventory' was further extended as the checking stage proceeded. Finally, the corpus was 'spot-checked' before releasing Version 1 in 1998. Error-correction has continued on an *ad hoc* basis, and new amendments will be incorporated into subsequent releases.

1.9 Digitization

The sound recordings in ICE-GB were made using cassette tapes on analogue equipment. In total, they consist of about 70 hours of speech. These recordings have now been digitized in mono,[3] and have been transferred to CD-ROM. After digitization, the sound files were divided into separate, smaller files which correspond, in most cases, to individual parsing units. This means that in ICECUP, users can play back each spoken parsing unit while examining the corresponding syntactic tree on the screen, or while examining concordance

---

[3] More precisely, they are stored as 16kHz, 16-bit single-channel (mono) 'wave' files.

lines. In some cases, however, the sound units correspond to more than one parsing unit. This is always the case with overlapping speech, when one sound file may correspond to several parsing units. Similarly, very brief utterances, or utterances delivered at high tempo, may occur in the same sound file with adjacent parsing units. In all cases, however, the user can play the sound file, either on its own, or in the context of the whole text, using the 'continuous play' mode. The details of this operation are discussed in Section 4.11.

1.10 Examining ICE-GB texts

To conclude this introductory chapter, we will look at a selection of text types in the corpus. As described in Section 1.2, each text has been assigned a unique textcode, which corresponds to its place in the hierarchical text classification scheme (Appendix 1).

The texts may be viewed using ICECUP III, the retrieval software which is supplied with the corpus (see Part 2). When you first start ICECUP, the program displays a corpus map, as shown in Figure 6. The corpus map provides a convenient method of browsing the corpus (Chapter 4), looking at individual text categories and individual texts.

The default view is based on the sampling variable 'text category', though other variables are also available, including speaker gender, speaker age, and speaker education (see Section 4.1). Here we will concentrate on the

Figure 6: The corpus map window.

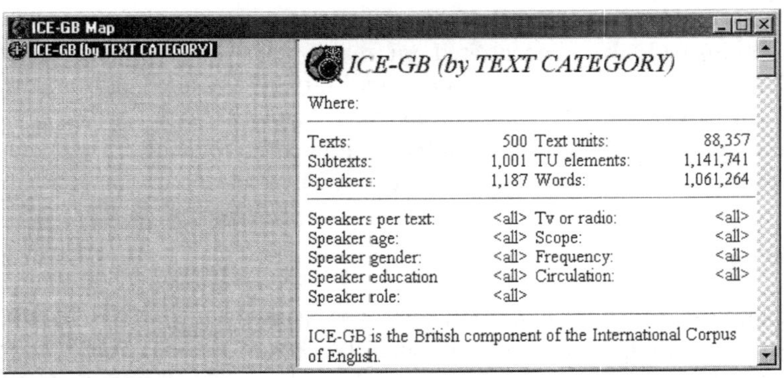

Figure 7: Navigation buttons for the corpus map.

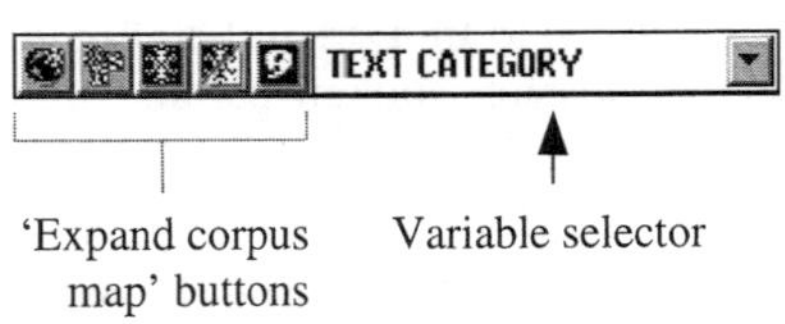

Figure 8: The corpus map expanded to view the values of the 'text category' variable.

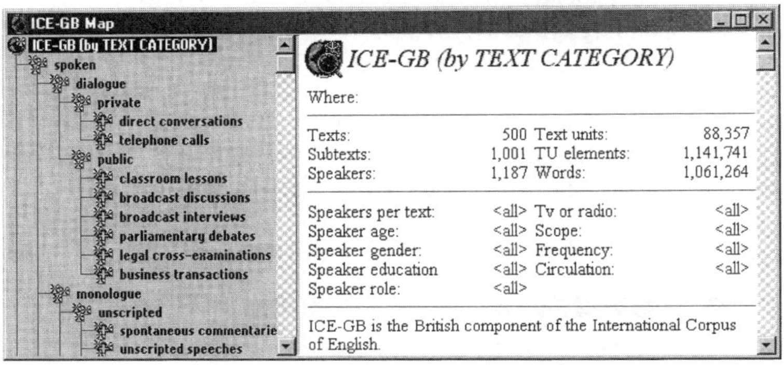

text category variable.

The corpus map may be navigated using a number of small 'buttons', which appear in the secondary bar window below the main 'command bar' in ICECUP. These are shown in Figure 7.

These five buttons expand or collapse the corpus map in different ways. The first button (from the left), '', expands or collapses the map down to just the single variable label, in this case, the text category variable (as in Figure 8). The next button ('') expands or collapses the map to show the different values of the variable, in this case, the different text categories in the corpus (Figure 8). Using the other three buttons (see also Section 4.2), you can expand the map further to display: the individual 2,000 word texts and (where texts have been composed from several sources, *e.g.*, letters) subtexts. Finally, individual speakers may be listed. At all times elements in the corpus map that may be expanded further are indicated by a yellow 'plus' symbol.

To examine any of the text categories, 'double-click' on the label with the mouse in the corpus map, press function key <F4>, or click on the Browse 'button' at the far right of ICECUP's command bar. The category opens in a new window. The following Figures (9-12) show, respectively, the start of the categories direct conversations, legal presentations, social letters, and press news reports.

In these views, each line corresponds to one text unit ('sentence') in the corpus. If you are using ICECUP 3.0 you may have to scroll right in order to read the entire text unit.[4] The textcode and the text unit numbers appear on the left of the screen. For details of the various display conventions used, see Chapter 4.

[4] In ICECUP 3.1 you can use the 'word wrapping' facility. Select the last option, '', under concordancing. See Section 4.6.

As they appear here, texts show only the minimum of information. In particular, no grammatical information is shown. To see how a text unit has been analysed grammatically, the user can simply 'double-click' on the relevant line. The corresponding syntactic tree will be then displayed in a new window.

In this section we (very briefly) introduced ICECUP and the corpus map, and showed how they may be used for viewing the texts in the corpus. Part 2 looks at ICECUP, and the corpus map, in much greater detail. We discuss the wealth of detail available in ICE-GB and how to explore it. In Part 3 we show how one can carry out scientific research in grammar using the corpus.

Figure 9: Start of the text category 'direct conversations'.

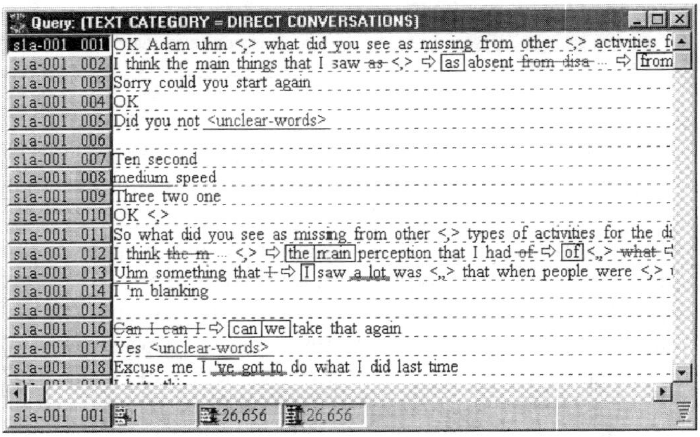

Figure 10: Viewing the text category 'legal presentations'.

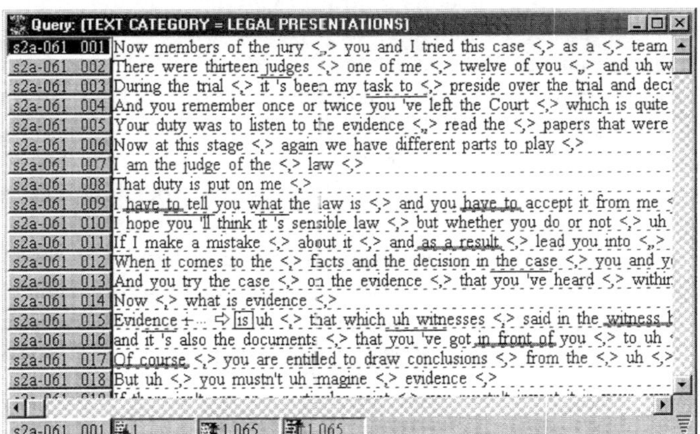

Figure 11: Start of the category 'social letters'.

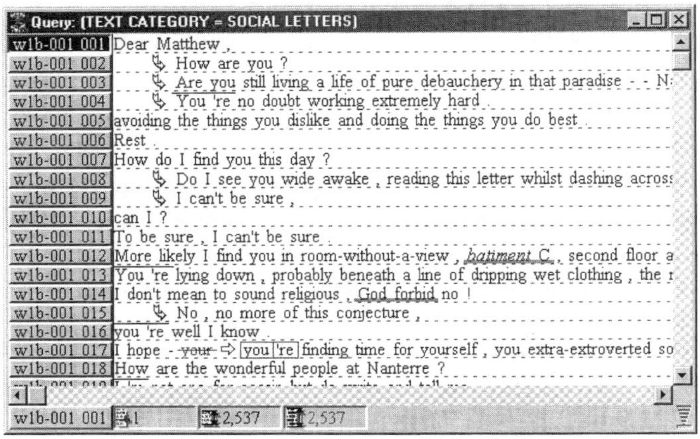

Figure 12: Start of the text category 'press news reports'.

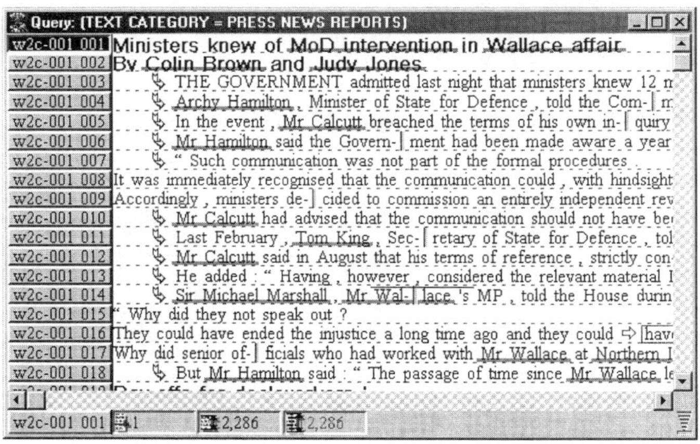

2. THE ICE-GB GRAMMAR

2.1 *Introduction*

The ICE-GB corpus was grammatically annotated in two separate, though closely related stages. During the first stage – part-of-speech tagging – we assigned a word class label to every word in the corpus. Word class labels consist of a main part-of-speech label, such as '**N**' for noun or '**V**' for verb, as well as – in most cases – additional features. We refer to the repertoire of word class labels ('tags') in ICE-GB as the *ICE Tagset*. This tagset was developed at the Survey of English Usage, in collaboration with the TOSCA Research Group at the University of Nijmegen, and is discussed in Section 2.2.

The tagged corpus formed the input to the second annotation stage, syntactic parsing. Using the TOSCA automatic parser, we analysed every parsing unit ('sentence') in terms of its clause and phrase structure, and represented this in the form of a syntactic tree. Figure 13 shows the tree for the text unit "Many have tried" (S2B-024 #6).

Figure 13: Tree for "Many have tried" (S2B-024 #6).

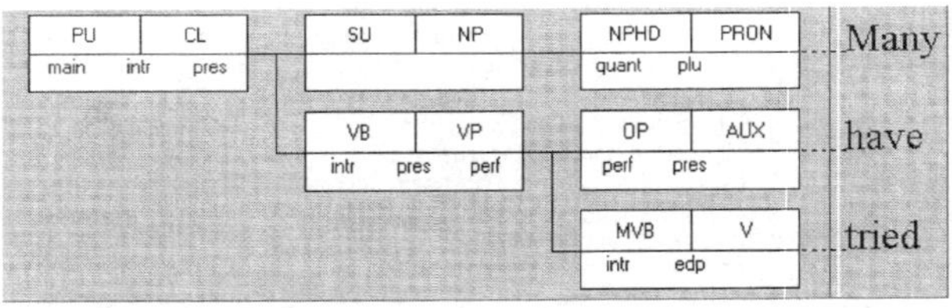

Each node on the tree consists of the three sectors indicated by Figure 14. The function and the category/word class sectors are always labelled, but on many nodes the features sector is blank. In many cases no features are applicable. Function, category, and word class labels are shown in upper case. Feature

Figure 14: The sectors of a node.

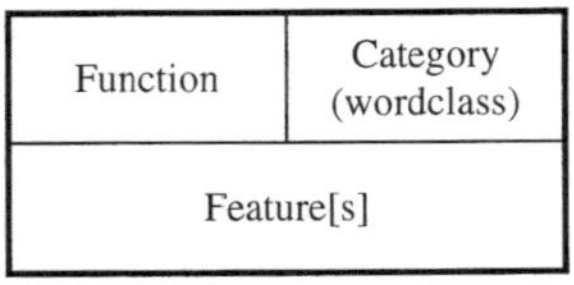

labels always appear in lower case.

In this chapter we list and exemplify the grammatical labels used in ICE-GB. Section 2.2 discusses the word class labels. The function and category labels employed in the parse analysis are discussed in Section 2.3, and the feature labels are discussed in 2.4.

2.2 *ICE Word Classes*

The ICE Tagset consists of the 20 main word classes listed in Table 4 below. Word class tags consist of one of these main word class labels, in upper case, followed (usually) by tag features in lower case within parentheses. Tags, then, have the general form shown below on the left. For example, adjectives carry the main word class symbol '**ADJ**' followed by a feature indicating their form. So comparative adjectives are labelled as on the right below.

pattern	example
WORDCLASS(feature)	**ADJ(comp)**

If the tag carries more than one feature, these are separated by a comma. For example, verbs carry the main word class tag '**V**', followed by a feature indicating their transitivity and another indicating their form. Transitivity and form are *feature classes* of verbs. A monotransitive ('**montr**') verb in the present tense ('**pres**') is tagged:

WORDCLASS($feature_1$, $feature_2$, ...) **V(montr,pres)**

In general, each lexical item is assigned its own word class tag. However, certain compound expressions are assigned compound tags if they are considered to function grammatically as single units. Each word in the expression is assigned the tag of the expression as a whole.

Table 4: ICE word classes.

Word class	Word class tag	Word class	Word class tag
Adjective	**ADJ**	Interjection	**INTERJEC**
Adverb	**ADV**	Nominal adjective	**NADJ**
Article	**ART**	Noun	**N**
Auxiliary verb	**AUX**	Numeral	**NUM**
Cleft *it*	**CLEFTIT**	Preposition	**PREP**
Conjunction	**CONJUNC**	Proform	**PROFM**
Connective	**CONNEC**	Pronoun	**PRON**
Existential *there*	**EXTHERE**	Particle	**PRTCL**
Formulaic expression	**FRM**	Reaction signal	**REACT**
Genitive marker	**GENM**	Verb (lexical)	**V**

Thus, the compound particle (see Section 2.2.18) "in order to" is tagged as follows.

in	`PRTCL(to):1/3`
order	`PRTCL(to):2/3`
to	`PRTCL(to):3/3`

We will illustrate this kind of compound simply as, for example

And the story was written *in order to* reflect the discontent... [S1B-001 #28] `PRTCL(to)`

Personal names, book titles, and headings, are tagged in the same way, as singular, proper nouns, without any internal analysis.

Clare	`N(prop,sing):1/2`
Hayes [S1A-004 #104]	`N(prop,sing):2/2`
King	`N(prop,sing):1/4`
Charles	`N(prop,sing):2/4`
the	`N(prop,sing):3/4`
Bald [W2A-008 #13]	`N(prop,sing):4/4`
Patterns	`N(prop,sing):1/4`
in	`N(prop,sing):2/4`
Human	`N(prop,sing):3/4`
Geography [W1A-006 #107]	`N(prop,sing):4/4`

Compounding was also used to avoid the need to analyse some particularly difficult constructions, usually complex NPs:

I'm not playing *oh no you're not oh yes you are games* with you [W2F-001 #102]
It's just *a question and answer session* [S1A-005 #117]
... *endless hormones and glands problems*... [S1A-031 #90]

We refer to these compound tags as *ditto tags*. In ICECUP's main display window, ditto-tagged items are indicated by yellow underlining. In the tree window, they are indicated by a yellow brace. The index numbers ('`1/2`', '`2/2`', *etc.*) appear only when you save the results of a search as 'tagged text' (see Chapter 5, Section 5.1.12).

2.2.1 Adjective (ADJ)

Adjectives carry the main word class label '**`ADJ`**', and are further distinguished by the types listed in Table 5. Adjective features are grouped into two main sets of alternatives, the main type, called 'morphology', and an optional 'comparison' feature.

The 'general' subclass consists of all adjectives that do not belong to any of the other subclasses. Adjectives in periphrastic, comparative constructions,

Table 5: Features of the word class 'adjective'.

class	feature	code
morphology	general	**ge**
	-ed participle	**edp**
	-ing participle	**ingp**
comparison	comparative	**comp**
	superlative	**sup**

such as *more expensive* and *most expensive*, are tagged '**ADJ(ge)**', since they are not formally marked.

2.2.2 *Adverb (ADV)*

Adverbs carry the main word class label '**ADV**'. The class is divided into eight subclasses, which appear as features in the tag. These subclasses are summarised in the upper part of Table 6.

The following are examples of additive adverbs in ICE-GB, tagged '**ADV(add)**'.

But he was *both* intelligent and industrious [W2B-015 #86] **ADV(add)**
They *either* loved it or loathed it [W2B-001 #10] **ADV(add)**
In addition, the NOAA satellites act as relays... [W2A-037 #92] **ADV(add)**

Exclusive adverbs are tagged '**ADV(excl)**'.

He *merely* shrugged his shoulders [W2B-012 #20] **ADV(excl)**
He is *simply* saying officially that you've got to be a Levite [S1B-001 #104] **ADV(excl)**
The puppet is *purely* an algorithmic object... [W2A-035 #73] **ADV(excl)**

Intensifying adverbs denote a place on a scale of comparison, and include amplifiers and downtoners. They are tagged '**ADV(inten)**':

It's *very* cute [S1A-039 #85] **ADV(inten)**

Table 6: Features of the word class 'adverb'.

class	feature	code
type	additive	**add**
	exclusive	**excl**
	intensifying	**inten**
	particularizing	**partic**
	phrasal	**phras**
	relative	**rel**
	wh-	**wh**
	general	**ge**
comparison	comparative	**comp**
	superlative	**sup**

Quite impossible [S1A-040 #134]	**ADV(inten)**
The intro's *extremely* readable [S1A-053 #15]	**ADV(inten)**

Particularizers emphasize that the utterance is restricted to the focused part. They are tagged '**ADV(partic)**'. There are a number of compound particularizers, including *at least*, *at most*, and *in particular*.

It was *mostly* about the weather [S1A-055 #11]	**ADV(partic)**
But *in the main* it's going to be... [S1A-086 #229]	**ADV(partic)**
At least I think I will [S1A-023 #107]	**ADV(partic)**

Adverbs are tagged '**ADV(phras)**' when they enter into a combination traditionally known as a phrasal verb.

How did it come *about* [S1A-003 #43]	**ADV(phras)**
...you're having to build *up* the muscles... [S1A-003 #22]	**ADV(phras)**
Let's move *on*... [S1A-001 #115]	**ADV(phras)**

The adverb in the traditional phrasal-prepositional verb is tagged in the same way. For example, *up* in *put up with* is tagged '**ADV(phras)**', and the phrasal preposition *with* is tagged '**PREP(phras)**'. For prepositions in prepositional verbs, see Section 2.2.20.

Relative adverbs are tagged '**ADV(rel)**'. The relative adverbs *when*, *where*, *whereby*, and *why* introduce postmodifying relative clauses.

... at a time *when* unemployment has halved [S1B-059 #10]	**ADV(rel)**
... the school *where* I teach [S1A-082 #9]	**ADV(rel)**
... a chart *whereby* I can date all of the rocks... [S2A-046 #56]	**ADV(rel)**
The reason *why* I am now writing to you... [W1B-024 #36]	**ADV(rel)**

Wh-adverbs are tagged '**ADV(wh)**'. This subclass comprises all adverbs beginning with *wh-* plus the adverbs *how* and *however*. The adverbs in this subclass introduce clauses that are exclamatory, independent interrogative, dependent interrogative, and nominal relative.

How stupid [S1A-014 #198]	(independent exclamatory)	**ADV(wh)**
Why has intelligence evolved? [W1A-009 #1]	(independent interrogative)	**ADV(wh)**
D' you know *how* much... [S1A-008 #182]	(dependent interrogative)	**ADV(wh)**
I'll just have to see *how* things go [W1E-002 #144]	(nominal relative)	**ADV(wh)**

If *when*, *whenever*, *where*, and *whenever* introduce an adverbial clause, they are tagged as subordinating conjunctions ('**CONJUNC(subord)**'). See also 2.2.6.

The general subclass consists of all adverbs that do not belong to any of the other subclasses. They are tagged '**ADV(ge)**' and the subclass includes *arguably*, *often*, *recently*, *slowly*, *there*, and *yesterday*, as well as *AD.*, *BC.*, *am.*, *pm.*, *ibid.*, *etc.*, *et al.*, and *per cent*.

Inflected adverbs – mostly general and intensifying adverbs – have an additional comparison feature indicating comparative ('**comp**') or superlative ('**sup**') form. For example, *fast* is tagged '**ADV(ge)**' whilst *faster* is tagged '**ADV(ge,comp)**' and *fastest*, '**ADV(ge,sup)**'.

2.2.3 *Article (ART)*

Articles are assigned the main word class label '**ART**', and they carry one of the feature labels '**def**' (definite) or '**indef**' (indefinite).

the	**ART(def)**
a, an	**ART(indef)**

2.2.4 *Auxiliary verb (AUX)*

Auxiliary verbs are tagged '**AUX**' for word class. This is followed by at least two features. The first feature indicates the subclass ('type') of the auxiliary, shown in Table 7.

The *do* subclass consists of the dummy operator *do* and the introductory imperative marker *do*. All instances are marked '**AUX(do,...)**'.

How *did* you... [S1A-046 #88]	**AUX(do,past)**
Simon *doesn't* pay but Laura the student does [S1A-007 #231]	**AUX(do,pres,neg)**
Don't let him worry you [S1A-005 #37]	**AUX(do,infin,neg)**
*D'*you remember [S1A-007 #309]	**AUX(do,pres,procl)**

The introductory imperative marker *let* is tagged '**AUX(let,imp)**':

Let's just stop there [S1A-001 #84]	**AUX(let,imp)**

This auxiliary use of *let* is distinguished from the lexical verb *let* ('*allow*'), as in *Let me go*.

Modal auxiliaries are tagged '**AUX(modal,...)**'. The modal auxiliaries are *can*, *may*, *shall*, *will*, *must*, *could*, *might*, *should*, and *would*.

You *can* apply for help... [W2D-001 #47]	**AUX(modal,pres)**
...all this *will* start again tomorrow [W1B-007 #25]	**AUX(modal,pres)**
She *should* wait at the airport [S1A-006 #316]	**AUX(modal,past)**
I*'ll* go and get one [S1A-079 #14]	**AUX(modal,pres,encl)**

The passive auxiliaries *be* and *get* are tagged '**AUX(pass,...)**'.

No they *were* given a fairly good write-up [S1A-008 #194]	**AUX(pass,past)**
It can *be* used to measure out a parade ground... [S2A-011 #118]	**AUX(pass,infin)**
The census form has *been* designed so that... [S2B-044 #56]	**AUX(pass,edp)**
... that's why I *got* sent home... [S1A-011 #135]	**AUX(pass,past)**

Table 7: Features of the word class 'auxiliary verb'.

class	feature	code
type	*do* auxiliary	**do**
	let auxiliary	**let**
	modal	**modal**
	passive	**pass**
	perfect	**perf**
	progressive	**prog**
	semi-auxiliary	**semi**
	semi-auxiliary + *-ing* participle	**semip**
tense/mood/form	present	**pres**
	past	**past**
	imperative	**imp**
	-ed participle form	**edp**
	-ing participle form	**ingp**
	infinitive	**infin**
clitics	enclitic	**encl**
	proclitic	**procl**
	negative	**neg**
ellipsis	elliptical	**ellipt**
coordination	coordination	**coordn**

The perfect auxiliary *have* is tagged '**AUX(perf,...)**'.

B A *has* already reacted by withdrawing... [S2B-002 #70] **AUX(perf,pres)**
Because you *haven't* got a history... [S1A-006 #284] **AUX(perf,pres,neg)**
Had he [S1A-006 #275] **AUX(perf,past)**
Nothing*'s* ever happened about it [S1A-007 #286] **AUX(perf,pres,encl)**

The progressive auxiliary *be* is tagged '**AUX(prog,...)**'.

We *were* having a discussion... [S1A-008 #102] **AUX(prog,past)**
But they think they*'re* getting a good deal... [S1A-012 #157] **AUX(prog,pres,encl)**
Laura's not meant to *be* talking [S1A-017 #147] **AUX(prog, infin)**
She's *been* collecting second hand books [S1A-025 #320] **AUX(prog, edp)**

Semi-auxiliaries are tagged '**AUX(semi,...)**'. This subclass includes modal idioms and catenatives, including *appear to*, *be about to*, *be likely to*, *have to*, and *tend to*. All semi-auxiliaries are ditto-tagged (see above).

Now Jeeves and Wooster *is about to* burst upon us again [S1B-042 #7] **AUX(semi,pres)**

If the parts of a semi-auxiliary do not occur adjacent to one another, they carry an additional feature, '**disc**' (discontinuous):

... I *was* just *going to* say [S1B-021 #70] **AUX(semi,past,disc)**

However, if modifiers of the adjectives in semi-auxiliaries are present, they are included in the ditto tags.

...*is almost certain to* be acting in his own interests [W2B-014 #58]	**AUX(semi,pres)**

A repeated semi-auxiliary may be elliptical, but it is tagged in the same way as the full form, except that it is given the added feature ellipt:

Well I *am* [S1A-043 #101]	**AUX(semi,pres,ellipt)**
...but you *needn't* turn it up as I say [S2A-061 #93]	**AUX(semi,pres,neg,ellipt)**

When *be* performs more than one function at the same time, by convention we tag only the first function. In the following example, *was* is both a progressive auxiliary (*was listening*) and a main verb (*was fascinated*). The tag is determined by the first function:

I *was* listening and fascinated [S1A-069 #101]	**AUX(prog,past)**

Semi-auxiliaries followed by an *-ing* participle are tagged '**AUX(semip,...)**'. The ***-ing*** participle is not part of the semi-auxiliary.

I *keep* thinking I must do something about it. [S1A-010 #45]	**AUX(semip,pres)**
He *began* running, feeling light and purposeful... [W2F-008 #96]	**AUX(semip,past)**
I'll have to *stop* talking about the place [W1B-001 #79]	**AUX(semip,infin)**
Outside, it had *started* snowing again... [W2F-004 #205]	**AUX(semip,edp)**

2.2.5 Cleft it *(CLEFTIT)*

The *it* in cleft constructions is tagged '**CLEFTIT**', without any further features.

It was you that told me that... [S1A-099 #272]	**CLEFTIT**
Is *it* pleasure that makes you paint [S1B-008 #144]	**CLEFTIT**

2.2.6 Conjunction (CONJUNC)

The ICE grammar distinguishes two type of conjunctions: coordinating conjunctions ('**coord**') and subordinating conjunctions ('**subord**'). Both carry the main word class label '**CONJUNC**'.

Coordinating conjunctions are labelled '**CONJUNC(coord)**'. The following items are tagged as coordinating conjunctions: *and*, *as well as*, *but*, *for*, *let alone*, *nor*, *or*, *plus*, *rather than* and *yet*. However, when the conjunctions *and*, *but*, *for*, *nor*, *or*, *plus*, and *yet* occur at the beginning of a text unit, they are tagged as general connectives (see 2.2.7 below), rather than coordinators. *Nor* and *yet* are also tagged as connectives when they follow *and* or *but*.

The subordinators are tagged '**CONJUNC(subord)**'. They include *after*, *if*, *since*, *so*, *that*, *unless*, *until* and *when(ever)*. Multi-word subordinators may also be discontinuous.

2.2.7 *Connective (CONNEC)*

The ICE grammar distinguishes two types of connectives: general connectives, '**CONNEC(ge)**', and appositive connectives, '**CONNEC(appos)**'.

General connectives are used to establish a relation between the current clause or sentence and (one or more) previous clauses or sentences.

And we are suspicious again [W2C-001 #56]	**CONNEC(ge)**
But his own position is well known [W2C-003 #47]	**CONNEC(ge)**
However there have been delays [S2A-063 #6]	**CONNEC(ge)**

Appositive connectives are tagged '**CONNEC(appos)**'. They typically occur between items which are in apposition.

... certain aspects of my life *such as* work and exams [S1A-059 #19]	**CONNEC(appos)**
...national capitals (*e.g.*, Oslo and Athens) [W2A-020 #16]	**CONNEC(appos)**

The feature '**disc**' indicates discontinuous appositive connectives.

that	**CONNEC(appos,disc):1/4**
is	**CONNEC(appos,disc):2/4**
perhaps	ADV(ge)
to	**CONNEC(appos,disc):3/4**
say	**CONNEC(appos,disc):4/4**

2.2.8 *Existential* there *(EXTHERE)*

Existential *there* is tagged '**EXTHERE**'. This tag does not carry any features. The main verb in existential constructions is tagged *intransitive*.

...within this particular class *there* are limitations [S1A-002 #24]	**EXTHERE**
How many are *there* [S1A-010 #128]	**EXTHERE**

2.2.9 *Formulaic expression (FRM)*

Formulaic expressions are tagged '**FRM**', without any further features. The class includes greetings and farewells (such as *adieu*, *bye*, *goodbye*, *hello* and *Merry Christmas*), thanks (*cheers*, *thanks*, *thank you*), and apologies (*excuse me*, *I beg your pardon*, *sorry*). It also include expletives (*Christ*, *damn*, *fuck*, *shit*) and the discourse markers *I mean* and *you know*.

2.2.10 Genitive marker (GENM)

In ICE-GB, the genitive marker – written either as an apostrophe (') or as an apostrophe followed by *s* (*'s*) – is separated from the word preceding it. It is assigned the tag '**GENM**'.

...Napoleon *'s* bedroom [S1A-009 #9]	**GENM**
...we are different from boys *'* schools [S1A-012 #210]	**GENM**

2.2.11 Interjection (INTERJEC)

Interjections are emotive words that do not enter into syntactic relations. Examples include *aha*, *boo*, *ha*, *oops* and *wow*. The class also includes the voiced pauses *uh* and *uhm*. All interjections are tagged '**INTERJEC**', without any features.

2.2.12 Noun (N)

Nouns carry the word class label '**N**', followed by two features. The first distinguishes between common ('**com**') and proper ('**prop**') nouns, and the second indicates number – singular ('**sing**') or plural ('**plu**').

The assignment of singular and plural relies predominantly on form. No distinction is made between singular count nouns and noncount (or mass) nouns. The following nouns in boldface are therefore tagged '**sing**':

Tubular steel *furniture* [S1A-074 #65]	this *research* [S1A-056 #39]
all the *information* [S1A-016 #301]	white *wine* [S1A-038 #210]

Singular collective nouns are tagged '**sing**'; for example: *board*, *gang*, *team*, and *committee*. So too are *news*, names of disciplines, *etc.*, ending in *-ics* (for example, *mathematics*, *physics*, *politics*, and *athletics*), names of diseases ending in *-s* (*measles*, *mumps*); and names of certain games ending in *-s* (*dominoes*, *darts*). However, some of these nouns may be used with number contrast, and in such cases the final *-s* marks the plural; for example: a *statistic* / some *statistics*, a *dart* / two *darts*.

Some nouns that are not morphologically marked as plural are tagged '**plu**' because they require a plural verb:

... the *police* are not directly accountable... [S1B-033 #110]	**N(com,plu)**

The distinction between common and proper nouns is made simply on the basis of the absence or presence of an initial capital letter. If a noun begins without a capital it is a common noun, if it begins with a capital it is a proper noun (unless the capital is only required to mark the beginning of a sentence).

...just being involved in *dance* [S1A-001 #69] **N(com,sing)**
I'm graduating in *June*... [S1A-002 #138] **N(prop,sing)**

To facilitate the parsing process, the concept of a compound noun has been broadened to encompass every sequence of two or more nouns with a noun as Head that constitutes a unit. The nouns in the sequence are assigned ditto tags, determined by the Head of the sequence.

I'm actually involved in an integrated *youth group*... [S1A-002 #122] **N(com,sing)**
...a *London Tourist Board information giver* [S1A-005 #202] **N(com,sing)**
...*interest rate cuts* [W2C-005 #58] **N(com,plu)**

Expressions that are mentioned as linguistic objects are treated as common singular nouns:

You're not telling me *looking-glass* is correct [S1A-023# 44] **N(com,sing)**
Well *heck* is pretty strong [S1B-042 #31] **N(com,sing)**

Genitive nouns with determiner function (or in a noun phrase with determiner function) are not part of the sequence and are therefore tagged independently, for example, *soldier's* in the following.

That's the old [*soldier*]'*s* [*way*] isn't it [S1A-009 #187] **N(com,sing)**

Nouns in apposition are also tagged independently:

...[*chief executive*] [*John Conlon*] ... [W2C-013 #84] **N(prop,sing)**

Contrast this with the tagging of *Professor Roger Scruton*, where *Professor* is a title and the sequence is treated as a compound.

Professor Roger Scruton... [S1B-030 #37] **N(prop,sing)**

Some noun compounds consist of an adjective plus a noun. They are treated as compounds on the basis of their stress pattern (main stress on the first word) or their idiomaticity (for example, *hot dogs* and *French windows*).

If a compound premodifies a noun, the compound is tagged with the Head noun under the sequence rule stated at the beginning of this chapter.

How do... the *Mike Heafy group* feel... [S1A-001 #052] **N(com,sing)**

The titles of books, plays, songs, newspapers, *etc*. are tagged as compound singular proper nouns, without regard to the word classes of their constituents:

Have you seen *The Silence of the Lambs* [S1A-006 #58] **N(prop,sing)**

In titles, punctuation, including the genitive marker (Section 2.2.10), is included in the ditto tags.

...*Young People's Guide to Social Security*... [W2D-002 #74] **N(prop,sing)**

2.2.13 Nominal Adjective (NADJ)

Nominal adjectives carry the main word class label '**NADJ**' and additional features. One major subclass denotes members of a nationality and has plural reference. These carry the feature '**prop**' (proper) because they have an initial capital. Nominal adjectives with this feature cannot have any other features.

... the *English* are branded on their tongue... [S1A-020 #44] **NADJ(prop)**
Not being a lover of the *French*... [S1A-088 #206] **NADJ(prop)**

Three further subclasses of nominal adjectives are distinguished.

1. Words with plural reference to classes of people: these are tagged '**NADJ(plu)**'.

the *weak* against the *strong* [S2A-039 #82] **NADJ(plu)**

2. Words with abstract and singular reference.

If the *worst* comes to the *worst* [S1A-071 #366] **NADJ(sing)**

3. Words with a participial ending. They carry a form feature '**edp**' or '**ingp**', and a number feature '**sing**' or '**plu**'.

the *unemployed* [W2B-019 #56] **NADJ(edp,plu)**

Like other adjectives, nominal adjectives may also be marked for the comparison '**comp**' or superlative '**sup**' form (Section 2.2.1).

The *younger* calmed down eventually [W1B-008 #36] **NADJ(comp,sing)**
I think it's for the *best* [S1A-042 #58] **NADJ(sup,sing)**

2.2.14 Numeral (NUM)

Numerals carry the main word class label '**NUM**'. This is followed by a feature label indicating one of the subtypes given in Table 8.

Each of these subclasses is discussed below. Where relevant, numerals are also marked for number according to their form; hence, *thousand* is singular ('**sing**') and *thousands* is plural ('**plu**'). In written texts, numerals may appear in words (*a hundred*) or as digits (*100*). In spoken texts, they are always spelled out (*nineteen ninety-eight*, or *nineteen hundred and ninety-eight*, not *1998*).

Cardinal numerals carry the feature label '**card**', and a number feature '**sing**' or '**plu**'. Examples include *one* (with singular nouns), *two*, *threes*, *forty-two*, *one hundred*, *a hundred*, *two thousand*, *thousands*, *millions*, *a dozen*, *scores*. The subclass also includes *zero* and its synonyms.

Table 8: Features of numerals.

class	feature	code
type	cardinal	**card**
	ordinal	**ord**
	fraction	**frac**
	hyphenated	**hyph**
	multiplier	**mult**
number	singular	**sing**
	plural	**plu**

I think *nineteen eighty-two* was the last time... [S1A-013 #191] **NUM(card,sing)**
And he died in his *forties* quite recently [S1A-003 #52] **NUM(card,plu)**

The subclass of ordinals includes the primary ordinals, such as *first*, *second*, *10th*, *twenty-first*. It also includes the following: *additional*, *another*, *extra*, *following*, *former*, *further*, *last*, *latter*, *next*, *other*, *others*, *preceding*, *previous*, *same*, and *subsequent*.

Fractions include *a half*, *one fifth*, *three-quarters*, *four-fifths*, *1/8* and *3/5*. They carry the feature label '**frac**' and a number feature '**sing**' or '**plu**'.

I was at a job for three and *a half* days [S1A-017 #204] **NUM(frac,sing)**
So that means over *two thirds*... [S1B-030 #24] **NUM(frac,plu)**

Hyphenated numerals denote an inclusive range. They are simply labelled '**NUM(hyph)**', with no other feature. The 'hyphen' is more properly in print a short dash or en-dash. The range may also be indicated by a slash.

1 Corinthians 13 *4-8* [W1B-006 #32] **NUM(hyph)**
21/11/90 [W1A-006 #01] **NUM(hyph)**

Multipliers include *once*, *twice*, *double*, *triple*. They carry the feature label '**mult**', and no number feature.

Triple the price [S1A-048 #37] **NUM(mult)**

2.2.15 Preposition (PREP)

Prepositions carry the main word class label '**PREP**', followed by the feature label '**ge**' (general), '**phras**' (phrasal), or '**inter**' (interrogative)

General prepositions are tagged '**PREP(ge)**'. These may be simple prepositions, consisting of just one word, such as *about*, *by*, *for*, *of*, *to*, and *with*.

We also recognise a large number of complex prepositions. This group includes *according to*, *by means of*, *except for*, *prior to*, *with reference to*, *thanks to*. Complex prepositions are ditto-tagged, and may be also marked as elliptical ('**ellipt**') or discontinuous ('**disc**').

...in relation to international images and *to* ... identity... [S1B-036 #25]	**PREP(ge,ellipt)**
... *subject* only *to* the limited category... [S2A-065 #38]	**PREP(ge,disc)**

Prepositions that combine with verbs to form intransitive prepositional verbs are tagged '**PREP(phras)**'. The verb and preposition are tagged separately, since prepositional verbs and phrasal-prepositional verbs are not regarded as multi-word verbs:

he	PRON(pers,sing)
looked	V(intr,past)
at	**PREP(phras)**
me [S1A-014 #209]	PRON(pers,sing)

Similarly, in transitive prepositional constructions, such as:

to	PRTCL(to)
protect	V(montr,infin)
it	PRON(pers,sing)
from	**PREP(phras)**
frost [W2D-012 #40]	N(com,sing)

The preposition may be stranded after the verb, without its complement:

... that's what I'm talking *about* [S1A-010 #37]	**PREP(phras)**

Finally, *what about*, *how about*, and *what of* are tagged '**PREP(inter)**':

What about the father [S1A-019 #37]	**PREP(inter)**
And *how about* your general health apart from this [S1A-051 #292]	**PREP(inter)**
And *what of* British political reaction... [S2B-018 #79]	**PREP(inter)**

2.2.16 Proform (PROFM)

Proforms carry the main word class label '**PROFM**'. There are two subtypes, proform conjoin, '**PROFM(conj)**', and proform *so*, '**PROFM(so)**', which replaces phrases and clauses.

Proform conjoins include the following items, all introduced by a coordinating conjunction: *(or) so*, *(and) so forth*, *(or) whatever*, *(and/but/or) the reverse*. The conjunction is not part of the proform.

It comes on after ten minutes or *so* anyway [S1A-099 #215]	**PROFM(conj)**
Never mind the size feel the width or length or *whatever* [S1A-027 #266]	**PROFM(conj)**
Is Bim at the Slade now or *not* [S1A-015 #72]	**PROFM(conj)**

The following are examples of '**PROFM(so)**'.

I think *so* [S1A-003 # 131]	**PROFM(so)**
It says *so* on the tape recorder [S1A-039 # 104]	**PROFM(so)**

The proform *so* has a negative counterpart in the word *not*.

No I suppose *not* [S1A-099 #125]	**PROFM(so)**

2.2.17 Pronoun (PRON)

Pronouns carry the main word class label '**PRON**' and a feature label for the subclass. We distinguish the subclasses of pronoun indicated in Table 9. Where a distinction in number is relevant, the feature '**sing**' or '**plu**' is assigned. There is no assignment of case features.

Anticipatory *it* is tagged '**PRON(antit)**'.

It's pretty hard to park there anyway [S1A-006 #258]	**PRON(antit)**
But he made *it* clear he would continue to co-operate... [S1B-008 #64]	**PRON(antit)**

The assertive pronouns are *some*, *somebody*, *someone*, and *something*. Except for *some*, they are tagged '**PRON(ass,sing)**'.

The demonstrative pronouns are *that*, *these*, *this*, *those* and *such*. Except for *such*, they are marked for number as '**PRON(dem,sing)**' or '**PRON(dem, plu)**'.

The exclamative pronoun *what*, as in *what a great week it has been!*, and *what fun!*, is tagged '**PRON(exclam)**'.

Negative pronouns are marked with the feature '**neg**'. These pronouns

Table 9: Features of pronouns.

class	**feature**	**code**
type	anticipatory *it*	**antit**
	assertive	**ass**
	demonstrative	**dem**
	exclamative	**exclam**
	negative	**neg**
	nonassertive	**nonass**
	one	**one**
	personal	**pers**
	possessive	**poss**
	quantifying	**quant**
	reciprocal	**recip**
	reflexive	**ref**
	relative	**rel**
	universal	**univ**
number	singular	**sing**
	plural	**plu**

are *neither*, *nobody*, *no one*, and *nothing* (which are tagged '**PRON(neg, sing)**'), and *no* and *none* (tagged '**PRON(neg)**').

The nonassertive pronouns ('**PRON(nonass)**') are *any*, *anyone*, *either*, *anybody* and *anything*. All except *any* are also marked as '**sing**' (singular).

The pronoun *one* subclass comprises *one* and *ones*. *One* can be either a substitute pronoun, with *ones* as plural, or a generic (indefinite) pronoun. Generic *one* does not have a plural.

Is that the *one* [S1A-011 #124]	(substitute)	**PRON(one,sing)**
I like the sweet *ones* [S1A-019 #17]	(substitute)	**PRON(one,plu)**
One can't have everything [W2F-016 #63]	(generic)	**PRON(one,sing)**

Personal pronouns are tagged '**PRON(pers)**', and except for *you*, they are also tagged for number, but not for case. Examples include *she*, *he*, *it* (tagged '**PRON(pers,sing)**'), *us* ('**PRON(pers,plu)**') and *you* ('**PRON(pers)**').

Also tagged '**PRON(pers,sing)**' are abbreviations or combinations such as *s/he* and *him/her*. Proclitic *it*, as in *'tis*, is tagged as '**PRON(pers,sing, procl)**'), while proclitic *you*, as in *y'know*, is tagged '**PRON(pers,procl)**', and enclitic *us*, as in *let's*, is tagged '**PRON(pers,plu,encl)**'.

Prop or dummy *it*, as in *It's raining* and *It's nine o'clock*, is tagged '**PRON(pers,sing)**'.

Possessive pronouns are tagged '**PRON(poss)**', and except for *your* and *yours* they are also tagged for number. Combinations such as *his/her* are tagged '**PRON(poss,sing)**'.

Quantifying pronouns are tagged '**PRON(quant)**', and some are tagged for number ('**sing**' or '**plu**'). The quantifying pronouns are shown in Table 10.

There are only two compound reciprocal pronouns, *each other* and *one another*, ditto-tagged as '**PRON(recip)**'.

Reflexive pronouns are tagged '**PRON(ref)**', and carry an additional feature label for number.

Relative pronouns (*which*, *who*, *whom*, *whose*, *that*, and *whereby*) are tagged '**PRON(rel)**'. Number and case are not marked.

Universal pronouns (*all*, *both*, *each*, *every*, *everyone*, *everybody*) are tagged '**PRON(univ)**'. *All* is not tagged for number, *both* is tagged as plural. All other universal pronouns are tagged as singular.

Table 10: Quantifying pronouns.

PRON(quant)	**PRON(quant,sing)**	**PRON(quant,plu)**
enough, plenty		
least, less	*little*	*few, fewer, fewest*
more, most	*much*	*many, several*

2.2.18 Particle (PRTCL)

Particles are assigned the main word class label '**PRTCL**' and one of the following identifying subclass features – '**to**', '**for**', or '**with**'. If the particle is discontinuous, the feature '**disc**' is also used.

Particle *to* ('**PRTCL(to)**') introduces an infinitive clause. The subclass includes *to*, *in order to*, and *so as to*.

Oh I'd love *to* see that [S1A-065 #329]	**PRTCL(to)**
In order to make that assessment did you examine... [S1B-068 #38]	**PRTCL(to)**
...be punctual *so as to* reduce waiting time. [W2D-009 #102]	**PRTCL(to)**
...*in order* better *to* discharge my responsibilities [S1B-059 #94]	**PRTCL(to,disc)**

Particle *for* ('**PRTCL(for)**') introduces the subject of an infinitive clause. The subclass includes *for* and *in order for*.

Have you got to pay *for* Betty to go [S1A-030 #20]	**PRTCL(for)**
In order for you to claim additional tax relief I enclose... [W1B-022 #82]	**PRTCL(for)**

Particle *with* ('**PRTCL(with)**') introduces the subject of a nonfinite or verbless clause. The subclass includes *with* and *without*.

Don't turn around *with* a microphone on [S2A-029 #80]	**PRTCL(with)**
They have reasons enough, *without* being handed more. [W2F-007 #64]	**PRTCL(with)**

2.2.19 Reaction signal (REACT)

Reaction signals express agreement or disagreement with a previous speaker. They are tagged '**REACT**', without any feature. The class includes *all right*, *fine*, *good*, *no*, *ok*, *right* and *yes*.

2.2.20 Verb (V)

Lexical verbs are tagged '**V**', followed by at least two features (see Table 11). The first feature specifies the complementation pattern. The ICE grammar recognises seven complementation patterns, and these are discussed in more detail below.

The second feature indicates the form of the verb, selected from the set labelled 'tense/form' in Table 11. The clitic features '**encl**' and '**neg**' apply only to the lexical verbs *be* and *have*. Verbs with imperative mood carry the feature label '**infin**' (infinitive). The imperative mood feature ('**imp**') is carried by the clause which dominates the VP (see Section 2.5.3).

With the exception of transitive ('**trans**'), the complementation patterns in the ICE grammar conform to those described in Quirk *et al* (1985: 1170ff.). Intransitive verbs ('**intr**') are not followed by any object or complement.

...life *begins* at forty [W2B-010 #230]	**V(intr,pres)**
You *graduated* in the summer... [S1A-034 #3]	**V(intr,past)**
Just don't know where to *stop*... [S1A-084 #235]	**V(intr,infin)**

Copular verbs ('**cop**') require the presence of a subject complement.

Food *is* available but not fuel to cook it with [S2B-005 #80]	**V(cop,pres)**
Uh so you actually *aren't* a member of staff [S1B-062 #54]	**V(cop,pres,neg)**
It*'s* on the ground floor [S1A-073 #54]	**V(cop,pres,encl)**
Somehow he *looks* nice [S1A-065 #188]	**V(cop,pres)**
I *felt* quite ignorant [S1A-002 #83]	**V(cop,past)**
If anything it *seems* lighter [S1A-023 #164]	**V(cop,pres)**

All instances of *be* as a lexical verb are tagged as copular, with the exception of the verb in cleft and existential constructions. In these constructions, *be* is tagged as intransitive.

Monotransitive verbs ('**montr**') are complemented by a direct object only.

I *buy* books all the time for work [S1A-013 #4]	**V(montr,pres)**
I *used* the wrong tactics [W2C-014 #106]	**V(montr,past)**
just... *sign* your name there [S1B-026 #160]	**V(montr,infin)**
Have you *seen* it [S1A-006 #103]	**V(montr,edp)**
I *haven't* a clue [S1B-080 #189]	**V(montr,pres,neg)**

Dimonotransitive verbs ('**dimontr**') are complemented by an indirect object only. They include *show*, *ask*, *assure*, *grant*, *inform*, *promise*, *reassure*, and *tell*.

...when I *asked* her, she burst into tears [S1A-094 #110]	**V(dimontr,past)**
I'll *tell* you tomorrow [S1A-099 #396]	**V(dimontr,infin)**
Show me [S1A-042 #219]	**V(dimontr,infin)**

Table 11: Features of verbs.

class	feature	code
transitivity	intransitive	**intr**
	copular	**cop**
	monotransitive	**montr**
	dimonotransitive	**dimontr**
	ditransitive	**ditr**
	complex-transitive	**cxtr**
	transitive	**trans**
tense/form	present	**pres**
	past	**past**
	-ed participle	**edp**
	-ing participle	**ingp**
	infinitive	**infin**
clitics	enclitic	**encl**
	negative	**neg**

Ditransitive verbs ('**ditr**') are complemented by both an indirect object and a direct object.

We *tell* each other everything [S1A-054 #2] **V(ditr,pres)**
So they *built* themselves a magnificent amphitheatre [S2B-027 #21] **V(ditr,past)**
Give us the answers [S1B-004 #156] **V(ditr,infin)**

Complex transitive verbs ('**cxtr**') are complemented by a direct object and an object complement.

... some people just *find* it very difficult [S1A-037 #31] **V(cxtr,pres)**
A glass of wine would *make* me incapable... [W2B-001 #51] **V(cxtr,infin)**
I hope you *take* that as a compliment [S1B-028 #93] **V(cxtr,pres)**

The transitivity is unclear in many instances where the main verb is transitive and is followed by a noun phrase that may be the subject of the nonfinite clause or the object of the host clause. In all such cases, we avoid deciding the type of transitivity by tagging the main verb '**V(trans,...)**'.

You *wanted* them to recognise your experience... [S1A-060 #151] **V(trans,past)**
I *saw* myself launching off into a philosophical treatise [S1A-001 #89] **V(trans,past)**
Is it pleasure that *makes* you paint [S1B-008 #144] **V(trans,pres)**

However, the '**trans**' label is *not* applied if:

1. the lexical verb is *be*:

   The aim *is* to help pupils to acquire knowledge and skills... [S2A-039 #20] **V(cop,pres)**
   What they actually did *was* send 6 huge C.I.D. men... [W1B-007 #6] **V(cop,past)**

2. the nonfinite clause does not have an overt subject:

   We just *wanted* to go to sleep [W1B-012 #16] **V(montr,past)**
   No I've *enjoyed* doing it [S1B-026 #227] **V(montr,edp)**

3. the noun phrase is followed by a *wh*-clause whose verb is a *to*-infinitive:

   I'll *tell* you why I had to phone then [S1A-099 #389] **V(ditr,infin)**
   The Document *shows* the buyer how to do this [W2D-010 #58] **V(ditr,pres)**

The following points should also be noted:

a) In passive constructions, the tagging of the main verb is the same as it would be if the verb were active:

   He's been *caught* in a challenge... [S2A-014 #72] **V(montr,edp)**
   (*cf.* They caught him in a challenge)
   ...the unions were *told* of the impact on jobs [S2B-002 #71] **V(dimontr,edp)**
   (*cf.* They told the unions of the impact on jobs)
   ...I may be *proved* wrong... [S1A-054 #79] **V(cxtr,edp)**
   (*cf.* Someone may prove me wrong)

b) Constructions tagged **`V(trans,...)`** are generally tagged the same in the passive:

Then the wall is plastered and *allowed* to dry [S2A-052 #87] **`V(trans,edp)`**
(*cf.* You allow the wall to dry)
...which is commonly *found* growing wild in Egypt [S2A-048 #75] **`V(trans,edp)`**
(*cf.* You commonly find it growing wild in Egypt)

c) Prepositional verbs and phrasal-prepositional verbs that are tagged as intransitive in the active are tagged as monotransitive when they occur in the passive:

I'll *deal* with it [S1A-007 #190] **`V(intr,infin)`**
...the problem was *dealt* with... [W1B-020 #49] **`V(montr,edp)`**

The prepositions which collocate with these verbs are tagged '**`PREP(phras)`**', described in Section 2.2.15.

d) In existential sentences and in cleft sentences, the lexical verb is labelled **`intr`** (intransitive):

Existential: There *are* lots of deer and lots of rabbits [S1A-006 #264] **`V(intr,pres)`**
Cleft: It *was* Connie who had been deceitful [W2F-006 #17] **`V(intr,past)`**

In sentences with anticipatory *it*, the lexical verb is tagged as in regular sentence patterns:

...so it *makes* sense to use it [S1A-088 #31] **`V(montr,pres)`**
(*cf.* ...so to use it makes sense)
Well it sometimes *happens* that... you can't go back [S2A-008 #53] **`V(intr,pres)`**
(*cf.* That you can't go back sometimes happens...)

2.2.21 Miscellaneous tags

Punctuation marks appear only in written texts. They are tagged with the main label '**`PUNC`**', followed by a feature specifying their type. Table 12 summarises the tagging of punctuation marks.

Pauses carry the main label '**`PAUSE`**', followed by a single feature. For

Table 12: Punctuation types.

class	feature	code	comments
type	closing bracket	**cbrack**	')', ']', '>', *etc.*
	colon	**col**	
	closing quote	**cquo**	single, double.
	comma	**comma**	
	dash	**dash**	dashes, including '~'.
	ellipsis	**ellip**	*i.e.*, '...'.
	exclamation mark	**exm**	
	opening bracket	**obrack**	'(', '{', '«', *etc.*
	opening quote	**oquo**	single, double.
	period	**per**	full stop.
	question mark	**qm**	
	semicolon	**scol**	
	other	**other**	various, *e.g.*, '★', '■'.

silent pauses, the feature simply indicates the length of the pause ('**short**' or '**long**'). This tag is also used for pauses due to laughter ('**PAUSE(laugh)**') and vocalising ('**PAUSE(vocal)**'). In the transcription of spoken texts, short pauses are marked as <,> and long pauses are marked as <,,> (see also Section 1.4 on structural markup).

The tag '**UNTAG**' is used to label incomplete words. These occur most commonly in spoken texts, though they may also be found in handwritten texts.

...Uhm while I was there as a *pai* [S1A-004 #41] **UNTAG**

'**UNTAG**' is also used to label words whose word class is indeterminate because of a false start or incomplete utterance:

She *had* [S1A-018 #85] **UNTAG**

Here, *had* is indeterminate between lexical *have* and auxiliary *have*, so it is tagged '**UNTAG**'. This tag does not carry any features.

Items are tagged with a question mark ('**?**') if they are so unclear as to make it impossible to decide their word class. These items usually appear as "<unclear-syllable(s)>" or "<unclear-word(s)>" in the transcriptions. The markup label "<unclear>" is also used, which is indicated with a blue underline in ICECUP (see Section 4.4 and Appendix 4).

It has to be tried <unclear-words> [S1A-056 #102] **?**

In other cases, words may be unclear, but it may still be possible to determine their word class, for instance in personal names.

...our friend Michael <unclear-word>... [S1A-057 #156] **N(prop,sing)**

2.3 Functions and categories

In this section we discuss the function and category labels used in the ICE grammar. The feature labels are discussed in Section 2.4. Appendix 5 contains an alphabetical list of all the syntactic labels – functions, categories, and features. We indicate the type of label below using the following abbreviations.

[Function]	Function Label
[Category]	Category Label

2.3.1 Adverbial (A) [Function]

Principally a top-level function, adverbial usually appears as one of the primary constituents of a clause. However, adverbials can appear at practically any level

Figure 15: Typical Adjective Phrase (AJP) structure (S1A-005 #157). The lighter boxes are optional.

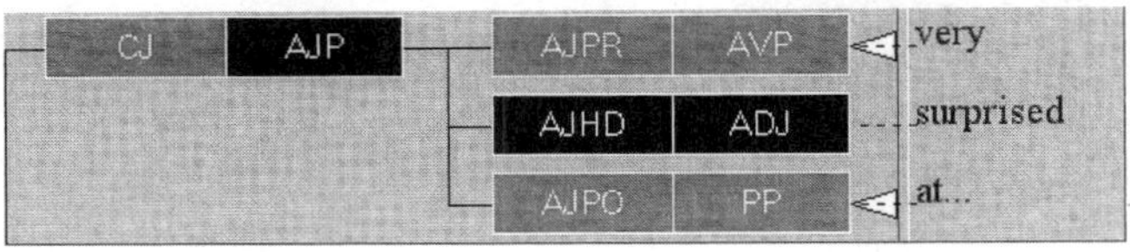

of the tree and within any category on the tree. An adverbial can be realised by the categories '**AVP**', '**CL**', '**NP**', '**PP**', and '**DISP**'.

Sorry could you start *again* [S1A-001 #3]	**AVP**
That appeals to you *both* [S1A-002 #97]	**NP**
I'm just going to go berserk *for a while* [S1A-001 #22]	**PP**

2.3.2 Adjective Phrase (AJP) [Category]

An adjective phrase consists of a Head (with function '**AJHD**'), and optional premodifiers ('**AJPR**') and postmodifiers ('**AJPO**'). This structure is exemplified in Figure 15.

2.3.3 Adjective Phrase Head (AJHD) [Function]

Realised by the word class category '**ADJ**'. See Figure 15.

2.3.4 Adjective Phrase Postmodifier (AJPO) [Function]

May be realised by the categories '**AVP**', '**PP**', '**CL**' and '**DISP**'. See Figure 15.

2.3.5 Adjective Phrase Premodifier (AJPR) [Function]

Related categories: '**AVP**', '**NP**', '**DISP**'. See Figure 15.

2.3.6 Adverb Phrase Head (AVHD) [Function]

Realised by the word class category '**ADV**':

I finished *yesterday*[S1A-040 #174]	**ADV**
A little too *quickly* perhaps [S2A-001 #222]	**ADV**

2.3.7 Adverb Phrase (AVP) [Category]

An adverb phrase consists of a Head ('**AVHD**') and, optionally, premodifiers ('**AVPR**') and postmodifiers ('**AVPO**'). Figure 16 shows an adverb phrase with all of these elements.

Figure 16: Typical Adverb Phrase (AVP) structure (W1B-014 #12).

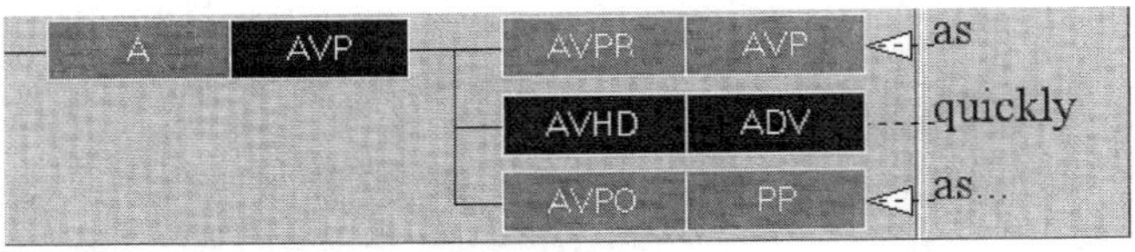

2.3.8 Adverb Phrase Postmodifier (AVPO) [Function]

Related categories: '**PP**', '**VP**', '**CL**', '**AJP**'. See Figure 16.

No because I plan to be out of phonetics as quickly *as possible* really [S1A-008 #15]	**PP**
Had I been hassling you so much *you couldn't bear it* [S1A-068 #128]	**CL**

2.3.9 Adverb Phrase Premodifier (AVPR) [Function]

Related categories: '**AVP**', '**NP**'. See Figure 16.

You do get to know everybody *quite* well [S1A-002 #111]	**AVP**
and then he rings up *two months* later [S1B-065 #88]	**NP**

2.3.10 Auxiliary Verb (AVB) [Function]

The function label '**AVB**' is applied when the auxiliary is *not* the first auxiliary in the verb phrase. Related category: '**AUX**'.

Everything else has *been* stopped [S1A-012 #251]	**AUX**

The typical structure of a verb phrase is shown in Figure 24 on page 55. See also: operator ('**OP**', see Section 2.3.45).

2.3.11 Central Determiner (DTCE) [Function]

Related categories: '**ART**', '**NP**', '**PRON**', '**NUM**'.

I won't be *a* second Richard [S1A-001 #21]	**ART**
Just like *any* other dance group we would be self-financing [S1A-001 #97]	**PRON**
It's *another* language [S1A-015 #169]	**NUM**
That's *the old soldier's* way isn't it [S1A-009 #187]	**NP**

See also: determiner ('**DT**', Section 2.3.17), determiner phrase ('**DTP**', 2.3.18), determiner premodifier ('**DTPR**', 2.3.20), determiner postmodifier ('**DTPO**', 2.3.19), postdeterminer ('**DTPS**', 2.3.48) and predeterminer ('**DTPR**', 2.3.49) .

Figure 17: Some constituents of a clause (S1A-001 #19).

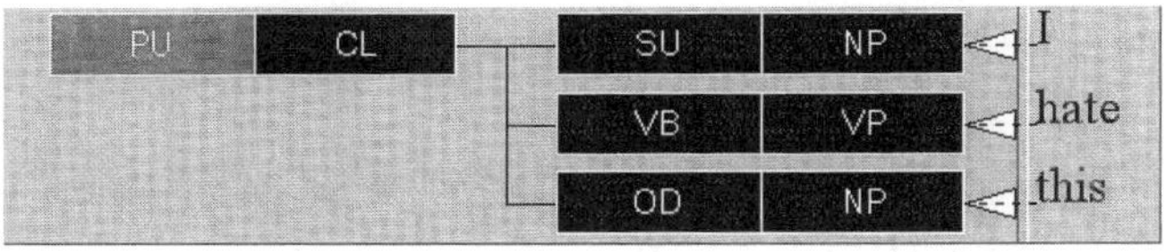

2.3.12 Clause (CL) [Category]

Some of the standard constituents of a clause can be seen in Figure 17. Clause is one of the principal realisations of the parsing unit ('**PU**') function, and often appears at the top-most level of the tree.

2.3.13 Cleft Operator (CLOP) [Function]

The function label applied to cleft *it* (with category '**CLEFTIT**').

It's exercise you need, not rest [W2F-013 #45]	**CLEFTIT**

See also: cleft *it* ('**CLEFTIT**', Section 2.2.5), focus ('**FOC**', 2.3.28), focus complement ('**CF**', 2.3.29).

2.3.14 Conjoin (CJ) [Function]

Conjoin is discussed properly in relation to coordination in Section 2.5.4. Related categories: '**NP**', '**CL**', '**AJP**', '**AVP**', '**PP**', '**PREDEL**', '**VP**', '**NONCL**', '**DISP**'.

You play this back and *I'll kill you* [S1A-069 #80]	**CL**
With working now in *movement* and *dance* [S1A-003 #12]	**NP**
It's only *two hundred* and *fifty* sods [S1A-008 #239]	**DTP**

2.3.15 Coordinator (COOR) [Function]

Related category: '**CONJUNC**'. See Section 2.5.4 on coordination.

Because me *and* John said [S1A-005 #4]	**CONJUNC**

2.3.16 Detached Function (DEFUNC) [Function]

DEFUNC is applied to parenthetical clauses and vocatives. Related categories: '**NP**', '**CL**', '**AJP**', '**DISP**'.

You could *I suppose* commission some prints of you yourself [S1A-015 #37]	**CL**
You're a snob *Dad* [S1A-007 #180]	**NP**

See also Section 2.5.5 on the treatment of direct speech.

2.3.17 Determiner (DT) [Function]

Related category: '**DTP**'. See Figures 18 and 19.

2.3.18 Determiner Phrase (DTP) [Category]

Determiner phrases occur within noun phrases, and have the typical structure defined by Figure 18. The elements on the right-hand side are (reading downwards), determiner premodifier, predeterminer, central determiner, postdeterminer and determiner postmodifier. This complete configuration does not appear in ICE-GB, however. Figure 19 shows some actual examples.

2.3.19 Determiner Postmodifier (DTPO) [Function]

Related categories: '**AVP**', '**PP**'. See Figures 18 and 19.

About thirty *odd* pounds... [S1A-048 #313] **AVP**

Figure 18: Typical Determiner Phrase (DTP) structure.

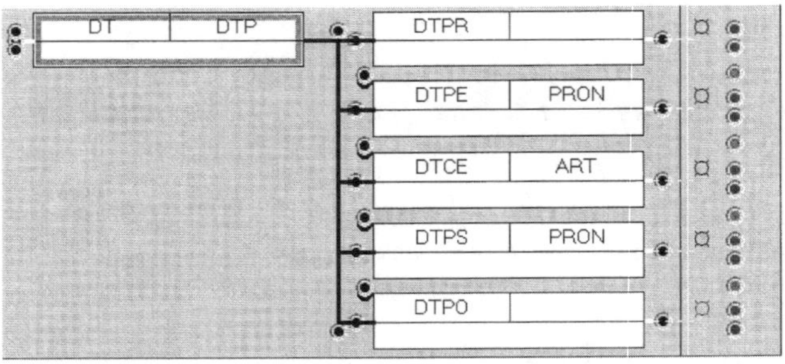

Figure 19: Examples of DTPs (upper, S1A-075 #77; lower, S1A-048 #313).

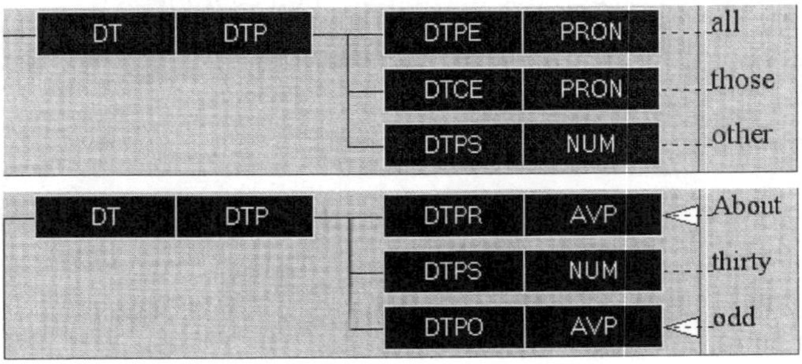

2.3.20 Determiner Premodifier (DTPR) [Function]

Related categories: '**AVP**', '**AJP**', '**NP**'.

About three miles probably [S1A-006 #297]	**AVP**
That's a *good* ten minutes I should think [S1A-006 #297]	**AJP**
Half a year [S1B-080 #199]	**NP**

2.3.21 Direct Object (OD) [Function]

Direct objects occur with monotransitive ('**montr**'), ditransitive ('**ditr**'), or complex transitive ('**cxtr**') verbs. Related categories: '**NP**', '**CL**', '**AJP**', '**REACT**', '**INTERJEC**', '**DISP**'.

I hate *this* [S1A-001 #19]	**NP**
Excuse me I've got to do *what I did last time* [S1A-001 #18]	**CL**

2.3.22 Discourse Marker (DISMK) [Function]

Discourse markers may appear at any level in the tree, *e.g.*, at the top-level of a clause, within a phrase, or alone in a non-clause, as in the second example below. Related categories: '**INTERJEC**', '**FRM**', '**CONNEC**', '**REACT**'.

and I'll then start again [S1A-001 #23]	**CONNEC**
You know [S1A-010 #46]	**FRM**
Ah thank you [S1A-001 #24]	**INTERJEC**

2.3.23 Disparate (DISP) [Category]

See Section 2.5.4 on coordination.

2.3.24 Element (ELE) [Function]

Phrases occurring in a non-clause ('**NONCL**') have the function element ('**ELE**').

Ten second [S1A-001 #7]	**NP**
Uh *Monday or Tuesday* anyway [S1A-001 #7]	**NP**
Quite sad [S1A-014 #121]	**AJP**

2.3.25 Empty (EMPTY) [Category]

The category label applied to a parsing unit ('**PU**') that contains only non-textual material, *e.g.*, editorial references to graphics, photos, or editorial comments.

2.3.26 Existential Operator (EXOP) [Function]

The function label applied to existential *there*. Related category: '**EXTHERE**'.

there're many projects that they have on hand uhm [S1A-003 #71] **EXTHERE**

2.3.27 Floating Noun Phrase Postmodifier (FNPPO) [Function]

An NP postmodifier which does not immediately follow the Head. Related categories: '**AJP**', '**CL**', '**PP**', '**DISP**'.

I mean one bloke did get married *from our course* [S1A-014 #157] **PP**

See also noun phrase postmodifier ('**NPPO**', Section 2.3.42)

2.3.28 Focus (FOC) [Function]

The focus of a cleft construction. Related categories: '**AVP**', '**CL**', '**PP**', '**NP**'.

And it was *then* that he felt a sharp pain [S2A-067 #68] **AVP**
It is *what you put in and what you achieve* which counts [S2B-035 #4] **CL**
Is it *your brother* who knew Peter [S1A-019 #291] **NP**

2.3.29 Focus Complement (CF) [Function]

The function label applied to the relative clause in a cleft construction. Related category: '**CL**'.

Is it your brother *who knew Peter* [S1A-019 #291] **CL**

2.3.30 Genitive function (GENF) [Function]

The function label applied to genitive markers ('**GENM**'). See Figure 20.

Uh do you remember the ones you took of Napoleon*'s* bedroom [S1A-009 #9] **GENM**

Figure 20: Typical Genitive Construction (S1A-009 #9).

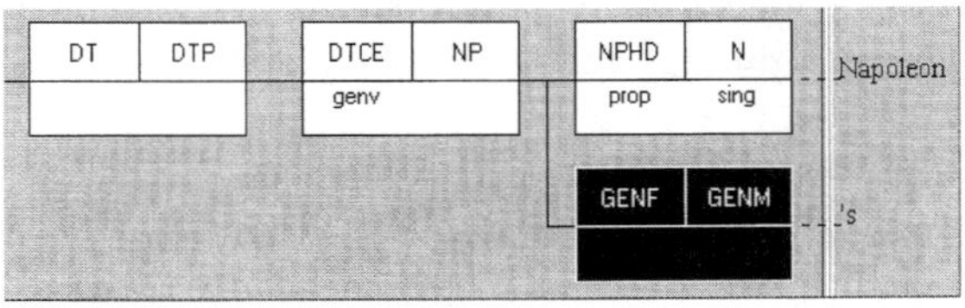

2.3.31 Imperative Operator (IMPOP) [Function]

The imperative operator function is only used when an auxiliary is detached from the verb phrase. See the discussion on imperatives in Section 2.5.3. Related category '**AUX**'.

> *Let*'s stop it for the moment [S1A-001 #50] **AUX**

2.3.32 Indeterminate (INDET) [Function]

An element that has an indeterminate syntactic function. The function may be indeterminate for a number of reasons. For instance, the utterance may break off before it is finished, leaving stranded a number of elements whose function cannot be determined. Related categories: '**UNTAG**', '**?**', '**AJP**', '**AVP**', '**CL**', '**NP**', '**PP**', '**VP**', '**DTP**', '**DISP**'.

> Did you not <*unclear-words*> [S1A-001 #5] **?**

2.3.33 Indirect object (OI) [Function]

Indirect objects occur with ditransitive and dimonotransitive verbs. Related category: '**NP**'.

> Tell *him* we are waiting for the order [S1A-004 #46] **NP**

2.3.34 Interrogative Operator (INTOP) [Function]

The interrogative operator function is only used with an auxiliary when it is detached from the verb phrase. See the discussion on interrogatives in Section 2.5.2. Related categories: '**AUX**', '**V**'.

> Sorry *could* you start again [S1A-001 #3] **AUX**
> *Is* Michelle in here [S1B-079 #11] **V**

2.3.35 Inverted Operator (INVOP) [Function]

The inverted operator function is only used with the auxiliary when it is detached from the verb phrase. Inversion is discussed in Section 2.5.1. Related categories: '**AUX**', '**V**'.

> So *do* I [S1A-005 #149] **AUX**
> Here*'s* a napkin [S1A-061 #142] **V**

2.3.36 Main Verb (MVB) [Function]

Related category: verb ('**V**').

2.3.37 Nonclause (NONCL) [Category]

A non-clause is defined as a string of words which constitutes a complete parsing unit but not a clause.

OK [S1A-001 #4] **PU**
Three two one [S1A-001 #9] **PU**

2.3.38 Notional Direct Object (NOOD) [Function]

See the feature extraposed direct object ('**extod**') in Section 2.4. Related category: '**CL**'.

They're not finding it a stress *being in the same office* [S1A-018 #9] **CL**

2.3.39 Notional Subject (NOSU) [Function]

See extraposed subject ('**extsu**') in Section 2.4. Related category: '**CL**'.

It's pretty hard *to park there* anyway [S1A-006 #258] **CL**

2.3.40 Noun Phrase (NP) [Category]

A noun phrase consists of a noun phrase head ('**NPHD**') and optional premodifiers ('**NPPR**') and postmodifiers ('**NPPO**'). Determiners, if any, are also dominated by the NP node. The typical structure of an NP is shown in Figure 21.

2.3.41 Noun Phrase Head (NPHD) [Function]

Related categories: '**N**', '**NADJ**', '**NUM**', '**PRON**', '**PROFM**'. See Figure 21.

medium *speed* [S1A-001 #8] **N**
It's like *Turkish* [S1A-015 #164] **NADJ**
I presume this is the *first* [S1A-002 #121] **NUM**

Figure 21: Typical Noun Phrase (NP) Structure (S1A-006 #172).

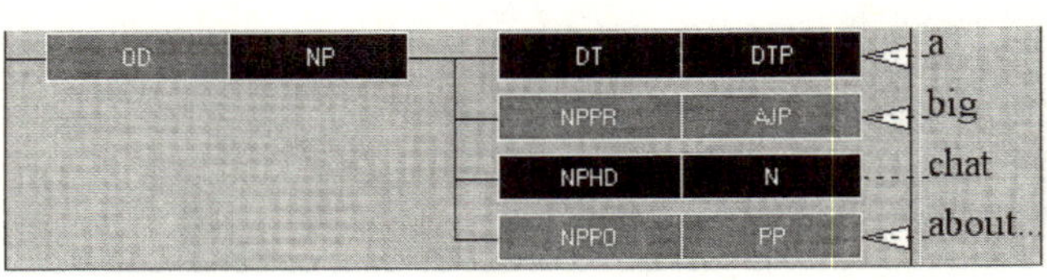

2.3.42 Noun Phrase Postmodifier (NPPO) [Function]

Related categories: '**PP**', '**CL**', '**AVP**', '**AJP**', '**NP**', '**DISP**'. See Figure 21.

A sense *of evil* [W2F-020 #42]	**PP**
... a programme *called Don't Mention the War* [W2B-001 #14]	**CL**
Someone *else* [S1A-005 #100]	**AVP**

See also: floating noun phrase postmodifier ('**FNPPO**', Section 2.3.27).

2.3.43 Noun Phrase Premodifier (NPPR) [Function]

Related categories: '**AVP**', '**AJP**', '**NP**', '**DISP**'. See Figure 21.

Global problems [W2A-030 #24]	**AJP**
... the Observer's *then* deputy editor [W2B-015 #17]	**AVP**
That was the horrible *nine o'clock* one on a Tuesday [S1A-008 #34]	**NP**

2.3.44 Object Complement (CO) [Function]

Object complements occur with complex transitive verbs. Related categories: '**AVP**', '**AJP**', '**CL**', '**NP**', '**PP**', '**DISP**'.

Leave that battery *alone* [S1A-007 #184]	**AJP**
What do they call it [S1A-006 #16]	**NP**

2.3.45 Operator (OP) [Function]

The function label applied to the *first* auxiliary verb in a verb phrase. Related category: '**AUX**'.

He *has* been a full time writer since 1979. [W2B-005 #54]	**AUX**

The typical structure of a verb phrase is shown in Figure 24, page 55. See also auxiliary verb ('**AVB**', Section 2.3.10).

2.3.46 Parataxis (PARA) [Function]

The function label '**PARA**' is applied to direct speech and reported speech. Related categories: '**CL**', '**DISP**', '**NONCL**'.

And he said *oh yes I agree with you* [S1A-005 #25]	**CL**
So I said *yes here* [S1A-008 #274]	**NONCL**

2.3.47 Parsing Unit (PU) [Function]

The function label '**PU**' is applied to the topmost node on *every* tree. Related categories: '**CL**', '**NONCL**', '**EMPTY**',' **DISP**'.

2.3.48 Postdeterminer (DTPS) [Function]

Related categories: '**NUM**',' **PRON**'. See Figure 18, page 46.

one *more* thing [S1A-002 #154]	**PRON**
Anybody got any *other* ideas [S1A-007 #32]	**NUM**

2.3.49 Predeterminer (DTPE) [Function]

Related categories: '**NUM**', '**PRON**'. Again, refer to Figure 18, page 46.

Half a stone [S1A-011 #206]	**NUM**
We don't need *all* this [S1A-004 #57]	**PRON**

2.3.50 Predicate Element (PREDEL) [Category]

A predicate element is part of the predicate of a clause, but it is only categorised explicitly when it is coordinated with another predicate element.

Have you *taken something off* or *put something on* [S1A-007 #299]	**CJ**

The coordination of predicates is discussed in more detail in Section 2.5.4.

2.3.51 Predicate Group (PREDGP) [Function]

The function label applied to the node immediately dominating coordinated predicate elements. Related categories: '**PREDEL**', '**DISP**'. See also 2.5.4.

2.3.52 Prepositional (P) [Function]

The function label applied to the Head of a prepositional phrase ('**PP**'). Related category: '**PREP**'.

I'm just going to go berserk *for* a while [S1A-001 #22]	**PREP**

2.3.53 Prepositional Complement (PC) [Function]

Related categories: '**AVP**', '**AJP**', '**CL**', '**NP**', '**PP**', '**DISP**'.

I'm just going to go berserk for *a while* [S1A-001 #22]	**NP**
...a valid way of *comprehending the war* [W2A-009 #53]	**CL**

Figure 22: Typical Prepositional Phrase (PP) Structure (S1A-008 #121).

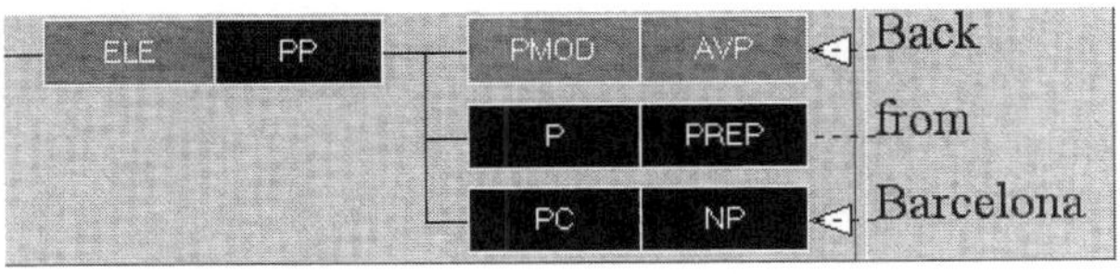

Prepositional Modifier (PMOD) [Function]

Premodifier of a preposition. Related categories: '**AVP**', '**NP**'.

It goes *straight* across the face of the goal [S2A-010 #38]	**AVP**
Yeah *all the way* down there [S1A-036 #137]	**NP**

2.3.54 Prepositional Phrase (PP) [Category]

A prepositional phrase consists of a Head ('**P**'), a prepositional complement ('**PC**') and optional prepositional modifiers ('**PMOD**'). The typical structure of a '**PP**' is shown in Figure 22. See also stranded preposition ('**PS**', Section 2.3.57).

2.3.55 Provisional Direct Object (PROD) [Function]

See also extraposed direct object ('**extod**') in Section 2.4. Related category: '**NP**'.

They're not finding *it* a stress being in the same office [S1A-018 #9]	**NP**

2.3.56 Provisional Subject (PRSU) [Function]

See also the feature extraposed subject ('**extsu**') in Section 2.4. Related category: '**NP**'.

It's pretty hard to park there anyway [S1A-006 #258]	**NP**

2.3.57 Stranded Preposition (PS) [Function]

The function applied to a preposition ('**PREP**') when separated from its phrase.

How long did you do English *for* [S1A-006 #1]	**PREP**

2.3.58 Subject (SU) [Function]

Related categories: '**AVP**', '**AJP**', '**CL**', '**NP**', '**PP**', '**DISP**'.

I'm blanking [S1A-001 #14]	**NP**

And obviously *buying books* is very special [S1A-013 #119] **CL**

2.3.59 Subject Complement (CS) [Function]

Subject complements occur with copular verbs. Related categories: '**AVP**', '**AJP**', '**CL**', '**NP**', '**PP**', '**DISP**'.

I won't be *a second* Richard [S1A-001 #21] **NP**
I was *lucky* [S1A-001 #90] **AJP**

2.3.60 Subordinator Phrase Head (SBHD) [Function]

Related categories: '**CONJUNC**', '**PRTCL**'.

I don't know *that* awkward is the word [S1A-002 #82] **CONJUNC**
Have you got to pay *for* Betty to go [S1A-030 #20] **PRTCL**

2.3.61 Subordinator Phrase Modifier (SBMO) [Function]

Related categories: '**AVP**', '**NP**'.

It's *just* cos you're not used to them [S1A-042 #304] **AVP**
About a fortnight before your vehicle license expires... [W2D-010 #108] **NP**

2.3.62 Subordinator (SUB) [Function]

Related category: '**SUBP**'. The parent clause will have the dependent clause type subordinate ('**sub**').

He said *that* she's coming soon [S1A-045 #160] **SUBP**

2.3.63 Subordinator Phrase (SUBP) [Category]

A subordinator phrase consists of a subordinator phrase Head ('**SBHD**') and an optional modifier ('**SBMO**'). The typical structure is shown in Figure 23.

Figure 23: Typical Subordinator Phrase (SUBP) Structure (S1A-042 # 216).

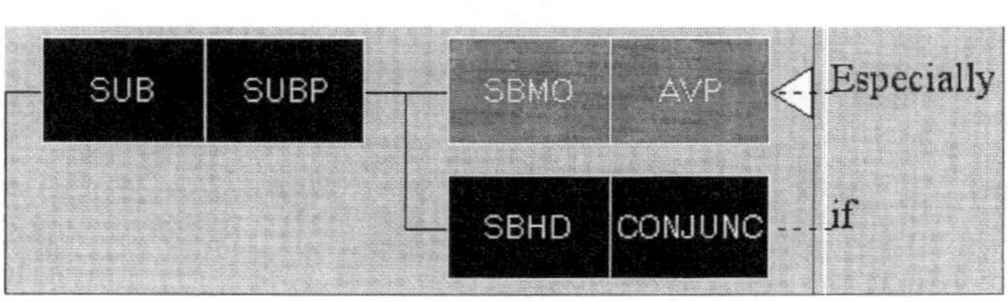

2.3.64 Tag Question (TAGQ) [Function]

Related category: '**CL**', which has the clause level feature '**main**' and markedness value reduced ('**red**').

Oh Xepe turned up *did he* [S1A-005 #139]	**CL**
It was very good *wasn't it* [S1A-053 #189]	**CL**

2.3.65 Particle To (TO) [Function]

The function label applied to particle (infinitival) *to*. Related category: '**PRTCL**'.

I like *to* watch sport [S1A-003 #7]	**PRTCL**

2.3.66 Transitive Complement (CT) [Function]

Transitive complements occur with transitive verbs. Related categories: '**CL**', '**DISP**'.

They asked *me to cover for them.* [W2F-006 #143]	**CL**
I don't want *you dribbling on those* [S1A-007 #141]	**CL**

2.3.67 Verbal (VB) [Function]

The function label applied to a VP. Related categories: '**VP**', '**DISP**'.

2.3.68 Verb Phrase (VP) [Category]

A verb phrase consists of a main verb ('**MVB**') and optional auxiliaries. Figure 24 shows the typical structure of a VP. See also: auxiliary verb ('**AVB**', Section 2.3.10) and operator ('**OP**', 2.3.45).

Figure 24: Typical Verb Phrase (VP) Structure (S1B-071 #36).

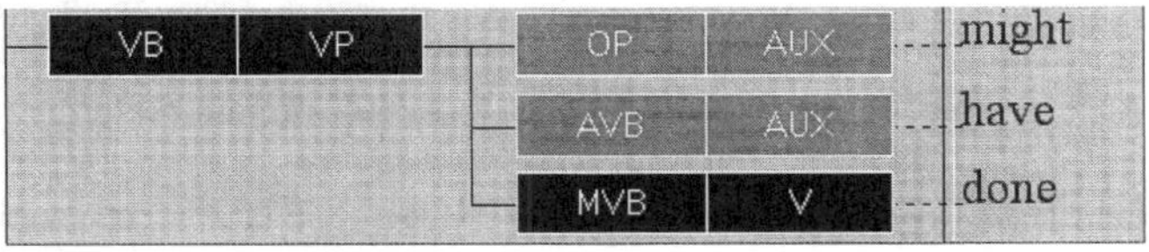

2.4 Feature Labels

The feature labels encode a wide range of information, including clause type, VP transitivity, the tense, mood, and form of a clause, and the markedness of a clause. Feature labels appear in the lower sector of a node (see Section 2.1), and by convention are written in lower case. Appendix 5 contains an alphabetical list of all the syntactic labels – functions, categories, and features.

Table 13: Feature labels in the ICE grammar

feature	code	explanation
additive	`add`	**Adverb type** feature of additive adverbs (*also*, *too*).
anticipatory *it*	`antit`	**Pronoun type** feature of anticipatory pronoun *it* (*It* is possible that he'll be late).
appositive	`appos`	**Connective type** feature of appositive connectives (*namely*, *in particular*) and **detached function** feature of appositive clauses and NPs.
assertive	`ass`	**Pronoun type** feature of assertive pronouns (*somebody*, *some*).
deferred attributive	`attrd`	**Adjective phrase syntax** feature of deferred attributive adjective phrases (something *rotten*).
attribute	`attribute`	**Detached function** feature of an "attribute" adjective phrases (*Red with rage*, she stormed out).
attributive	`attru`	**Adjective phrase syntax** feature of unmarked attributive adjective phrases (a *happy* child).
cardinal	`card`	**Numeral type** feature of cardinal numerals (*one*, *100*).
closing bracket	`cbrack`	**Punctuation**.
colon	`col`	**Punctuation**.
common	`com`	**Noun type** feature of common nouns.
comma	`comma`	**Punctuation**.
comment	`comment`	**Detached function** feature of parenthetical clauses, including reporting clauses (This, *he said,* is the real problem). These clauses are analysed as *main* clauses with a detached function. See Section 2.5.5.
comparative	`comp`	**Comparison** feature of adjectives (a *bigger* increase) and adverbs (walk *faster*).
complex transitive	`cxtr`	**Transitivity** feature of verbs complemented by a direct object (**OD**) and an object complement (**OC**) (It *makes* me ill). The feature also appears on the clause (**CL**) containing the verb. See Section 2.2.20.
conjoin	`conjoin`	**Proform type** feature of conjoin proforms (and *so on*, or *whatever*, or *something*).
coordinating	`coord`	**Conjunction type** feature of coordinating conjunctions (*and*, *but*, *or*).
coordination	`coordn`	**Coordination** feature carried by coordinated items. See Section 2.5.4.
copular	`cop`	**Transitivity** of verbs complemented by a subject complement (**SC**) (David *is* a lawyer, She *seems* unwell). The feature also appears on the clause (**CL**) containing the copular verb. See 2.2.20.
closing quote	`cquo`	**Punctuation**.

feature	code	explanation
dash	**dash**	**Punctuation**.
definite	**def**	**Article type** feature of definite article *the*.
demonstrative	**dem**	**Pronoun type** feature of demonstrative pronouns (*this* page, *that* book).
dependent	**depend**	**Clause level** feature of dependent clauses, which carry a further value for dependent clause type. The dependent clause type is selected from: subordinate, relative, zero subordinate, zero relative, and independent relative. Dependent clauses can stand alone as parsing units, but are always linked to another clause and so, in this sense, are distinct from main clauses.
dimonotransitive	**dimontr**	**Transitivity** of verbs complemented by an indirect object (**OI**) only (*Tell* me). The feature also appears on the clause (**CL**) containing the verb. See 2.2.20.
ditransitive	**ditr**	**Transitivity** of verbs complemented by a direct object (**OD**) and an indirect object (**OI**) (*Give* her the news). The feature also appears on the clause (**CL**) containing the verb. See Section 2.2.20.
auxiliary *do*	**do**	**Auxiliary type** feature of auxiliary *do*.
***-ed* participle**	**edp**	(1) **Adjective morphology** feature of *-ed* participial adjectives (a *talented* singer) and nominal adjectives (the *disabled*), otherwise it is a **tense/form** feature of (2) *-ed* participial verbs (has *broken*) and (3) *-ed* participial auxiliaries (has *been* stolen). The feature also appears on the clause (**CL**) containing a participial verb or auxiliary.
ellipsis mark	**ellip**	**Punctuation**.
elliptical	**ellipt**	**Ellipsis** feature of (1) semi-auxiliaries (we have to grow and *to* develop), (2) particles (in order to grow and *to* develop), and (3) complex prepositions (according to John and *to* Mary).
enclitic	**encl**	**Clitics** feature used in an (1) enclitic auxiliary (What*'s* happening?), (2) enclitic verb (That*'s* the idea), and (3) enclitic pronoun (Let*'s* go).
exclusive	**excl**	**Adverb type** feature of exclusive adverbs (It's *only* a game).
exclamative	**exclam**	**Pronoun type** feature of exclamative pronouns (*What* a great idea!) and **tense/mood/form** feature of exclamative clauses (*How true that is!*).
existential	**exist**	**Markedness** feature of existential clauses. (*There is a burglar in the house*). Existential *there* is analysed as an existential operator (**EXOP**), and *a burglar in the house* is analysed as the subject (**SU**). The verb in an existential clause is analysed as intransitive.
exclamation mark	**exm**	**Punctuation**.

feature	code	explanation
extraposed direct object	`extod`	**Markedness** feature of a clause with an extraposed direct object (*I find it hard to forgive*). *It* is analysed as a provisional direct object (**`PROD`**), and the extraposed element, *to forgive*, is analysed as the notional direct object (**`NOOD`**).
extraposed subject	`extsu`	**Markedness** feature of a clause with an extraposed subject (*It is difficult to park here*). *It* is analysed as the provisional subject (**`PRSU`**), and the extraposed element, *to park here*, is analysed as the notional subject (**`NOSU`**).
***for* particle**	`for`	**Particle type** feature of particle *for* (It's not *for* me to decide).
fraction	`frac`	**Numeral type** feature of numerals in the form of fractions (*a half, three quarters*).
general	`ge`	The element is a general (1) adjective (where it is an **adjective morphology** feature), (2) adverb or adverb phrase (**adverb type**), (3) connective (**connective type**), or (4) preposition (**preposition type**).
genitive	`genv`	**Genitive** feature of genitive NPs (*David's new job*).
hyphenated	`hyph`	**Numeral type** feature of hyphenated numerals (*1998-99*).
imperative	`imp`	**Mood** feature of imperative clauses (*Put it down*). See Section 2.5.3 on imperatives.
incomplete	`incomplete`	**Completeness** feature of an incomplete clause or phrase.
indefinite	`indef`	**Article type** feature of indefinite articles.
independent relative	`indrel`	**Dependent clause type** feature of independent (nominal) relative clauses (*What we need* is more money).
infinitive	`infin`	**Tense/mood/form** feature of an infinitive verb.
-*ing* participle	`ingp`	**Type/form** feature of (1) -*ing* participial adjectives (an *amusing* story) and nominal adjectives (the *dying*), (2) -*ing* participial verbs (is *leaving*), and (3) -*ing* participial auxiliaries (is *being* sold). The feature also appears on the clause (**`CL`**) containing a participial verb or auxiliary.
intensifier	`inten`	**Adverb type** feature of intensifying adverbs (*very* unusual, *quite* recently).
interrogative	`inter`	**Preposition type** feature of interrogative prepositions (*How about* a drink?) and interrogative pronouns (*Who* is there?). On interrogative sentences, see 2.5.2.
intransitive	`intr`	**Transitivity** of verbs with no complement. (The mail *arrived* early, She *sang* beautifully). The feature is also carried by the clause containing the intransitive verb.
inverted	`inv`	**Inverted** feature of inverted clauses. See 2.5.1.

feature	code	explanation
laughter	`laugh`	**Pause length** feature of a laughter segment. The feature is carried by a **PAUSE** node.
***let* auxiliary**	`let`	**Auxiliary type** feature of auxiliary *let* (*Let*'s go).
long pause	`long`	**Pause length** feature of long pauses.
main	`main`	**Clause level** feature of main clauses. Main clauses are realised by the functions parsing unit (**PU**), detached function (**DEFUNC**), parataxis (**PARA**) and tag question (**TAGQ**).
modal auxiliary	`modal`	**Auxiliary type** feature of modal auxiliaries.
monotransitive	`montr`	**Transitivity** of verbs complemented by a direct object (**OD**) only (He *says* he *likes* it). The feature is also carried by the clause containing the monotransitive verb. See Section 2.2.20.
multiplier	`mult`	**Numeral type** of multiplier numerals (*twice*, *double*).
negative	`neg`	**Pronoun type** feature of negative pronouns (*no*, *nothing*, *none*) and **clitic** feature of negative auxiliaries (*doesn't*, *won't*, *shouldn't*).
nominal relative	`nom`	**Pronoun type** feature of nominal relative pronouns (Let's see *what* happens).
nonassertive	`nonass`	**Pronoun type** of nonassertive pronouns (*any*, *anybody*, *anything*).
opening bracket	`obrack`	**Punctuation**.
pronoun *one*	`one`	**Pronoun type** feature of the pronoun *one* (*One* shouldn't laugh).
without operator	`-op`	**Markedness** feature of clauses from which an operator has been ellipted (*You leaving soon?*).
opening quote	`oquo`	**Punctuation**.
ordinal	`ord`	**Numeral type** feature of ordinal numerals (*first*, *second*).
other punctuation	`other`	**Punctuation**.
particularizer	`partic`	**Adverb type** feature of particularizer adverbs (*mainly*, *chiefly*).
passive	`pass`	(1) **Voice** feature of passive clauses (*The house was sold*). Clauses not labelled as passive are assumed, by default, to be active. (2) **Auxiliary type** feature of passive auxiliaries (The house *was* sold).
past	`past`	**Tense/mood/form** feature of past tense verbs. The feature is also carried by the clause.
period	`per`	**Punctuation**.
perfect auxiliary	`perf`	**Auxiliary type** of perfect auxiliaries (He *has* retired).
personal	`pers`	**Pronoun type** feature of personal pronouns.
phrasal	`phras`	(1) phrasal adverb (**adverb type** feature: Look *up* the reference) and (2) phrasal preposition (**preposition type**: Look *at* the picture).

feature	code	explanation
plural	**plu**	**Number** feature of nouns, pronouns, numerals, nominal adjectives, and proforms.
possessive	**poss**	**Pronoun type** feature of possessive pronouns.
predicative	**pred**	**Adjective phrase syntax** feature of predicative adjective phrases (She was *very rich*).
preposed object complement	**preco**	**Markedness** feature of clauses containing a preposed object complement (I don't know *what it's called*).
preposed subject complement	**presc**	**Markedness** feature of clauses containing a preposed subject complement (*What station is that?*).
preposed direct object	**preod**	**Markedness** feature of clauses containing a preposed direct object (*Which car did you take?*).
preposed indirect object	**preoi**	**Markedness** feature of clauses containing a preposed indirect object (*Everyone that cooks I ask how they make pastry*).
preposed prepositional complement	**prepc**	**Markedness** feature of clauses containing a preposed prepositional complement (I know *what you're waiting for*).
present	**pres**	**Tense/mood/form** feature of present tense verbs. The feature is also carried by the clause.
preposed subject	**presu**	**Markedness** feature of clauses containing a preposed subject. This feature is only used in the analysis of pushdown (**pushdn**) constructions (see below).
proclitic	**procl**	**Clitic** feature of proclitic auxiliaries (*D'*you want some?).
progressive	**prog**	**Auxiliary type** feature of progressive auxiliaries (Snow *is* falling).
proper	**prop**	**Noun type** feature of proper nouns (*London, Mary*) and **adjective morphology** feature of nominal adjectives (the *French*).
pushdown	**pushdn**	**Markedness** feature of clauses containing a pushdown construction, *i.e.* a type of embedding in which a category has not been extracted from the immediate clause in which it appears, but from a subordinate clause, as in *That's what they're trying to do.*
question mark	**qm**	**Punctuation**.
quantifier	**quant**	**Pronoun type** feature of quantifying pronouns (*more, many, much*).
reciprocal	**recip**	**Pronoun type** feature of reciprocal pronouns (*each other, one another*).
reduced	**red**	**Markedness** feature of reduced clauses, usually tag questions (**TAGQ**).
reflexive	**ref**	**Pronoun type** feature of reflexive pronouns (*myself, themselves*).

feature	code	explanation
reference	`reference`	**Detached function** feature of noun phrases used for reference (*One*, there is widespread dissatisfaction, *two*...). NPs of this type are analysed as having a detached function (**`DEFUNC`**).
relative	`rel`	(1) **Pronoun type** feature of relative pronouns (people *who* read), (2) **adverb type** feature of relative adverbs (That's *where* I found it), and (2) **dependent clause type** feature of relative clauses (people *who read*).
semi-colon	`scol`	**Punctuation**.
semi-auxiliary	`semi`	**Auxiliary type** feature of semi-auxiliaries (He*'s going to* fall).
semi-auxiliary + participle	`semip`	**Auxiliary type** feature of semi-auxiliaries followed by a participle (He *keeps* shouting).
short	`short`	**Pause length** feature of a short pauses.
singular	`sing`	**Number** feature of nouns, pronouns, numerals, nominal adjectives, proforms, *etc*.
proform *so*	`so`	**Proform type** feature of proform *so* (I think *so*).
without subject	`-su`	**Subject** feature of a clause (**`CL`**) which lacks a subject (*In doing so*, we behave hypocritically).
subordinate	`sub`	**Dependent clause type** feature of subordinate clauses. (I don't think *that he cares*). Subordinate clauses contain an overt subordinator (**`SUB`**). See Section 2.5.4.
subjunctive	`subjun`	**Mood** feature of subjunctive clauses (*If I were you...*).
subordinating	`subord`	**Conjunction type** feature of subordinating conjunctions (He thinks *that* he'll be late).
superlative	`sup`	**Comparison** feature of (1) superlative adjectives (the *oldest* child) and nominal adjectives (I wish you the *best*), and (2) superlative adverbs (John worked *hardest*).
***to* particle**	`to`	**Particle type** feature of infinitival *to* (I'd like *to* see you).
transitive	`trans`	**Transitivity** of verbs complemented by a nonfinite clause (I *asked* him to leave). The complement *him to leave* is analysed as a transitive complement (**`CT`**). See Section 2.2.20.
universal	`univ`	**Pronoun type** feature for universal pronouns (*all*, *everyone*, *everything*).
without verb	`-v`	**Tense/form** feature of clauses from which the main verb has been ellipted (*Has he?*).
vocative	`voc`	**Detached function** feature of vocative NPs (I'll be there soon, *Sam*).
vocalising	`vocal`	**Pause length** feature of a vocalising (non-verbal) segment. The feature is carried by a **`PAUSE`** node.
***wh-* (adverb)**	`wh`	**Adverb type** feature of *wh*-adverbs (*How* did it happen?).

feature	code	explanation
***with* particle**	`with`	**Particle type** feature of particle *with* (I can't concentrate *with* you talking).
zero relative	`zrel`	**Dependent clause type** feature of zero relative clauses. Zero relative clauses contain no relative pronoun or adverb (There's the man *I met yesterday*).
zero subordinate	`zsub`	**Dependent clause type** feature of zero subordinate clauses. Zero subordinate clauses contain no subordinator (**`SUB`**) (I don't think *he cares*).

2.5 Special Topics in the ICE-GB Grammar

In this section we discuss some aspects of the ICE-GB grammar which require more detailed treatment. Specifically, we are concerned here with constructions which may be analysed in a variety of ways in ICE-GB.

2.5.1 Inversion

Figure 25 illustrates a simple case of inversion:

...and on her right is standing the Lord Mayor of London [S2A-019 #62]

The clause contains a prepositional phrase *on her right* which has been inverted

Figure 25: A simple case of inversion: "...and on her right is standing the Lord Mayor of London" (S2A-019 #62).

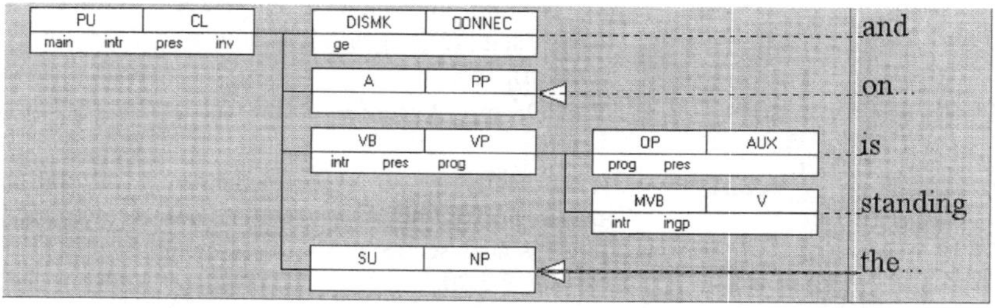

Figure 26: A second case of inversion: "Here's a napkin" (S1A-061 #142).

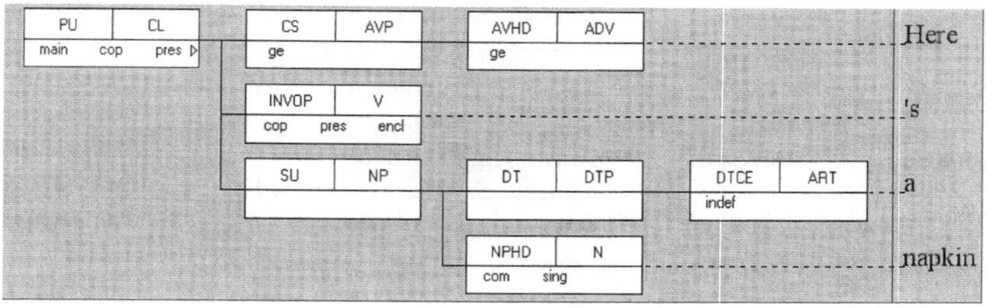

with the whole verb phrase *is standing*. The inversion is indicated by assigning the inversion feature '**inv**' to the clause node.

A second example, containing a simpler VP, is shown in Figure 26. Since this contains a single verb, we use the inverted operator ('**INVOP**') function with the verb category. As well as the inverted feature on the clause node, we also have the '**precs**' feature (preposed subject complement), indicating that the subject complement ('**CS**') *here* has been moved.

2.5.2 *Interrogative*

One of the simplest cases of interrogatives is shown in Figure 27. The interrogative mood feature ('**inter**') is carried by the clause node.

A slightly more complex example is illustrated by Figure 28. Here the

Figure 27: A simple interrogative: "Who knows" (S2A-039 #71).

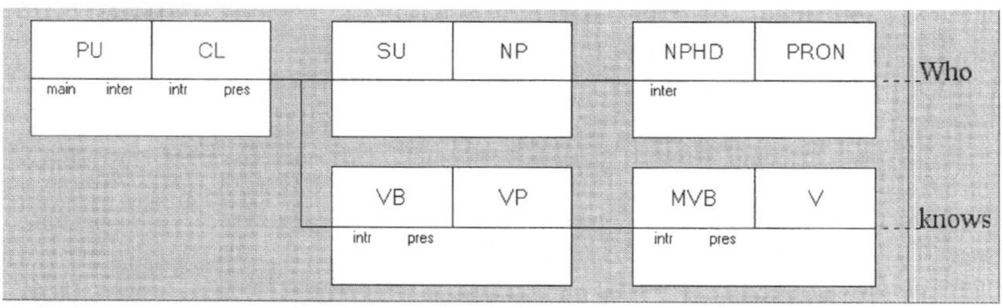

Figure 28: "Is it important" (S1A-003 #18).

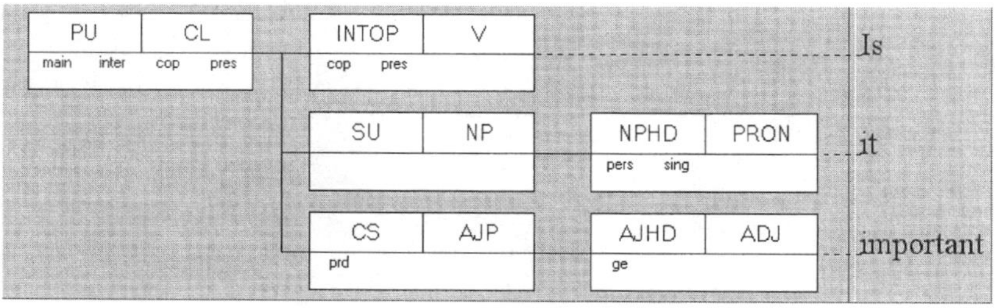

Figure 29: "Sorry could you start again" (S1A-001 #3).

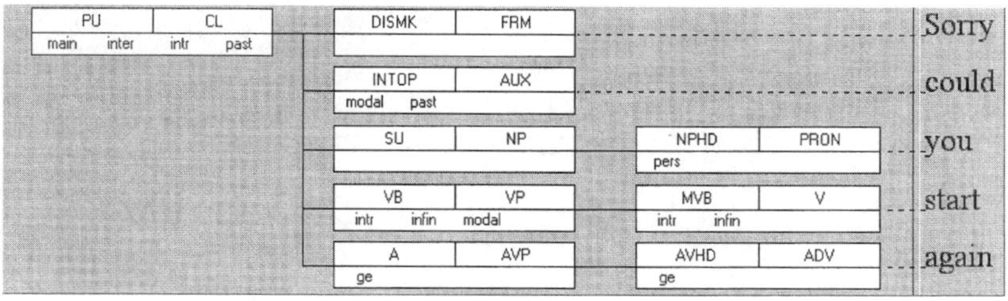

verb *is* has been fronted in the clause. This verb is analysed as an interrogative operator ('**INTOP**'). Note that there is no inversion feature in addition to the interrogative feature.

Finally, Figure 29 contains an auxiliary that has been separated from the main verb. In this case, the auxiliary is assigned the function of interrogative operator ('**INTOP**').

2.5.3 Imperative

The verb or auxiliary in an imperative clause carries the infinitive ('**infin**') feature for tense/mood/form, while the clause itself carries the imperative ('**imp**') feature label. This is illustrated in Figure 30. The clause also carries the feature '**-su**' (without subject).

When the introductory imperative marker *let* is present, the analysis is somewhat different (Figure 31). Here, auxiliary *let* functions as an imperative operator ('**IMPOP**'). The VP has infinitive form, and carries a '**let**' feature to indicate the presence of the auxiliary. The clause has the imperative mood feature ('**imp**'), as in the previous example, and gains the tense/form value infinitive ('**infin**') from the VP. Note that in this case the subject *'s* (*us*) is present.

Figure 30: "Have a seat" (S1A-004 #38).

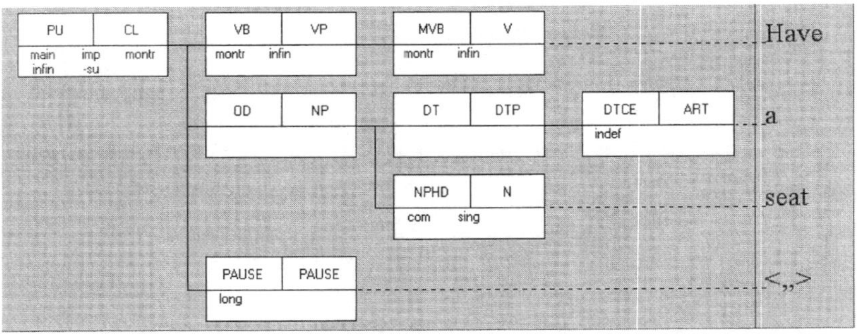

Figure 31: "Let's be honest" (S1A-006 #168).

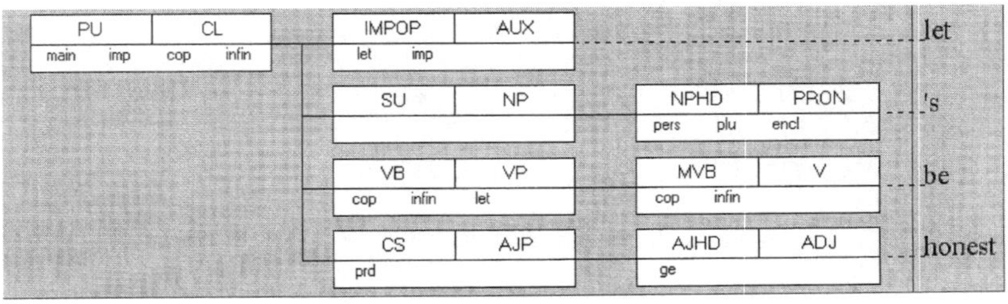

2.5.4 Coordination

Most coordination involves two or more like categories, for example:

> We have *tutorials lectures and practicals* [S1A-059 #40]

This is coordination of three object NPs. ICE-GB treats *tutorials lectures and practicals* as a constituent, functioning as a direct object. The direct object node carries the coordination feature ('**coordn**'), and has four daughters: the coordinator ('**COOR**') *and*, and the three conjoined NPs. The latter each carry the function label conjoin ('**CJ**') to indicate their participation in a coordinated structure.

The tendency in ICE-GB is to coordinate at the phrasal level if possible,

Figure 32: Coordination of like categories (S1A-059 #40).

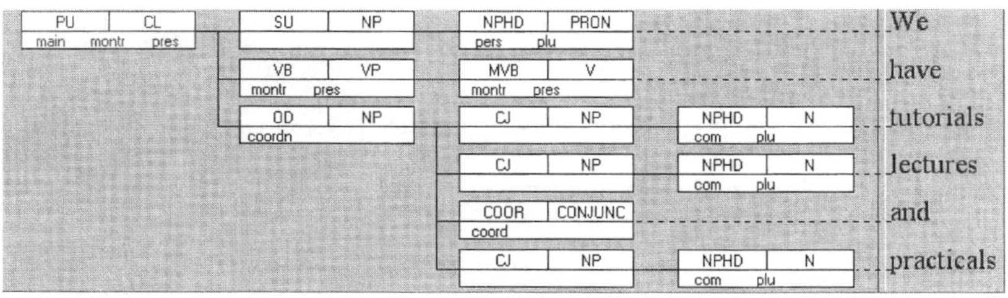

Figure 33: Coordinated prepositions (W2B-022 #99).

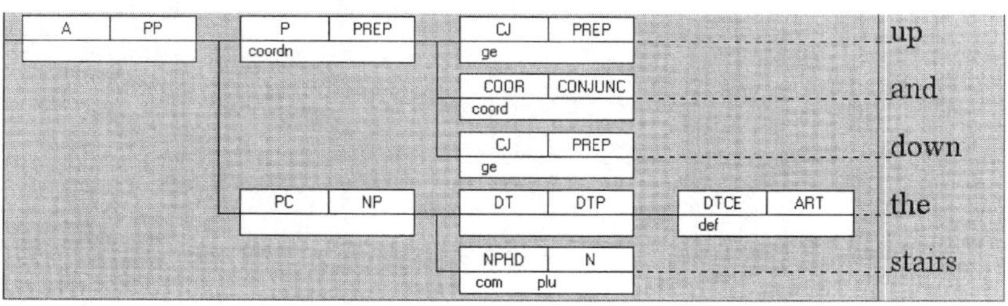

Figure 34: Coordination of unlike categories (S1B-015 #202).

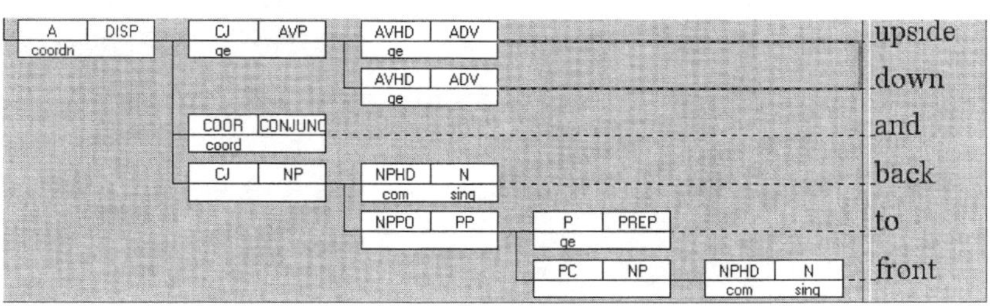

but coordinated Heads may also occur. Consider the following:

At home run *up and down* the stairs a few times every day [W2B-022 #99]

The prepositions *up* and *down* are coordinated, giving the analysis in Figure 33.
Consider a case in which the conjoins are not of the same category:

It's turned *upside down or back to front* [S1B-015 #202]

This is coordination of an adverb phrase ('**AVP**') with an NP. We use the category-neutral label '**DISP**' (disparate) to label the superordinate node, as in Figure 34. The '**DISP**' node carries an obligatory coordination ('**coordn**') feature.

The analysis of coordinated VPs is usually comparable with that of coordinated NPs (Figure 32 above). Figure 35 shows the analysis of the following:

I *listened and listened* to that [S1B-044 #77]

A more complicated case for ICE-GB is:

Well they *bring it to the boil and whip it off the stove* [S1A-009 #184]

In Government-Binding Theory, where verbs and their complements form con-

Figure 35: Coordinated VPs: "I listened and listened to that" (S1B-044 #77).

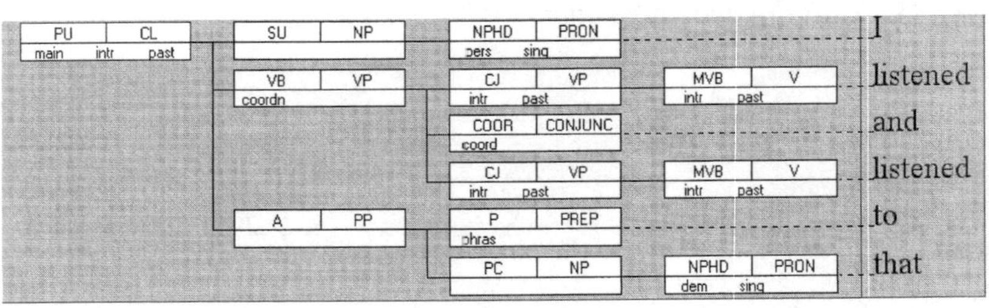

Figure 36: A predicate group: "Well they bring it to the boil and whip it off the stove" (S1A-009 #184).

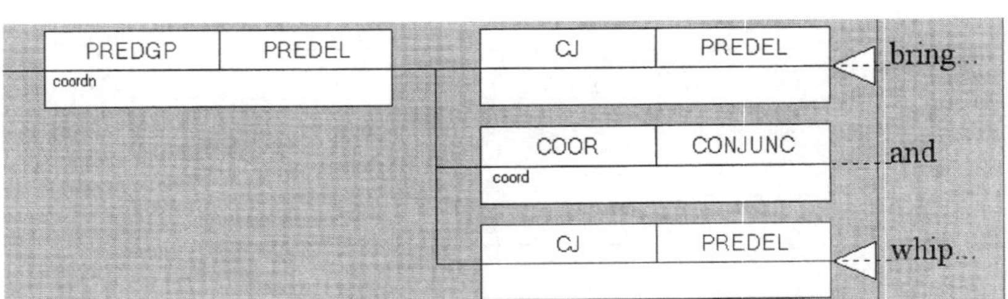

Figure 37: "Is that an irritation..." (S1A-013 #92).

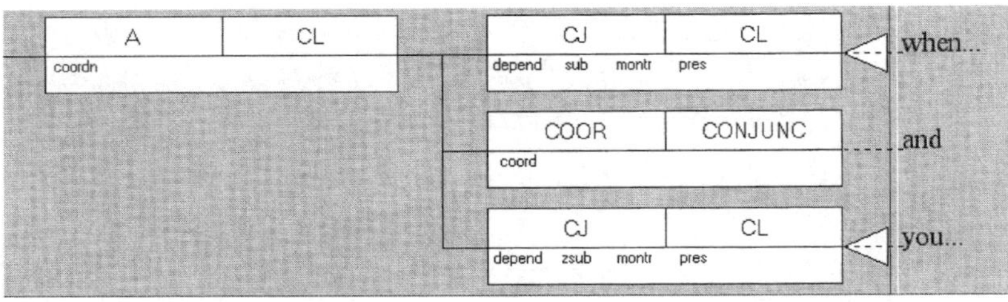

stituents, this example would be treated identically to the one in Figure 35. This is not possible in ICE-GB, however, where VPs contain only auxiliaries and verbs, with the complements of the verb attached directly to the clause node.

In ICE-GB, this example is analysed as shown in Figure 36. The elements *bring it to the boil* and *whip it off the stove* are analysed as conjoined constituents with the special category predicate element ('**PREDEL**'). The superordinate node also has the category predicate element, and a coordination ('**coordn**') feature. The function label of this node is predicate group ('**PREDGP**').

Finally, consider the following:

> Is that an irritation *when you have a vague feeling you've lent a book to somebody and you can't quite figure it out* [S1A-013 #92]

This contains two coordinated adverbial clauses. In categorial terms, we have two identical conjoins, so the analysis is as in Figure 37.

Strictly speaking, *when* is common to both clauses, as in *when you have a vague feeling... and (when) you can't quite figure it out*. However, ICE-GB does not allow the subordinator to be shared by both conjoins. *When* is only part of the first clause, which therefore has the dependent clause type feature subordinate ('**sub**'). The second clause, *you can't quite figure it out*, does not contain a subordinator, so it carries the feature zero subordinate ('**zsub**').

2.5.5 Direct Speech

Direct speech is normally assigned the function label parataxis ('**PARA**'), as in Figure 38. Notice that the verb *said* is intransitive ('**intr**') here. A similar analysis applies if the parataxis appears before the reporting clause (*'It's fine,' he said*).

A different approach is used when the reporting clause is embedded within the direct speech.

> 'I think,' *said Selena*, 'that the current expression is bimbo'. [W2F-011 #82]

Figure 38: He said it's fine (S1A-008 #276).

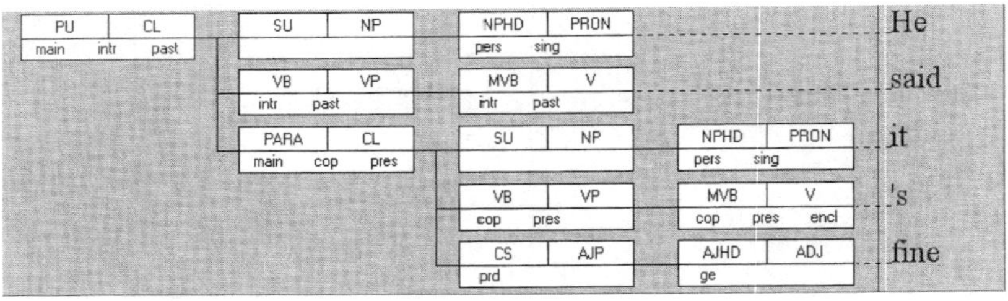

Figure 39: "I think, said Selena..." (W2F-011 #82).

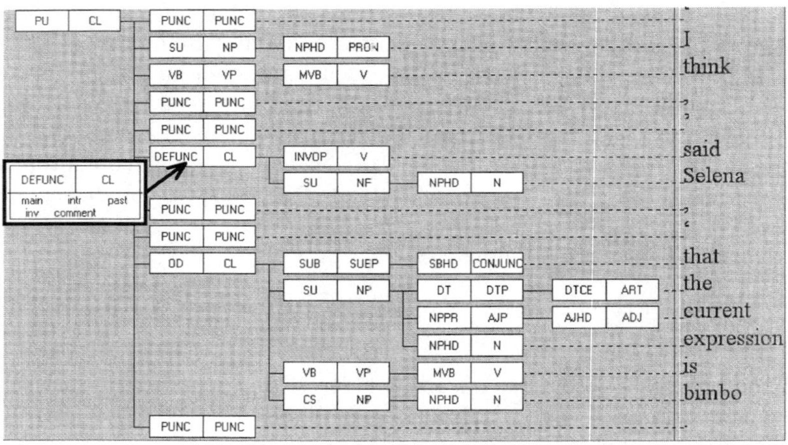

In this case, *I think that the current expression is bimbo* is treated as the "principal" sentence, and *said Selena* is analysed as an intransitive comment clause. The comment clause carries the function label detached function ('**`DEFUNC`**'), and the clause level feature '**`main`**'.

PART 2:
Exploring the corpus

3. INTRODUCING THE ICE CORPUS UTILITY PROGRAM (ICECUP)

3.1 First impressions

The *International Corpus of English Corpus Utility Program* (ICECUP III) is supplied with the ICE-GB corpus. The initial display will look like Figure 40.

Figure 40: ICECUP III on startup, with 'about' dialog box.

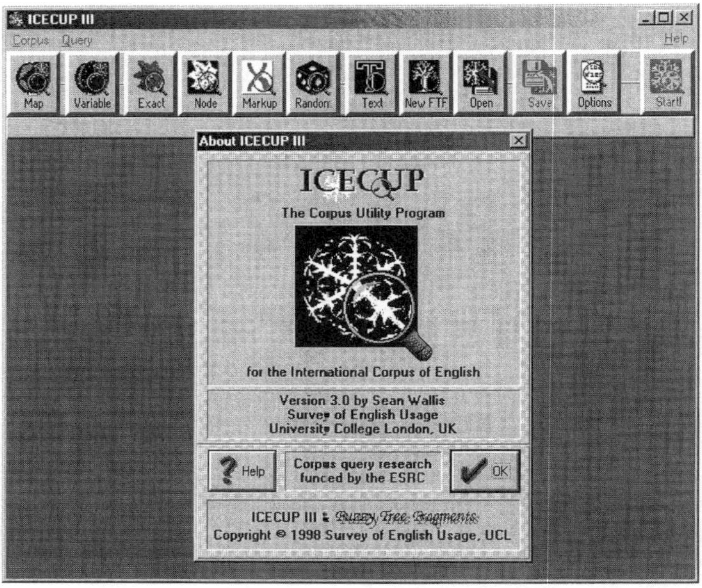

ICECUP is an advanced system for helping you to explore the corpus. It uses multiple windows to show different aspects of the corpus side-by-side. If you have used tools with other corpora before, some aspects of the program may appear novel. There are two reasons for this.

1. ICE-GB is a *parsed corpus*, and therefore the structure of each text unit is considerably more complex than it would be in a 'flat' grammatically tagged corpus.
2. ICECUP is a *complete system* for exploring the corpus (see the introduction to Chapter 4). As you search ICE-GB, you view results in ICECUP, refine your queries and explore.

As you use ICECUP, therefore, you will gain practical knowledge of ICE-GB. In Section 1.9 we introduced the corpus by using ICECUP.

Along the top of the main ICECUP window is a series of large buttons, each containing an icon and a label. This is the main “command button” menu bar. It summarises the principal available actions, which are also found in the menus.[1] (With the exception of the *Corpus Map*, they are all to be found under the ‘Query’ menu.)

The button on the far right hand side (shown in Figure 40 disabled and labelled ‘Start!’) is different from the others. This is a kind of general purpose ‘go’ button, reproduced by the function key <F4>. It performs a variety of different tasks depending on the situation. In the Corpus Map, for instance (Figure 41), it opens another window which displays the text of the currently-selected subcategory of the corpus.

The other buttons provide a number of different functions. In this chapter we will briefly introduce each function in turn. We suggest that if you can, experiment as you read, to familiarise yourself with what each command does.

3.2 *The corpus map*

When you first start ICECUP, the program should display a map of the ICE-GB corpus, as in Figure 41.

The Corpus Map shows the structure of ICE-GB, organised according to

Figure 41: ICECUP III with a corpus map of ICE-GB.

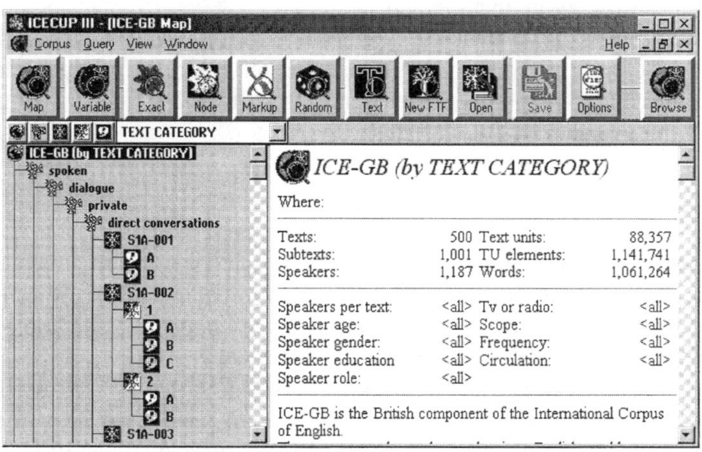

[1] The main menu bar is optional (go to ‘Corpus | Viewing options...’ to hide it). However, we recommend that you keep it visible until you are more familiar with the program.

a particular sociolinguistic variable. The most important of these is the main sampling variable, ‘text category’, which defines the categories of text (genres) included. This variable is hierarchically structured, which means that texts can be classified at a number of different levels of granularity.

The corpus map illustrates this hierarchical structure on the left-hand side of the window. Thus, in Figure 41 we can see that ‘direct conversations’ are a named subclass of ‘private dialogues’. Private dialogues are a subclass of ‘dialogues’. This class is, in turn, a subclass of the ‘spoken’ part of the corpus, which is a major subclass of the corpus. Furthermore, within each text category, we can view the structure of each individual text. So text S1A-001 has two named speakers, ‘A’ and ‘B’, and it is an instance of a ‘direct conversation’. Text S1A-002 contains two subtexts (two different conversations), labelled ‘1’ and ‘2’, which contain three and two speakers, respectively.

This hierarchical structure repeatedly subdivides the corpus, that is, each sub-category represents a smaller subset of the corpus contained within a parent category, but the elements in this hierarchy are not all of the same type. A speaker, for example, is not the same kind of element as a subtext or a sociolinguistic category. We indicate the type of element in the hierarchy by a small icon to the left of the label.

Section 4.2 describes the corpus map in more detail. You can expand and collapse the entire hierarchy according to the type of element to be viewed (for example, to the level of each text) by clicking on the smaller buttons (from ‘’ onwards) in the lower menu bar. You can use cursor keys (arrows marked ‘↑’, ‘→’, *etc.*) and the scroll bar to move through the elements in the hierarchy. Note also that as you change the currently selected element, the view on the right changes to describe that element.

If you press the control key (marked “Ctrl” on many keyboards) and a cursor key together, you can move around the tree by following its structure. A final tip: Pressing <Ctrl> plus the <Right> cursor together makes a single node open to show its children if it was closed.

3.3 Browsing the results of queries

As we mentioned, you can *browse* the content of any selected subcategory of the corpus (single text, speaker or sociolinguistic category) by either pressing the function key <F4> or pressing the ‘Browse’ button at the top right. In Figure 42, the whole text is selected.

This query viewer is a general purpose window that is used to view text units selected from the corpus. The same window is used regardless of whether the selection is “the whole corpus”, as shown here, or a small set of results. For now, note that you can browse through the text using cursor keys and the scroll bars. You can also make the text larger or smaller using the small ‘magnifying glass’ tools in the button bar. If you wish to see what the other buttons do, simply place the mouse arrow cursor over the button. A small yellow 'banner' will appear, summarising the button's function. We discuss browsing text in the 'query window' in detail in Chapter 4.

Figure 42: Browsing ICE-GB (the 'query' is simply 'text category = <all>').

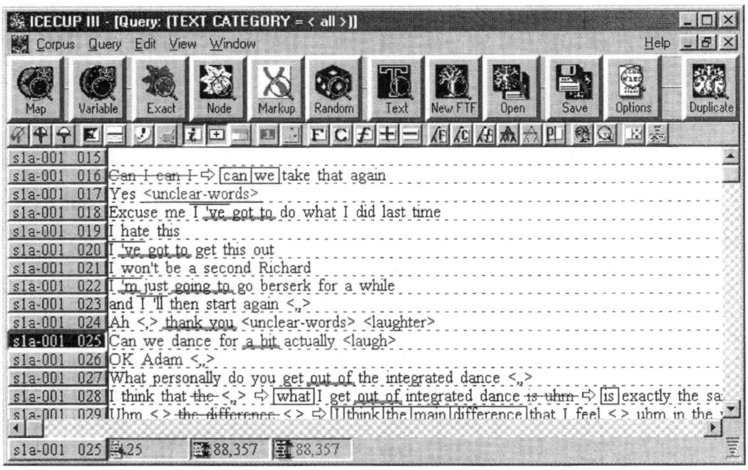

Figure 43: The selected sentence and tree in Figure 42 (S1A-001 #25).

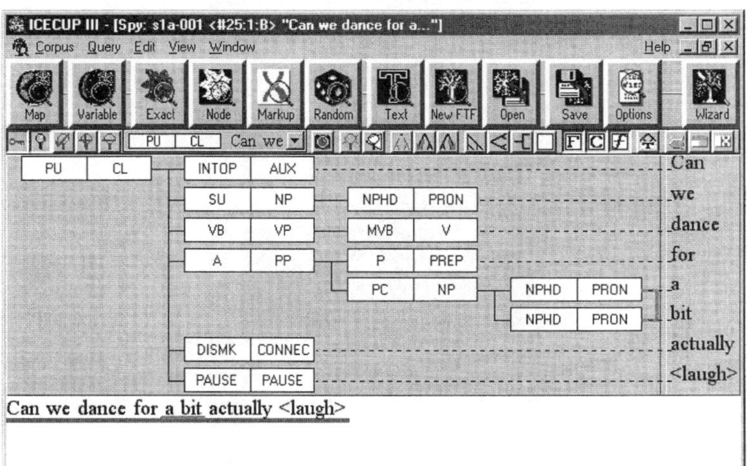

3.4 Viewing trees in the corpus

If you perform a 'double-click' operation with the left mouse button on a line in the query viewer, another window opens. This "spy", or inspection window, shows a view of the single line, and the grammatical tree analysis associated with the view. Figure 43 illustrates the tree for the line selected in Figure 42 (*i.e.*, S1A-001 #25). By default, trees are drawn from the left toward the right (rather than top-down, say), the parent is positioned above the first child, the diagram employs regular right-angled links and constituent nodes are divided into three sectors for function, category and features.

In this "spy" mode, if you change your current selection in the query window, the spy window changes accordingly. (Hint: if you select the 'Window | Tile' command from the menu bar it is easier to manipulate the pair of windows.)

3.5 Variable queries

The corpus map is not the only way of selecting material from the corpus on sociolinguistic terms. The *Variable query* window allows you to perform simple grouped selections from a variable. Figure 44 shows an example.

This window employs a multiple selection system that is sensitive to the hierarchy. If you select, say, 'dialogue' with the mouse, 'dialogue' and (by implication) all its subvalues are highlighted. If you then select 'private' with the mouse, this, and all its subvalues are deselected. If you work from the top,

Figure 44: A 'Variable' query for all dialogues apart from private ones.

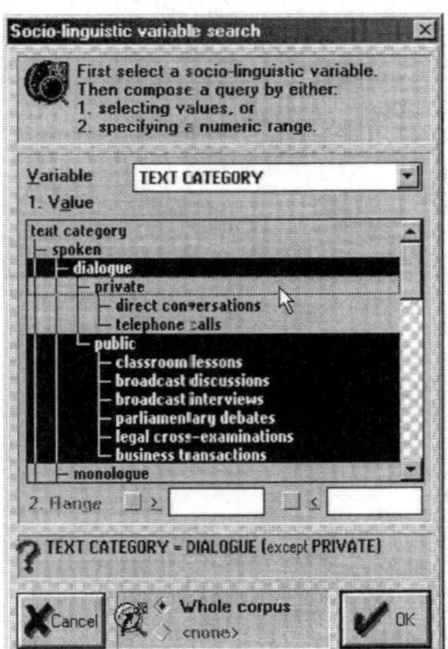

down, this is a rapid method of selecting from a hierarchical variable. Press 'OK' at the bottom of the window and the results of the query are shown in a new window.

If you choose a variable that can be given a number value, *e.g.*, speaker age, then you can also use the 'Range' controls below the main 'Value' panel. Thus, you can click on '≥' and type a number (say, 30), to state that the variable must be greater than or equal to that number. Click on both range controls to specify a closed range (*e.g.*, from 30-50).

A panel below these variable selection windows summarises your current selection. In Figure 44, for example, this reads "TEXT CATEGORY = DIALOGUE (except PRIVATE)". Finally, between the two buttons at the bottom, there is a panel marked with a magnifying glass and arrow that allows you to apply your query to either the whole corpus or, alternatively, a preselected subset. This is similar to the idea of searching a subcorpus, or combining searches.

You can apply a variable query to any selected subset of the corpus. The way you do this is either to (a) first select a specific element in the corpus map or the lexicon, or (b) apply it to the currently selected text viewer window. Chapter 6 discusses how to combine queries in detail.

Try the following.

- ➢ Perform the selection from the text category variable according to Figure 44. You should get a view of the corpus consisting of over fourteen thousand text units.
- ➢ Now press 'Variable' again and select "SPEAKER GENDER = F" (female). Note that you change the variable by the pull-down selector at the top of the dialog box.
- ➢ If you now choose to apply this query to the previous query, you will get a new query results window with a title that reads "Query: (SPEAKER GENDER = F and TEXT CATEGORY = DIALOGUE...)". In ICE-GB (Release 1) this will contain 3,449 text units.

3.6 'Single grammatical node' queries

ICE-GB is a parsed corpus, which means that for every text unit in the corpus, we have provided a grammatical analysis in the form of a tree. (Some texts also contain unparsed units consisting only of extra-corpus material, but these are not strictly part of the corpus.)

How can we search for information in these trees? The simplest way is to retrieve all trees that contain nodes which exactly match a node that we specify. This is what the *Exact Node* query does. By 'exactly match' we mean that you must specify every detail (function, category and features) of the node in order to perform the search. If you omit a feature, this means that it shouldn't be present in the trees you are looking for, not that it is unimportant. You specify an exact node query by typing the codes directly into a 'dialog box' window.

There is a slight difference between ICECUP 3.0 and later versions of the software. ICECUP 3.0 has a separate 'Exact node' search facility (Figure 45,

Figure 45: Node query windows.

left), which is not required from ICECUP 3.1 onwards. Instead, an 'Exact match' option is available in the 'node search' box (Figure 45, right).

Queries are written in the format: "<function>, <category> (<features>)". The following are examples of this format.

CJ,NP	a conjoined noun phrase, with no features.
DISMK,INTERJEC	an interjection functioning as a discourse marker.
VB,VP(intr,pres,prog)	an intransitive present tense, progressive verb phrase.

However, performing an exact match for nodes is usually too restrictive. Suppose, for example, that you want to find all cases of conjoined noun phrases, labelled '**CJ,NP**'. You wouldn't want to have to perform a separate search for, say, appositive instances (labelled '**CJ,NP(appos)**'). Some conjoined NPs are marked 'incomplete', 'vocative', and so on.

If you want a list of all conjoined NPs, regardless of their features, you should search for cases matching only a subset of the function, category and features (*e.g.*, function plus category, as here; or just a single function or category, *e.g.*, "find me all the noun phrases in the corpus").

This is what the *Inexact Node* search does. It is a fast general query, ideal for when the information you are looking for can be determined by just one node. As before, you must still type the "<function>, <category> (<features>)" directly, but as you can leave information out, it is less burdensome. If you need to extend the query by adding other nodes, you can press the 'Edit' button instead of 'OK' and turn it into a general Fuzzy Tree Fragment (FTF). We introduce FTFs in Section 3.11 below. Chapter 5 discusses them in more detail.

3.7 Markup queries

The corpus is annotated in a number of non-grammatical ways, which are indicated by general annotation or 'markup'. This is expressed in a number of ways. For example, bold text is indicated by <bold> and italic text by <it> (see Appendix 4). You type these directly into the query window (Figure 46, left).

Figure 46: Searching for markup elements (left) and defining a random sample (right).

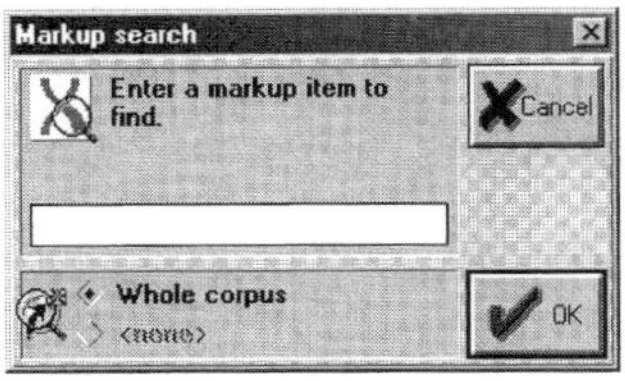

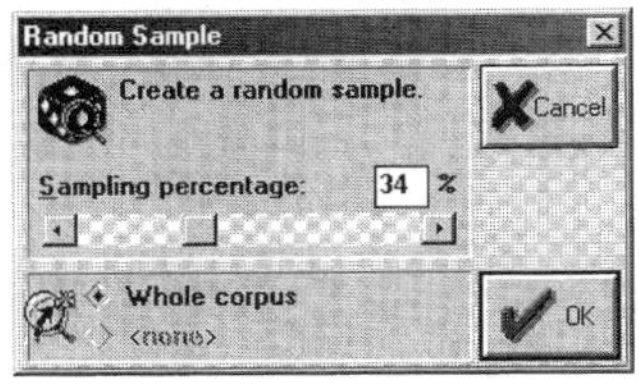

3.8 Random sampling

In many circumstances you may want to generate a *random sample* of the corpus. One motivation for this is just to 'thin out' or reduce the number of cases that you want to consider. The 'Random sample' command creates a unique random sample of the entire corpus. You can then make copies of this sample, and combine it with any other search, using the "drag and drop" facility and the query editor (this is described later in Chapter 6).

If you choose 100% you will obtain the entire corpus, 0%, an empty list. With any number between 1 and 99%, a random sequence across the corpus is generated. Each time that you create a random sample, the sampling will be different. Note that you will probably not get the exact percentage of the corpus. ICECUP randomly samples each text unit in the corpus, that is, it independently throws a notional 'dice' for each one.

You can save a random sample for later use using the normal 'Save and cache' command (see Section 3.13). You can then retrieve these samples later with the 'Open' command.

3.9 Text fragment queries

So far we have only considered relatively simple queries, such as the search for a particular tree node. If ICECUP only allowed you to retrieve single nodes, words, and so on, it would not be very powerful. The analogy would be a "find" button in a word processor that could only find a single word at a time!

In many cases, you cannot specify what you want to look for in terms of a single element in a sentence. Instead, you have to search for several words, nodes, *etc.*, at the same time.

Figure 47: Searching for two successive words in the corpus.

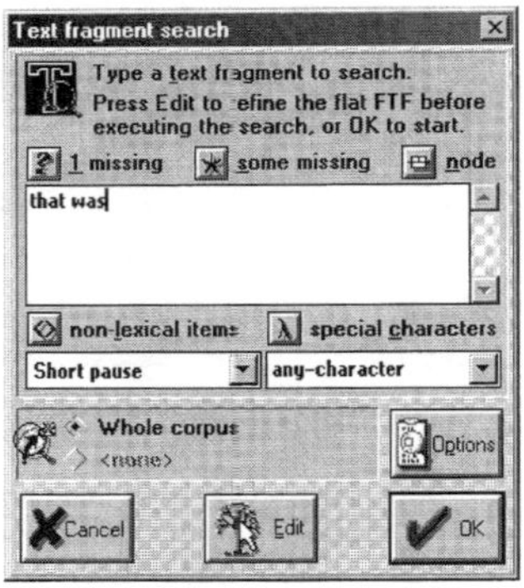

You can define this kind of search using the ‘Text Fragment’ button. This produces a query window like the one in Figure 47. This search is very much like the traditional word processor “find” command (except that it works across the entire corpus and finds all the text units containing the words you type).

➢ Try typing a single word into the query window, say, “**that**” and press ‘OK’. Then try a couple of words, say, “**that was**”.

What happens next may be surprising. Some searches are almost instantaneous, while others, usually those that are more complex, can take a while. In the second case (*that was*), an empty window was opened and then each matching case was added, one-by-one, as it was found (see Figure 48). The box overleaf discusses this in a little more depth. The actual speed of this kind of search depends on the speed of your computer, network, or hard disk (or, if you are running the software from your CD drive, the speed and ‘caching’ capacity of your CD drive).

*Figure 48: The query viewer actively searching the corpus for “**that was**”.*

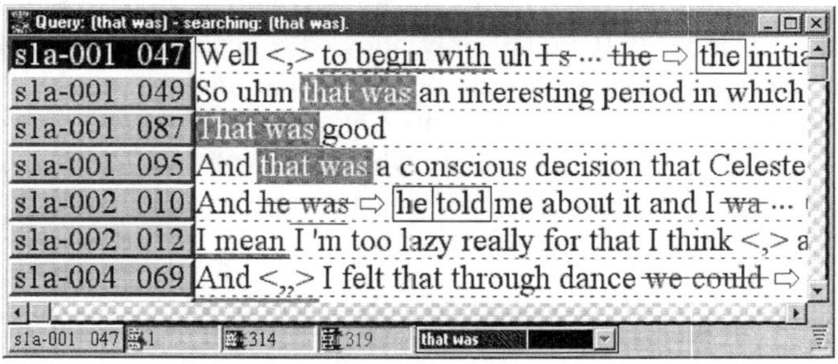

Background and quick searches

ICECUP uses two kinds of search procedure. Note that all queries in principle are exhaustive, that is, they apply to the entire, one million word ICE-GB. The software is not doing what a word processor does: looking for the next case of a word or pattern of characters in a file, usually held in main memory. We are looking for all cases of a pattern of words in a big, structured, database stored on a disk.

The quick search is possible because, to some extent, the program can 'cheat'. For example, ICECUP stores the location of each instance of every word in the corpus. This information is supplied on the CD with the corpus, and it is installed on your hard disk or network. When you search for the word "that", ICECUP looks it up, discovers that the word "that" is mentioned, say, 16,660 times in the corpus, and simply reads in the appropriate list of references.

Unfortunately, we can't precalculate every search! Any query that is not stored[2] has to be performed with a different method.

The background search sifts through the corpus unit-by-unit, checking to see if the entire query that you specified can be found in each text unit. This can take some time, so instead of demanding that you stop work while the program 'thinks', ICECUP searches behind the scenes. A query results window is created to receive the results of your search. Whenever ICECUP finds a successful match, the case is added to this window, as we have seen. ICECUP can work out the minimum set of cases to examine, so some background queries may be quite swift.

Meanwhile, you can continue to use ICECUP. However, you can only perform one background search at a time. You can also stop the search at any point and continue it later, by releasing the button on the right of the main command bar (labelled 'Stop!', see Figure 49) or hitting the function key <F4>. You can also press <Esc> (escape) to stop. If the main command bar is hidden, a monitor window appears.

Figure 49: Part of the command bar during search. The upper time is the total (estimated) time for the search, the lower, the time remaining.

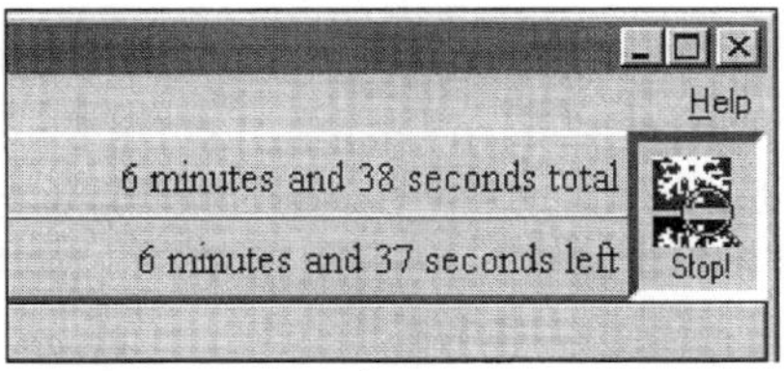

[2] In ICECUP 3.0, the following atomic searches have been precalculated and stored: all lexical items (words), constituent nodes and inexact combinations of nodes, all markup symbols, all values of sociolinguistic variables and all texts, subtexts and speakers are stored. The rule is that if a query consists of two or more elements *with some kind of relationship between them*, or a single element *with some kind of structural restriction placed upon it*, then a background search must be performed. The introduction of the *lexicon* into ICECUP 3.1 (see Chapter 7) means that some 'structural' searches also become quick, *e.g.*, 'tagged word' combinations and plain tags.

The 'Text Fragment' query window contains a number of additional elements. You can add a missing or unknown word, or specify that an arbitrary number of intermediate words can be found between the words. These are specified with the computerese question mark ('?') and asterisk ('*') symbols. They are shown in unemboldened text to distinguish them from actual question marks and asterisks. The question mark stands for a single missing 'word' (lexical item, punctuation, *etc.*). The asterisk stands for any number of words, including zero, within the same text unit.

You can also add word class tags to your search. You do this with the 'Node' button, which inserts a pair of angled brackets ('<>') in the text window. You may then type an 'inexact' specification of the node between the brackets, using the "<function>, <category> (<features>)" style (see Section 3.6).

You can write "**work** <N>", meaning the word *work* followed by a noun. Note that word class tags are at the word level, one for every word. Although this is a parsed corpus, the only noticeable difference from searching a tagged corpus at this stage is that you can also introduce the grammatical function (say, noun phrase head, "<NPHD>") into the node.

Note one important distinction: if there is a space between a word and a node (in that order), it means that they follow one another. If there is no space before the node, ICECUP puts a little 'plus' symbol between the two elements. This means that the node grammatically annotates the word. So, "**work**+<V>" (*work* as a verb) is different from "**work** <V>" (*work* followed by a verb).

As in the 'Inexact Node' query window, you can press the 'Edit' button and produce what we call a "Fuzzy Tree Fragment" from your query (Figure 50). *Fuzzy Tree Fragments* (FTFs) are more flexible than the text fragments that we have been discussing here.

3.10 Fuzzy Tree Fragment searches

Pressing the 'New FTF' button on the main command bar produces an empty Fuzzy Tree Fragment in a new window (see Figure 51, left). Pressing the 'Edit' button in either the 'Inexact Node' or the 'Text Fragment' query windows

*Figure 50: Visualising "**work**+<V>" (left) and "**work** <V>" (right) as Fuzzy Tree Fragments.*

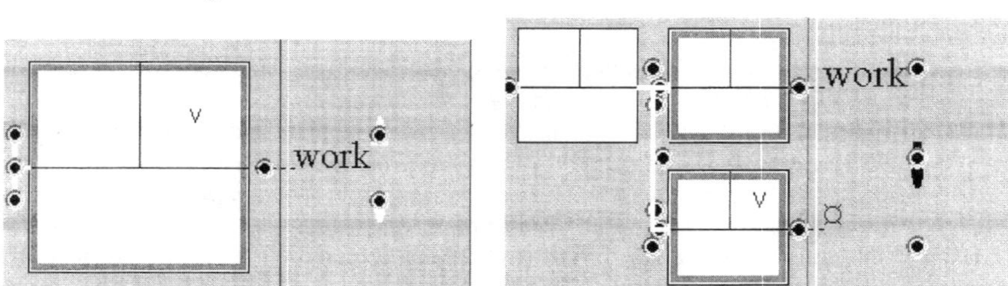

*Figure 51: Editing a simple FTF: (left) an empty FTF, and (right) after editing, defined as a single conjoined noun phrase ('**CJ,NP**').*

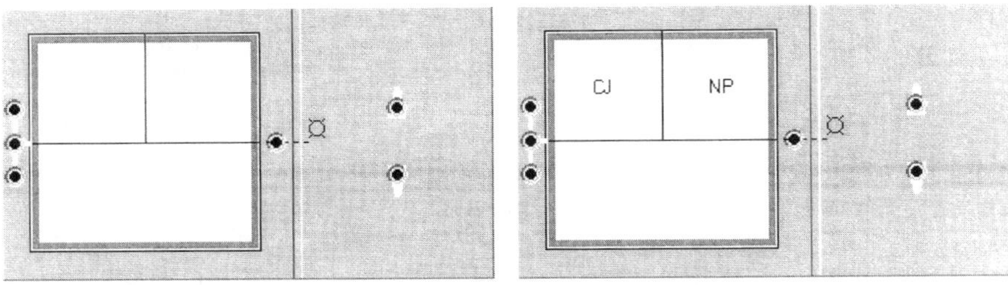

produce specialised FTFs. (Note that this window is not a temporary 'dialog window' but a more lasting 'document window' in ICECUP.)

There are a number of special commands for editing the FTF, indicated by the set of multi-coloured buttons on the secondary menu bar. However, the basic idea of FTFs is very simple. An FTF is a 'sketch' of the grammatical structure that you are looking for. We discuss the editing of FTFs in some detail in Chapter 5. For now, try the following.

- Press 'New FTF' to get an empty FTF.
- Press the function key <F2>, which opens the "Edit function and categories" dialog box shown in Figure 52. Alternatively, press the little '' button in the button bar.
- Select "conjoin" from the function list and "noun phrase" from the category list (hint: look in the list of all functions for conjoin, and then select "noun phrase" from the list

Figure 52: Assigning the function and category of a node.

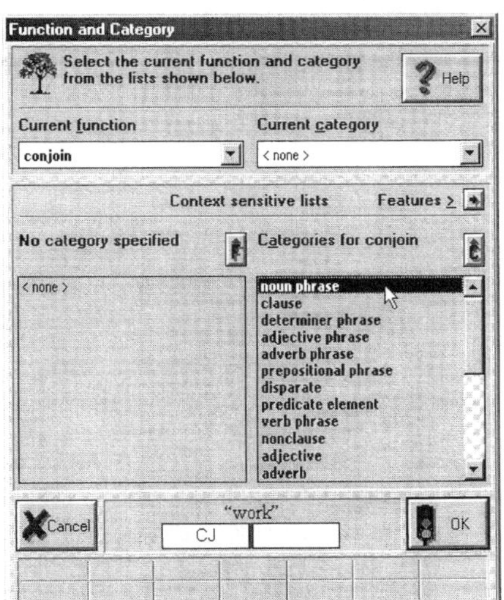

of categories that 'go' with "conjoin": see Figure 52).

- Press 'OK'. If you have been successful, the top two panels of the FTF node will read "CJ" and "NP" respectively (Figure 51, right).
- Now press the function key <F4> or press the 'Start!' button at the top right in the command bar. You should get the results of a quick search for '**CJ,NP**', just as if you had typed them into the (inexact) nodal query window.

This seems a very roundabout way to specify a simple query that we can do already. However, FTFs can do a lot more than these simple queries. In particular, FTFs are most effective in specifying relationships between grammatical elements. In Chapter 5 we discuss how to perform sophisticated grammatical queries using FTFs.

3.11 Open file

'Open' reads a Fuzzy Tree Fragment or random sample from the disk. FTF files are, naturally enough, distinguished by the suffix '.ftf', random samples are labelled '.rnd' and selection lists '.sel'. Some FTF files are saved with the results of precalculated searches (suitably compressed). This means that once a calculation has been made, the search can be swiftly repeated. (If the FTF is modified, naturally, these results are no longer applicable and ICECUP must perform another background search, see box on page 79.)

3.12 Save to disk

The 'Save' command is intuitive, saving material to disk depending on the current window. In the FTF editor window, 'Save' stores the current FTF.

If you perform 'Save' from the query browser, however, a number of options are available, illustrated by Figure 53, which determine what to store.

Figure 53: Saving material to disk.

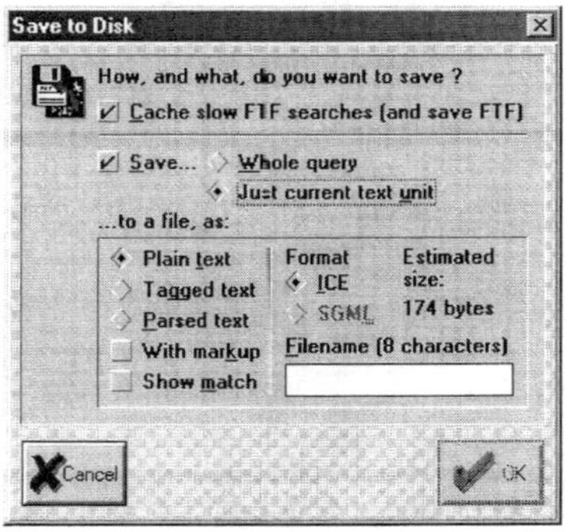

The first of these is to "cache" the results of all background FTF searches used to construct the current query window. 'Quick' FTF searches are not saved (they are already stored). If the FTF was saved previously the search results are stored with it. Otherwise, after you hit 'OK', the program asks for a file name for each FTF in the conventional way. You can also save random samples and *selection lists* (see Chapter 4) in this way.

The second major option, labelled 'Save...', dominates the rest of the window. This allows you to save ('export') material from the query to a standard ASCII file, for use in other programs apart from ICECUP. You can save just the current query, or the entire set of results. You can also choose the level of annotation, from plain text, tagged text, and parsed text. You can opt to include structural markup. Finally, if the search involves the matching of one or more FTFs to text units, you can choose to include information indicating how they have matched. These files are saved to a standard output directory ('c:/output'), with '.txt', '.tag' or '.tre' suffixes. ICECUP 3.1 also gives you the option of outputting files in a more verbose SGML style.[3]

3.13 Search options

This button allows you to specify a set of important search options which control the FTF search process. They determine how queries are applied to the corpus, how FTFs and text fragments are matched and so forth.

We mentioned that lexical matches are affected by two factors: the ability to ignore *case* (capitalisation) and *accents*. By default, searches are case and

Figure 54: The search options dialog box (default settings).

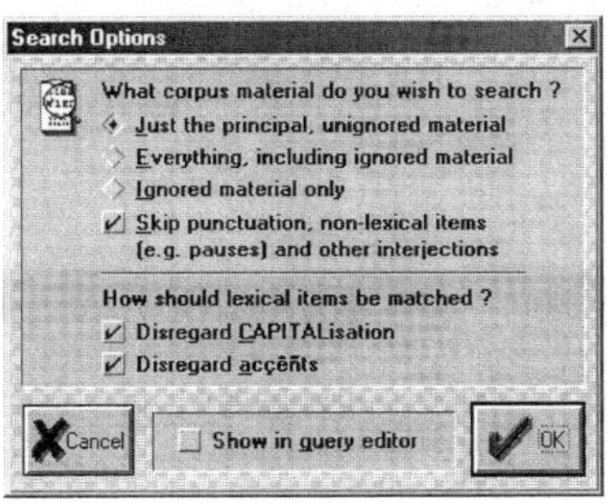

[3] Note that you can also use copy and paste to insert text and tree diagrams into word processor documents such as research reports. The tree viewer's Edit menu has two commands: 'Copy Sentence to Clipboard' and 'Copy Image to Clipboard'. These compose a copy of the sentence text and a line drawing of the tree that you can then paste into a document. If you want to include any diagram image or fragment of a concordance display, you can 'capture' pictures from the screen with a program such as Paint Shop Pro™.

*Figure 55: The results of a search for "***saw as***" with the 'skip' option enabled.*

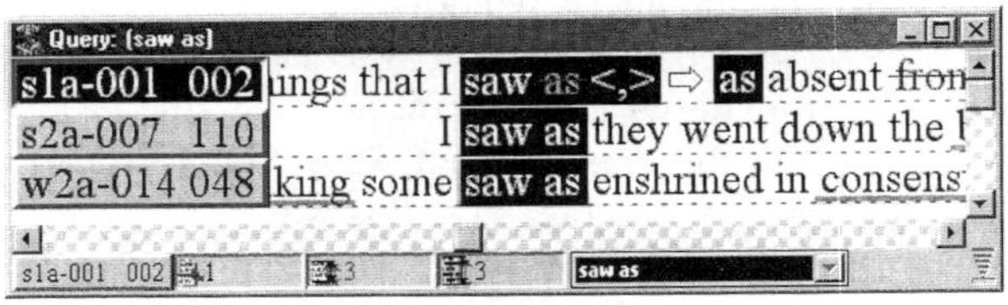

accent insensitive. Obviously these two options affect the matching of individual words. They do not affect the interpretation of the relationship between words.

The other search options are different. The principal choice is whether to include or exclude the 'ignored material' in the corpus (see Chapter 4). The default is to exclude it. In the case studies in Chapter 8, for example, we only search this material. In some circumstances, however, it is useful to include ignored material in your search: if you are studying self-correction, for example, you will sometimes have to include it. For completeness' sake, we also allow the option of searching *only* ignored material.

An associated option allows you to 'skip over' what are essentially 'extra-grammatical' terms: punctuation, non-lexical items such as pauses, and interjections (*e.g.*, "uh"). This allows ICECUP to stretch its notion of 'what immediately follows what' (note that you can still include, a pause, say, in your query). Thus, in Figure 55, without the 'skip over' option, we would only find two examples of "saw as". These options affect the matching of grammatical expressions as well as lexical matches.

The final option at the bottom of the search options window (Figure 54) let you see, as a series of small icons, the status of any FTF search in the query editor. We will see come back to this in Chapter 6.

This concludes our brief tour. The rest of Part 2 discusses the main facilities of ICECUP in more detail.

4. BROWSING THE CORPUS

4.1 The idea of corpus exploration

In the previous chapter we summarised the different search facilities in ICECUP, from the corpus map to individual 'Node' queries and Fuzzy Tree Fragments. In this section we will discuss, in more detail, some of the facilities

Figure 56: Exploring the corpus: from the top, down (left), and, using the Wizard (Section 5.14), in an exploration cycle with FTFs (right).

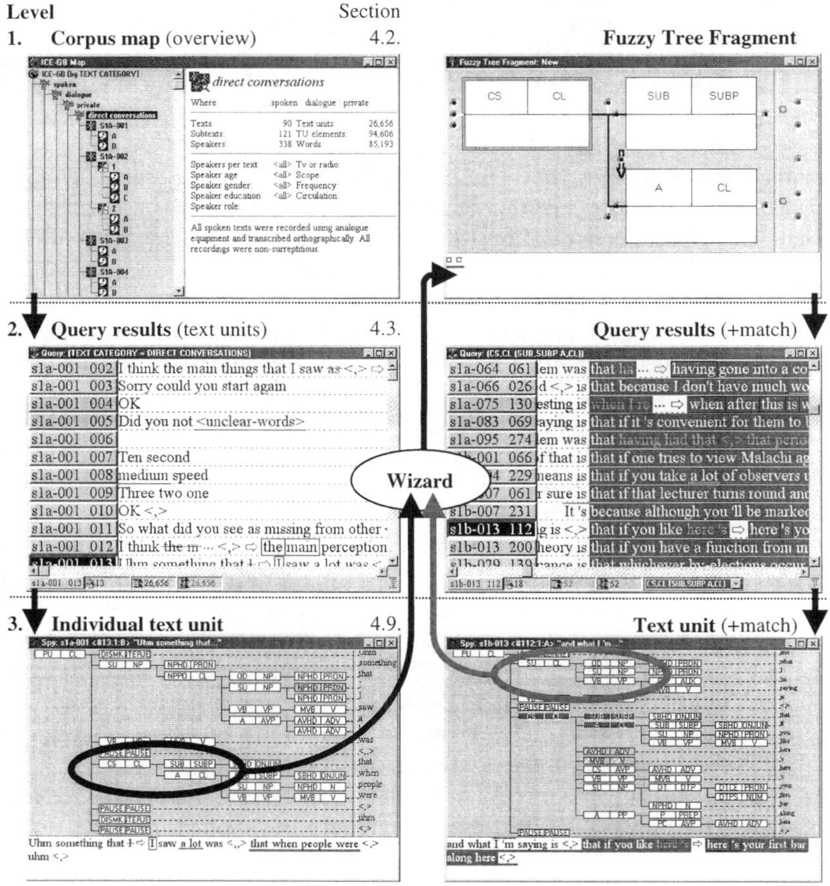

provided by ICECUP for browsing corpus texts and the results of queries. Having performed a query, you need to know how to investigate the results effectively. Before getting down to the 'nitty-gritty', however, it would be appropriate to discuss the perspective behind ICECUP. This was first outlined in (Wallis, Aarts and Nelson 1999).

The fundamental problem facing any new user of any large and complicated data source – and a parsed corpus is a good example of this – is that it is very difficult to know in advance precisely what an appropriate query should look like. Even the most experienced grammarian could not be expected to learn, not only the formal grammar in Chapter 2, but also the realisation of that grammar in ICE-GB – quirks and all – before constructing his or her query.

We get around this problem in two ways. First, we provide a forgiving interface that allows a researcher to be imprecise and experimental, and second, we provide a facility to 'use the corpus to query the corpus'. The 'Wizard' facility, indicated schematically at the centre of Figure 56, is described later in the book (Chapter 5, Section 14). This constructs an FTF query based on the grammatical analysis in part of a corpus tree.

The corpus may be explored at the three levels shown in Figure 56. At the top of the figure is the relatively abstract 'overview' level represented by the corpus map. ICECUP 3.1 also includes a lexicon overview. The corpus map, like other query systems (*e.g.*, the FTF on the right), can produce a query.

The next level is the results of performing such a query (in this case, the text category "direct conversations"). This view displays the results of a query as a sequence of text units, one after another. It also lets you modify the logical structure of combined queries (Chapter 6). If the query is an FTF, text fragment or nodal query, ICECUP indicates the number of times the FTF matches the same tree. It can also concordance matching cases, illustrated by the window on the middle right of Figure 56.

The final level is that of a single text unit and tree. This 'tree viewer' window displays the full grammatical analysis for a particular text unit. If an FTF was applied, it also shows how the FTF matches constituent nodes (shaded nodes, bottom right).

Typically, experimental research proceeds in a 'top down' direction: from the abstract to the concrete. This, of course, presumes that we know what we are looking for, and how to express it as a query. As we commented, the issue is particularly crucial with respect to parsed corpora, where the prime difficulty is in learning the grammar. ICECUP permits a researcher to extract a prospective query from the corpus and to explore the corpus in cycles, either by defining a new FTF (the grey arrow in Figure 56) or, more usually, by modifying an existing one in the light of search results.

The aim of this process is, as ever, to develop a set of well-defined, linguistically meaningful queries for research purposes. Sometimes, as we shall see in one of the case studies (Section 4.4), we may need to experiment first in order to define these queries appropriately.

This chapter describes the process of browsing the corpus at these three levels: the corpus map (below), browsing the texts (Sections 4.3 to 4.8) and trees (4.9 and 4.10). We end by discussing a couple of features that are new to ICECUP 3.1: playback of recorded speech and creating selection lists.

4.2 Navigating the corpus map

In previous sections (1.10, 3.2) we briefly introduced the corpus map. Here we consider it in greater detail. The corpus map is organised by a single selected sociolinguistic criterion in the form of a hierarchical variable. Texts, subtexts and speakers are then grouped under this variable. By default, the view is based around the "text category" variable used to sample the corpus. When you open the corpus map for the first time, the view should look like Figure 57.

Some buttons specific to the corpus map appear in the secondary bar below the main command bar in ICECUP. These are shown in Figure 58. These five buttons expand or contract the corpus map to a varying extent, determined by the type of element selected. Thus ‘’ collapses the map down to the single variable, ‘’ expands or collapses the map to show just the different values of the variable (groups, or classes), while ‘’ shows all the individual text units. If you press ‘’ the map extends as far as distinct subtexts, ‘’ and it will

Figure 57: The corpus map initial view.

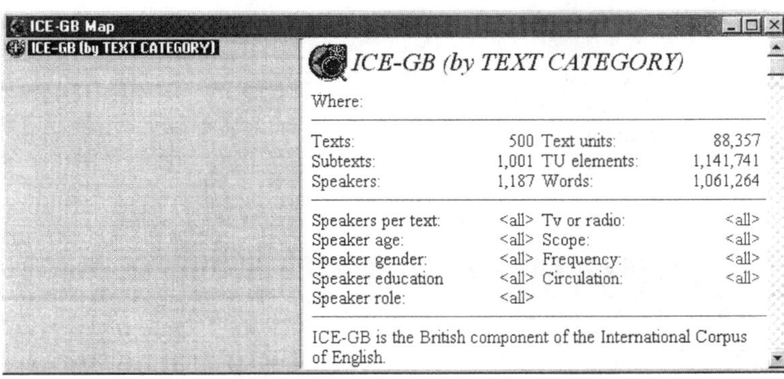

Figure 58: Corpus map buttons and variable selector.

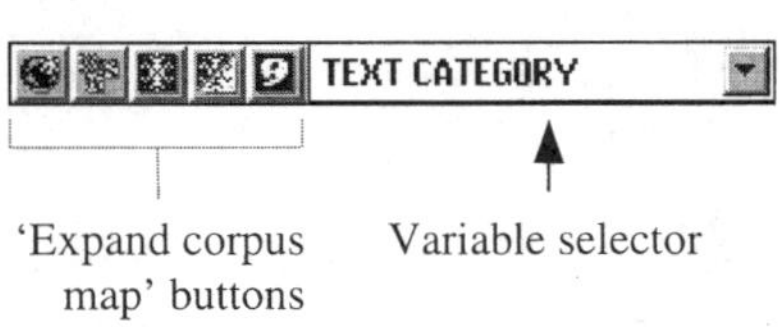

Figure 59: The corpus map showing the values of the 'text category' variable.

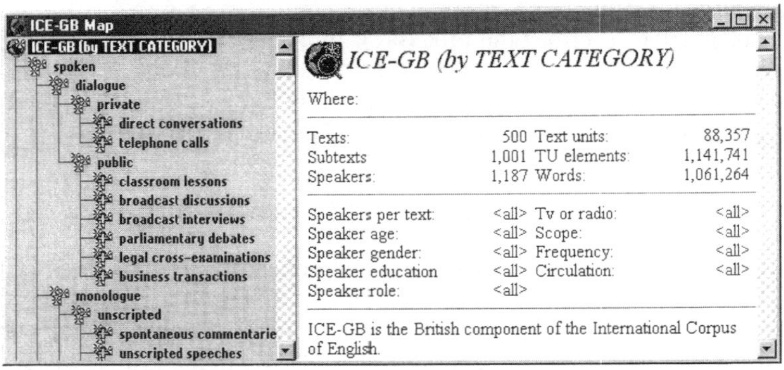

include speakers within subtexts as well (this generates the entire map). You can replicate the action of these buttons from the 'Browse' menu, or with the control key and a numeric key from '0' to '4'.

> If you expand the map to show just the values of a variable (hit '', or <Ctrl>+'1'), it will look like Figure 59. Elements in the corpus map that may be expanded further are indicated by a yellow 'plus' symbol.

You should experiment with the other expansion options. The full expansion of the corpus map is illustrated by Figure 60.

You can expand and contract individual branches if you wish. For example, you may wish to concentrate on the written part of the corpus, and hide the spoken branch of the 'tree'.

> Place the mouse cursor arrow over the icon designating the main division marked "spoken", and perform a 'double click' with the left mouse button. It will expand or collapse accordingly.

Figure 60: A full expansion of the corpus map.

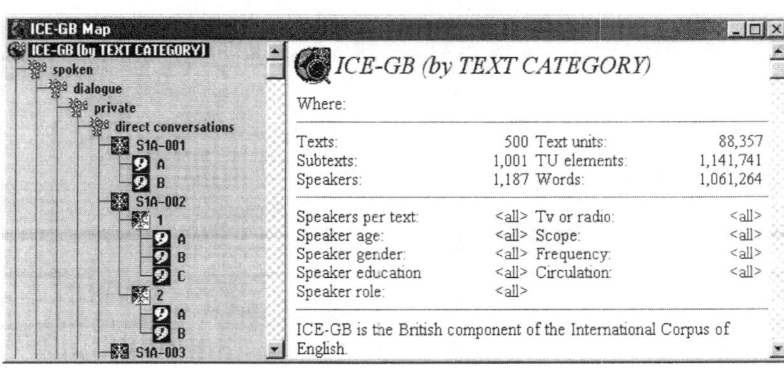

You can also navigate the map using the keyboard. Cursor keys (the 'arrow' keys on the keyboard) move you up and down the view. The keys <Home>, <End>, <Page Up> and <Page Down> operate as they would in a regular scrolling window. That is, <Home> will move you to the top of the viewer, and <End> to the last element in the viewer. <Page Up/Down> will move you through entire screenfuls of information.

In addition, you can move around the corpus map using the structure of the tree. This topological navigation system works with the 'control' button. Press <Ctrl> and the <Up> cursor key (marked '↑') together, and your current location moves to the 'preceding sibling' in the tree.

> In Figure 60, if you have text S1A-003 selected and you press <Ctrl>+<Up>, you will move to S1A-002. You can move down through the texts with <Ctrl>+<Down>.

> Pressing <Ctrl> plus the <Left> cursor moves the current point to the parent node, for example, from S1A-002 to "direct conversations". Finally, note that descending the hierarchy by pressing <Ctrl> and <Right> together will also open up branches.

The sampling category of the text is not the only way of subdividing the corpus. In fact, a number of different sociolinguistic variables, listed in Table 14, are provided, each describing different aspects of the texts, subtexts and speakers. These may all be applied to the corpus map.

The pull-down selector in the button bar specifies the organising variable. Note that some of the variables only apply to certain subtexts, such as newspaper articles. Variables pertaining to the speaker (age, gender, *etc.*) include an element for co-authored written material (marked '<co-authored>').

Table 14: Summary of sociolinguistic variables.

name	**by**	**applicable range**	**description**
text category	text	all	principal text sampling variable
speakers/text	subtext	all	number of speakers per subtext
speaker age	speaker	all	age of speaker
speaker gender		(some written	gender of speaker
speaker education		material is	education level attained by speaker
speaker role		co-authored)	role of speaker within discussion
TV or radio	text	broadcast material[1]	broadcast medium
scope	subtext	press news reports	geographical scope of newspaper
frequency		press editorials	frequency of periodical or newspaper
circulation			audited circulation of newspaper

[1] 'Broadcast material' includes broadcast interviews, discussions, news, talks and spontaneous commentaries.

Figure 61: A full expansion of the corpus map, by "speaker gender".

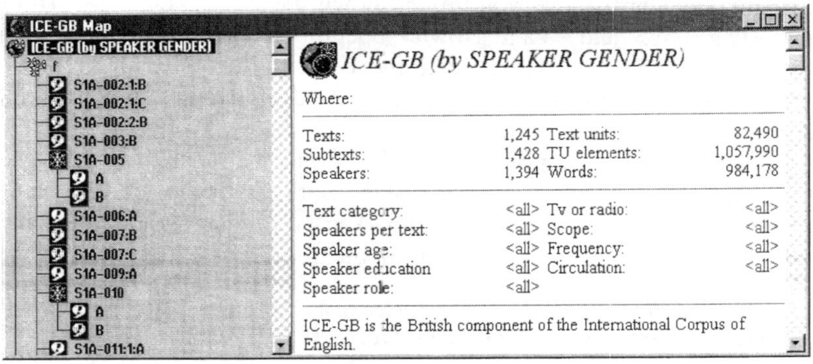

➢ Select the "speaker gender" variable and expand the map fully. The picture will look like Figure 61.

So far we have been looking at how different texts, or portions of texts, can be classified and grouped. The corpus map is really only an overview or 'index', describing a selected sociolinguistic facet of the corpus. Moreover, we can browse the text of any subpart of the corpus very easily from the corpus map.

➢ Press the large button in the right hand corner of the main command bar, marked 'Browse', or hit <F4>. Alternatively, you can briskly click twice with the left mouse button, with the mouse cursor over the text label in the variable hierarchy.

4.3 Browsing single texts

As we saw at the start of this section, ICECUP employs just one type of window to browse text units in sequence. This is the text viewing window, or, more correctly, the "query results" window (see Chapter 6). This window is used whether you want to look at a single text or the results of a complex search. It displays text units in sequence, one per line.

In order to allow a fair degree of control over the presentation of material, the query window is quite complex, and provides the user with a number of different options. Among other things, these reveal annotation, both structural and grammatical, and control concordance displays. ICE-GB contains two major classes of annotation.

- **Structural markup**: texts and subtexts, speakers, self-correction and overlapping speech, and typographic styles.
- **Grammatical analysis**: tags and aspects of the tree structure, and the top-most parse unit label.

'Structural markup' refers to a diverse class of general annotation, from indicating which speaker is currently speaking, to paragraphing, fonts and symbols in written text. This information, in some sense, is an artifact of the source: for example, it tells us who spoke when and where. Although much of this information may have been entered by hand when texts were transcribed or retyped (Section 1.5), there is a relatively unambiguous system for encoding this material (see Appendix 4).

On the other hand, the grammatical analysis of a corpus such as ICE-GB is more problematic. The text may be ambiguous. Annotation schemes, such as ICE, are highly complex, and are therefore difficult to apply consistently. Any grammatical scheme dealing with a significant amount of material, particularly with spoken English, is subject to dispute and even change.

The grammatical information in the corpus is the result of a synthesis between the annotation scheme and the source material. Since human annotators find it difficult to apply grammatical decisions consistently, and checking automatic annotation is extremely skilled and time-consuming, some other corpora have been annotated only by applying an algorithm to the corpus. This has the advantage of minimum effort and maximum consistency. However, the result will be systematically biased by the performance of the algorithm, which means that researchers' results will also be so biased.

The ICE-GB corpus has been grammatically annotated twice: first with stand-alone algorithms, and second, in repeated passes, by hand (see also Section 1.8). In fact, in the later stages of checking, ICECUP was used to search systematically for potential errors and edit the trees. In this way, we can guarantee that remaining errors are human, and therefore erratic!

4.4 The text browser window

The browser window displays text units on a series of lines, by default with **no** line breaks. This means that text can disappear beyond the right-hand or left-hand edges of the window, but it guarantees a regular, line-by-line display. ICECUP 3.0 does not provide a word-wrapping mode (Figure 63).[2] This can be a drawback if you want to read an entire long sentence without scrolling back and forth.

The window shows two parts: a status bar at the bottom, and a scrolling text browser. The browser is divided into two sections: a left-hand margin composed of 'buttons', and the text view itself. The margin indicates the current text code and unit number (and optionally, subtext and speaker codes). The margin remains stationary when the text is scrolled sideways but moves up and down with the view.

[2] See also Table 21, page 100. There is a way around this, however. 'Show text' in the tree viewer window can be used to show a single sentence with word wrap. See page 109.

Figure 62: Elements of the text browser and status bar.

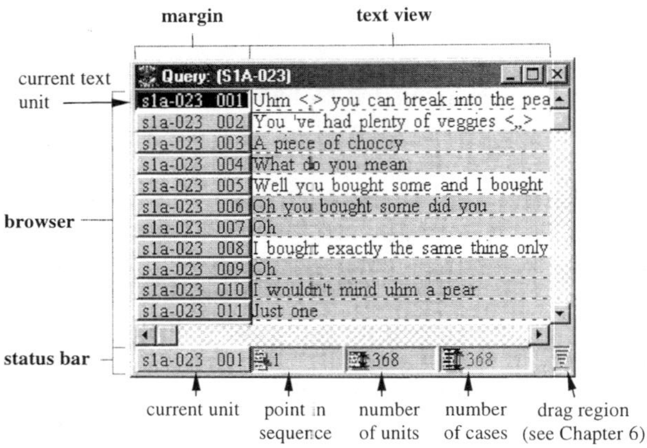

Figure 62 illustrates the result of a 'Browse' action from the corpus map with the single text S1A-023 selected. The status bar contains a series of indicators: the current text code (S1A-023) and text unit number (001); the current location in the browser sequence; and two totals, indicating the length of the sequence. The first of these is the total number of units in the sequence. In this figure, the text contains 368 numbered units, including some which may only consist of extra-corpus material (see Section 1.3).

The second total is a number never smaller than the first. This is the total number of cases in a search sequence. Note that more than one instance of a search argument may appear within a single text unit.

These two totals are distinct when performing FTF or text fragment queries. They will be the same when browsing a text, or the results of a corpus map or variable query, where each text unit is a 'case'. The concordance display options show a separate case, rather than text unit, per line. The total number of cases becomes the maximum number of lines in the text browser.

As we shall see, the status bar can hold further information controlling concordance elements, and a 'drag region' that exposes the query editor. We will return to these in Chapter 6.

The basic text browser is shown in Figure 62 – predominantly black text against a cream background, each text unit separated by a pale dotted line, one line per view.

In order to control the view, a menu button bar, placed under the main command bar, is provided (Figure 63). These buttons replicate commands in the 'View' menu, and can be usefully divided as follows.

- **Select text unit control** (ICECUP 3.1 only). This command marks the selected text unit in the corpus using a query element called a 'selection list' (see Section 4.12). If no list exists in the current window a new one is created. The current text unit is added

Figure 63: Evolution of the text map button bar to support grammatical concordancing, text unit selection and sound playback.

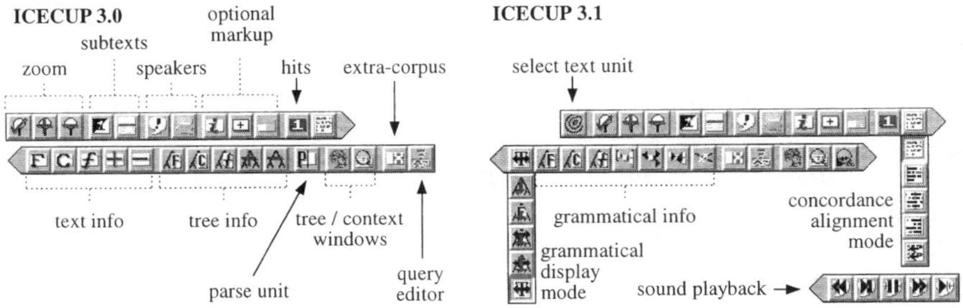

to this selection list and the margin is marked. You can remove the mark by performing the operation again.

- **Zoom controls**. Default, larger and smaller scale adjust the text size.
- **Text and subtext controls**. These reveal, or hide, the subtext number (1, 2, 3...) and division lines separating texts, subtexts and paragraphs.
- **Speaker controls.** These reveal, or hide, the speaker code (A, B, C...) and speaker highlight shading.
- **Optional markup controls**. These reveal or hide: ignored material, text added by corpus editors and overlap shading.
- **Concordance controls**. These reveal or hide the number of cases per line and set concordancing alignment.
- **Grammatical annotation controls**. Grammatical information is controlled differently in versions 3.0 and 3.1 of ICECUP. In 3.0, text and tree information is controlled independently. ICECUP 3.1 uses a 'display mode' button (Figure 63, right) to switch between five different modes, including three new 'grammatical concordancing' modes. In either case the first three buttons determine the grammatical elements to show – function, category and features – the remainder control the quantity of material by modfying the size of the 'neighbourhood'.
- **Show/hide parse unit** (ICECUP 3.0 only). The parse unit is the topmost node in each tree, containing summary grammatical information about the entire text unit.
- **New window controls.** These buttons activate new windows. The first creates a 'spy' tree window of the currently selected text unit. The second creates a simple browse window of the whole text.
- **Show/hide extra-corpus material.** This reveals descriptive annotation and material excluded from the corpus, typically on the grounds of sample size (texts should be approximately 2,000 words) and speaker (sometimes non-British speakers are part of a conversation or news report). See also Section 1.3.
- **Show/hide logical query editor.** This performs a task equivalent to the drag region in Figure 62 and is described in Chapter 6.

- **Sound playback controls** (ICECUP 3.1 only). These are: rewind, quick play, pause, fast forward and continuous play. Quick play plays the current unit, while continuous play tracks through the browser list playing each available unit in turn.

You can explore a text in three main ways: exposing more or less of the view by zooming or resizing the window, scrolling the view up and down, and thirdly – which is really an extension of the second – jumping directly to a specific point in the text.

Zooming is controlled by three buttons on the toolbar at the top of the screen, or alternatively a series of key strokes or menu options. Table 15 summarises these. There are eight face sizes, from a very pinched 'nine point' to a large 'thirty point'. When the text is very small, the inter-word spacing is slightly exaggerated. The default scale is 'twelve point', which is the smallest face that doesn't appear cramped, yet is comfortable to work with.

To move through the text you can scroll the view as in a conventional window. Scroll bars disappear when you can see all the view in one direction. In ICECUP 3.1, scrolling and zooming may be performed by 'dragging' the display with the mouse. Use the left mouse button to drag the view. To zoom with the mouse, hold down <Ctrl> at the start. See Chapter 7 for more details.

If you want to move to a specific point in the list, there are a number of 'hidden' controls in the status bar. Three of these are within the "current text unit" 'button' at the left hand end of the status bar.

> If you press down with the left mouse button over the initial (alphanumeric) part of the text code (the part labelled S1A, *etc.*) a pop-up menu appears which will move you to the start of any such initial text code within the range of the query results.

> If you press down on the second part of the button text, namely the secondary numeric code, you can 'type over' the number. Similarly, you can adjust the unit number within a text by overtyping the final three digits.

The 'sequence position' index ranges from 1 to the length of the entire sequence and can also be edited.

> Press down with the left mouse button here and you can type over this number.

As we have seen, text codes and unit numbers are always shown in the margin. These uniquely identify every text unit in the corpus. However, some texts are

Table 15: Scaling commands.

	name	**keyboard action**	**menu command**
	Default scale	<Ctrl>+<Home>	**View | Default scale**
	Larger scale	<Ctrl>+<Cursor Up>	**View | Larger**
	Smaller scale	<Ctrl>+<Cursor Down>	**View | Smaller**

Table 16: Subtext and speaker information commands.

	name	keyboard action	menu command
	Show subtext number	<Ctrl>+'B'	**View | Subtext**
	Show dividers	<Ctrl>+'D'	**View | Dividers**
	Show speaker identifier	<Ctrl>+'S'	**View | Speaker**
	Show speaker highlight	<Ctrl>+'L'	**View | Highlight**

composed of a number of subtexts. For example, text W1B-012 is composed of two social letters; W2C-023, seven short newspaper reports. ICECUP visualises these divisions in the query results browser in two ways: showing subtext codes in the margin, and marking division lines between subtexts. The commands for these are given in Table 16.

Text dividers are horizontal lines which overrule the light dotted lines. A black line indicates a division between one text and another; a red line, between subtexts in the same text; and a dashed blue line, between paragraphs.

In dialogues, it can be difficult to keep track of who is speaking when. For example, in Figure 62, it is not clear that text units 003 and 004 are spoken by a second speaker, while the first returns briefly in unit 005, to say,

> Well you bought some and I bought some [S1A-023 #5]

As with text and subtext markers, there are two viewing options to help you see speakers and turn taking (Table 16, lower): an explicit speaker identifier in the margin ('A', 'B', 'C', *etc.*), and a coloured background for the text. In ICECUP 3.1, the speaker element also indicates sentences where sound recordings are available (with a white disc in the margin 'button').

In Figure 64, speakers are indicated by both identifier and coloured highlight: cream for speaker 'A', sky blue for 'B', lime green for 'C', and so on. These colours are also reflected in the corpus map 'speaker' icons.

This figure also illustrates two other common features of spoken texts:

Figure 64: Viewing speakers.

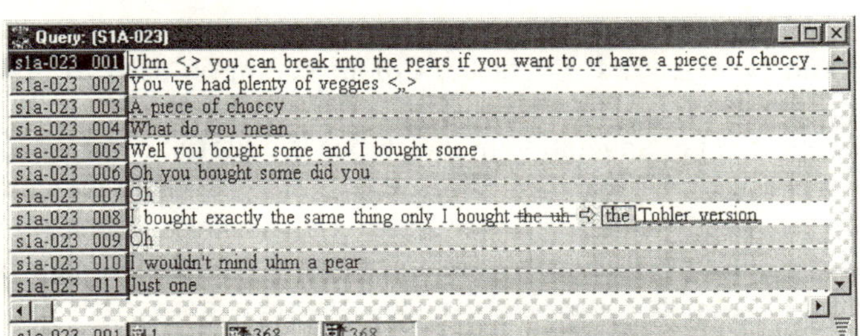

self-correction and *speaker overlap.*

Speakers often correct themselves. In Figure 64, line 8, speaker **A** says

> ...I bought the uh the Tobler version [S1A-023 #8]

In plain text, it is difficult to see self-correction, but you can 'hear' it by speaking the text aloud to yourself. We annotate this by:

1) **Marking the corrected material**: (a) as ignored (shown as red text), and (b) as self-removed (with a red horizontal bar through the middle).

2) **Marking the replacement material**. This is shown by a black box around the words and a red arrow before the text, thus:

   ...I bought ~~the uh~~ ⇨ [the] Tobler version [S1A-023 #8]

No text is actually removed. The speaker *did* say all of this, after all. Another way of thinking about this is that the marking described here is of two types:

- **Illustrative marking** which describes a particular aspect of the text (this is not typically searched).
- **Formal marking** specifies a fundamental, 'logical' change that affects the grammatical interpretation of the sentence (it also has an impact on searching).

The formal marking employed here, *ignore*, means that *the* and *uh* are ignored when considering the grammar of the sentence. It also has implications for *searching the corpus*, as we discuss in Chapter 5. Ignored material, visible by default, can be hidden by the 'hide ignored text' command (Table 17).

Incomplete words, for example, where a speaker tails off, are depicted with a trailing centred ellipsis, *e.g.*,

> ...~~from disa~~··· from work with disabled... [S1A-001 #002]

In dialogues, a further issue concerns *speaker overlapping*. In Section 1.5, we discussed examples like the following.

> [speaker B] I mean you have to completely suspend disbelief
> [speaker A] who knows [S1A-006 #149-150]

Overlaps are displayed by a system of coloured highlights, controlled by the 'speaker overlap' command (Table 17). Here the first utterance is interrupted by the second 'who knows' utterance. Colour coding is used to differentiate different pairs of overlapping speech.

A further kind of annotation in the corpus is editorial correction. In order to allow the corpus to be searched effectively, and to facilitate the grammatical annotation, the corpus is corrected for spelling mistakes. In the spoken part of the corpus, a similar process deals with nonstandard pronunciations which have established orthographic forms. For example, *dunno* is transcribed as such, and

Table 17: Switches for ignored text, overlaps and editorial additions.

	name	keyboard action	menu command
	Show ignored text	<Ctrl>+'I'	**View | Ignored text**
	Show overlaps	<Ctrl>+'O'	**View | Overlap**
	Show text additions	<Ctrl>+'A'	**View | Text additions**

then 'normalised' as *don't know*. In part of the written corpus, (albeit a little inconsistently) punctuation errors have been corrected.

This 'annotator correction' is marked differently from self-correction. When speakers overrule their previous utterance, their replacement speech is marked with a black box around it. When annotators replace material, this is marked with a red box around it. Further, this material can also be hidden when browsing the corpus. The 'show text additions' command does this (Table 17).

Some of the material in the corpus is ambiguous or missing, which is unavoidable for a variety of reasons. For example, the spoken material may not be fully transcribed. If the transcriber was uncertain about a word, the word is depicted in royal blue, rather than black, and underlined in blue. Indecipherable material is shown as a notional element – the non-lexical items '<unclear-syllable(s)/word(s)>' as appropriate, again in blue.

A similar problem exists in some of the written texts, particularly hand-written material, where text has been crossed out by the author and characters may be imperfectly formed. A final problem of this type is when a recording is broken, either by accident or deliberately. Intentional breaks in the source can arise from, for example, a commercial break in a radio broadcast, or a break for an interview or report which has been removed.

Written material in the corpus presents a different set of problems to its spoken counterpart. Although we do not attempt to present printed text exactly in its original form, we have reproduced the following formatting.

- **Paragraphs and headers**. A new paragraph is shown as an indented line with a blue arrow pointing down and right – '↳' – preceding it. (Paragraph breaks are also indicated by a blue dotted line if 'text dividers' are shown.) Headers are shown in a slightly enlarged, heavy sans-serif typeface, *e.g.*,

  "**REFERENCES :**" [W1A-004 #104]

- **Bold, italic and underlined fonts**. These are illustrated by an appropriate change of typeface.

- **Capitalisation, special symbols and accents**. Capital letters, including 'small-capitals' are reproduced. The current ICE 'special character' set includes most conventional accented characters, as well as the upper and lower-case Greek alphabet, and a variety of non-alphabetic symbols (see Table 18). The latter includes math-ematical and 'bullet' symbols, and some more unusual symbols, such as the 'female'

Table 18: Alphabetic special characters used in ICE.

	description	**coding**	**examples**
ÁÈÎÕÜ	Upper case accents	<capital letter><accent>	Aacute, Egrave...
áèîõü	Lower case accents	<lower case letter><accent>	aacute, egrave...
ΑΒΓΔ	Greek capitals	<capitalised English>	Alpha, Beta...
αβγδ	Greek lower case	<lower case English>	alpha, beta...
Æœ	Ligatures	<two letters>ligature	AEligature

('Venus') symbol (Appendix D). These can be viewed in the Text Fragment dialog box 'special characters' pull-down list (see Section 5.3).

- **Linebreaks and hyphenation**. Hyphenated words are presented with their hyphen. Where words are hyphenated over the end of a line, we have an 'embedded' line break marker within a word, indicated by a vertical 'raised bar' in the word.

  A slightly rarer occurrence is ambiguous line break hyphenation. This is when a word was hyphenated in the text at a line break, but it is unclear whether the hyphen was inserted because the text met the end of the line, or because the word would have been hyphenated anyway, *e.g.*, "disease-causing" (W2B-030 #108). Ambiguous hyphenation is indicated by a long hyphen ('—') before the line break.

- **Other typological conventions**, such as references, superscripts and subscripts, are depicted accordingly (see Table 19).

Just as in the spoken texts, written material can be ambiguous, albeit for different reasons. Although images are not included in the corpus, we include indications, in the markup, of the location of photographs and diagrams.

We briefly summarise miscellaneous annotations below.

- **Single-word joins**. When a word is orthographically represented as a single word, but split for tagging purposes, it is drawn with a black overline:

  $\overline{\text{I'm}}$ blanking [S1A-001 #14]

Table 19: Miscellaneous typological conventions.

description	**coding**	**depiction**
Footnotes	<footnote>	blue text
Footnote reference	<fnr>	underlined superscript
Superscript	<sp>	superscripted text
Subscript	<sb>	subscripted text
Roman numeral	<roman>	sans-serif bold
Marginalia	<marginalia>	(not visualised differently)
Typeface change	<typeface>	

- **Quotations**. Quoted material is indicated in bold italics, as in the following example. We have marked the quotation marks themselves, as well as the material within them.

  Proust 's symbolism is an ***' autosymbolism '***... [W2A-004 #65]

- **Mentioned words**. References to a word, or 'mentions', are in a bold blue type.

  Well **still** isn't really the word [S1A-015 #115]

- **Foreign words**. Non-English words are indicated by a blue italic type.

  All those *châteaux* you went to visit <,> [S1A-009 #242]

- **Aliases**. To preserve anonymity, aliases have sometimes been used. Aliases are written in a green pen.

4.5 Viewing word class tags

ICE-GB is a tagged and parsed corpus. This means that, first, for each 'word' or text unit element, there is a word class tag,[3] and second, each text unit contains a full parse analysis – a grammatical tree – which relates these tags together and specifies their function.

In the text browser you can view the text and tags together. Note that you have to specify *which* elements and *how much* you want to see.

> Select 'View | Syntax | Tags', or press the keys <Ctrl> and '5' together to specify that you want to see word class tags.

> Now we must specify how much grammatical annotation we want to see, *e.g.*, all. Select 'View | Focus | All' to specify that you want everything to be shown tagged (the 'Focus' submenu is below the 'Syntax' one). The result is in Figure 65.

As we can see in Table 20, three buttons control the content of the 'tags' shown. Two buttons increase or reduce the amount of material. Additional

Figure 65: Viewing tags in text.

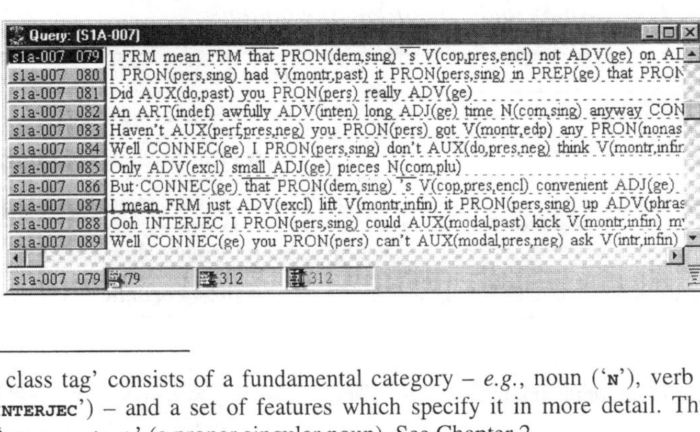

---

[3] A 'word class tag' consists of a fundamental category – *e.g.*, noun ('**N**'), verb ('**V**'), interjection ('**INTERJEC**') – and a set of features which specify it in more detail. Thus *Adam* is tagged as '**N(prog,sing)**' (a proper singular noun). See Chapter 2.

Table 20: 'Grammatical information' commands (ICECUP 3.0)

tags	trees[4]	name	keyboard action[4]	menu command
		Functions	<Ctrl>+'1'	**View | Syntax | Functions**
		Categories	<Ctrl>+'2'	**View | Syntax | Categories**
		Features	<Ctrl>+'3'	**View | Syntax | Features**
		Expand focus	<Ctrl>+<Page Up>	**View | Focus | More**
		Reduce focus	<Ctrl>+<Page Down>	**View | Focus | Less**

shortcuts are provided in the menu system. A slightly different system is used for later versions of ICECUP, which we explain below.

Tags are displayed following each word, in a plain, blue type, presented in the ICE style. The category comes first, in capitals, followed by a set of features enclosed in brackets and written in lower case, where they apply.

4.6 Concordancing a query

Concordancing is a popular method for viewing the results of searches that is often used in corpus linguistics. Many systems offer a method called 'key word in line' (KWIL) concordancing,[5] which lists each instance of a key word, one per line, within their surrounding text. Lines are centred around the key word. The method allows a researcher to rapidly scan a series of cases.

Concordancing can be used for plain text files. In tagged corpora, however, one can search and display word class tags. Thus 'key *word* in line' becomes 'key *tag* in line', *i.e.*, first, we can perform a query for a word class tag, and second, we may display tags in the sentence (or, at least, in the region

Table 21: Line display and concordancing options.

	name	menu command
	Concordance left	**View | Concordance | Left**
	Concordance middle	**View | Concordance | Middle**
	Concordance right	**View | Concordance | Right**
	No concordancing	**View | Concordance | None**
	Word wrap (new in ICECUP 3.1)	**View | Concordance | Word wrap**

[4] To specify a 'tree' command, press <Shift>. The equivalent menus are under 'View | Tree'.

Figure 66: Concordancing nouns.

simple: with no annotation specified

with tags: i.e., 'categories and features' specified

after increasing the range by one

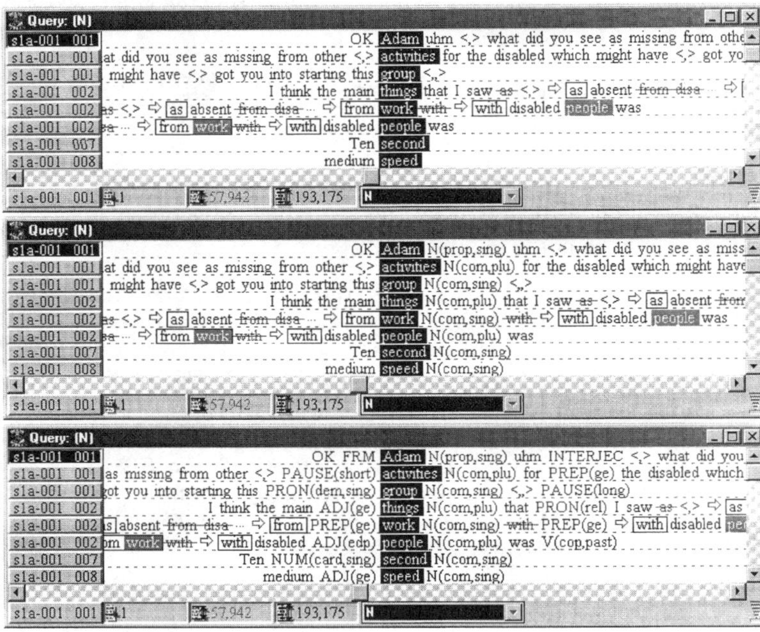

near the element).

We perform a 'key tag in line' concordance in ICECUP as follows.

- ➢ Perform an FTF query for a word class tag (*e.g.*, an inexact 'nodal' query for '**N**').
- ➢ Press <F2> to change the display to a concordance mode (alternatively, select 'View | Concordance | Left' or hit the 'concordance' button, '', Table 21). The view should look like the upper window in Figure 66.
- ➢ We can now view neighbouring tags by selecting 'View | Syntax | Tags', or <Ctrl>+'5' as before. Then increase the size of the neighbourhood gradually using the 'expand focus' command. Figure 66 shows what happens to the concordance display as tags are revealed.

The two 'expand and reduce range' buttons adjust the range of the tag display. The tag range varies from 'none' to 'all'. The default, '1', means 'just the highlighted elements' (Figure 66, middle); '2' means 'these plus one text unit element either side' (Figure 66, bottom), and so forth. Distance is measured by counting lexical items along the text. Thus, for example, one of the matches in Figure 66 expands as shown in Figure 67 overleaf.

---

[5] Some people refer to this as 'key word in context' (KWIC) concordancing. We would use this to mean a way of viewing material which displays more than one line of surrounding text.

Figure 67: Lexical distance along a text unit from the noun "work" in S1A-001 #002.

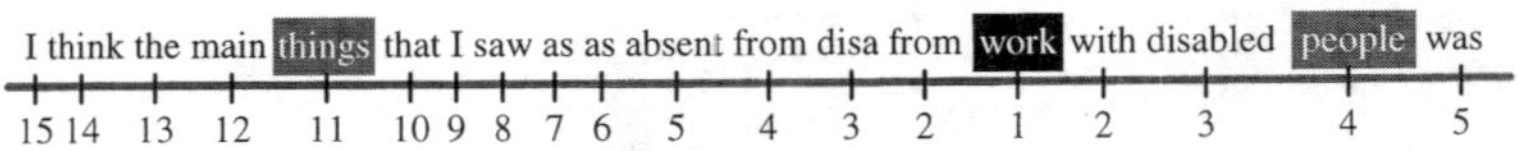

ICECUP extends the concept of concordancing to a parsed corpus. We have what we might call 'key *constituent* in line' concordancing. The following points should be borne in mind.

1) *Any* grammatical query that is expressed as a Fuzzy Tree Fragment may be concordanced. This includes single node queries (inexact nodes only in ICECUP 3.0, nodes containing logical expressions in 3.1) and text fragment queries. ICECUP can perform queries on complex grammatical structures and concordance the results.

2) Concordancing is based on the 'focus' of an FTF. For a single word, the focus point is the tag node, while for a word sequence, it is the entire set of tag nodes. For a single node query (*e.g.*, 'N'), it is that constituent. Where FTFs have more structure, however, the focus point may be separately specified within the structure (see Section 5.10). For example, in Figure 56 (page 85, upper right), the subject complement node ('CS,CL') has been given the focus.

3) The focus point determines the *marked text range*, which is defined as the part of the text dominated by the focus node or nodes. This range determines the notion of a 'neighbourhood' measured in terms of lexical distance (Figure 67). Additionally, in ICECUP 3.1, further grammatical concordancing modes are available in which tree nodes in *structural* proximity to the focus point may be revealed (see 4.8).

4) Concordancing operates in conjunction with the logic of combined queries. For more on this, see Chapter 6.

4.7 Displaying trees in the text

As we noted, it is quite common to display word class tags in text. Yet ICE-GB consists of parsed text units: each sentence has been analysed as a grammatical tree. How does ICECUP support the exploration of these trees?

One facility is a line-by-line display of tree structure using brackets, expanded from the top, down. An example is given in Figure 68.

➢ In ICECUP 3.0, press the 'expand tree' button once (marked '' – see Table 20, page 100). In ICECUP 3.1, you must first change mode (press <F3> to set 'show mode' to 'top down' – ''), and then press 'expand' (shown as '') twice.

➢ We can add function, category and feature information to the brackets. Press '' to display functions in the tree (Figure 69).

However, while we can expand trees 'in line' like this, we will be quickly swamped by excessive irrelevant detail. We have to either limit the number of

Figure 68: Bracketting the topmost tree constituents in the browser.

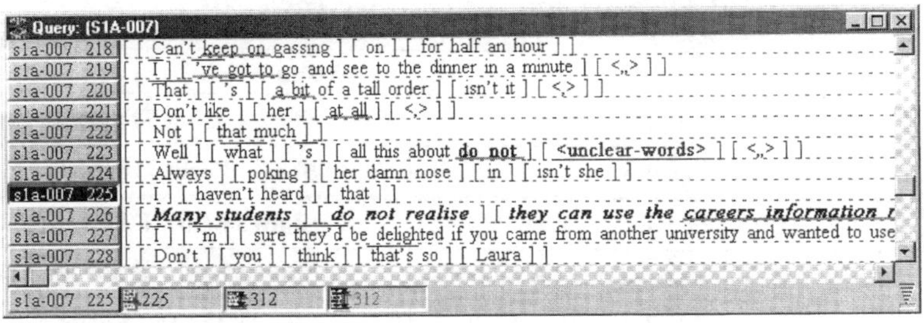

Figure 69: Visualising the major functional constituents of trees.

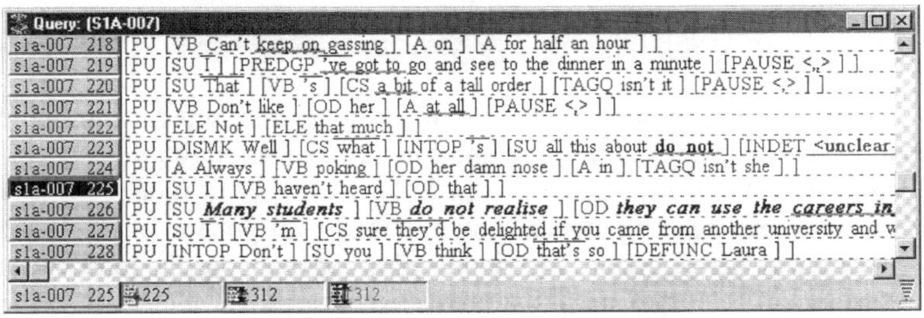

Figure 70: Viewing the topmost node of each tree.

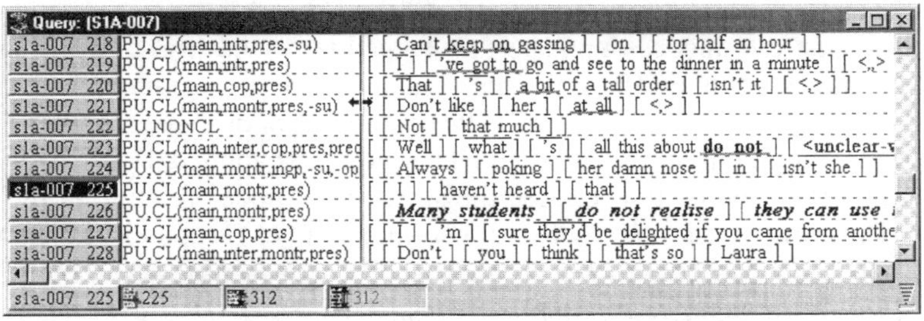

visible trees at any one moment in time, or control the display of grammatical information in a more precise manner.

Another possibility is to consider only the most summary information about a parse, specifically features contained in the 'parse unit' node. ICECUP allows you to view this information in a separate column using the 'show parse unit' command ('[icon]' or 'View | Parse Unit', Figure 70). The divider can be moved with the mouse.

Table 22: Display modes in ICECUP 3.1. The first two are provided in ICECUP 3.0 as separate options (see Table 20).

	name	menu command
	Display tags along text	**View | Show | Along (Tagged) Text**
	Display tree from top, down	**View | Show | From Top of Tree**
	Display tree from FTF focus, down	**View | Show | Below FTF Focus**
	Display tree from focus, down and siblings	**View | Show | Below & Beside Focus**
	Display tree around FTF focus	**View | Show | Around Focus**

4.8 Grammatical concordancing in ICECUP 3.1

When we are examining a particular set of query results, relevant grammatical information may not be at the top of the tree, but *in the neighbourhood of the matching part* of the tree. ICECUP 3.1 includes a number of more sophisticated *grammatical concordancing* modes shown in the lower portion of Table 22.

The button bar gains an additional 'show mode' button (and the menu gains a further set of commands) that provides five options. Function key <F3> rotates through these modes. We no longer require two sets of display commands – as in Table 20 – a single set is provided which is dependent on the mode. These commands are summarised in Table 23.

The first two modes duplicate the 'tagged text' and 'top-down bracketting' commands of ICECUP 3.0. The remainder display grammatical information in the tree *relative to the FTF focus* node or nodes (see Chapter 5.10). They are therefore only available if an FTF search was applied.

The three new options expose the structure of nodes relative to the FTF focus. Thus the 'from the focus, down' mode ('') expands as follows.

Table 23: 'Grammatical information' commands, ICECUP 3.1 (cf. Table 20).

	name	keyboard action	menu command
	Functions	<Ctrl>+'1'	**View | Syntax | Functions**
	Categories	<Ctrl>+'2'	**View | Syntax | Categories**
	Features	<Ctrl>+'3'	**View | Syntax | Features**
	Show all	<Shift>+<Home>	**View | Focus | All**
	Expand range	<Shift>+<Page Up>	**View | Focus | More**
	Reduce range	<Shift>+<Page Down>	**View | Focus | Less**
	Show none	<Shift>+<End>	**View | Focus | None**

'1' means just the node, '2', plus all daughters, '3', daughters of daughters, *etc.* If you wish to see grammatical information contained in siblings of the focus, you can use the 'below and beside' option (''); to reveal parent nodes use 'all around' (''). Try the following:

- Perform an 'inexact' 'Node' query for all clauses ('CL') in the corpus. Many clauses realise entire parse units, many are recursively 'nested' (*i.e.*, there are clauses within clauses) and some are conjoined together. We can use grammatical concordancing to separate these out.
- Press <F2> for a leftward concordance. Then press <F3> or hit the 'show mode' button until it indicates 'Show below focus' (''). Now press <Ctrl>+'9' or each of the 'function', 'category', 'features' buttons. The result should look like the window in the upper part of Figure 71.

It is now easy to identify both the function and the features of each clause. Of course, the category is strictly superfluous in this example ('**CL**'), but it improves the readability of the display. Suppose we wish to identify the set of constituents forming the clause (*i.e.*, the nodes immediately below).

- For legibility, we will hide the features. Click on the 'features' button ('') or press <Ctrl>+'3'. Then extend the range by hitting the 'expand' button, ''. The display

Figure 71: Concordancing clauses.

from the focus down, function, category and features displayed

including nodes below the current one, hiding features

including sibling nodes

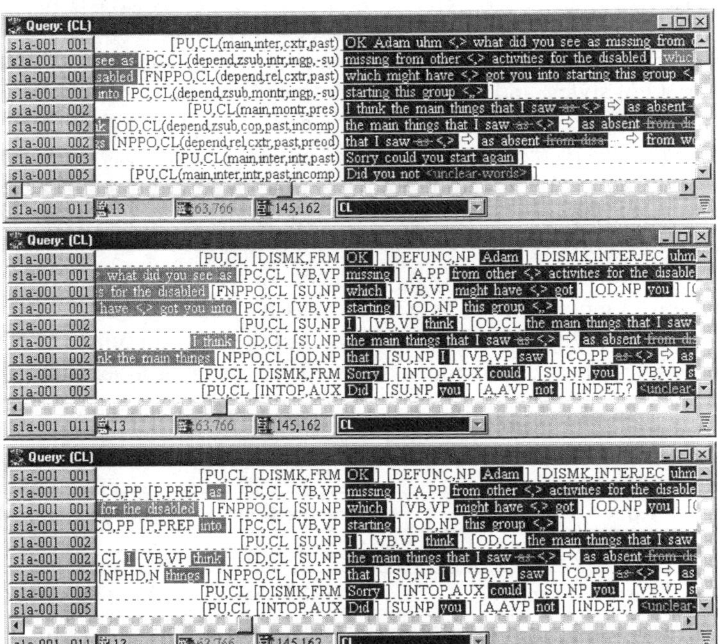

should now resemble the second window of Figure 71.

- We can also reveal sibling nodes (Figure 71, bottom). Press <F3> or hit the 'show mode' button again.

The central problem is managing the sheer quantity of information in the corpus. There is only so much space within a single line in the view. Nonetheless, this approach is useful if you want to identify variation in the 'grammatical neighbourhood' of the FTF focus.

As we commented before, grammatical concordancing works in conjunction with the focus. In Chapter 5 we discuss the construction of more complex FTFs, including how the focus is specified. Defining the focus separately from the grammatical query provides a high degree of flexibility, letting us to change the focus and then reveal constituents near it. Grammatical concordancing provides a 'drill-down' method which can reveal relevant comparable elements in a sequence of grammatical trees. In order to inspect the trees themselves, however, we require a different approach.

4.9 Displaying trees in a separate window

The basic problem with a concordance display is that we are limited to a series of single portions of lines, of fixed width. Expressing an essentially two-dimensional structure in one dimension is always bound to be problematic! Fortunately, as we have already seen, ICECUP has a viewer for displaying trees (it is also used for editing Fuzzy Tree Fragments, of which, more later). This window includes a multi-line version of the annotated text, draws trees in a variety of styles, and shows how the tree is related to the text.

The tree viewer is invoked as a 'spy window'. This means that *the tree window always reflects the current sentence in the browser* that it originated from. Thus, in Figure 72, if you were to move the current selection in the query window from text unit #222 to #223, the tree in the other window would change accordingly.

You can use the first command in Table 24 or perform a left mouse button 'double-click'. These operations may also be found in a 'popup menu' (press the right mouse button down with the mouse pointer over the text in the browser). The other commands listed below open a second browser window

Table 24: Commands to activate new windows.

	name	**keyboard action**	**menu command (also popup)**
	View spy tree	<Space>	**View | Browse | Spy tree**
	View text / context	<Ctrl>+<Space>	**View | Browse | Text / Context**
	View map (ICECUP 3.1)	<Ctrl+Shift>+<Space>	**View | Browse | Corpus map**

Figure 72: Employing a spy window in conjunction with the query browser.

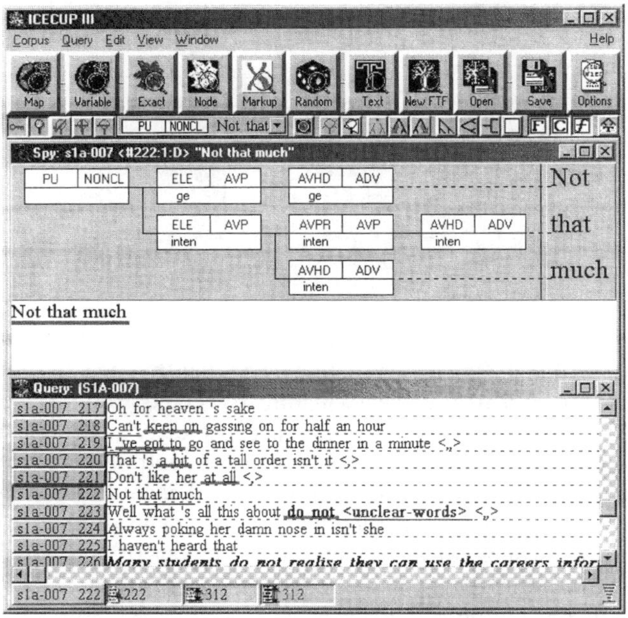

revealing the context around the current text unit and open the corpus map to show the current location (and hence other sociolinguistic information).

A browser and its spy window is illustrated in Figure 72 overleaf. Only a single spy window may be connected to a text browser at any one moment. Opening a second spy window disconnects the first and makes it 'passive'. A passive window can hold a text unit and tree when you find something interesting.[6]

This implicit 'spying' connection is very flexible. There is no restriction on resizing or moving either window: the connection is 'live' while both are open. To be effective with spy windows, therefore, you need to master Windows' methods for arranging windows.

A good rule of thumb is: minimise or close unwanted windows and use a 'Tile' command (in the 'Window' menu) to tidy the display as much as possible. Avoid obscuring your spy window when you are exploring text units in the browser. When you have found a tree or text unit that you are interested in, you can maximise the spy window to the entire ICECUP window in order to explore it in more depth.

[6] This is not the only way of recording 'interesting' text units. ICECUP 3.1 allows you to mark texts manually by creating a *selection list*. This is summarised in Section 4.12.

Figure 73: The tree viewer button bar.

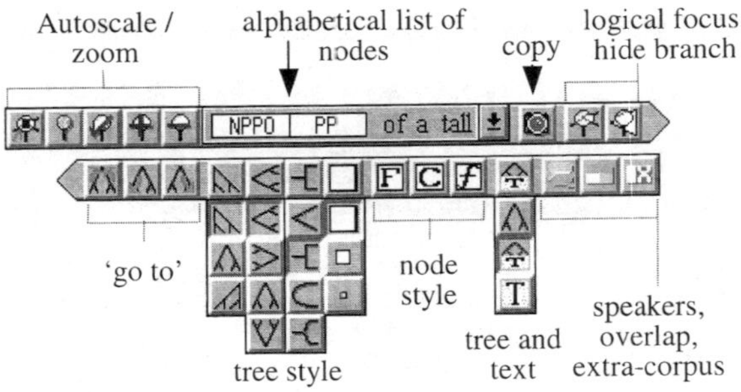

You can make the tree window active by clicking down with the left mouse button inside it. (It becomes active when you first open it, but typical use of the spy window may involve switching back and forth between the two windows.) When the window is active, it accepts keyboard commands and the small button bar changes to display commands for controlling the tree viewer.

These buttons are shown in Figure 73, and include a number of those provided for editing FTFs (see Section 5.6). The main difference is that you cannot edit corpus trees. Instead, you gain a number of additional buttons to control the view of the tree.

As with the button bar for the query results window, it is useful to discuss the buttons in groups.

- **Scaling buttons.** At the far left is a group of scaling buttons which change the size of the view. New to ICECUP 3.1 is a *zoom to focus* button (top left). This automatically tracks each matching case in a concordance view by zooming in on the focus of each one in the tree. By default, the window will be in *autoscale* mode (the second button at the top). This automatically fits the tree into the window, which is useful if you want to see the overall structure of the tree. However, it is less useful if you want to explore the tree in detail. Switching off autoscale enables zooming and scrolling within a tree.
- **Alphabetical list of nodes.** The second element in the button bar is a pull down selector which selects from an alphabetically ordered (by function, then category, then text) list of the nodes in the tree. Selecting a node here moves the current selection in the tree to that point.
- **Copy button.** This records the contents of the current node. You may then paste this into an FTF (see also Chapter 5.9).
- **Focus and close branch buttons.** These commands are useful for hiding irrelevant parts of a large tree, particularly in autoscale mode. *Focus* hides all of the tree above the current point. *Close branch* hides all of a branch below the current point.
- **'Go to' buttons.** These move you to the *top* of the tree, and the *first* or *last child* under the current node.

- **Tree style buttons.** These four buttons change the current tree-drawing style. They do this globally, so all trees shown are simultaneously changed. These buttons are 'multi-state', in other words, they rotate through a set of possibilities, and depict the current setting. You can use the left and right mouse buttons to rotate in alternate directions. The buttons are: *justification, orientation, line style,* and *box size,* respectively.
- **Node style buttons.** These three buttons determine what should be shown within the node box. By default, all three are down (set). At least one value must be set, because nodes must be depicted with something within them.
- **Show text button.** This button is another multi-state button which allows you to show the *tree only*, the *text only*, or *both* (the default). Hint: if you show *text only* in a spy window you obtain a resizable multi-line sentence viewing window which expands the text of a single line in the text browser into a large font and let you see the entire line without scrolling.

Moving around the tree is very simple. You can use the keyboard to move in logical steps around the tree, and the mouse to move directly to a node (just click down on it with the left mouse button). Logical (or topological) movement around the tree means moving to the next node according to the tree structure, not the geometric distance on the screen. This kind of navigation is used in the corpus map when you press <Ctrl> down. In the tree window, this is the only kind of keyboard-controlled movement permitted.

If you have the spy window open from before, try the following.

> Move the current position in the list to unit #220, and click down again on the spy window. Figure 74 shows the default condition of the tree in that window.

Grammatical features are hidden in this figure due to lack of space. The tree is autoscaled to fit the window and the entire tree is visible. By default your current position is at the top of the tree. This node 'box' is shown highlighted in the current Windows 'selection colour'. The 'shadow' of the selection falls across the text, marked by (a) the colouring of the words on the right of the tree, and (b) a broad 'underline' placed under these words in the lower, text part of the spy window. This underline is not shown in Figure 74.

As we mentioned, keyboard-driven movements take account of the tree structure, which can be drawn in a variety of different orientations ('left-to-right' being the default) and justifications ('align with the first child' being the

Figure 74: Default view of tree for text unit S1A-007 #220.

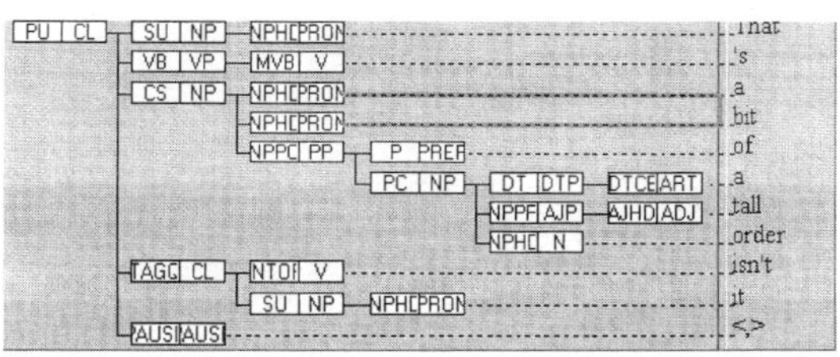

Table 25: Keyboard commands to move around the tree following the topology, assuming the left-to-right view in Figure 74.

name	**cursor**	**result**
Go to parent	<Left>	Moves to parent of the current node.
Go to adjacent child	<Right>	Moves to the nearest child under the current node.
Go to previous sibling	<Up>	Moves to prior sibling in sequence.
Go to next sibling	<Down>	Moves to posterior sibling in sequence.

default). These affect the way in which cursor keys are interpreted. Thus, if the tree is drawn from left to right, cursor <Left> means ‘go to the parent of the current node’. If it is drawn from right to left, on the other hand, it means ‘move to the closest child of the current node’.

Basically, there are four distinct actions corresponding to the four cursor keys, but the orientation determines which actual key does which action. (This is much more intuitive in practice than it is to describe.) Available actions are listed in Table 25, with cursor keys indicated for the default left-to-right view (consider Figure 74). You can also press <Home> (or ‘’) to go to the top of the tree, and <Page Up> and <Page Down> (‘’ and ‘’) to go to the first and last leaf node relative to the current position.

Another way of moving around the tree is to use the ‘node selector’ in the button bar. This shows an alphabetical list of all the nodes, less their features, with the initial part of the text under them. If you change the selection here the current selection will move in the tree to match.

The best way to learn these different ways of navigating the tree is to experiment.

> Try moving around this tree, using the keyboard, mouse and menu buttons. Move to the prepositional phrase (‘PP’) *of a tall order*, marked as a noun phrase postmodifier (‘NPPO’) and located towards the centre of Figure 74.

> When you have located this node, press down on the ‘focus’ button, ‘double-click’ with the left mouse button on the node, or press the space bar. This focuses the view on this branch, and hides other parts of the tree (Figure 75).

Figure 75: Focusing on a branch of the tree.

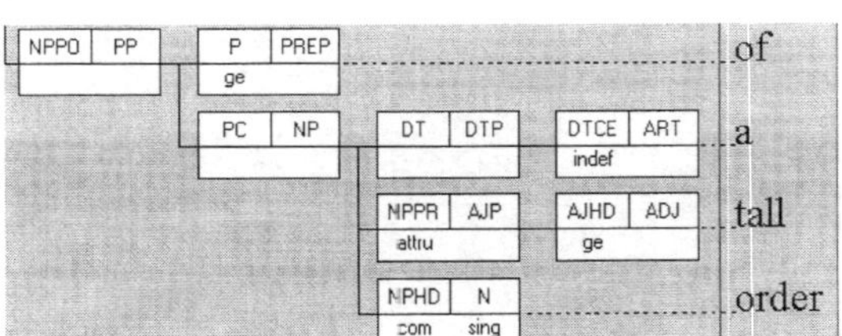

To ‘unfocus’, simply move the current position towards the root (you can select ‘’ or press <Home>). In autoscale mode, the view will focus on the current node if you move in any direction apart from towards the text.

The complementary action to focusing on a branch is called ‘hide branch’ (‘’). This closes the entire branch and hides every node beneath the current node. A triangle is drawn in place of the branch and the text is contracted.

> Press <Home> to go to the top of the tree and unfocus the view. Now find the prepositional phrase branch again and press ‘’ or <Ctrl> and the space bar. The result is shown in Figure 76.

Note that the text below the node is marked with an ellipsis (‘...’), but it is still visible in the text view. This branch will remain closed unless you either release the ‘’ button or move into the closed branch (*e.g.*, with the keyboard or node selector). In such cases the branch will expand sufficiently to show the relationship between the new position and the rest of the tree. It will not necessarily expand completely. To reveal an entire branch, press ‘’ once to close the branch entirely and a second time to re-open it entirely.

These commands pay dividends when you want to focus on part of a tree and explore the grammatical analysis. However, sometimes you may find that a more traditional ‘scrolling’ approach is preferable.

The autoscale mode may be switched off by pressing <Scroll Lock> on the keyboard or releasing the ‘autoscale’ button on the far left hand side of the menu buttons (‘’). You then gain the three zoom buttons in Table 27 and two scroll bars (Figure 77). Note that the text on the right-hand side is always visible, like the text unit buttons in the query window. You can adjust the margin by dragging the ‘dip’ divider sideways with the mouse.

Scrolling works with zoom. As we noted, the text margin is always

Figure 76: Hiding a branch of the tree.

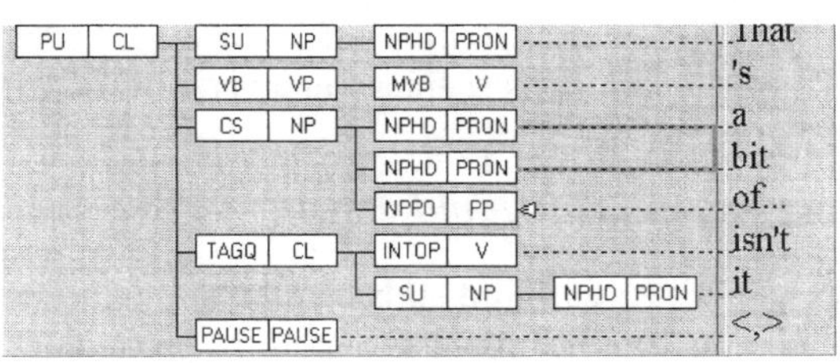

Table 26: Focus and hide branch commands.

	name	keyboard action	menu command
	Focus on branch	<Space>	**Edit | Focus on branch**
	Hide branch	<Ctrl>+<Space>	**Edit | Hide branch**

*Table 27: Scaling commands (available if autoscale is **off**).*

	name	keyboard action	menu command
	Default scale	<Ctrl>+<Home>	**View | Default scale**
	Larger scale	<Ctrl>+<Cursor Up>	**View | Larger**
	Smaller scale	<Ctrl>+<Cursor Down>	**View | Smaller**

Figure 77: Scrolling the tree window in ICECUP 3.0.

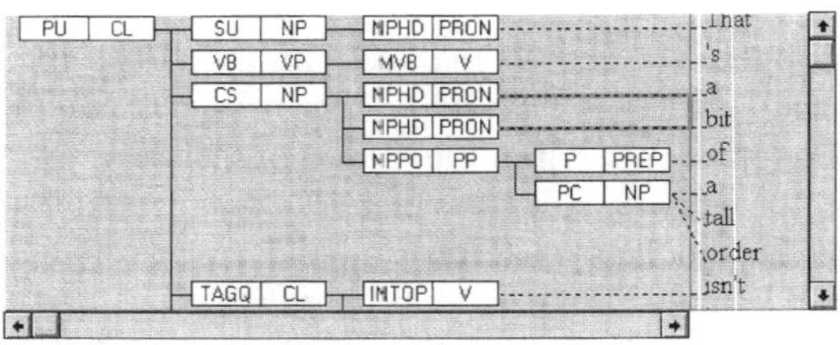

visible, so if you scroll towards the text, hidden tree structure is revealed. In Figure 77, the text *a tall order* is shown to be found under the node marked '**PC,NP**' (noun phrase as prepositional complement). This is indicated by a series of connecting dotted lines. These text unit elements are actually connected directly to nodes below this node, but these nodes are hidden in this view. If you were to scroll right in Figure 77, these would be revealed.

A useful enhancement in ICECUP 3.1 is the ability to scroll and zoom around the entire tree view smoothly, using the mouse. This is controlled in an identical manner as the text browser (see Section 4.4). To scroll in any direction, place the mouse pointer over the background panel, press the left mouse button and drag the mouse in that direction. If you want to zoom, hold the control key down at the start. This zoom facility also lets you to adjust the height and width of the tree independently. Finally, if you lose sight of your currently-selected position, press <Shift> and <Space> together to position the view around it. Chapter 7 summarises enhancements in ICECUP 3.1.

4.10 Concordancing, matching and viewing trees

To conclude this chapter, we will look at how this 'spy window' system can be used to help you examine the results of a search. In particular, the most useful search facilities make use of a 'matching' system based around the Fuzzy Tree Fragment system. This system is discussed in more detail in the remainder of the chapter, but for now, let us try the following.

If you perform a search using the 'inexact Node' query, ICECUP will not only retrieve a set of results with a count of the number of cases in the set, but will highlight, first, how the query has matched the tree, and second, how the matched 'focus' of the query casts a 'shadow' over the text.

> Type '**CJ,NP**' into a Node query window to obtain a text browser.

> Switch to a concordance mode by pressing the function key <F2>. Now double-click in a sentence to open a spy tree.

If you close all other trees and tile the windows, you can then browse through the list of results. ICECUP will look something like Figure 78.

Some of these trees are very large, and you may wish to practice exploring them with the zoom, focus and scroll controls discussed above. In ICECUP 3.1 you can also apply the 'Zoom to Focus' option (see below), which tracks each FTF focus through the concordance display. However, the point of this illustration is to show how matches are depicted.

As before, each case in the browser is allocated a distinct line. Hence, we can see two matches in unit S1A-004 #080, for example. You can show the number of matches per text unit by pressing down on the '▣' button (or press <Shift> and <F2> together). We can see how these two matches differ by the distinct text alignment (in this case, to the left of the elements) and by the shaded range itself (see also Figure 66). In a text unit with more than one match, the other matches are indicated by a lighter shading.

*Figure 78: Concordance centred on '**CJ,NP**', plus a spy window.*

Table 28: How 'zoom to focus' and 'autoscale' work together.

zoom to focus	autoscale: on	autoscale: off
off	Show entire tree, regardless of scale.	
on	Autofocus on FTF match, so only material below the match is shown.	Position match in the centre of the view and show surrounding material.

In the spy window, however, we can also see the matching nodes in the tree. This allows us to directly inspect the grammatical consequences of a particular search. In ICECUP 3.0 each tree is initially displayed in its entirety, automatically scaled to fit the window. However, we are often interested in the context immediately surrounding the focused nodes, which can be difficult to see if the tree is sizable. A new option in ICECUP 3.1 is 'Zoom to Focus' (''), which is available when tracking through a set of cases in concordance mode. The option automatically selects and zooms in on the focus of each case. With autoscale on, only the part of the tree under the focus is visible (Table 28); when off, focused nodes are centred in the spy window, allowing you to view material above and around the case.

The ability to inspect matching cases like this is very useful when you need to refine a search or abstract a new search using the Wizard. This returns us to the perspective outlined at the beginning of this chapter.

You could start an investigation with a 'text fragment' query consisting of a few words, and then browse the results and explore trees to identify the grammatical construction corresponding to your area of interest. You can build an FTF from the tree using the 'FTF Creation Wizard' described in Section 5.14). You can then use this FTF to find other similar grammatical constructions, irrespective of where they occur or how they are realised.

ICECUP is a system for exploring parsed corpora like ICE-GB. A query should be thought of as less an attempt at obtaining an 'ideal definition' in advance, than as an integral part of the exploratory process. Chapter 5 describes some of the more sophisticated query systems available.

4.11 Listening to speakers in the corpus

If you have access to digitised sound recordings from the spoken part of ICE-GB, you can use ICECUP 3.1 to play them back. (ICECUP 3.1 is supplied with the CD-ROM.) Suppose we have a CD-ROM that includes S1A-050.

➢ Use the corpus map to find S1A-050 (in the direct conversations) and open it.

Table 29: Sound playback controls.

	name	keyboard action	menu command
	Back		**View I Playback I Back**
	Quick play	<F8>	**View I Playback I Quick play**
	Pause		**View I Playback I Pause**
	Forward		**View I Playback I Forward**
	Continuous play	<Shift>+<F8>	**View I Playback I Continuous play**

You must let ICECUP know that a CD-ROM has been inserted.

> Press the large 'Speech' button on the button bar or select, from the menu, 'Query I Detect Speech CD'. This detects and 'registers' the CD by collecting track information and comparing it with current open browser windows.

You can now play the CD. The commands in Table 29 control playback.

> Press 'Quick play' ('' or <F8>). This will play the current text unit (#001).

You can move through the text and play text units in this way. Note that some of the text units in the recordings were not entirely separated out, in which case the 'segment' in which the utterance may be heard will be played.

You can listen to more than one text unit in sequence by selecting 'Continuous play' (''). This tracks through the corpus, playing each text unit in sequence. Note that the current selection in the browser moves automatically to the next unit when each sound segment finishes playing. (If a spy window for the browser is open ICECUP will update this automatically as well.)

Finally, the 'forward' and 'back' buttons move to the next and prior available sound segment. If 'continuous play' is active, then the next segment is played. 'Pause' simply pauses the playback.

There is a final advantage in allowing ICECUP to play sound recordings. You can listen to the results of any corpus query, provided that the recording is available. Finally, note that you must let ICECUP know when you change CD. Stop playback, eject and replace the CD, and then press 'Speech' again.

4.12 Selecting text units in ICECUP 3.1

Among the new text browser features in version 3.1 of ICECUP is a button on the far left of the button bar, with a 'thumb print' on it. This is the 'select unit' button ('', 'Query I Select Unit', or <Insert>, or pressing the right mouse button down in the margin).

In a (non-empty) browser window, try the following.

➢ Press <Insert> or place the mouse pointer over a margin 'button' and hit the right mouse button.

The button should change from grey to a marking colour, indicating that the current text unit is selected. If the browser contains a concordanced display and the current unit contains more than one case, each case will be highlighted together. If you reapply the command, the selection will be removed.

Notice also that the title of the window will change, from something like 'Query: (*x*)' to 'Query: (*x* or Selection #1)'. This indicates that a new query element (a 'selection list') has been automatically inserted into the underlying query expression. You can copy, negate and otherwise edit the logic of the underlying query. Editing the logic of the query is described in Chapter 6. For now, note the following.

1) The selection list element is similar to an FTF, in that it contains a matching range shown as a coloured highlight. Unlike an FTF, this range is simply the entire text unit.

2) At any one time you can have several windows open showing the same selection list. Press 'Duplicate' or use drag and drop to achieve this. When you modify the selection list in one window, it will be modified globally.

3) As a consequence, the 'undo' command (<Alt> and <Backspace> together) *does not* revert selection list actions. Instead, it will remove the selection list element from the query expression, eliminating the entire list.

4) Selection lists work with logic (see Chapter 6). This means, for example, that expressions of the form

(*x* or selection)	will list all elements in *x* with the highlights in the list (the default),
(*x* and selection)	will only show elements in *x* that are also in the list (note: this makes it difficult to add elements to the list),
(*x* and ¬selection)	will show elements in *x* that are *not* in the list (here you cannot remove elements from the list), and
(selection)	will show just the list, with no highlights.

5) You can have more than one selection list in a window at once. (You have to drag the element out of the window and then back.) This can make editing the list difficult. The rule is that the 'select unit' command works on the 'current, or nearest following, selection list in the query expression'. You switch between selection lists by selecting a different unit in the query expression.

To save the content of a selection list, create a query window for '(selection)' alone and then press 'Save' to output the content. To include FTF matches, save the query '(*x* and selection)' and tick the 'include matches' box. You can save the actual selection list for re-use in ICECUP by ticking the 'cache' flag.

5. FUZZY TREE FRAGMENTS AND TEXT QUERIES

At the heart of ICECUP is a method for carrying out structured queries in the corpus. This method is based on models of approximate grammatical trees, called *Fuzzy Tree Fragments*, or "FTFs" (Aarts, Wallis and Nelson 1998; see also the "FTF home" website at http://www.ucl.ac.uk/english-usage/ftfs/). FTFs are used when we search for simple individual *tree nodes* (Section 3.6). They are also used to search for sequences of words and tags, which we introduced in Section 3.9. When you specify a node or text query, ICECUP generates an appropriate FTF and applies it to the corpus. If you just press 'OK' in the query window, the search is performed and the FTF itself remains hidden. You may reveal the underlying FTF by selecting the 'Edit' button.

In this chapter we explore text queries in rather more detail. The *Text fragment* search window lets you relate fragments of text to categorical tags, and thus the deeper tree annotation, in the corpus. In the first part of the chapter, Sections 5.1-5.4, we construct increasingly complicated text queries, ending by turning a text fragment into an FTF and extending the query into the tree, in our case, by insisting that two words must be within the same noun phrase.

In the next part we turn to FTFs themselves. Sections 5.5-5.10 form an extended tutorial into constructing FTFs, and in 5.11 we apply our newfound knowledge to text queries. The final set of sections (5.12-5.14) describe how FTFs work. So Section 5.12 discusses what the links mean and 5.13 how they work together when FTFs match examples in the corpus. Section 5.14 describes the FTF Creation Wizard, a tool that lets you grab part of a corpus tree and turn it into an FTF. But for now, let's experiment with text fragment queries.

5.1 The Text Fragment query window

Choosing 'Text Fragment...' from the 'Query' menu or pressing the 'Text' query command button produces the following window. In Section 3.9 we saw some simple uses of this query system. Now we will consider text fragment searches in more detail.

The window is divided into a number of sections. The main centre panel is where you type your query. The flashing line, or 'caret', on the left hand side of this box indicates that it is ready to accept text. Placed around the outside of the box are a number of little buttons, and two 'pull-down selectors' are located at the bottom of the main panel. A second, smaller panel, offers the option of applying the search to a selected query (see Chapter 6). The 'Options' button allows you to change the current search options. These options specify which

Figure 79: The Text Fragment search dialog window.

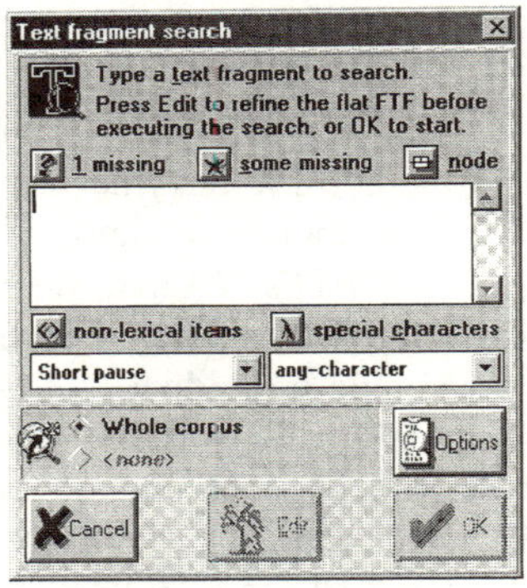

material to search and how to match lexical items (case sensitive, accent-sensitive, *etc.*).

Below this are three big buttons: 'Cancel', 'Edit' and 'OK'. 'Cancel' quits this window at any time, while 'OK' starts the search. 'Edit' allows you to make your query more complex (and hopefully more subtle) by turning it into a Fuzzy Tree Fragment. We will discuss this option last.

5.2 Searching for words, tags and tree nodes

The most basic query is to search for a single word. Try typing "**magic**" and hit 'OK' or Return on the keyboard: you should get seventeen cases. Note that by default, matching is not case sensitive.

Try a few other single words. ICECUP will show you an hourglass cursor, to say that it is 'thinking', before retrieving the examples. If you enter a single word, it can retrieve all the cases quickly. This is what we called a 'quick search' in Section 3.9.

If you type more than one word ICECUP has to 'think' rather harder. Try typing "**and so on**" and press <Enter>. If you have the main command bar visible (you will have large buttons along the top of the display), then the search

*Figure 80: The results of searching for "**magic**" in ICE-GB.*

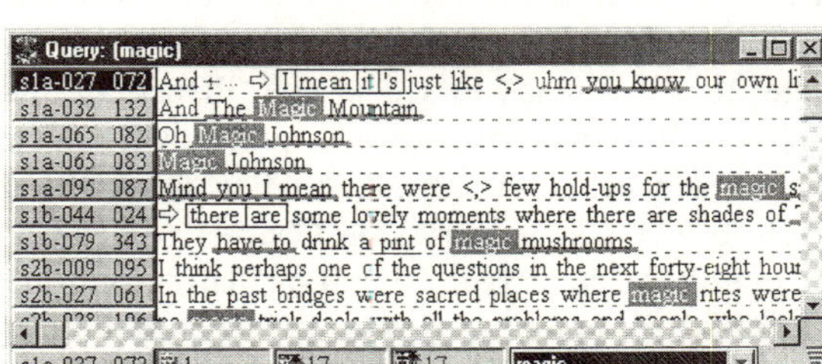

Figure 81: Two ways of viewing the search in progress. Left, estimated time of completion in the main command bar – right, a monitor window.

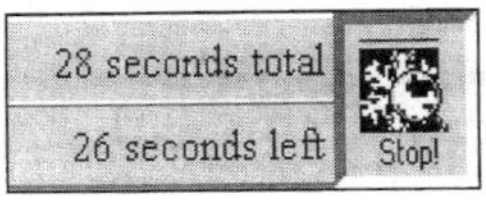

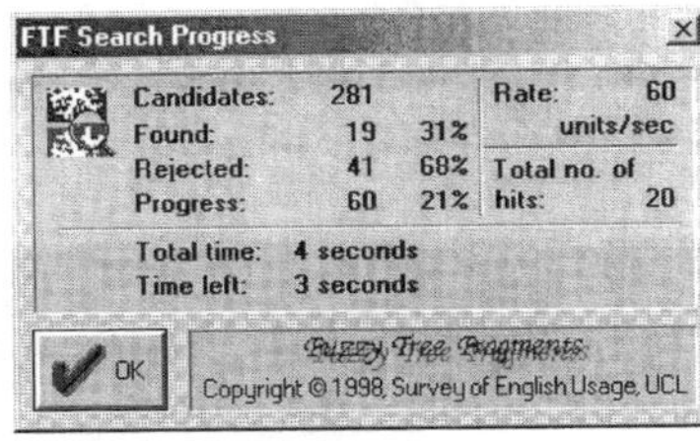

process is indicated by an animation in the top right corner of the main ICECUP window (Figure 81, left). If you hide this bar, a monitor window will pop up to let you know how the search is proceeding (Figure 81, right).

In either case, the search operates behind the scenes. When ICECUP finds a case, it adds it to an (initially empty) query results window. The fact that this is receiving a search is indicated by the window title.

Figure 82: The search in progress.

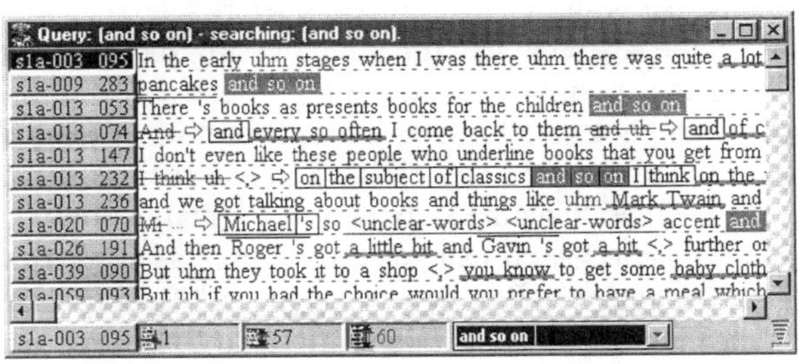

We also discussed this kind of background search in Section 3.9. ICECUP has a database that lets it find a complete list of cases for every single lexical item in the corpus. When you type the lexical item into the Text Fragment query window and press 'OK', it looks up this list. By working out the overlap between the lists for *and*, *so*, and *on*, ICECUP generates a list of potential cases that might match the sequence *and so on*. This is only a potential, or 'candidate', list. The fact that a sentence contains these three words doesn't necessarily mean that they are in the right order!

The background search establishes that the different elements of the query are in the correct arrangement (in this case: in sequence, with no intervening words). Part of the art of specifying a query is in defining the right relationship between words (and other terms, as we shall see).

The monitor window or the indication in the main command bar lets you know how the search is progressing. The monitor window is more informative: it tells you how many candidates there were to start with, for example, and the

Figure 83: Components of the status bar.

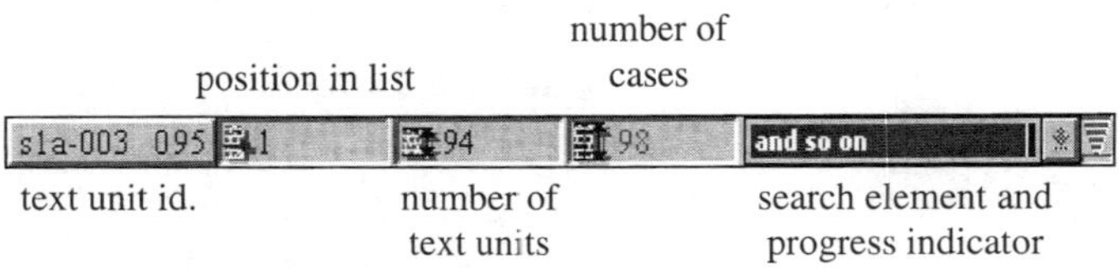

proportion of successful matches from the candidate set (the 'hit rate'). The two most important figures are the following.

1. The number of successfully-discovered independent matching cases (hits).
2. The number of sentences (text units) containing these cases.

In the monitor window (Figure 81, right), "Found:" indicates the second of these, the total number of text units (all the figures in this column are given in text units), while the total number of hits is shown on the right. However, if you do not have the monitor window visible, this information is reproduced in the 'status line' at the bottom of the receiving query viewer window. Your current progress through the list is shown by a 'thermometer' search element indicator.

You can stop the search at any time, by pressing the Escape (<Esc>) key. Alternatively, from the monitor window you can press 'Accept', or from the command bar you can click to release the 'Stop!' button, or from the searching query window, press the function key <F4>. You can then restart the search by pressing <F4> again or the 'Continue!' button in the main command bar.[1]

The Text Fragment search can search for tags as well as words. If we return to the Text Fragment dialog box (do 'Query | Text fragment...' again), text is shown in the central edit control in a slim bold font, *e.g.*, "**magic johnson**".

We introduce a tag by pressing the button marked 'Node'. Since this is a parsed corpus, we can actually refer to the grammatical function that has been assigned, as well as the categorisation of text unit elements, but as an initial example, we'll just introduce a plain noun tag. Press 'Node', and type *N*. This is shown as a fine-text capital letter inside angled brackets: "<N>". Press 'OK' to start the search.

What if you specify the part of speech of an existing word, *e.g.*, *magic* as an adjective, rather than a noun? Leave out the space between the word and the tag. ICECUP shows this with a little '+' sign between word and tag. So *magic* as an adjective is written "**magic**+<ADJ>" and finds eight cases. The word *magic* **followed by** an adjective is written "**magic** <ADJ>", and finds no cases.

When you are editing the text fragment you've typed, you may discover some interesting effects. Deleting the space in the middle of "**magic** <ADJ>"

[1] If you start a second search while a first is running, the first is stopped before the second commences. You can restart the first by switching windows and pressing <F4> or 'Continue!'

produces "**magic**+<ADJ>". Pressing <Backspace> after a node removes the whole node. Editing these logical elements, tags and so on, 'in line' is perfectly possible. Just place the blinking 'caret' where you wish to insert and type. Note that functions and categories are shown in capitalised faint text, features in lower case. So a general adjective is written "<ADJ(ge)>", a conjoined general adjective, "<CJ,ADJ(ge)>". These nodes are tag nodes, *i.e.*, they must directly annotate a word in the corpus.

5.3 Missing words and special characters

You can introduce missing words into a Text Fragment search. If you've used "wild card" systems to search databases, you may be familiar with the "?" and "*" convention. You can use these to find files in Windows, for example.

In these schemes, the 'query' character (?) substitutes for *any single character*, while the asterisk (*) means *any number of characters, including zero*. So, "fr*d" would match *Fred* and *freed* as well as *frightened*, while "fr?d" would only match with *Fred.*[2] ICECUP uses a similar idea to introduce missing words into a text fragment search.

At the top left and middle of the window are two buttons, marked with a query and an asterisk respectively, and labeled '1 missing' and 'some missing'. You can't type, for example, "**do ? mind**", directly, though. This would search for a question mark between the two words. Instead, you have to enter the word *do*, then click on the question mark button in the window and then type *mind*. This produces "**do** ? **mind**", as in Figure 84. You can press <Alt> and the (number) '1' key together, if you prefer. The query symbol is drawn in a light font. Pressing

*Figure 84: Searching for the sequence "**do**", <one element>, "**mind**".*

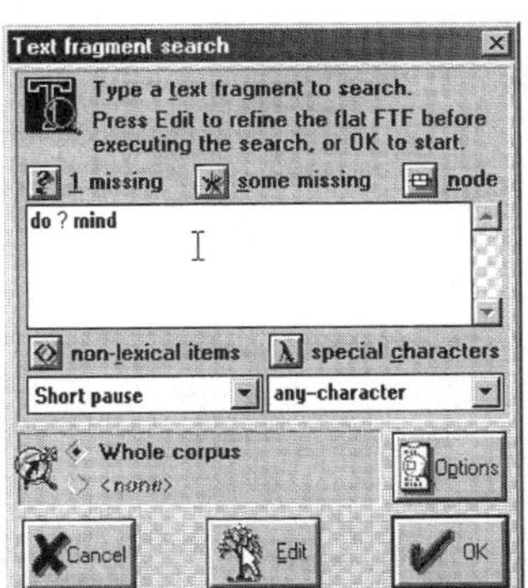

[2] ICECUP 3.1 lets you specify an approximate lexical pattern by using a *lexical wild card* instead of a specific word. See Chapter 7.4.

'OK' eventually produces three cases, two where the '?' stands for *you*, and one where it stands for *with* (*to do with mind*...).

The asterisk, or 'some missing' symbol is introduced in a like manner. So we can write "**do * mind**", remembering, of course, to introduce the 'some missing' element by pressing <Alt> and 'S', or clicking on the button. Pressing 'OK' then produces a list of eleven matches, including, naturally, the three we found with "**do ? mind**", and eight others. Note that this kind of wild card substitution, as it doesn't restrict the search very much, is rather general, insisting only that *do* precedes *mind* in the sequence. If we wish to limit the range in a more sophisticated way, for example to insist that it is within the same phrase, we need to use an FTF.

What if you want to insert non-lexical items, such as pauses or laughter, into the Text Fragment? You can type them directly. For example, "<,,>" stands for a long pause. There is, however, an easier way which is less prone to error. Select the particular non-lexical item you want from the left-hand pull-down control, marked 'non-lexical items', either with the mouse or by pressing <Alt>+'L' and using the cursor keys. This produces a list of all such items in the corpus. Press the graphical button above the pull-down to insert the element into the text fragment.

Special characters in the written corpus present a different problem. These are represented in an 'ampersand' notation, which means that each code is spelled out between an initial ampersand (&) and a semicolon (;), thus:

Ω Ω **Á** Á **½** ½ **&black-square;** ■

Codes include Greek and accented characters, mathematical and graphical symbols. The convention for alphabetic characters is that an initial capital letter indicates capitalisation. So 'Γ' is displayed as 'Γ' while 'γ' is 'γ'. Likewise, 'á' produces 'á'.

A similar procedure is used to insert these characters into the text fragment, using the right-hand pull-down selector and its corresponding 'insert' button. One difference is that special character codes are introduced without separating spaces, so typing "coup" followed by inserting 'é' produces "coupé". On the other hand, inserting a short pause after "coup" would produce "coup <,>", because the pause marker is a distinct element. Be careful with punctuation and genitives (*'s* and *'*), because these are treated as distinct items in the corpus. Finally, what about ampersand itself? This is spelled out as "&ampersand;". Note that the semi-colon, braces ('{ }') and square brackets are spelled out in this way.

When you search for lexical items that include special characters, you may want to be less than exact. Accents can be ignored by making the lexical match 'accent insensitive' via the 'Search Options' dialog. This mode ignores the accent, so you can write "coupe" to search for *coupé*. However, for most special characters, in ICECUP 3.0 there is no natural way of specifying a more

Figure 85: Part of the 'special character' pull-down hierarchy.

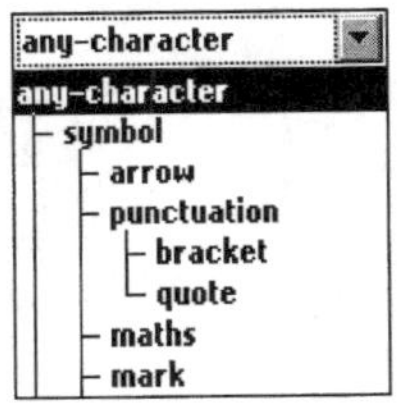

general character than a specific symbol. To make things easier, we have arranged many of these single elements into a set of hierarchical groups.

Suppose we want to specify a quotation mark in our search, but do not wish to distinguish between left or right, or double or single, quotes. We can simply introduce the general 'quote' marker, written "&quote;". Select 'quote' in the pull-down in Figure 85 and press the 'special characters' button. The special characters used by ICECUP, and the names of the groups that they belong to, are listed in Appendix 6.

5.4 Extending the query into the tree

What if you want to do something more complex than the options provided by the Text Fragment dialog box will allow? The following possibilities are in order of increasing complexity.

1) Specify that a text unit element (a lexical or non-lexical item) is at the start or end of the text unit. For example, state that *this* is the last word in the unit.
2) Permit two elements to be reversible, for instance, *this time* or *time this*.
3) Alter the 'focus' of the FTF to highlight only parts of the search.
4) Introduce tree-like elements into the fragment. This includes the possibility of specifying that two words must be found within the same clause or phrase.

Pressing the 'Edit' button introduces a wide number of possibilities. We mentioned at the beginning of this chapter that the text fragment search was based on something called 'Fuzzy Tree Fragments' (FTFs for short). The FTF on the left of Figure 86 illustrates the query "first * person". Type "first * person" into the Text Fragment window and then press the 'Edit' button.

*Figure 86: FTFs for (left) "first * person", and (right) "first * person" within an NP.*

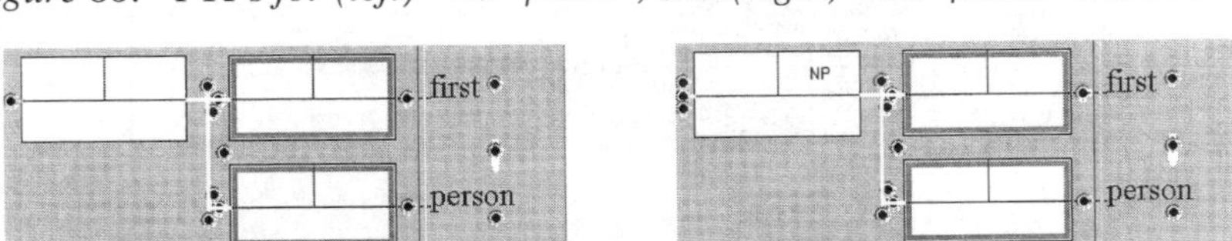

Figure 87: Using the edit node window to specify a category. Left, an empty node – right, during the selection of 'noun phrase'.

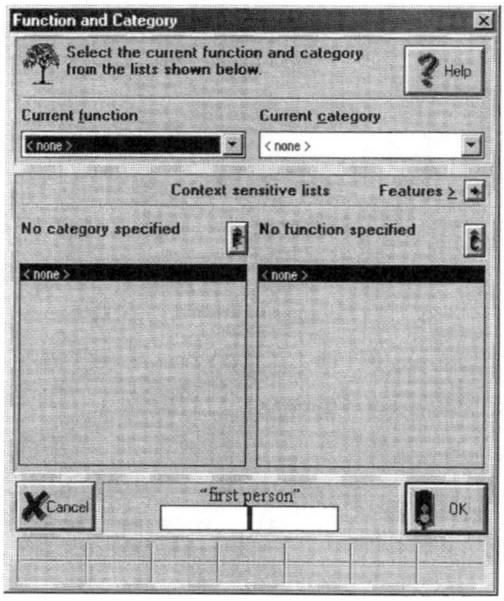

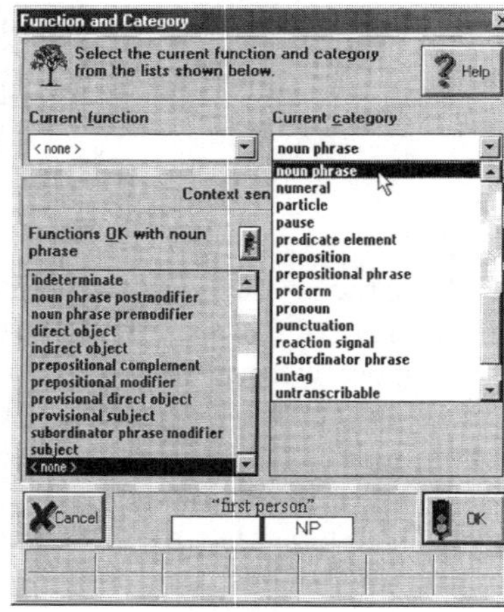

The rest of the chapter discusses FTFs in detail. For now, we will just perform a simple modification to this search. The current search finds seven cases in six text units in ICE-GB (try it). We would like to limit the search to find only those cases where both words are within the same noun phrase. The new FTF is shown on the right of Figure 86.

To change the FTF on the left of Figure 86 to that on the right, we have to do two things to the left-most box, or 'node', in the tree structure. Obviously, we have to specify that this stands for a noun phrase, or '**NP**'. Second, and rather less obviously, we have to release this node from its obligation to stand for the *root* – indicated by the absence of a line on the left of the box and the single dot. This is done very simply by clicking down with the left mouse button over this dark blue dot, or 'cool spot' at the far left of the FTF.

Changing the category of this node to '**NP**' is slightly more complicated. If you place the mouse over the top right quadrant of the box (where we see the '**NP**' logo appear in Figure 86) and press the function key <F2>, the 'edit node' dialog window appears (Figure 87, left). Select 'noun phrase' in the 'Current category' pull-down at the top right hand side. The window should change

Figure 88: Results from the second FTF in Figure 86.

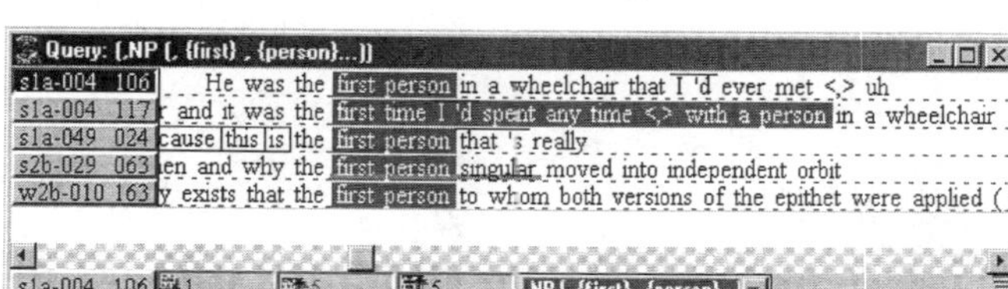

accordingly (Figure 87, right). Press 'OK' to close the dialog. The FTF should now look like the structure on the right of Figure 86.

Press function key <F4> to run, select 'Query | Start Search!' or press the 'Start!' command button. The result is five cases in five text units (Figure 88).

Text fragment searches can be very powerful. In particular, they offer a simple way of finding sequences of lexical terms, and uncovering the detail of the grammatical analysis for each case. You can use the "spy tree" facility (Figure 89) to expose this analysis and identify how the search has matched it. As we will see, ICECUP can even create a query from the tree.

You can then move on to a new stage of searching, one more appropriate for grammatical research. This next stage looks for similar grammatical constructions which may be realised by other lexical items.

5.5 *Introducing Fuzzy Tree Fragments*

Fuzzy Tree Fragments are approximate 'models', 'diagrams' or 'wild-cards' for grammatical queries on a parsed corpus. Because they are models, they are essentially *declarative*, that is, there is no right or wrong order for evaluating elements – like logical statements, all elements must be true together.

More specifically, FTFs are generalised grammatical subtrees that represent the grammatical structure sought. They retain only the essential elements of a matching case – they are a 'wild-card' model for grammar. The idea is fairly intuitive to linguists while retaining a high degree of flexibility. Nodes and text unit elements may be approximately specified, as may links between components, and 'edges' (simple structural properties such as **First child**).

FTFs are diagrammatic representations: they make sense as drawings of partial trees rather than as a set of logical predicates. Such diagrams have the

Figure 89: Spying the results of the search.

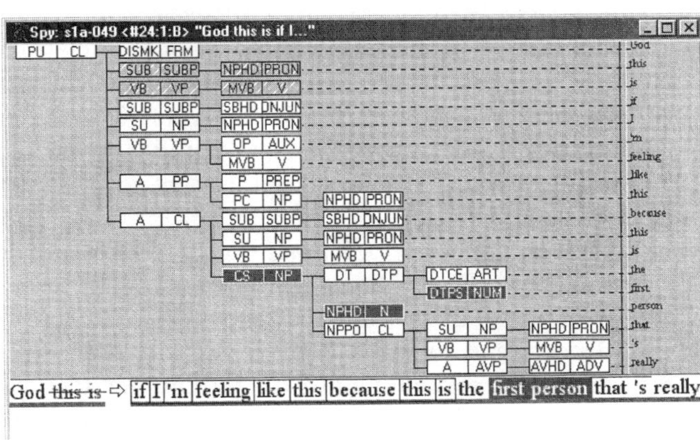

Figure 90: Components of FTFs.

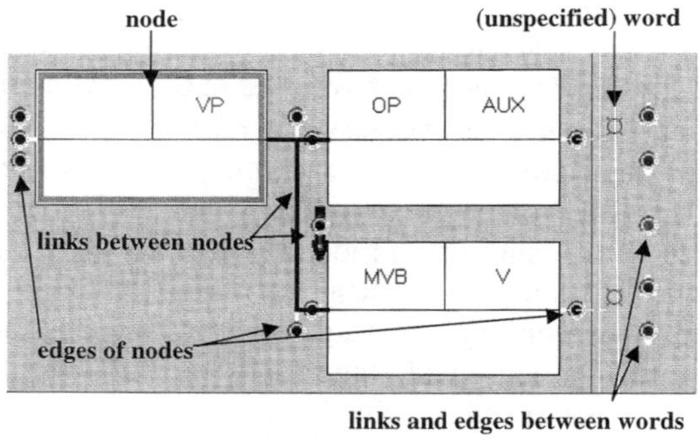

property of *structural coherence*, that is, it is immediately apparent if an FTF is feasible and sufficient (grammatically and structurally). You can't draw a tree containing two nodes where each one is the parent of the other, but in logic you might write "**Parent**(*x*, *y*) and... **Parent**(*y*, *x*)" by mistake.

Fuzzy Tree Fragments consist of the following components.

- '**Nodes**', which are drawn as white 'boxes' divided into *function*, *category* and *feature* partitions (see Chapter 2 and Figure 93, right). At least one node must be marked as the '**focus**' of the FTF (see Section 5.10). ICECUP employs this focal point to indicate the portion of text 'covered by' the FTF and to concordance text units.
- '**Words**', including all lexical items and pauses (strictly, we should call them 'text unit elements'). These are drawn on the other side of the divider from the tree structure. In the example in Figure 90 no words are specified.
- '**Links**' joining two elements together. There are two kinds of link between two *nodes* (called '**Parent**' and '**Next**') and one type of link between two *words* ('**Next word**').
- '**Edges**', which are properties of single nodes or words. An edge might specify, for example, that a node is a leaf node, or a word is the first in the sentence.

Each link and edge is set to one of a number of different '**values**' or 'statuses'. The value of a link can be set by clicking with the mouse on the "dot" or '**cool spot**' in the middle of the element. To aid identification, *blue* dots are used for node edges and links, and *green* dots for words. In Figure 90, both **Parent** links are set to the immediate 'Parent' value, the **Next (child)** link is 'Immediately after' (hence the arrow), and the **Next word** link is <unknown>. All edges are set to <unknown> by default, *i.e.*, they are unspecified.

Links are coded for *adjacency*, *order* and *connectedness*, and depicted so as to exploit this notion of structural coherence. The general principle underwriting the set of possibilities is that they should be *as simple as possible but as complex as necessary*. A summary is given in Table 32 on page 137.

Thus, the *parent:child* relation in an FTF, **Parent**, is either immediately or eventually adjacent (called 'Parent' and 'Ancestor' respectively, and coloured black or white).[3] The link must be *ordered* (see Table 32). This means that a child node in an FTF can never match a node 'above' its parent.[4] The **Next (child)** sibling *child:child* relation may be set to one of a number of options, from 'Immediately following' (depicted by a black directional arrow), through 'Before or after' (a white bi-directional arrow), to '<unknown>' (no arrow). Note that two nodes with the same structural 'parent' in an FTF need not match siblings in a corpus tree, a facility, as we saw in the previous section, that is exploited by Text fragment queries.

A particular benefit of the graphical approach is that it is relatively easy to identify the relationship between an FTF and corpus trees. This applies to both *matching*, which is summarised in Subsection 5.13, and *abstraction*, *i.e.*, creating an FTF from a tree in the corpus (see 5.14).

One can construct an FTF from a variety of starting points in ICECUP. The simplest of these is the 'empty FTF'. This consists of a single, unspecified node and a single, unspecified text unit element, with an unspecified relationship between them, and no other restrictions placed on it.

> Press the 'New FTF' button, or select the Query | New FTF command from the menu. This creates the initial single-node fragment shown in Figure 91.

In the tutorial that follows, we commence by creating a new FTF. In Section 5.7 we add three daughters and label the nodes, then in 5.8 we extend the FTF by adding a clausal feature and making the subject stand for the single pronoun *I*. Section 5.9 illustrates two methods for rearranging nodes in the FTF and Section 5.10 describes the concept of the 'focus' of the FTF.

Earlier in this chapter we described another way of creating an FTF – by first defining a *text fragment* query. As we saw, this is useful if you want to search for words and other items in the text, but also wish to relate this to deeper grammatical annotation. You can type the words and tag nodes into the Text fragment window, and then press 'Edit' to turn it into an FTF. We return to the question of 'text-oriented' FTFs in Section 5.11.

The last parts of the chapter move away from our example FTF and discuss more general issues. In 5.12 we discuss the geometry of FTFs and their links. In Section 5.13 we discuss how FTFs match cases in the corpus, and in 5.14, how they may be abstracted from the corpus. Abstraction translates part of a tree in the corpus into a matching query using a tool called the *FTF Creation Wizard*. The wizard creates a general FTF by removing information from the

---

[3] For clarity we distinguish between the name of a link, written in a bold type (e.g., Parent), which means the link between one node and one above it in the tree, and the value of that link, which we place in quotes (e.g., 'Parent'). Thus Parent can take either the immediate 'Parent' or the eventual 'Ancestor' value.

[4] Having experimented with an <unknown> option, we do not believe that there is a linguistically useful query that could make use of it. Moreover, such an option makes it very easy to form a structurally nonsensical query – precisely what FTFs are meant to avoid.

Figure 91: A new FTF.

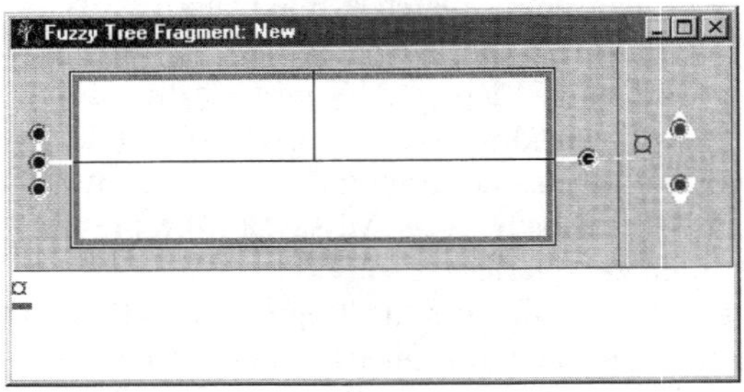

tree. You can edit the result manually. In the final section we discuss some advanced issues.

The following tutorial was written to be worked through with ICECUP and ICE-GB running on the computer in front of you, although you should be able to follow the discussion if this is not possible.

5.6 An overview of commands to construct FTFs

The menu bar of the FTF editor provides an overview of the commands for building FTFs. This editor is based on the *tree viewer* described in Chapter 4. Some of the commands, such as those specifying the way a tree is presented, navigated and explored, are identical. The menu bar is best understood as representing groups of commands (Figure 92). From left to right, these are as follows.

- **Disconnect editor button**. This is the first button in the bar, and is used in editing existing queries, otherwise it is disabled. See Chapter 6 (Section 6.7).
- **Scaling buttons.** At the far left of the menu bar are a group of scaling buttons, which change the size of the view. When creating an FTF it is unlikely that you will need to touch these. They allow you to zoom in or out on specific elements or nodes.
- **Alphabetical list of nodes**. This is a 'pull-down selector' which selects a node from an alphabetical list of the nodes in the tree (function first, then category, then word). It shows the function, category and text unit sequence under the current node. Selecting a node here moves the current selection in the tree to that point.
- **Main editing buttons**. These are: 'undo', 'delete', three different 'insert' buttons, 'move', and 'preview move'. We discuss these commands in Section 5.7 below.
- **Cut, copy and paste**. The next block contains 'cut', 'copy', and four 'paste' buttons. These cut and paste single nodes in the FTF. The four 'paste' buttons determine how the node is inserted relative to the current point.
- **Edit node data buttons**. The last block of editing commands allows you to edit the grammatical terms within an FTF node ('function and category'; 'features'), the

Figure 92: The FTF editor menu bar.

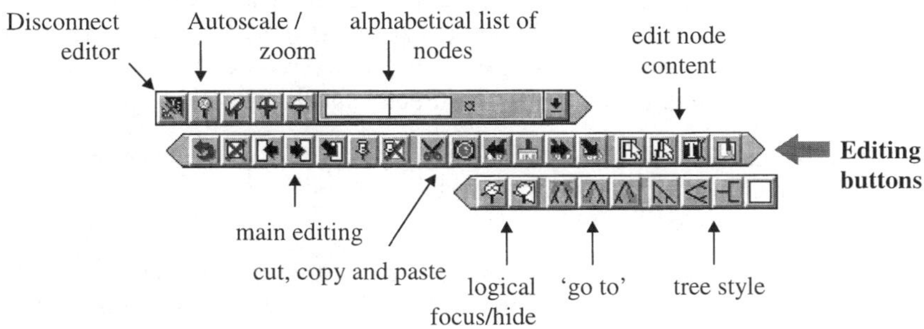

associated text unit element ('word'), and allows you to change the FTF focus. Links are edited by clicking on cool spots in the FTF diagram itself.

The remaining buttons in the menu bar perform a number of non-editing tasks:

- **focusing** on a branch or hiding a branch from view,
- **changing position** to the top of the tree or the first/last child, and
- adjusting the **style** by which trees are drawn (these are global settings).

5.7 *Creating a simple FTF*

For our first example, we will construct the simple FTF shown in Figure 93, left. This is a clause containing three nodes: a subject noun phrase, followed by a verb phrase and an adverb phrase (refer to Chapter 2).

We will construct this simple FTF in two stages: firstly building up the template structure and then introducing function and category terms.

First, we must construct the outline of the FTF.

➢ In the 'Query' menu, select 'New FTF' or press the main command button. This produces a window containing the simplest possible blank FTF (Figure 91).

The tree consists of a single node which is currently selected. The edges of the box and division lines are coloured by the selection colour. The box also

Figure 93: Left, our initial target FTF; right, sectors of a node.

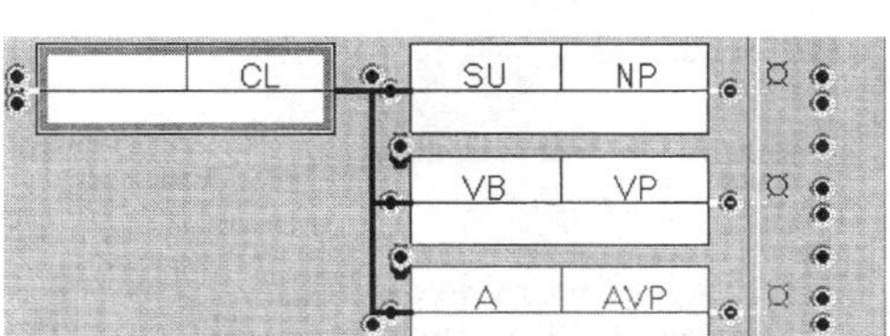

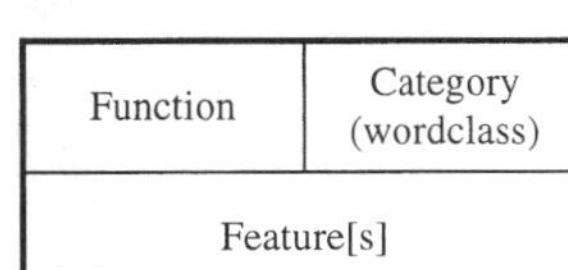

contains the focus, so it has a yellow border (see Section 5.10).

Even the simplest FTF has significant structure. The node is divided into three sectors for function, category and features (Figure 93, right). Optional links are indicated by white lines and other marks. As we shall see, white is used to mean that a link in an FTF is not directly specified.

> Now add three 'child' nodes immediately under this one. You do this by pressing the 'Insert child after' ('') menu bar button three times. You can also use the keyboard or menu commands (see Table 30).

There are three different 'insert' commands in this editor. The first two, illustrated by Figure 94, increase the depth of the tree. 'Insert node before' places a node 'above'[5] the current position, and the new node becomes the current one. Repeated pressing of this button creates a long sequence of nodes, from the start node towards the root (Figure 94, left). 'Insert node after' does the same thing except that each time it inserts a node 'below' the current one.

A third insert command is required to make the tree broader. 'Insert child after' adds a node below the current position if there are no nodes there. In this respect it is similar to 'insert node after'. If the current node does have a child, however, it inserts a node *in the last position* in the sequence of children. The current position does not change. Three presses of this button produces the FTF in Figure 95. Note that you can reverse the effect of all operations by pressing the 'undo' button (''), or <Alt> and <Backspace> together (or <Ctrl>+'Z',

Figure 94: Increasing tree depth with (left) 'Insert node before', and (right) 'Insert node after'.

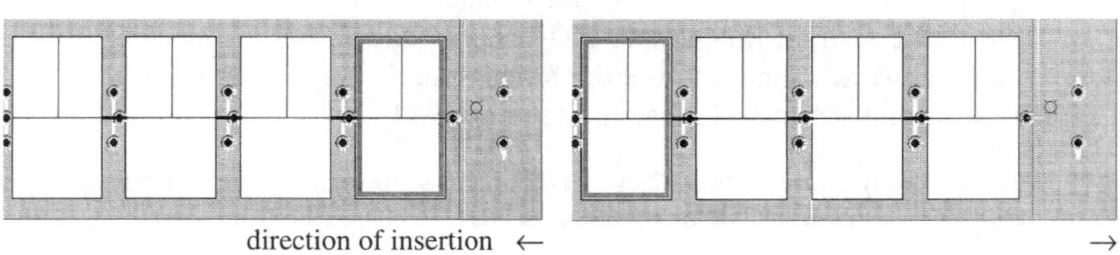

Figure 95: Increasing tree breadth with 'Insert child after'.

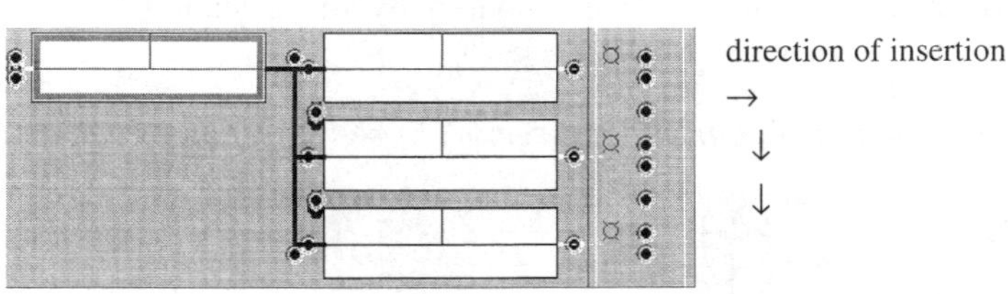

[5] In this orientation, with the tree drawn from left to right, 'above' in the tree means to the *left* of the current position. We use 'above' and 'below' here in this relative sense.

Table 30: Commands to insert nodes in an FTF.

	name	keyboard action	menu command
	Insert node before	<Insert>	**Edit | Insert Node Before**
	Insert node after	<Shift>+<Insert>	**Edit | Insert Node After**
	Insert child after	<Ctrl>+<Insert>	**Edit | Insert Child After**

which some prefer).

You can navigate this tree as you would in the tree viewer (Section 4.7), using the mouse or cursor keys to move around. <Home> (or '') moves to the top of the tree (the 'root'), and <Page Up> and <Page Down> ('' and '') goes to the first and last leaf node relative to the current position.

> If your FTF is different from Figure 95, press 'undo' to revert to a single node FTF and then press 'Insert child after' three times. We can then proceed to the next stage.

Next, we must specify what each node 'stands for' grammatically. Whereas trees in the corpus should be completely specified, FTFs should be as general as possible. But we still need to be more specific than this empty skeleton.

We will add function and category labels for each of the three 'child' nodes and the category for the left-hand 'parent' node (refer to Figure 93, page 129 for a guide). As we mentioned, each node consists of three panels or sectors, summarised in the figure. The basic method for specifying the

Figure 96: Specifying a category value with the 'Edit node' command – (left) before: unassigned, (right) selecting 'clause'.

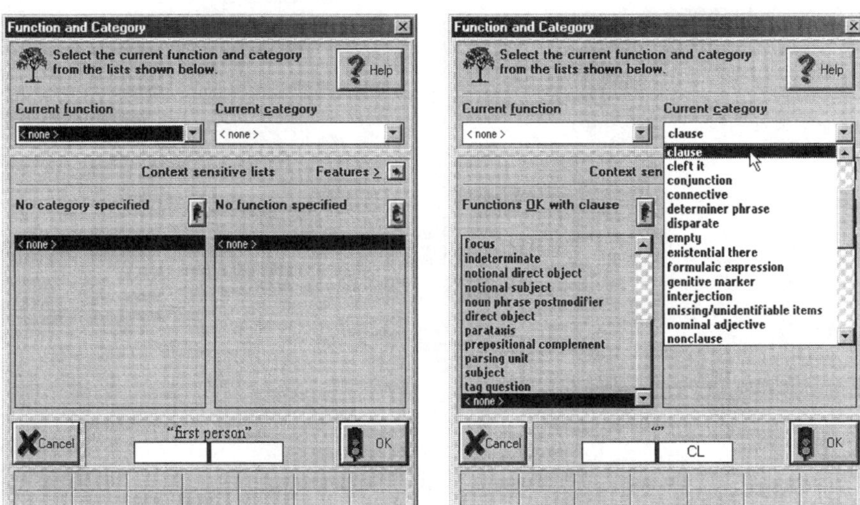

grammatical content of a node is to employ the ‘Edit node’ command.

- Press the function key <F2>, or the button ‘’, which produces the dialogue window in Figure 96, left.

You may select a function from the complete list of function codes labelled ‘current function’, or a category from the ‘current category’ list. As you specify the function or category, the identifier appears at the bottom of the window. In addition, a list of *complementary categories or functions* appears the middle of the window (Figure 96, right). By selecting from this list – with a double-click of the mouse[6] – you guarantee compatibility between function and category.

We may complete the target FTF in Figure 93 by the following steps.

- Choose the ‘top’ (in this view, leftmost) node and select <F2> or ‘’. If you selected another node by mistake, hit the ‘Cancel’ button or press <Esc> on the keyboard, choose the top node, and re-enter the dialog.
- This node should be given the category ‘clause’. Select ‘current category’ and press the key ‘C’ to locate the label ‘clause’ in the list (‘clause’ is the first category beginning with ‘C’). This action is illustrated in Figure 96. Press ‘OK’.
- Working through the FTF, select each node in turn, and set each function and category pair, referring to Figure 93. Thus, to assign the first element in our FTF as a subject

Figure 97: Selecting ‘subject’ function in the Edit node window (left) and ‘noun phrase’ from the list of complementary categories (right).

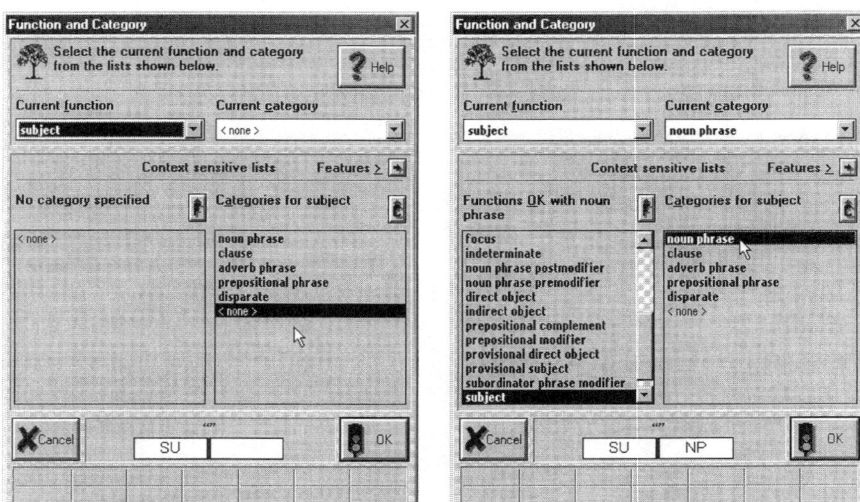

[6] You do need to perform a positive action (a ‘double click’, press <Space> when selected, or hit the nearby button) to change the currently selected function or category.

*Figure 98: Pop-up menu for **function** if the category is a clause.*

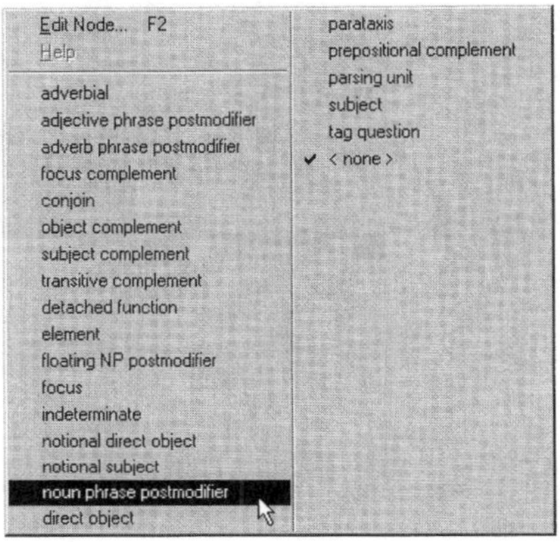

NP, select the node, enter the Edit Node dialog and press 'S' twice to find 'subject' in the list (the list of functions is selected by default). The categories compatible with 'subject' appear in the right-hand middle portion of the window (Figure 97, left). Double-click on 'noun phrase' with the mouse to select it (Figure 97, right).

With this technique you should be able to create the FTF in Figure 93 without much difficulty. Use 'undo' if you make an error.

> You can search the corpus at any time by selecting 'Start!' or pressing the function key <F4>. Press it now to see the search working. <Esc> or <F4> stops it.

There are other ways of constructing our FTF. Instead of using the Edit node window, you can use 'pop-up menus'. Try the following.

> Place the mouse cursor over the function sector of the top node and press the *right* mouse button down. This should produce a pop-up menu similar to Figure 98.

The pop-up menu lets you set a function or category that is compatible with an existing function. It also offers a number of additional commands including 'Edit Node...'. In ICECUP 3.1, the menu is extended to permit logic in nodes.

5.8 Adding a feature and relating a word to the tree

We can introduce features into the FTF using pop-up menus.

> Position the mouse 'arrow' cursor over the feature sector of the 'clause' node (Figures 93 and 99). Depress the right mouse button. This produces a pop-up menu containing a list of features which specify subtypes of the category (in this case, 'clause').

A node in the corpus has a single function and category. It may have many features. However, not all features can be defined together or are relevant to

Figure 99: Setting the feature 'dependent' for 'clause level' with a menu.

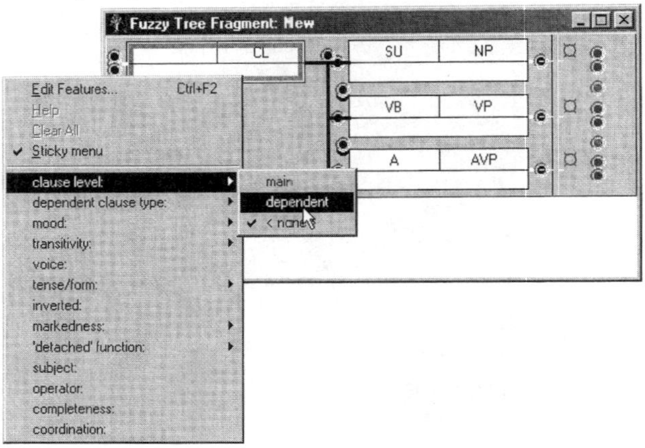

any category. Thus, 'main' is a feature of clauses, but no clause may be both 'main' and 'dependent' at the same time. Recall from Chapter 2 that we refer to a set of alternative features as *feature classes*. 'main' and 'dependent' belong to the class 'clause level'. We can say that 'clause level' *subcategorises* clauses. Some features are in classes by themselves: the 'completeness' class, for example, can be omitted or marked as 'incomplete' (*i.e.*, the feature is Boolean).

> Assign the 'clause level' feature 'dependent' to the topmost node using the pop-up menu. To do this, drag (hold down a button and move) the mouse down until 'clause level' is selected. The feature can be found under a secondary menu (Figure 99). Drag the mouse to the right, select 'dependent' and release the mouse button. Alternatively, press keys 'C' (to select 'clause level') and then 'D'.

The feature menu also contains a command to clear all the features from the node. The 'sticky menu' option causes the menu to reappear after each menu action (it disappears if you click outside the menu). This is useful if you wish to specify several features in a node, for example. ICECUP 3.1 additionally lets you specify that features are absent (select it twice).

You can also use the 'Edit Node' window to set features. If you press <Ctrl> and <F2> together, or select 'Edit Features...', the Edit Node window will appear listing the feature classes applicable to the current category.[7]

[7] The 'Edit node' window has two modes – 'Edit function and category' and 'Edit features' – which you can select using the arrow button at the middle right of Figure 100. You may scroll through the feature classes or jump to a particular feature by clicking on one of the spaces along the bottom of the window with the mouse (this area lists currently specified features). You can also change the current category or function in the window.

Figure 100: Specifying that a clause is dependent using the Edit Node dialog.

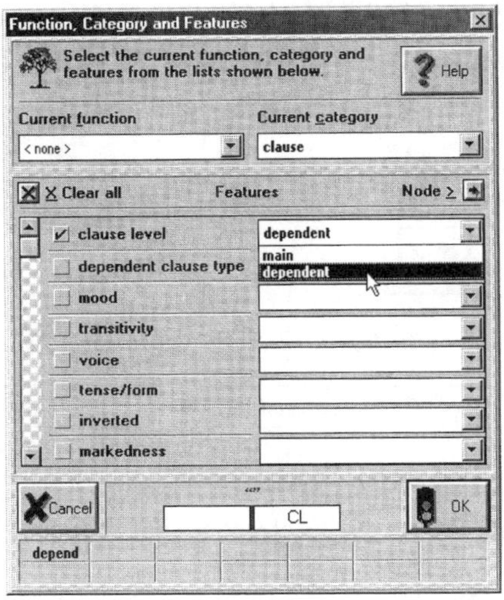

> Select 'Edit Features...' from the feature pop-up menu, press <Ctrl> and <F2> together, or select the button ''. You should get the window in Figure 100. Next, select the 'clause level' pull-down and choose 'dependent'. Press 'OK' to finish.

If you perform the search, only dependent clauses in this form will be retrieved.

Naturally, we may also add 'words' – text unit elements – to our FTF.[8] At the start of this chapter we described one way of creating an FTF containing these elements: using the Text Fragment search. Let us suppose that we wish to limit our FTF to those cases where the subject NP in Figure 93 is realised by the single word *I*. We will start by inserting the word.

> Select the node and hit the '' button, press <Ctrl>+'W' or use the menu command in Table 31 to invoke the 'Edit word' window (Figure 101, left). Alternatively, double-click with the left mouse button near the appropriate '¤' (empty word) symbol.

> Type *I*. Do not worry about non-lexical items or special characters. Press 'OK'. The result should look like the FTF in Figure 101.

If you perform a search now (press <F4>), you will get around 340 hits. Wait for the search to finish and examine the results. These should include the pair in Figure 102. The trees in these examples match the group of nodes defined by the FTF, but the word *I* may be *anywhere within the subject NP* (Figure 102, right). This is not exactly what we require! We want to find examples like

---

[8] More precisely, FTFs can contain "text unit elements", *i.e.*, lexical items, including punctuation, and non-lexical items such as pauses and laughter. ICECUP 3.1 (see Chapter 7.4) also lets you specify lexical wild cards.

Figure 101: Introducing the word "I" into the FTF: the Edit word window (left) and the resulting FTF (right).

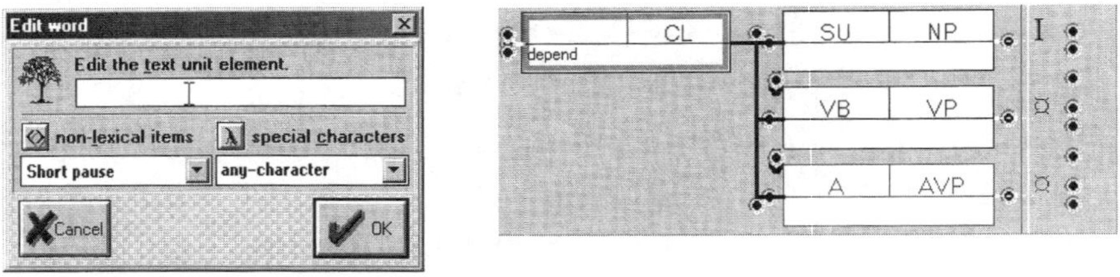

Table 31: Command to edit text unit elements in an FTF.

	name	keyboard action	menu command
	Edit word	<Ctrl>+'W'	**Edit | Edit word...**

Figure 102, left, where *I* is the sole element that realises the NP, and exclude examples like Figure 102, right.

How can we do this? The answer is to apply a little grammatical knowledge to the relationship between the word and the tree. Note that, first, the noun phrase realised by *I* alone must contain a single, further node, and second, this node is the only child of the subject NP (Figure 102, left).

We should therefore introduce a node into our FTF to stand for this additional node. We do not need to explicitly label it: the word *I* will be sufficient provided that the link between the word and this new node is marked as 'immediately connected' (*i.e.*, the node is a **Leaf**). We then insist that this node is the 'only child' of the subject node.

First, we introduce the blank node below the subject node.

> Select the subject and press 'Insert child after' ('') or 'Insert node after' (''). The result is illustrated in Figure 103.

Figure 102: Different matches for the FTF including the lexical item "I". The subjects are "I": S1A-002 #6 (left), and "the work that I was doing ~~in the~~ ⇨ in the fine art part of the course": S1A-004 #4 (right).

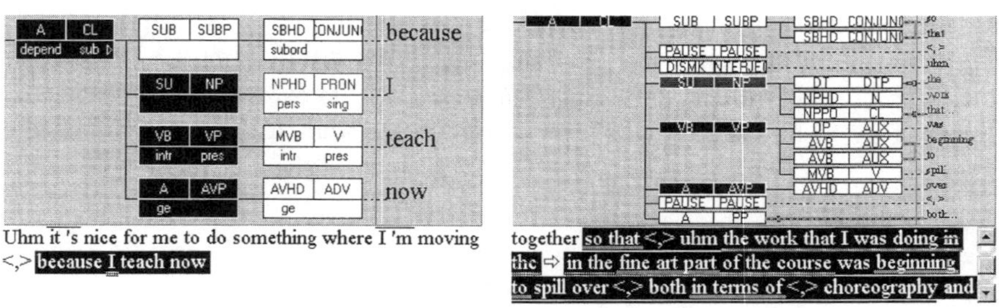

Figure 103: The result after inserting a child node under the subject.

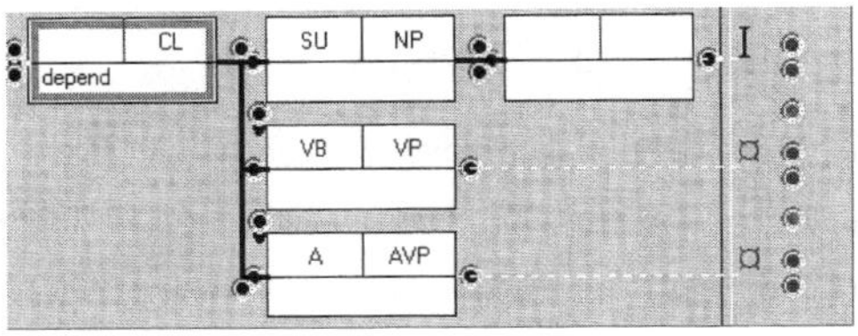

We then adjust the links. In Section 5.12 we discuss the geometry of FTFs in more detail. We content ourselves here with a brief discussion in the context of our worked example.

Table 32 lists the available links. Links are shown as black or white lines and arrows, and in some cases they can also be absent. Each link is separately indicated and controlled by a coloured 'dot' or 'cool spot' superimposed on the line. You can change the status of the link by selecting these spots with the mouse. The left and right buttons change the link by moving in opposite directions through the set of values. You can also use a pop-up menu to set the links directly (see Figure 105).

Table 32: Links and edges in FTFs.

Parent	*Name*	*Meaning*
	Parent	The child in the FTF must match a node *immediately* below the node matching the parent.
	Ancestor	The child must match a node below that matching the parent.
Next (child) and **Next word**		
	Immediately after	The second element in the FTF must match a node *immediately following* the node matching the first.
	After	The second element must follow the first.
	Just before or just after	The second element must *immediately precede or immediately follow* the first.
	Before or after	The second element must either precede or follow the first.
	Different branches ('**Next child**' only)	The second element must be *on a different branch to* the first (*i.e.*, one cannot be the parent of the other).
	<unknown>	No restriction is imposed.
Edges (in the sentence, they are drawn as triangles, see Section 5.12)		
	Yes	There may not be a node beyond this point in the corpus tree.
	No	There is at least one node beyond this point.
	<unknown>	No restriction is imposed.

Some links connect two elements in the FTF. Others, which we call 'edges', refer to a single element. Two links relate one constituent to another and a third connects a pair of words. These are

- Between a node and its child (the up-down, *parent:child* or **Parent** link).
- Between a node and its next sibling (the sideways arrow, **Next child** link).
- Between a word and the next in the text sequence (sideways, **Next word** link).

The **Parent** link is drawn as a thick line between parent and child according to the current line style (straight, curly, *etc.*). The other links may be directional and are depicted with arrows (Table 32). In addition to links, there are six types of *edge* property. By default these are unspecified, but they may be set to a Boolean value ('Yes' or 'No'). There are four edges in the tree structure (**Root**, **Leaf**, **First** and **Last**) and two in the text (**First word** and **Last word**).

- **Root**. We can specify that the uppermost node in the FTF, here drawn on the left, must *only* match the top of a corpus tree (**Root**: yes), or *never* match it (**Root**: no).
- **Leaf**. All nodes with no nodes below them (drawn to the right in Figure 104) may match leaf nodes in a corpus tree. Note that in the ICE grammar, if a node is a leaf, *it must be immediately connected to the word under it.*
- **First** and **Last** (child). These allow you to specify that a node must (or must not) match the first or last node in a sequence of child nodes in a tree.
- **First word** and **Last word**. These specify how a word should match against the first or last word in a text unit.

Figure 104 summarises the links in our FTF. By default, tree links are *immediately connected* (indicated by a thick black line or black arrow) as shown here, while inter-word links are *unspecified* (no arrows are visible at the **Next word** spots on the right of Figure 104).

Links and edges in Fuzzy Tree Fragments are drawn topographically, *i.e.*,

Figure 104: Links and edges in our FTF.

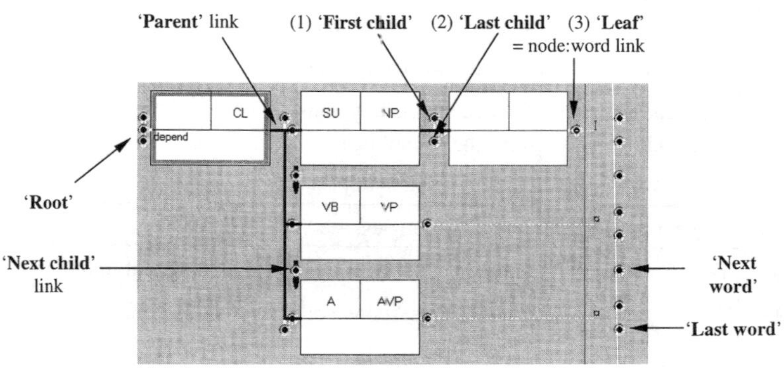

Figure 105: Using a pop-up menu to edit links.

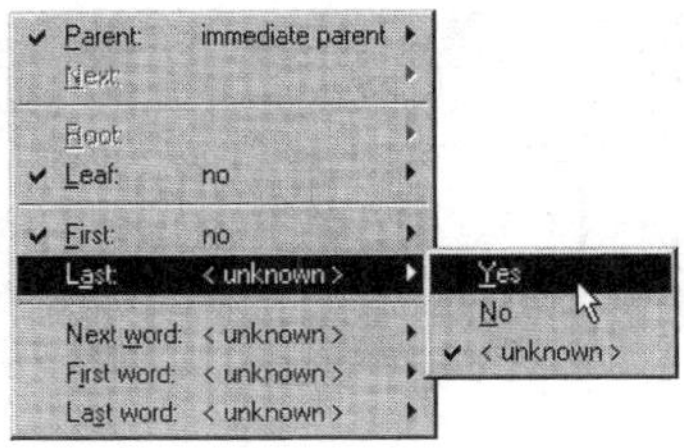

they make sense in relation to the overall structure. A black line between two elements means that, in the corpus, their corresponding elements must be found immediately adjacent to one another. White lines represent uncertainty or "fuzziness" and indicate *eventual* relationships between nodes.

This 'topological' approach leads to a slightly counter-intuitive labelling of 'edge' lines. Suppose a node is marked '**Root**: no'. The node matching it must have a parent, a fact we depict by drawing a black line toward this notional node. Conversely, if no line is visible, the matching node *cannot* have a parent, *i.e.*, it is the root ('**Root**: yes'). This principle applies to all edge links.

Armed with this knowledge, we can return to our FTF and make our newly inserted node an 'only child'. Refer to Figure 104.

- Place the mouse over the '**First child**' cool spot indicated by arrow (1) in Figure 104, and press the left button down. You will get a black line. If you leave the mouse over the spot, a yellow 'banner' will appear, reading '**First:** no' (*i.e.*, there must be a previous node although we need not specify what it is).
- Click on the cool spot a second time. The line disappears and the banner says '**First:** yes'. You may also click twice on the 'last child' spot (2). The unspecified node should now be an only child.

We are now ready to consider the final problem. How do we ensure that the word *I* is immediately connected to the blank node? The answer, as we hinted, is to modify the status of the blank node's **Leaf** edge. The default **Leaf** value is <unknown>. It follows that by default, the implicit relationship between a node and any text unit element below will be *eventual*. This was why any number of other nodes (and words) could be found under the subject in Figure 102.

- Click down with the mouse on the cool spot associated with the leaf status of the blank node (arrow (3) in Figure 104). The edge line first turns black (**Leaf:** no) and then disappears (**Leaf:** yes). When the status is 'Yes', the dotted line between *I* and the node turns black, meaning that the relationship is *immediate*.

You can also set link values with a pop-up menu. If you select a node and then do a 'right click' *outside* the node, you will see a menu like Figure 105.

This menu is very similar to that for features, except that a secondary menu is used to set the value of an edge, rather than specify a feature. Inapp-

*Figure 106: Revised FTF with an only child connecting "I" and '**SU,NP**'.*

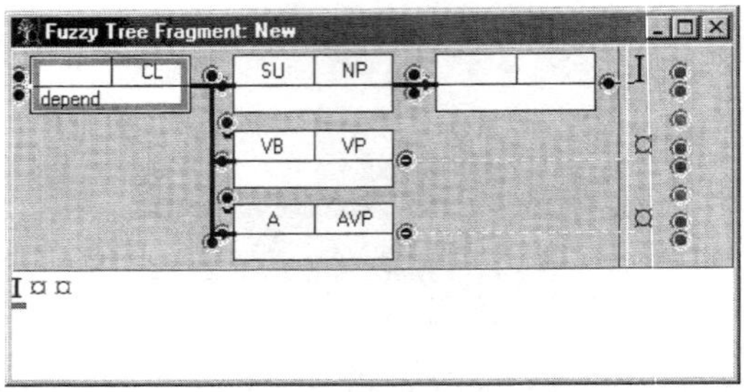

licable links are greyed out. The 'word' links and edges (**Next word**, *etc.*) refer to the text unit element immediately below the current node in the FTF.

Your FTF should now look like Figure 106. Pressing <F4>, or 'Start!' to search the corpus will now identify over 330 matching cases.

5.9 Moving nodes and branches

We constructed our FTF by 'slot filling': creating the structure first and then labelling nodes. However, we often need to move nodes during editing.

There are two different approaches to moving elements around an FTF. All commands are listed in Table 33.

1) **Moving branches**. This is typically performed by a 'drag and drop' operation using the mouse. Moving a node disconnects the node and all its children, and reconnects it at a new location in the tree. Obviously, you cannot connect a node onto itself or its children. The 'Move node' command window (Figure 107) performs the same task. 'Move' should be used in preference to 'cut and paste' when moving entire branches, specifically, when you want to move portions of a tree from point to point.

2) **Cutting and pasting single nodes**. 'Copy' copies the content of a single node, while

Table 33: Tree editing commands for FTFs.

	name	keyboard action	menu command
	Move node	<End>	**Edit | Move Node...**
	Cut node	<Ctrl>+X	**Edit | Cut Node**
	Copy node	<Ctrl>+C	**Edit | Copy Node**
	Paste node before	<Ctrl>+V	**Edit | Paste Node Before**
	Paste node over	<Shift>+V	**Edit | Paste Node Over**
	Paste node after	<Shift>+<Ctrl>+V	**Edit | Paste Node After**
	Paste child after	<Shift>+<Ctrl>+<Insert>	**Edit | Paste Child After**

Figure 107: The 'Move node' dialog box

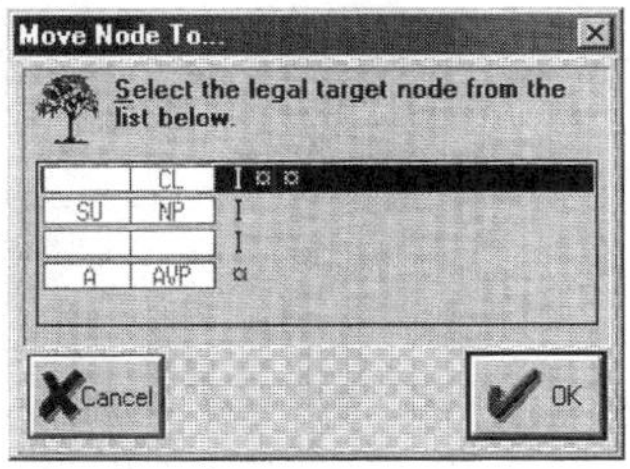

Figure 108: The FTF with the verb and adverbial phrase swapped around.

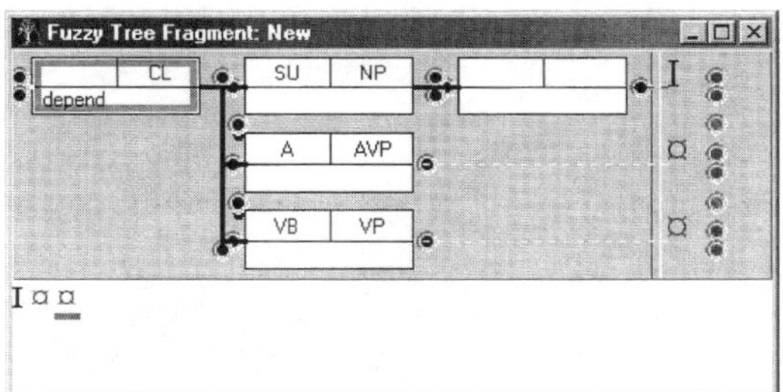

three of the various 'paste' commands replicate the 'insert' commands (*cf.* Table 30, page 131) to insert a new node into the tree. The fourth replaces an existing node. 'Cut' removes the node but remembers it for future paste operations. 'Cut and paste' is preferable to 'move' when inserting new nodes between existing ones.

To illustrate these approaches, consider how we can modify the FTF in Figure 106 so that the verb phrase follows the adverbial phrase (Figure 108).

Using the first method we move nodes from point to point.

> Place the mouse over the '**VP**' node, positioning it just inside the node, where the stem of the link connects with the node, press and hold down the left mouse button.

The link connecting the node to its parent should vanish, and the mouse pointer becomes a 'pin' ('⚲'). The link is replaced with a 'rubber band' connecting the pin to the node, as in Figure 109. Helpfully, all legal target nodes (everything apart from the current node and its descendants) turn green. If you drop the connection into one of these, the node will be reconnected and the tree is reorganised. Moreover, if the link is dropped into a node containing children, *the new node will be placed at the end of the set of children.* With a little practice this command can be used to rearrange the order of child nodes.

> Drop the link into the topmost clause node (Figure 109). This will shuffle the child sequence and place the verb phrase in the third position. The result is as Figure 108.

*Figure 109: One stage move: moving the '**VB,VP**' node with 'drag and drop'.*

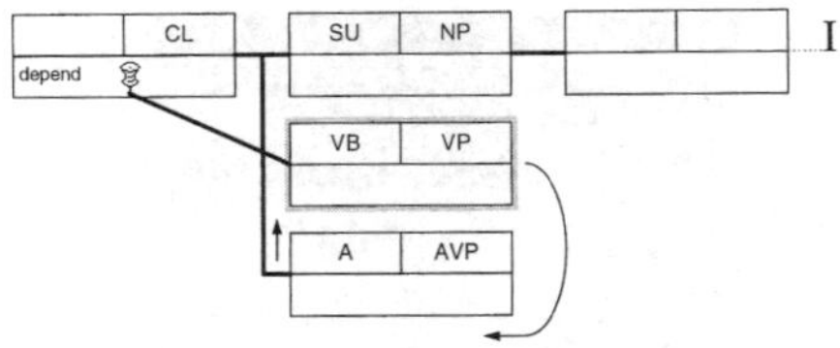

Figure 110: Two stage cut and paste – after the 'Cut node' operation (left) the clause is selected, following 'Paste child after' (right).

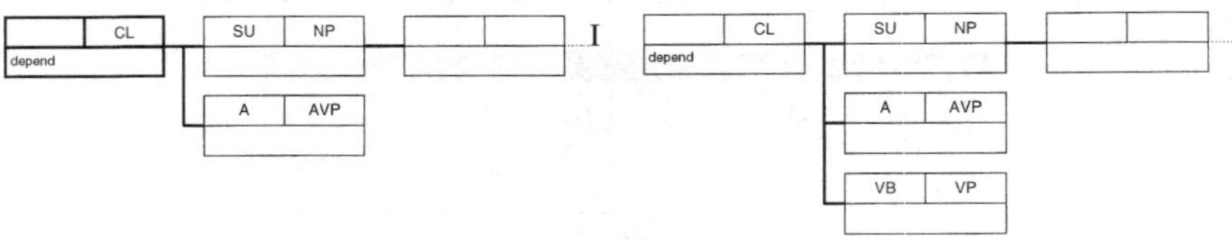

> Alternatively, press the 'Move node' command button ('') which opens the window in Figure 107. Pressing 'OK' without editing first breaks, and then reconnects, the connection with the node's parent, performing the same 'shuffle' operation.

The cut and paste method requires a two stage operation: cut the first node away, and paste it in elsewhere (Figure 110). To switch the order of the two nodes ('**VB,VP**' and '**A,AVP**'), you will find it simplest to cut out the '**VP**' node and then paste it in after the '**AVP**' node, using 'Paste child after'.

> Undo the move to try the 'cut and paste' approach. Now select the verb phrase node and hit the 'Cut node' button ('') or press <Ctrl> and 'X' together.

> Hit the 'Paste child after' button ('', or <Ctrl>, <Shift> and <Insert> together). This will insert the cut element in the tree into the last child position of the clause.

In this case we do not have to change our current position between cut and paste. If the current node has no children, cutting the node out will move us up the tree. This is exactly the right starting point to allow 'Paste child after' to reinsert the node into the last child position, after the adverb phrase.

Although we used these two methods to achieve the same result, the two techniques are quite distinct and should not be confused. The second method *removes a node and reinserts it at a new location*, whereas the first *alters the connection between a node and its parent* (and thereby the sibling order). Try moving the subject node in Figure 108 to the last position.

> Pick up the parent link from the subject node and drop it back into the clause. Then undo the operation.

> Cut the subject node. The result is that the node is removed and the blank child node is connected directly to the clause in the same position. If you then select the clause

and perform a "Paste child after" ('') operation, the subject (and only the subject) is inserted in the last position. Undo both instructions to reinstate our FTF.

With 'cut and paste', any constituents below the removed node are connected to the parent. 'Cut' excises a node from the structure, cutting above *and* below. On the other hand, 'move node' only affects the connection to the parent. Child nodes and words stay connected to the node being moved.

You should now be able to construct and modify any number of FTFs. You can add, remove and rearrange nodes; edit their function, category, features and associated text unit element; and edit the links between nodes.

We suggest that you experiment with FTFs, starting searches even if the FTF is not quite finished. As we demonstrated, observing how an FTF works in practice can help you refine it. You can save your FTF at any time via the 'Save' button in the main command bar.

5.10 Applying a multiple selection and setting the focus of an FTF

All the operations thus far described were performed by selecting a single node at a time. Only one node is the current node, which is acted upon by the chosen command. We cut and paste one node, we edit the content of one node, we set the links of one node.

In some circumstances, however, it can be useful to select more than one node at a time. Often this is just a question of speed: for example, it is quicker to delete several nodes together than each separately. Table 34 lists editing commands and how they exploit multiple selection.

There are two circumstances where a multiple selection is *necessary*. The first is in *assigning the FTF focus* to span several nodes, a task we turn to in a moment. The second is when creating an FTF from multiple siblings using the *FTF Creation Wizard* (Section 5.14).

Multiple selection is limited to a *contiguous set of siblings*. If two nodes

Table 34: Editing commands and multiple selection.

		Name	Result when several nodes are selected
		Delete / Cut node	Removes several nodes at one time
		Copy node	Copies just the first node in the sequence
		Insert / Paste node before	Adds a new common parent to the group
		Paste node over	Pastes over several nodes at once
		Insert / Paste node after	Adds a new child node below each one
		Insert / Paste child after	Adds new children below each one
		Move	Moves a group of nodes together

Figure 111: Performing multiple selection using the keyboard – (left) extend select:<Shift> + '↑' or '↓' (right) select children: <Shift>+ '→'.

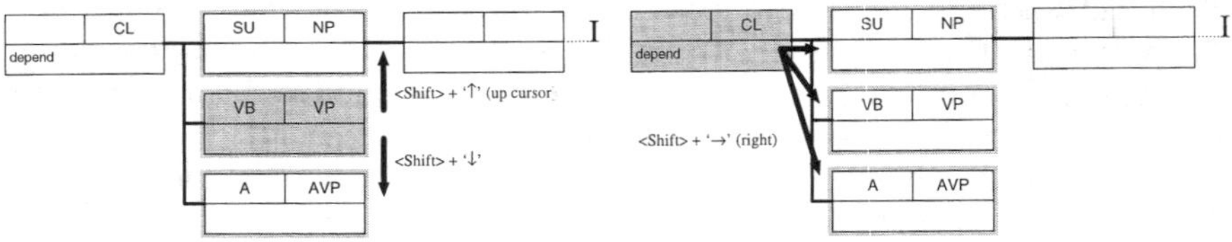

are selected they must be *siblings* (*i.e.*, they share the same parent), and *contiguous* (there cannot be an intermediate unselected constituent).

There are four different ways to perform a multiple selection.

1) **Using the keyboard**. Use <Shift> with the cursor keys. As with navigation, this takes tree orientation into account. If the tree is drawn left-to-right as in Figure 111, then '↑' and '↓' extend the selection over siblings, while '→' selects the set of children.

2) **Using the mouse**. If you press the left mouse button down in the space between the nodes, the cursor should change to a 'plus' symbol (Figure 112). You can then 'drag' this diagonally to create a 'selection box' from corner to corner, spanning part of the tree. When you release the button, the editor selects the longest contiguous set of siblings that are fully enclosed in the box. (In ICECUP 3.1 you usually need to press <Shift> to prevent the tree and window being scrolled sideways. See Chapter 7.)

3) **Selecting a node with the mouse and the <Shift> key together**. If you hold the <Shift> key down while selecting a second sibling, ICECUP will extend the selection. See Figure 111, left.

Figure 112: Multiple selection using the mouse.

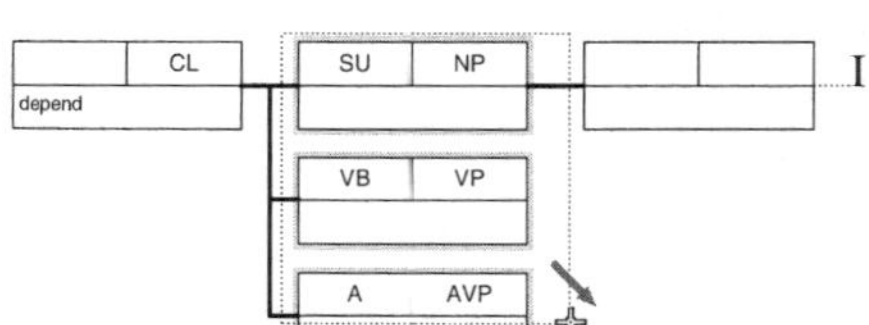

Figure 113: Selection via the text view – (left) single selection of tag node I, *(right) multiple selection by dragging "*I → ¤*".*

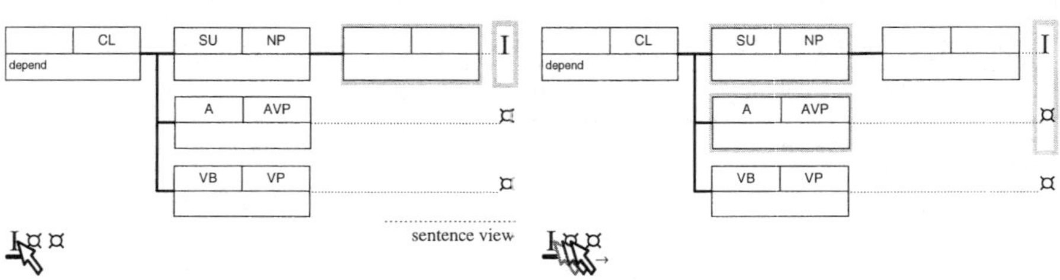

4) **Using the mouse in the sentence view** below the editor window. In our case, the view should consist of the sequence 'I ¤ ¤'. If you select one of these elements with the mouse, say, "I", the tree selection moves to *the node immediately dominating it* (Figure 113, left). If you drag the mouse over another element (say, the next '¤' symbol), the node selection becomes a multiple selection, and will move to the minimum set of contiguous siblings that dominate these text unit elements.

We are often interested in examining variation around *part* of the construction, what we might call the *point of interest*, or 'focus'. This is indicated by a yellow border in the node or nodes.

The tree view shows how the nodes of an FTF match against a tree (see, *e.g.*, Figures 102 and 106). Concordancing (see Section 4.6) exploits the focus, highlighting only *the text dominated by the nodes that match the focus* rather than the entire FTF. Note the following distinction:

- The *query* is defined by the entire FTF.
- The *point of interest* within the query is a specific location within the FTF.

When ICECUP performs a search, the FTF as a whole must match against trees it finds. If any part of the FTF is not in the tree in the specified arrangement, the match fails and the search process moves on. It follows that *the point of interest must be within the FTF* in order to specify how it relates to the rest of the structure. Changing the focus in ICECUP does not affect the set of queries retrieved but it does affect the display of example cases.

Returning to our example (Figure 108, page 141), suppose that we are interested in variation in say, the adjective phrase or the verb phrase (VP). We can examine how VPs are realised in the context of this FTF.

➢ Let us modify the focus of the FTF. Currently it is at the top of the tree. To make the *verb phrase* carry the current focus, select the VP node and press the 'Mark FTF focus' button (''), or press <Shift> and <F3> together.

➢ The focus will appear in its new position. Press <F4> to run the search. Then press the 'concordance button' ('') in the text browser menu bar or hit <F2>.[9]

Varying the focal point produces a number of distinct concordance displays (Figure 114). ICECUP can display varying amounts of information in the concordance view (refer to sections 4.6 and 4.8 for more on this). For example, you can reveal the word class tags for the lexical items covered by, or near, the focus. ICECUP 3.1 extends this by allowing us to selectively reveal grammatical information in the region around the focus node. This lets a researcher identify, *e.g.*, the function of each clause node in Figure 114.

---

[9] This process is clumsy because you are required to open a series of query results windows. Chapter 6 explains how the FTF focus for a *particular* query window can be altered.

Figure 114: Varying the focus of the FTF in Figure 108.

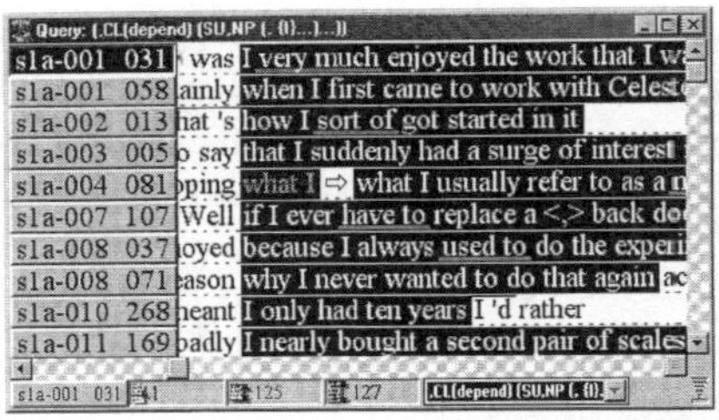

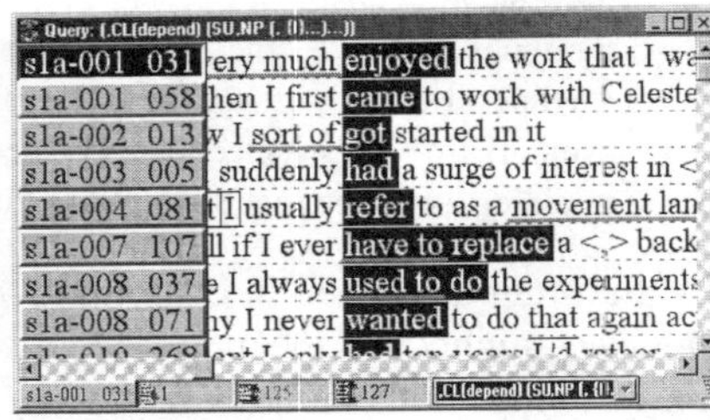

focus on:
entire ***clause***
(above)

*... **verb phrase***
(above)

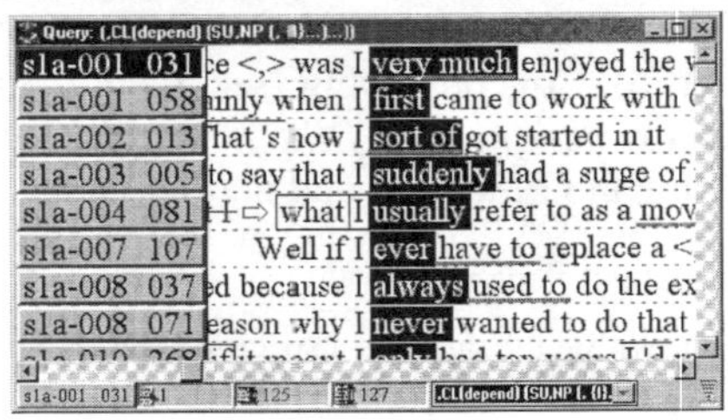

*... **adverb phrase***
(right)

Sometimes it is useful for the focus to span more than one node, *e.g.*, in text fragment queries. The rule is the same as for multiple selection – *the focus can extend over several contiguous siblings in the FTF*. To mark such a focus, you perform a multiple selection and then hit the 'mark FTF focus' button.

5.11 Text-oriented FTFs revisited

At the start of this chapter we discussed simple text fragment searches and demonstrated that text fragment queries are, in reality, specialised FTFs. We are now ready to return to text-oriented FTFs and apply some of the lessons we

Figure 115: The Text Fragment query window.

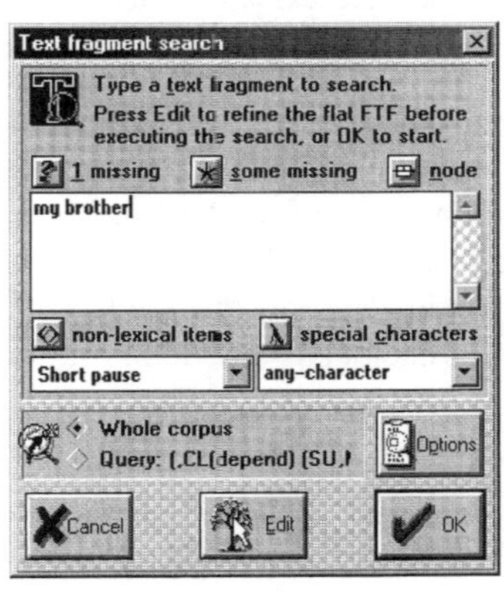

*Figure 116: Text-oriented FTFs for (left), "**brother**", and (right), "**my brother**".*

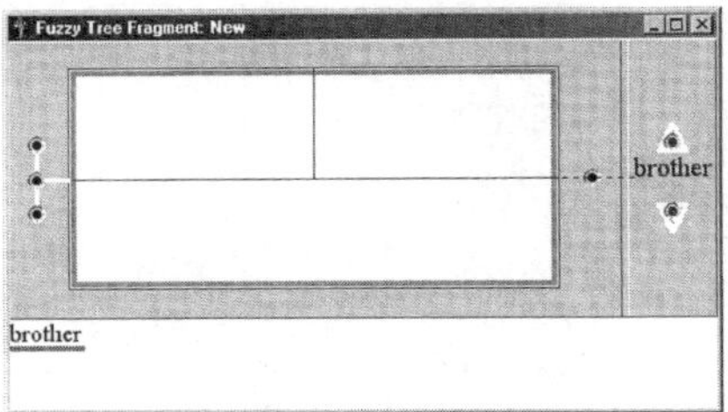

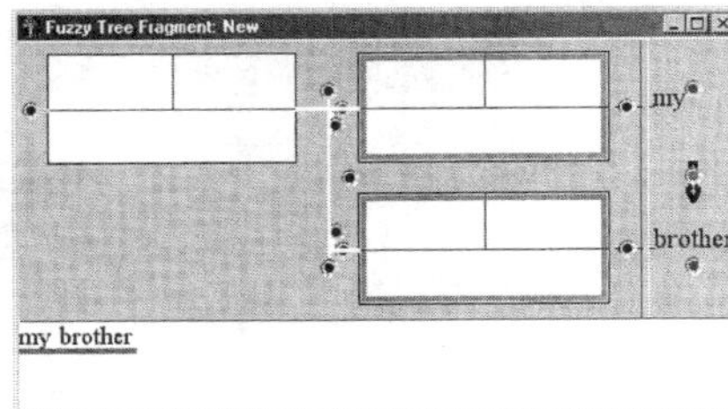

learned.

> Enter the text fragment query window (Figure 115).

> Type "**brother**" and press the 'Edit' button. You will get the FTF in Figure 116, left.

> Re-enter the Text Fragment query window. Type "**my brother**" and hit 'Edit'. The FTF should look like the second FTF in Figure 116.

This pair of queries have two things in common.

1) The node is directly, intimately, connected to the words, as evidenced by the black dotted line between the word and the node. Nodes are marked as "**Leaf**: yes", so there can be no intervening tree structure between the node and tree (see Section 5.8).

2) The leaf nodes have been given the FTF focus.

ICECUP creates a very simple FTF to search for the single word *brother*. This is just the word, plus an empty, immediately-connected leaf node. The empty node must be a **Leaf**, or the FTF will be *underspecified* (see Section 5.13). This node would hold the tag for "brother" if it were specified (*cf.* early examples in Section 5.13 and Figure 141, page 165). No other restrictions are placed on the node, except that it must be immediately connected to the word *brother*. Nor are there any restrictions on the location of the word *brother* in the sentence.

Compare this to the FTF produced by the two-word sequence *my brother* (Figure 116, right). Naturally, there are two directly attached tag nodes, one for each word. These nodes are not necessarily grammatical siblings. Instead, these are specified to be in *word* order by the black **Next word** arrow on the right.

An FTF must conform topologically to a tree, *i.e.*, the two sibling nodes must have a common parent. We must therefore have a third node acting as a 'parent' at the 'top' of the FTF (on the left here). This parent node must neither limit how the FTF matches against the corpus nor produce unnecessary duplicate matches (see Section 5.13). To see how we avoid this, consider Figure 117.

There is one unique location in a tree where this node can be safely made to match: the topmost 'root' of the tree. ICECUP marks the parent node with '**Root**: yes', it is disconnected from its children by setting '**Parent**: ancestor'

*Figure 117: Matching the "***my brother***" FTF (Figure 116, left) to a tree.*

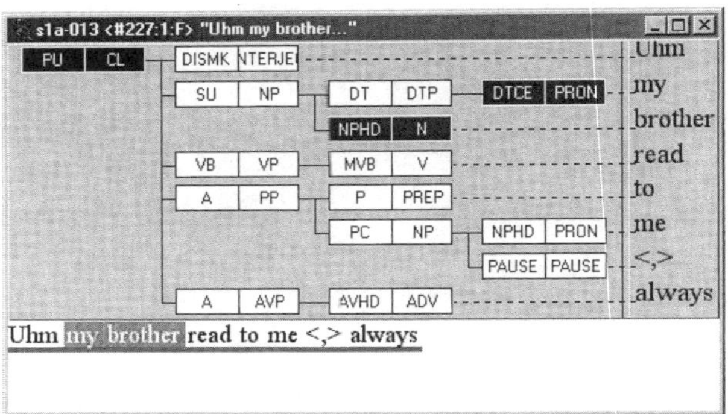

for each child. Sibling nodes are disconnected from one another by setting **Next child** to <unknown>. (Review Figures 116 and 118 if this is not clear.)

We remarked above that one could introduce *tags* into text fragments (using the 'Node' button in the Text Fragment query window).

Suppose we are interested in searching for a pair of intransitive verbs with a conjunction between them, as in *play and sing*. Note that tag searches tend to take longer than lexical ones.

Figure 118: An FTF generated from tags.

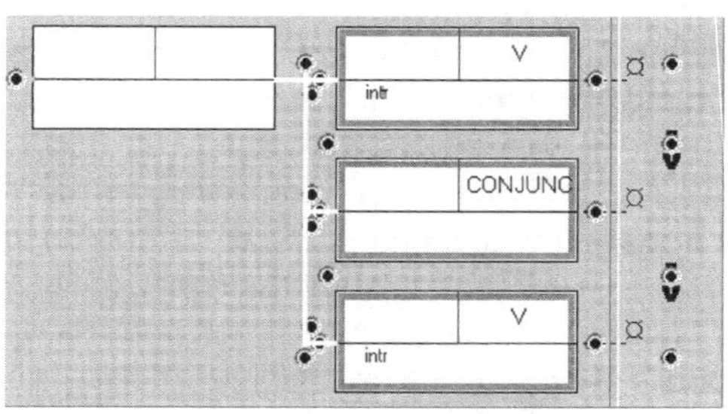

Figure 119: Search results from this FTF.

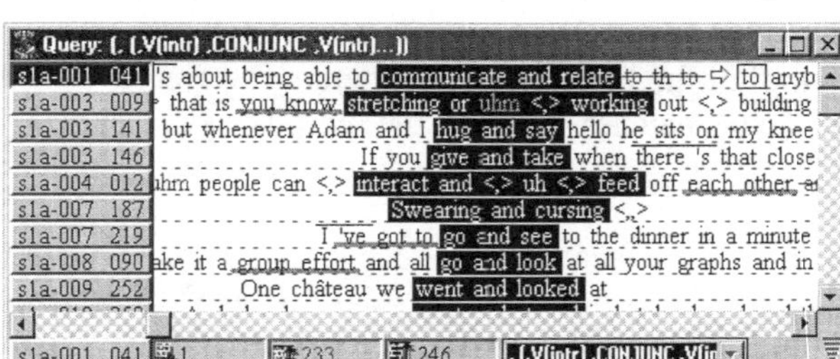

Figure 120: A case of conjoined predicate elements.

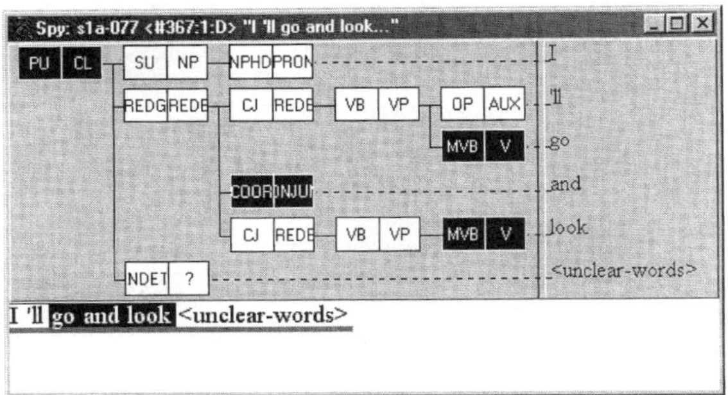

Try the following Text Fragment query.

> Select the 'Node' button (or <Alt>+'N'), then enter "V(intr)" between the '<>' symbols. Move the cursor to the end of the text (press <End>). Select 'Node' again and type "CONJUNC". Finally, move the cursor to the end, press 'Node', and enter "V(intr)".

> Now, if you press 'Edit', you will obtain the FTF in Figure 118. Pressing <F4> to search the corpus will generate a set of results similar to those in Figure 119.

Suppose we extend this text-oriented FTF from the tag nodes towards the root. Inspecting the tree analyses from the previous search, we notice that a large number of these cases are conjoined predicate elements (written '**CJ,PREDEL**', Figure 120), while others are conjoined verb phrases, *etc.* Let us identify just the conjoined predicate elements.

Our target FTF is shown in Figure 121. We must introduce two new conjoined predicate element nodes. We will then need to specify the relationship between these and the pre-existing nodes in the FTF.

> To introduce the first conjoin, move to the first (verb) tag node, and press the 'Insert node before' button ('[icon]', or press <Insert> on the keyboard). This introduces a blank node above the verb node as a prior sibling of the '**CONJUNC**' node.

Figure 121: Our target FTF.

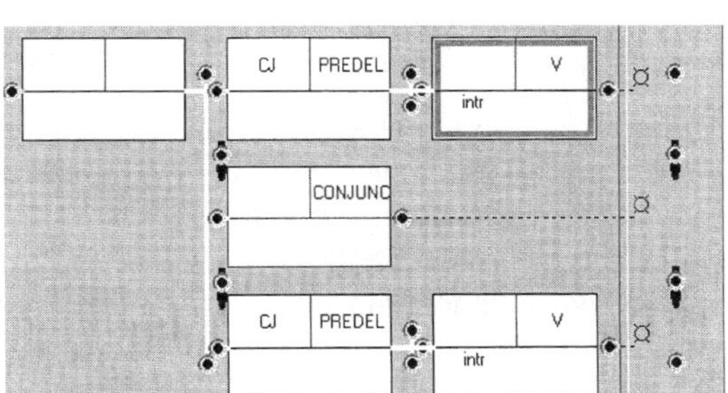

Figure 122: The result after inserting conjoined predicate element nodes.

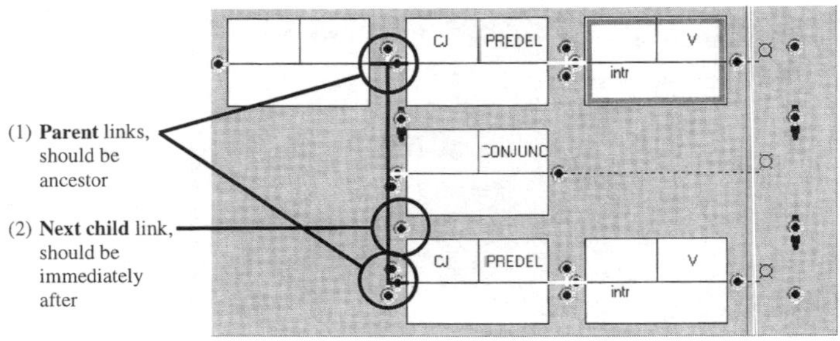

> We now mark this node as ('**CJ,PREDEL**'). Press <F2> or the '' button. Select 'conjoin' from the list of functions (hint: press 'C' three times). You may then locate 'predicate element' in the set of compatible categories (hint: you may need to scroll the view). Double-click with the mouse on 'predicate element' and hit 'OK'.

> To add the other node, we can copy the first and paste the second. Press the 'Copy' button ('', or <Ctrl> and 'C' together). Then move to the second of the two verb nodes, and press 'Paste node before' ('', or <Ctrl>+'V').

However, the resulting FTF (Figure 122) is not yet consistent with our target. The introduction of new nodes has rendered a number of links incorrect. We need to go through the FTF and modify these.

Firstly, the **Parent** links from the new nodes to the root (arrows (1) in Figure 122) are black ('Parent'), when they should be white ('Ancestor').

> Click once on the blue 'cool spot' on each link to the left of the '**CJ,PREDEL**' nodes.

Secondly, we want to ensure that both conjoined predicate elements match siblings in the tree 'on either side' of the conjunction node. This means specifying black 'Next child' arrows between them, thus:

CJ,PREDEL → CONJUNC → CJ,PREDEL.

When we inserted the first '**CJ,PREDEL**' we introduced this link by default. We just alter the second link (2), currently <unknown> (no arrow).

> Click once on the cool spot with the *right* mouse button (or several times with the left) or use the pop-up menu to set the link (see Section 5.8). Press <F4> again.

The structure should now be correct. However, only the first verb will have the FTF focus. To compare the two searches, you may find it easier to set the FTF focus to the three siblings ('**CJ,PREDEL**', '**CONJUNC**', '**CJ,PREDEL**'). To do this, perform a multiple selection across the three nodes, click on '', and press <F4> again. The results, when concordanced, will look like Figure 123.

Figure 123: Search results from the revised FTF (with spanning focus).

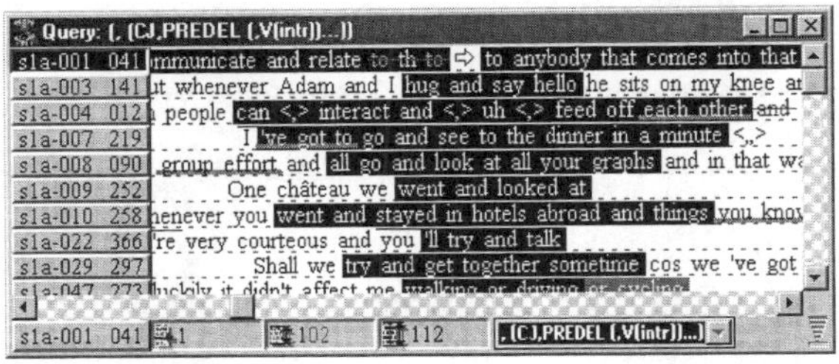

We have introduced three new nodes into our tag sequence, and specified the grammatical relationship between them. The nodes have to be specified in order for them to carry the FTF focus. However, inserting nodes into an FTF, even blank ones, can affect the matching process.

This brings us to a number of points about good practice. When introducing nodes into an existing FTF, or removing nodes, *pay attention to links*. Introducing a node can 'upset' existing links because new links are set to a potentially unexpected default. It is sometimes a good idea to make your links initially ambiguous, *e.g.*, to use ancestor instead of parent relationships if there is some doubt about the relative position of nodes.

You should be especially careful with unspecified 'empty' nodes. These can match against any node in a tree (see Section 5.13), so they should be 'tied down' as far as possible. To do this, specify an *immediate link* (immediately before or after, next child, parent) between the empty node and a more specified neighbour. You may be able to set the root or leaf status to 'yes'.

ICECUP's proof method is *exhaustive*, that is, it will try to find every combination in every candidate tree that matches the FTF. If you fail to tie down some nodes in the FTF, you can generate a very large number of meaningless combinations. ICECUP may stop with an error message and refuse to proceed in such a situation. In this case, correct your FTF and try again.

5.12 *The geometry of FTFs*

It is time to take stock. FTFs containing immediately-linked nodes are relatively easy to understand and construct. In the first place, such FTFs can only match a tree node-for-node. However, gaining mastery of FTFs means being able to employ the more indeterminate links. This is particularly important when the grammar does not quite express what you are looking for, and you need to use a more general FTF to get started.

In this section we navigate some of the main pitfalls of using some of the links in combination, and highlight a number of the less obvious issues. In the next section we examine the process of matching FTFs to trees in more detail.

Figure 124: Default topology introduced by the FTF editor (left), and a Text Fragment query (right).

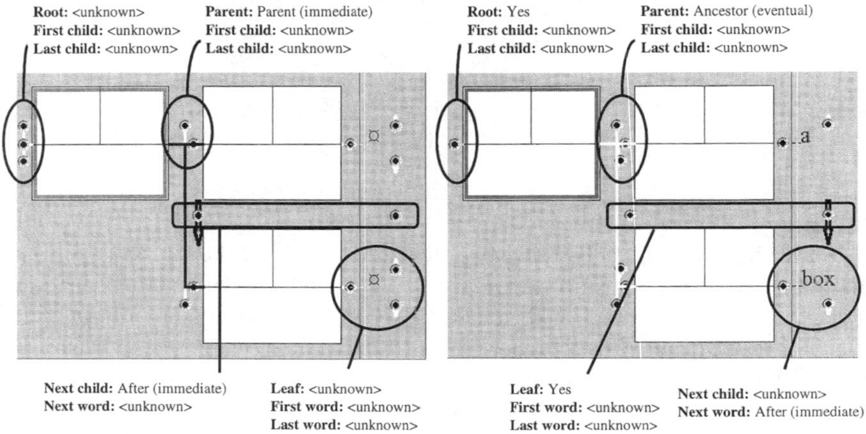

When the FTF editor is used, the default settings of links and edges are as follows: *inter-node links are immediate and ordered, all other values are marked as <unknown>*. This is illustrated by Figure 124, left. (Create it with 'New FTF' and add two leaf nodes with 'Insert child after'.)

This set of defaults is fine, of course, for 'tree-oriented' FTFs, which disregard the relationship between tree and text. These defaults are less useful for text fragment queries which are primarily concerned with textual elements. The two-word text query, "**a box**", is shown on the right of Figure 124.

The two queries are superficially similar – they consist of three nodes – but they are at opposite extremes with respect to the way that their nodes match the corpus. The first FTF matches tree geometry node-for-node, the second matches two leaves and the root, as we saw in the previous section.

Table 35 summarises ICECUP's current set of links and edges. This may be extended in later versions of the software (see Chapter 6) but it represents a topologically sufficient set for the ICE grammar.

There are only two possibilities for the **Parent** link, while there are a large number of values for **Next child** and **Next word**. **Parent** is always *ordered* (a parent in the FTF must match a dominating node in the tree). FTFs would otherwise be meaningless.

The **Next child** link takes one of the six values in Table 35. These are visualised using the 'arrow' representation with the 'black, white or absent' scheme common to all FTF links. The first four links (from 'Immediately after' to 'Before or after') are highly regular, consisting of either an *immediate* or *eventual* connection, and are either *ordered* or *unordered*. A slightly less obvious point is that, because they rely on sibling order, these four link values

Table 35: FTF links used in ICECUP 3.0 and 3.1 (cf. Table 32, page 137).

Parent link		
Parent (line in the current drawing style)		Ancestor
Next child and **Next word** links		
Immediately after		After
Just before or just after		Before or after
Different branches ('**Next child**' only)		<unknown>
Edges of the tree, in general		
Yes	No	<unknown>
Leaf (note implied *node:word* relation)		
Yes (direct)	No (indirect)	<unknown>
Edges of the sentence		
Yes	No	<unknown>

require *both nodes to have the same parent*. (This parent need not be the parent in the FTF.) The weakest of these four values, 'Before or after', states that siblings have the same parent and do not coincide.

The two remaining values, 'Different branches' and <unknown>, do not have this restriction. This is essential for lexical searches, among other things. Without this possibility, we would have to specify the grammatical arrangement of nodes in a lexical search! However, the use of these values is not limited to lexical searches, and understanding what they do can be very useful. The distinction between <unknown> and 'Different branches' is simple. Whilst <unknown> places no restriction on the relationship between nodes, 'Different branches' requires that siblings in the FTF must match nodes in different branches of the corpus tree. One sibling cannot dominate the other.

This means that values of **Parent** and **Next child** are not entirely independent. Although each link has a distinct meaning when considered in isolation, some combinations are redundant. 'Different branches' is only relevant when one of the **Parent** links is an 'Ancestor'. Consider the leftmost FTF in Figure 124. If the **Next child** link was changed to 'Different branches', it would behave no different from 'Before or after'. The only way that two nodes can share the same branch if they have the same parent is to be the same node! Similarly, if the second **Parent** link was set to 'Ancestor' but **Next child** was unchanged, both matching nodes would still share the same parent.

A similar issue arises when three or more siblings are partially ordered, as in Figure 125. Suppose we have three nodes which we label x, y and z, sharing a common parent. Now, if all three are in order ($x \rightarrow y \rightarrow z$) then we can be sure that z will follow x (*i.e.*, $x \rightarrow z$). If, on the other hand, we cannot be

Figure 125: A partially ordered sequence of child nodes.

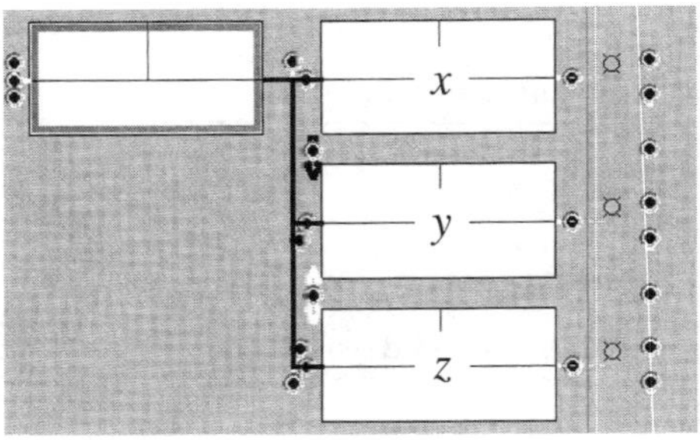

sure of the order of one of the pairs (say, $x \rightarrow y \leftrightarrow z$), then we cannot be sure that z will follow x. In the Figure, z could precede both x and y. This problem becomes even more complex with immediate and eventual links.

Alternatively, if the **Next child** link from y to z was immediate (*i.e.*, 'Just before or after'), z could be in one of only two positions: in order (after y) or in the same position as x. Typically the latter is ruled out by basic node incompatibility, whereupon the link effectively reduces to 'Immediately after', and the nodes must be in sequence. Bear in mind that each link refers only to two nodes – where they connect from and where they go to.

Take care with unordered links, and be prepared to experiment. If a search fails because you have underspecified the query, or you appear to get too many matches, it may be due to an unnecessarily weak ordering. You can always stop a search that appears to be going astray.

The **Next word** link is very similar to **Next child**, except that 'Different branches' no longer applies. 'Before or after' requires only that the two words, and therefore the nodes, cannot coincide. <Unknown> makes no restriction.

The main application of **Next word** is, of course, in standard text fragment queries (Figure 124, right). In grammatical FTFs, on the other hand, we would usually mark **Next word** as <unknown>, even if we might infer an ordering between attached words. So, for instance, in Figure 124, left, while we could set the **Next word** link to 'After', this is redundant.

However, if two sibling nodes are loosely connected together in the tree (*i.e.*, with a '**Next child** = Different branches' or '<unknown>' link between them and at least one '**Parent** = Ancestor' link), you *can* usefully deploy '**Next word** = After' to place branches in word order, or 'Immediately after' to specify that there may not be any intermediate elements. This compares the positions of the last word in the first branch and the first word in the second.

Edges in the tree take one of three values: 'Yes', 'No', and <unknown>. These are shaded in black or white as in Table 35 and employ the topological intuition that a line indicates 'a link to a point beyond the FTF'. Edges have darker spots to differentiate them from links. Like links, edges are only present

Figure 126: Two slightly different FTFs: without specifying the edges (left), the same example with node edges marked (right).

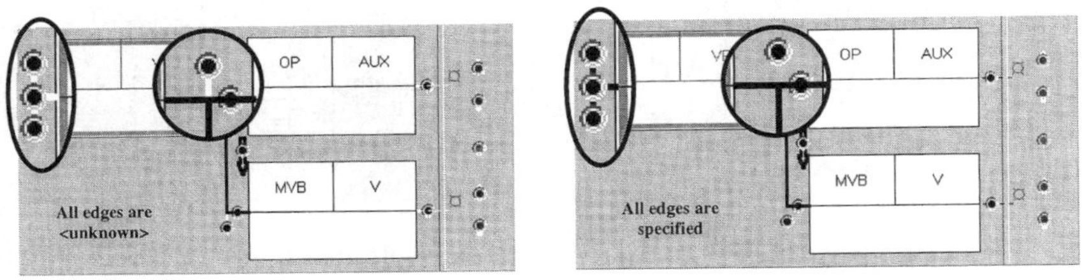

when relevant. For example, if you set the **Root** edge of a node to 'Yes', then the **First** and **Last child** links cannot be applied. If two sibling nodes are connected in order, the **Last child** edge of the first and the **First child** of the second must both be 'No'. The edges disappear. This phenomenon can be observed in Figures 124 and 125.

Two edges are applicable to text unit elements – **First word** and **Last word**, depicted by 'arrow head' triangles as per Table 35. These state whether the node is the first or last in the text unit. These edges are rarely used, because they are restrictive and of limited linguistic benefit.

Finally, the other edge that applies to text unit elements is the **Leaf** status – the 'edge of the tree' – and its implied relationship between word and tag node. We illustrate these in Table 35. As we commented in Section 5.8, the dotted line represents the status of the *node:word* relationship. Only if a node is a **Leaf** can we guarantee that the word is intimately connected to the node.

One can be too zealous when specifying edges. Compare the FTFs in Figure 126. The second FTF is almost the same as the first, except that it limits cases to those with nodes before and after the principal VP (*cf.* the links at the left of the figure). The VP is realised by *only* an auxiliary operator, '**OP,AUX**', and a main verb, '**MVB,V**'. Finally, these two nodes must be leaves (a fact that should be guaranteed by the grammar).

5.13 How FTFs match against the corpus

We should be able to apply our knowledge of links and edges to anticipate how FTFs match corpus trees. How does a program like ICECUP decide that an FTF matches (part of) a tree in the corpus? Recall that an FTF is *declarative*. In other words, all aspects of the FTF must be true together, and the order in which they are evaluated is not important.[10] We start with single node FTFs.

> Generate a single node FTF in ICECUP. Use the '(inexact) Nodal' query window, type the expression "**OD,CL**" and select the 'Edit' button.

---

[10] We will not trouble ourselves here with precisely *how* this process works. For a full discussion, see Wallis and Nelson 2000.

Figure 127: Matching a single-node FTF against a tree (S1A-010 #149).

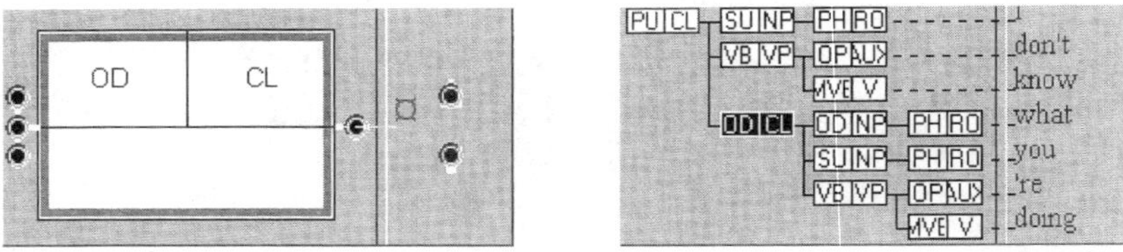

You should obtain an FTF looking like the example in Figure 127, left. Next, find an example of a matching case.

> Press <F4> or hit the 'Start!' button, you will get a complete list of examples (see Chapter 4). Double-click on an example to open a tree window.

An example tree is shown on the right of Figure 127. The matching case (the clause node) is inverted. In the text view, which is not shown here, the segment of text dominated by the node (the realisation of the clause) is shaded.

The FTF contains the focus and a number of unspecified edges, plus the '**OD,CL**' designation. But because the edges are unspecified, they do not limit the position of the matching case. So the query will match direct objects in the last position in the branch or in other positions, as in

I think [$_{OD}$ *you will agree*] because... they were dumbfounded [S1A-094 #52],

where "because... they were dumbfounded" is analysed as an adverbial clause.

Moreover, the FTF explicitly contains a 'word' element ('¤') which is unspecified. If we did specify the word, the FTF would only match examples that *contained* that word (the position of the word within the set of covered words is not specified). An FTF can match more than once in a single tree.

In the case of single *word* FTFs, that is, FTFs that search for a single text unit element, we must therefore specify that the (empty) node is a leaf.

> Using the 'Text fragment' command, type the word "**work**" and press 'Edit'.

The result should be the FTF shown on the left of Figure 128 with a matching example (W1B-001 #179) on the right. The empty node has the focus but is

Figure 128: A single-word FTF and a matching case.

Figure 129: A tagged-word FTF and a matching case.

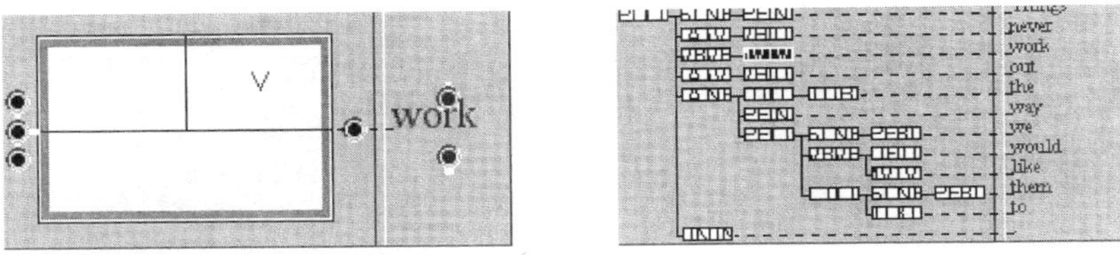

specified as a **Leaf**, so the word and node are immediately connected. No other edges have been specified.

This FTF finds examples of *work* as a noun or as a verb, as in

> We will have to [V *work*] very hard. [W2C-009 #44]

To limit *work* to verbs, you can edit the FTF or apply 'Text fragment' again.

> In the Text fragment window, type "**work**". Without pressing <SPACE>, press the 'Node' button. Position the input caret (blinking cursor) between the angled brackets and type "V". The query should look like this: "**work+<V>**". Then hit 'Edit'.

The FTF should be identical to Figure 129, left. The node is marked as a verb.

Thanks to the detail of the ICE grammar – and, in particular, the large number of features – you can do a lot with a single node query in ICE-GB. However, sooner or later you will want to perform a query that involves more than one node. We first look at FTFs where the **Parent** link is an immediate 'Parent' relationship, where matching child nodes are immediately connected to the node matching the parent. We end with some more complex examples which use the eventual 'Ancestor' link. In these cases the nodes matching the children may be some distance from the node matching the parent.

We could continue our discussion with a *two node* (parent and child) fragment, but this is rather limited. Anyway, this is similar to the 'tagged word' example that we have just seen. Instead, we turn to a more obviously tree-like example consisting of three nodes (Figure 130, left). This may be composed in the usual way (refer to Section 5.7 if in doubt).

Thanks to the black arrow ('**Next child** = immediately after'), one sibling must immediately follow the other in the sequence (the 'skip over' option may

Figure 130: A simple three-node FTF and a matching case.

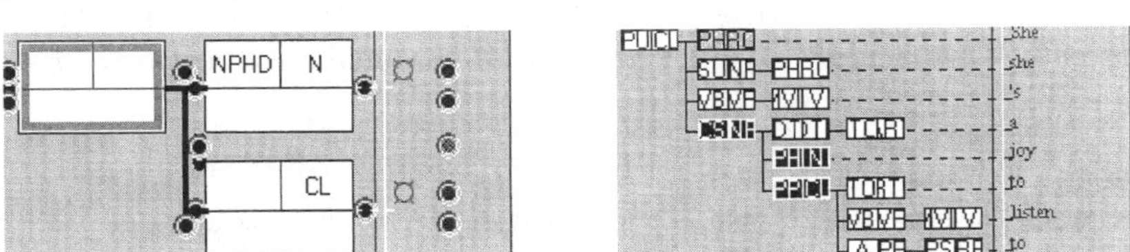

Figure 131: A three-node FTF with an eventual ***Next child*** *link, and two matching cases in the same tree.*

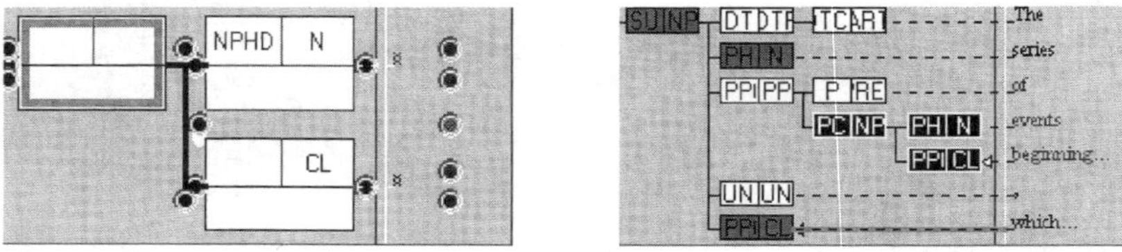

affect this, see Section 3.13). Secondly, the FTF specifies that the node acting as a parent for the other two, matches only the parent in the tree (in the case on the right, the subject complement NP).

It is relatively easy to anticipate the way that FTFs like this match trees in the corpus. If nodes are adjacent and in a particular order in the FTF, they will be adjacent and in that order in the tree. However, we are occasionally interested in weakening these restrictions. Suppose we modify the FTF to permit the clause to *eventually* follow the NP head node.

➢ Change the link to 'after' (the white arrow) by pressing down with the *right* mouse button over the blue cool spot in the middle of the arrow.

The FTF should now look like Figure 131, left. Performing the search again finds the previous cases plus a number of new ones. Figure 131, right, shows two matches, the second embedded within the first. The superordinate case (1) contains a postmodifying prepositional phrase ("of events beginning...") followed, eventually, by a (postmodifying) clause. In the second case the clause and head nodes are adjacent.[11]

(1) [*The* [N *series*] *of events beginning...* , [CL *which...*]

(2) The series of [[N *events*] [CL *beginning...*] , which... [W1A-001 #15]

What if we do not specify the *order* of nodes under the parent (*i.e.*, use a bi-directional arrow)? You may find that it does not appear to make much difference: grammatical terms are invariably (or almost invariably) in a particular order in the tree. If you substitute a 'Before or after' arrow for the 'After' arrow in this FTF and search ICE-GB there will be only a very few additional cases. In the ICE grammar, NP structure is highly ordered.

Not all structures are so regular, and the ability to specify either order can occasionally be useful. However, employing an unordered link can also cause problems. We will illustrate this with an example containing conjoined NPs.

[11] In passing, note that this example illustrates an interesting question regarding *sampling* that we discuss elsewhere (see Chapter 9, Subsection 6.4).

Figure 132: An FTF permitting order inversion with two matching cases.

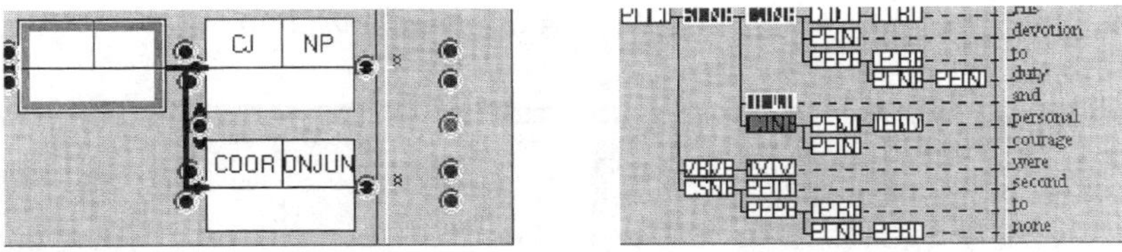

- Create a three-node skeleton as before, but this time, label the first node a conjoined noun phrase '**CJ,NP**' and the second node, a conjunction acting as coordinator '**COOR,CONJUNC**' respectively. Set the **Next child** link to 'Just before or just after'.

The resulting FTF is given on the left of Figure 131. Notice how, when you specified the unordered link between them, the two sibling nodes gained additional 'edge' options on the 'inside' of the branch (for the first, **Last child**, the second, **First child**). With ordered links (see above), FTFs can dispense with these edges, because the ordering itself guarantees that there must be a node after the first one (*i.e.*, **Last child** is 'No') and vice-versa.

This FTF will find examples of coordinated NP conjoins regardless of order. In Figure 131, right, it matches twice because there are two NPs and thus two distinct legal matching arrangements. The first example is in the same ordering arrangement as the FTF.

(1) [[$_{\text{NP}}$ *His devotion to duty*] [$_{\text{CONJUNC}}$ *and*] *personal courage*] were second to none

(2) [His *devotion to duty* [$_{\text{CONJUNC}}$ *and*] [$_{\text{NP}}$ *personal courage*]] were second... [S2A-011 #10]

The other example matches *in the other order*. It shares the same coordinating node in the middle and the same parent NP node.

If you replace 'Just before or just after' with 'Before or after' you will find even more combinations, particularly in cases of coordinated triples ("*x* or *y* or *z*"), *etc*. This kind of underspecified FTF may be useful for *exploration*, but should be avoided in *experimentation* at all costs (see Chapter 5).

A further issue arises when FTFs have to match compound, or 'ditto' tags (see also Section 2.1). 'Ditto' tags label lexical strings that are treated as single items for the purposes of parsing. They are most commonly applied to proper names (*John Brown*, *East Anglia*), compound nouns (*ice cream*, *computer keyboard*), and to semi-auxiliaries (*have to*, *be going to*).

Ditto tags therefore represent a mismatch between text and tree. In the tree, a ditto-tagged node is notionally a single grammatical element. This remains the case even when an intermediate element is inserted into the sequence, *e.g.*, *just* in *was* just *going to* (Figure 133, right).

The problem for Fuzzy Tree Fragments is that one node in an FTF must be able to match an entire set of dittoed nodes in a tree in the corpus, as in Figure 134, while word sequences are allowed to match word-for-word. This

Figure 133: Two examples of ditto tagging.

Two simple ditto tags: for adverbial and formulaic expressions.

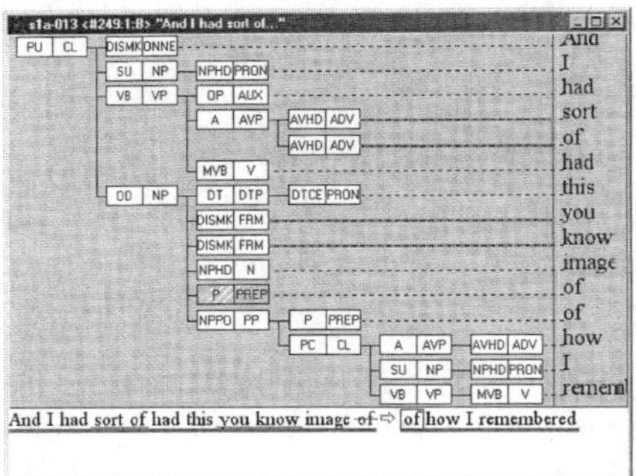

A discontinuous ditto tag for a semi auxiliary.

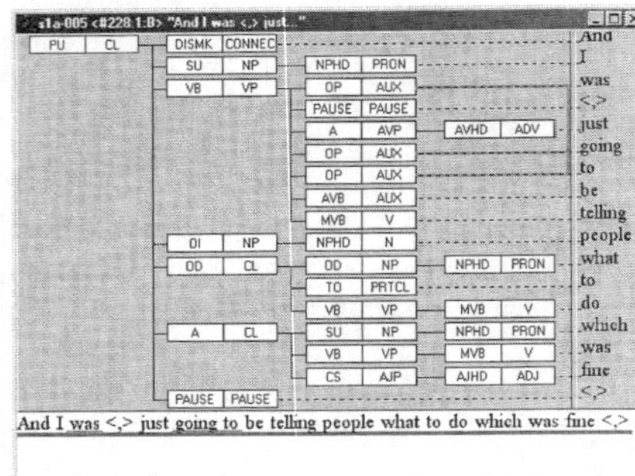

book is not the best place to discuss the technical details of our solution to this problem (instead, see Wallis and Nelson 2000). However, we need to grasp some of the implications. Compare the following searches.

- Use the Text Fragment search to find "**to** <V>" (*to* followed by a verb).
- Use the (inexact) 'Nodal' search to find the auxiliary operator '**OP,AUX**'.

Figure 134 shows a concordance display for the single-node FTF '**OP,AUX**'. FTFs match each compound ditto tag against a single node in the FTF, treating them as a grammatical whole and thus only counting them once in the search. Thus *[ha]'ve got to* and *are* both count as a single case. On the other hand, in our lexical example ("**to** <V>"), FTFs effectively ignore the ditto structure.

(1) I've got [*to* *do*] what I did last time [S1A-001 #18]

(2) ...that I was given ~~to~~ ⇨[*to study*] and [*to explore*] [S1A-001 #32]

In (1), *to* is part of the compound auxiliary operator, while in (2), it is analysed as a particle. The problem is complicated further with *discontinuous* ditto tags,

Figure 134: Concordance display of auxiliary operators in ICE-GB.

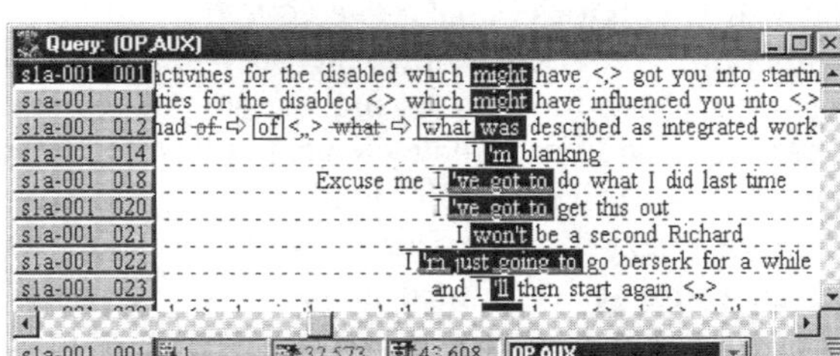

Figure 135: A search for an adverb phrase between two auxiliary operators and a matching case (note embedded ditto tags).

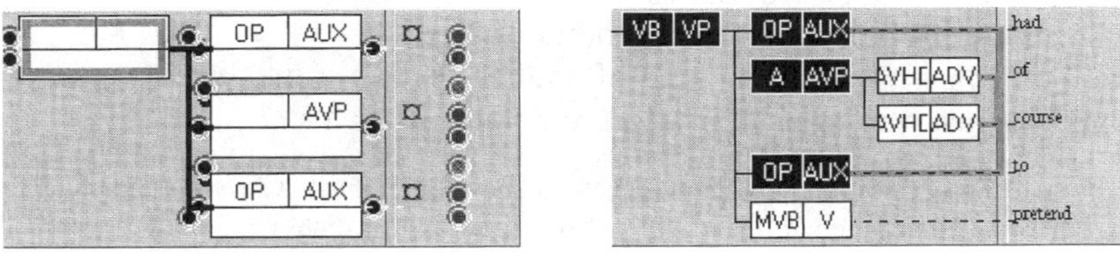

i.e., where an intermediate element is inserted into a compound. Suffice it to say that the FTF system matches by the following strategy.

1) It independently matches the FTF with the tree, node-for-node.
2) Then it reduces the number of cases by identifying dependent ditto-tagged nodes.

Employing this strategy means that ICECUP gives you 'the benefit of the doubt'. The FTF in Figure 135 matches an adverb phrase between a pair of auxiliaries. The only feasible way this might happen is as part of a discontinuous ditto-tagged structure. This search finds a few cases, from *'m [just] going to* (S1A-001 #22) onwards. An example is given in Figure 135.

Sometimes it is necessary or advantageous to specify that a parent in an FTF is not immediately related to a child. One motivation is to allow less strictly "tree-like" structures to be built, such as sequences of tags and words.

Suppose we look for clauses which dominate ordered 'auxiliary, verb' sequences. An appropriate FTF is given in Figure 136, left.

➢ To construct it, create a three-node FTF from scratch. Label the first node as an auxiliary operator and the second node as a main verb. Set *both* **Parent** links to 'Ancestor' (click on the cool spot on the link by the child nodes).

The FTF in Figure 136 obviously matches the tree on the right twice. However, there is a third, less obvious match. The three cases are as follows.

(1) [$_{\text{CL}}$ *I* [$_{\text{AUX}}$ *don't*] [$_{\text{V}}$ *know*] *what you're doing*]

(2) I don't know [$_{\text{CL}}$ *what you* [$_{\text{AUX}}$ *'re* [$_{\text{V}}$ *doing*]]

(3) [$_{\text{CL}}$ *I don't know what you* [$_{\text{AUX}}$ *'re* [$_{\text{V}}$ *doing*]] [S1A-010 #149]

Figure 136: A three-node FTF containing 'ancestor' links, and three cases.

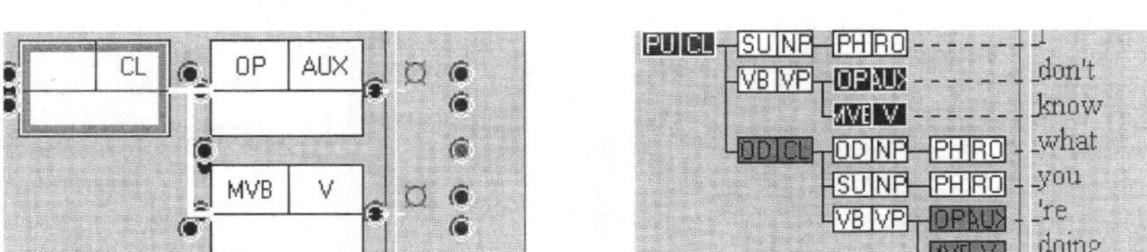

Matches (1) and (2) are structurally *separable*: they share no nodes nor do they subsume one another. The third case consists of the clause from (1) and the node pair from (2). As with our 'Before or after' examples, we obtain distinct combinations that do not match any additional nodes.

You can deal with this kind of ambiguity with a number of strategies. What if you just want to match the *nearest* clause to the pair?

- Apply observation and a little grammatical knowledge. Since ICE is a complete, rather than skeleton grammar, there will always be an intermediate (VP) node between the clause and the verbal elements. You therefore introduce this intermediate node into the FTF and insist that all parent-child relationships are direct 'parent' links. The result is shown in Figure 137, left. This would match (1) and (2) but not (3) above.

Another possibility is to restrict how the clause node matches in other ways.

- For example, if you were just interested in a list of different verb and auxiliary pairs which were within a clause, you could require that *the clause matched the root*. The FTF in Figure 137 (right) would exclude match (2) above. This would also exclude cases where the root node was not a clause, however.

In this 'auxiliary, verb' example, the 'child nodes' must match genuine siblings in the tree, *i.e.*, nodes that share the same parent. This restriction is entailed, not by the **Parent** link, but by **Next child**. 'Immediately after' means "immediately after *in the sequence of siblings in the tree*," and therefore requires that the nodes share the same parent. This property is shared by three other values of **Next child**: 'After', 'Just before or just after' and 'Before or after'. This property is depicted by the 'stem' of the arrow.

If you want to allow siblings to match nodes regardless of parenthood, you have to employ a different **Next child** option. If two nodes are connected by '**Next child** = <unknown>', and 'Ancestor' is employed, then their relative position is not restricted at all. This is how Text fragments are specified.

When we are studying grammatical structure, however, a more desirable constraint is to state that two nodes must be on *different branches* of the tree. This also means that any structure below the two nodes cannot coincide.

The 'Different branches' restriction can be rephrased as *one node cannot*

Figure 137: Two strategies for reducing indeterminacy in the FTF in Figure 136 – introducing an intermediate, immediately connected VP (left), and insisting that the clause is the root (right).

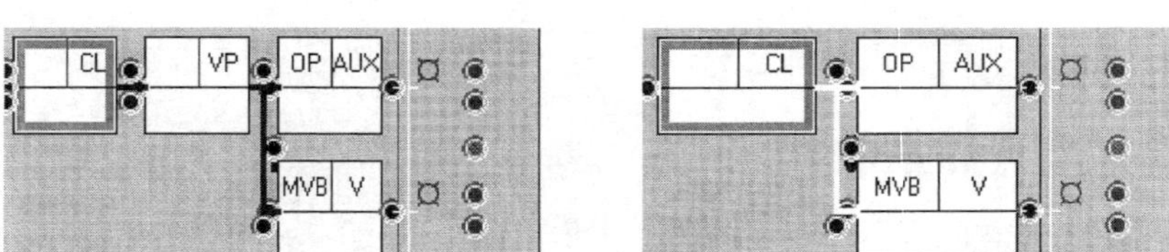

Figure 138: A three-node FTF with ancestor links, nodes on different branches but words in order; and three matching cases.

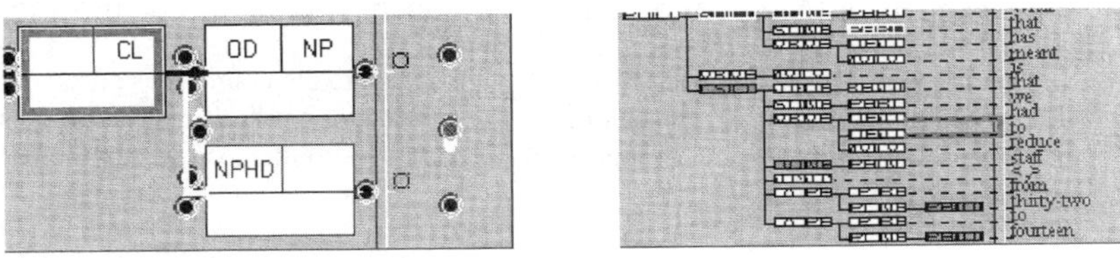

be the parent of the other. The nodes matching each FTF ‘sibling’ cannot share a path to the node matching their common ‘parent’. This option is more general than ‘Before or after’, because matching nodes need not share a parent. As we saw in Table 35 (page 153), the link is drawn like the white double arrow, but without the common stem.

The FTF in Figure 138 looks for examples of clauses containing a NP acting as a direct object (note that this is *directly linked* to the clause) and, somewhere within the clause, but not within the direct object, a NP head.

> Create a three-node FTF from first principles with a ‘New FTF’ command and ‘two child nodes after’. Label the nodes as shown using the ‘Edit node’ command (‘’, or <F2>). Next, click on the cool spot for the ‘Parent’ link for the noun phrase head node and then set **Next child** to ‘Different branches’.

In addition, we can insist that the NP head must *follow* the direct object in the *textual sequence* by specifying a **Next word** link.[12]

> Rotate the **Next word** link until it reads ‘After’ (white arrow).

You should get quite a lot of matches. The tree in Figure 138 contains three examples. Matches (2) and (3) are almost identical, save the position of the final noun phrase head, which is the head of one of two prepositional phrases, “from *thirty-two*” and “to *fourteen*”. The first case is distinct.

(1) [$_{\text{CL}}$ [$_{\text{OD}}$ *What*] [$_{\text{NPHD}}$ *that*] *has meant*] is...

(2) ...[$_{\text{CL}}$ *that we had to reduce* [$_{\text{OD}}$ *staff*] *<,> from* [$_{\text{NPHD}}$ *thirty-two*] *to fourteen*]

(3) ...[$_{\text{CL}}$ *that we had to reduce* [$_{\text{OD}}$ *staff*] *<,> from thirty-two to* [$_{\text{NPHD}}$ *fourteen*]] [S2B-002 #36]

As we discussed before, you should be careful using these ‘loose’ links when you are formalising your experimental design. You must eliminate multiple overlapping instances or at least account for them. We recommend that you

[12] ICE has a phrase structure grammar, so links cannot cross one another. This means that specifying word order also orders the nodes. **Next word** is interpreted generously to mean that a word under the first node precedes a word under the second.

experiment with structural variations on this theme using ICECUP. Try each of the following in turn, resetting the link after the experiment.

What happens if ‘**Next child** = different branches’ is set to <unknown>?

- You get many more matching cases, including those where the noun phrase head is the head of the direct object NP. In such cases, the ‘**Next word**: After’ restriction means that there must still be a word (and therefore a node) prior to the head within the NP: a determiner, for example.

What happens if you omit the word order restriction (*i.e.*, set **Next word** to <unknown>)?

- You get additional cases with NP heads prior to the direct object.

What happens if we weaken the restriction that the clause is the parent of the direct object?

- You obtain many more cases per tree, and eventually, an “out of memory” error (Figure 140). This is because the number of distinct matching arrangements can increase combinatorially.

The example in Figure 139 illustrates the principle. The first three highlighted locations, (reading left to right) match the clause element. The clause can be any distance above the direct object (*your S*). The two rightmost locations match the NP head element. Since all three locations of clause are legitimate for both positions of the NP head, we obtain six different match combinations. Now, suppose there was more than one direct object!

The problem is that the query may not be specific enough to be useful or to allow the query to proceed.

- An *underspecified query* is simply one that matches ‘cases’ that are neither useful nor informative. The simplest example of an underspecified search is an empty FTF. ICECUP 3.0 doesn’t even start a search for this.

Figure 139: An example of underspecification.

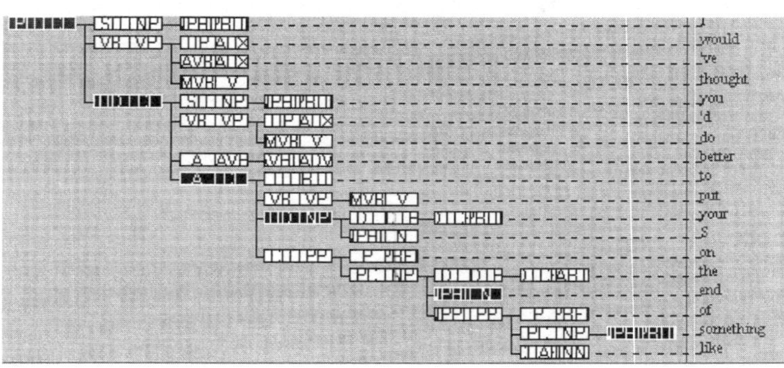

Figure 140: Search-time error indicating that a query is underspecified.

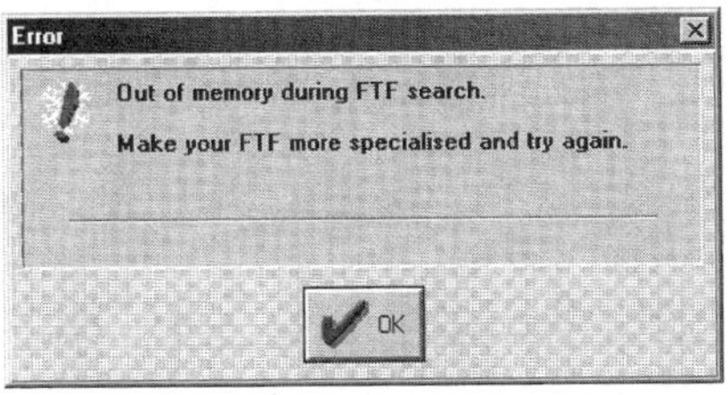

- We might say that a query is *structurally underspecified* if the same instance of a particular phenomenon matches the FTF more than once. This is a particular problem for *experimentation* (Chapter 9), where we need to identify every instance precisely. Press the 'show number of hits' ('▣') button or concordance the view (as in Figure 141, lower left) to reveal these multiple matches.
- If it is *radically underspecified*, the program will stop completely, preventing *exploration* as well as experimentation. ICECUP will report an *error message* (Figure 140) if the number of matches per text unit is too great.[13]
- Conversely, an *overspecified query* is one that fails to find all relevant cases.[14]

Figure 141: A common mistake: failing to make the empty node a leaf node.

*Searching for "**this**" as a text query.*

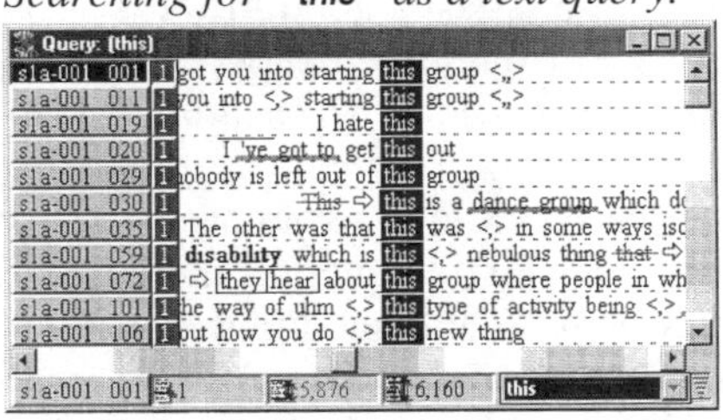

*A new FTF containing the word "**this**".*

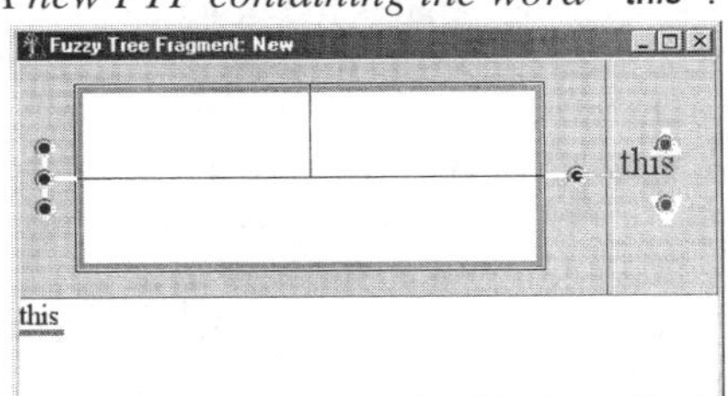

Part of the results of a search.

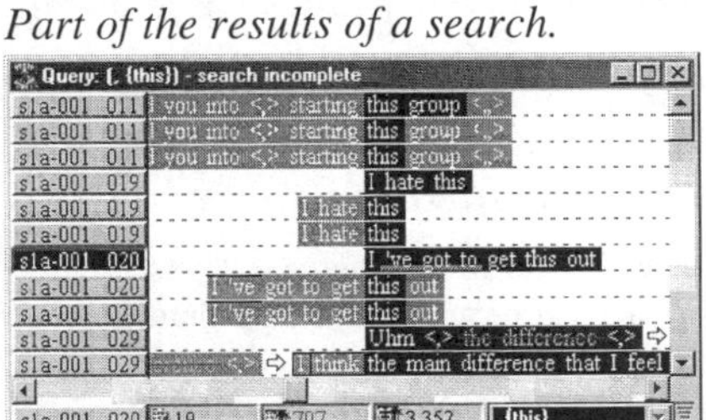

An example match in this search.

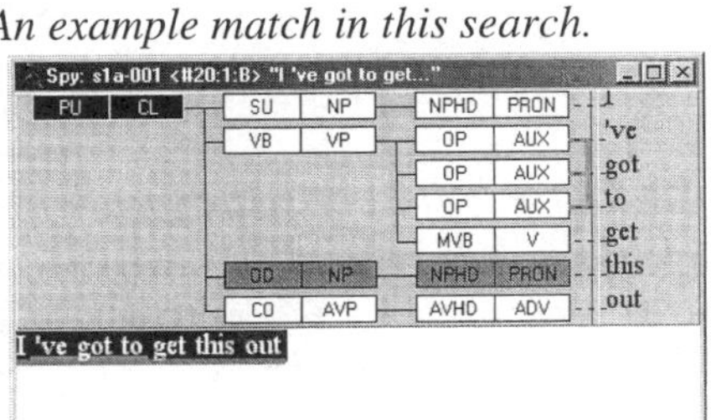

[13] In ICECUP 3.0, the precise relationship is as follows: *if the number of nodes in the FTF, multiplied by the number of independent matching combinations, exceeds 1,000*, the search is aborted. In practice this is more than adequate for plausible queries.

[14] The FTFs generated by the *FTF Creation Wizard* (see 5.14) can be overspecific. This is because the wizard copies information from a fully-specified tree wholesale.

The problem of underspecification can arise with very simple FTFs.

> Perform a Text Fragment' query for the word "**this**". You should get the set of results shown in the upper left window in Figure 141.

> Next, do the same thing using 'New FTF', but *do not* specify that the node is a **Leaf** (Figure 141, upper right). The result is a search that generates the same set of text units as before, but matches many cases per text unit (lower left). Inspection of any text unit reveals *a match for every node up to the root* (Figure 141, final window).

Now, it should be clear that we have not found any more instances of the word *this*! The extra 'cases' are simply variations in the position of the attached node. In this case, the solution is simply to specify that it is a leaf.

The problem can be avoided by increasing the specificity of our FTF, tying down the location of nodes in various ways (as we did in our example). You should link elements immediately if at all possible, even if this means introducing new nodes. You should *avoid* introducing very generally specified, loosely connected nodes, (clauses are common, and "empty" unspecified nodes will match anything). We therefore propose the following general advice (box).

None of the above should be taken to imply that you should *always* avoid the 'Different branches' or <unknown> options, or only use the 'Immediate parent' link. If you want to express a query consisting of two tightly-bound fragments linked by a loose relationship, the ability to specify that neither fragment dominates the other can be very useful. It is just a good idea to check that neither fragment is too general. Note that we distinguished between *exploration*, where you are trying to find example cases, and *experimentation* (see Chapter 9), where you are trying to *count* cases.

Just to prove this point, note that **Next child** is routinely set to <unknown> when you specify a *text fragment*. This kind of query is more like a 'comb' or 'hedge' than a 'tree'. Structure may be profitably modified by adding structure from the leaves toward the root (see Sections 5.4 and 5.11).

We can construct a two-element text fragment which finds cases of *this*

A general solution to the problem of underspecification

1. Eliminate all unnecessary empty nodes in the FTF, apart from where they preserve tree structure. Restrict nodes by introducing grammatical terms or text unit elements, but only where appropriate.
2. If you must have an empty node in your FTF, try to connect it directly to another, non-empty element, or to the root of the tree. You can insert an empty node safely if it is intimately bound to another node.
3. Failing that, specify the edge position of the node.

When you move from exploring the corpus to defining formal experiments, you may need to be stricter still. See Section 9.6.4.

Figure 142: A three-node text fragment and a matching case.

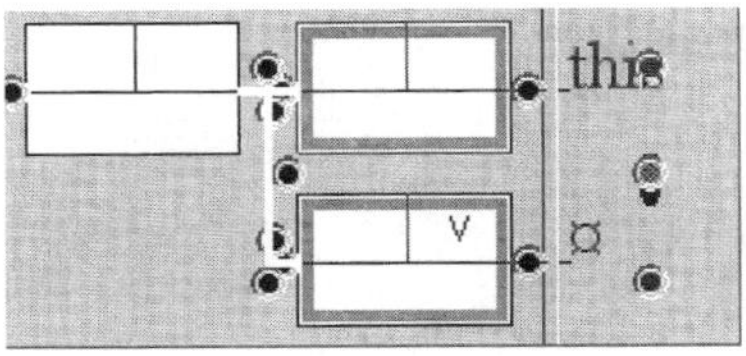

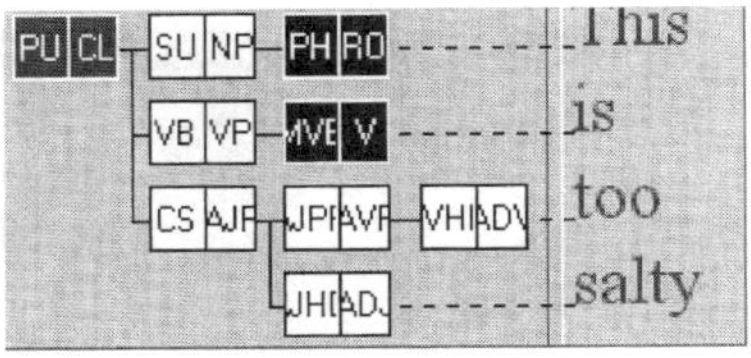

followed by a verb, as in "*This is* too salty." [S1A-010 #86].

➢ In the Text fragment window, type the word "**this**". Then, press <SPACE> and hit the 'Node' button. Position the input caret (blinking cursor) between the angled brackets and type "**V**". The query should look like this: "**this** <V>". Then press 'Edit'.

The FTF is shown in Figure 141, left. As expected, the upper node is the **Root** (matching the '**PU,CL**' element in the tree on the right); the nodes for *this* and the verb are leaves. **Parent** links are set to 'Ancestor' and **Next child** is <unknown>. The black 'Just after' arrow on the right hand side indicates that the verb must follow the word *this* immediately in the text sequence.

The FTF matches a series of examples, including the one in the figure. Although there is considerable ambiguity introduced on the tree side – empty nodes, ancestor links, unspecified **Next child** relations – the query is *not* at all underspecified (see above). One reason is that the nodes are bound to specific positions in the tree (root, leaf) and the 'Immediately after' link is employed. As a result, the leaf nodes are related to each other *via the sentence*, which dramatically reduces the ambiguity. A secondary point is that lexical items tend to be more specific than a simple node specification.

Setting up an FTF like this from scratch using the FTF editor requires some work, and it is easy to make mistakes (typically, forgetting to specify the **Root** or **Leaf** positions, as in Figure 141). However, as we have seen, the Text fragment command constructs queries like this very easily. You can then modify the query, for example, by adding superordinate nodes, but note that if you add elements you will need to set links appropriately.

5.14 The FTF Creation Wizard: a tool for making FTFs from trees

In the previous subsection we discussed how FTFs are matched against trees in the corpus. The beauty of FTFs is that it is quite easy to see how a tree-like query identifies cases in the corpus. Moreover, the matching process can be reversed. *We can take a tree and abstract a query from it.*

ICECUP includes a tool that can construct Fuzzy Tree Fragments from existing trees in the corpus. The *FTF Creation Wizard* extracts an FTF from the tree in the tree viewer. Hence you can perform a search, locate a construction in

Figure 143: Looking for candidates with a Text fragment query.

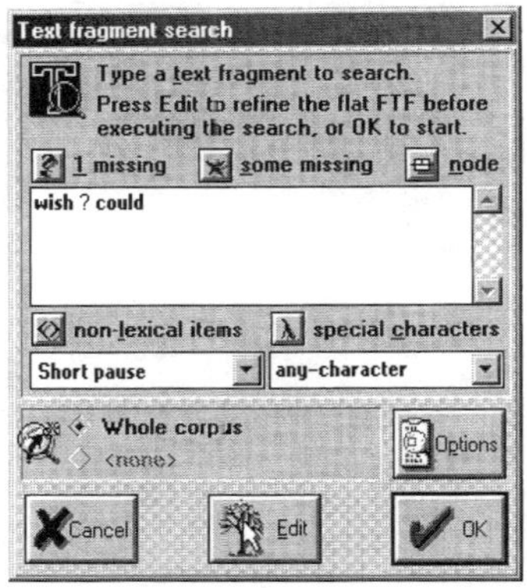

a text unit and extract an FTF from the tree in order to perform another search. The wizard completes the *exploration cycle* we mentioned in Chapter 4.

You can think of the way the wizard works as a two-stage process: *selecting nodes* and *selectively removing information* from these nodes. There are two kinds of wizard, which work slightly differently. The main difference is the way that they select nodes in the first place.

1) The original wizard, available in all versions of ICECUP, selects nodes from the branch of the tree below the current selection. It can 'prune' the tree according to a number of criteria controlled by the Wizard window.

2) A number of users found this confusing, however. So in ICECUP 3.1 we provided a second ('Version II') wizard that works slightly differently. Here the idea is that *you mark the nodes that you want to include first* and *then* request the wizard. ICECUP 3.1 uses the second approach if you first mark nodes in the tree.

In this subsection we discuss both of these approaches.

Let us motivate our discussion with an example. Suppose that we are interested in exploring clauses consisting of a subject, VP and direct object, where the direct object itself contains a subject and a verb. Consider clause (1).

(1) [$_{\text{SU}}$ *I*][$_{\text{VP}}$ *wish*][$_{\text{OD}}$ [$_{\text{SU}}$ *I*][$_{\text{VB}}$ *could swim*]]

Let's look for some examples of this kind of construction using the Text fragment search system.

➢ Enter "**wish** ? **could**" into the Text fragment window (Figure 143). The '?' is obtained using the "1 missing" button or by pressing <Alt> and '1' together. Do not type the question mark directly.

You should obtain five examples, all analysed in a very similar way. We can then use one of these cases to create a grammatical FTF.

Figure 144: Results of the text query (left), and an example tree (S1A-059 #19).

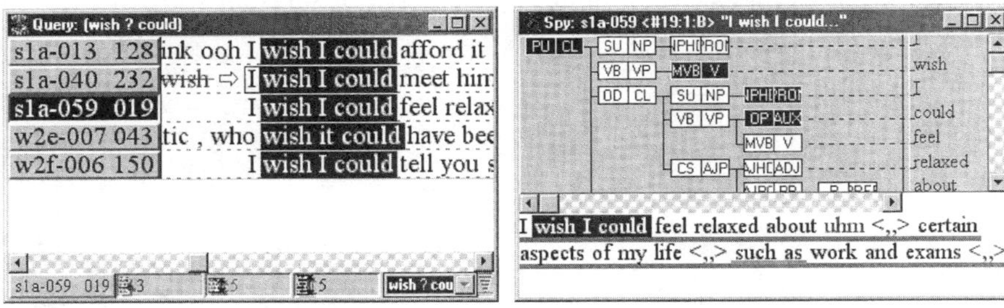

> Double-click on the sentence in S1A-059 #19 to open the tree window.

First we'll use the original Wizard. This will work in ICECUP 3.0. Suppose we want to create a grammatical FTF capturing the essentials of the three nodes under the clause – the subject, verb phrase and direct object. The simplest thing to do is to work from the clause down. To keep things simple we will not ask the Wizard to include features and work from the default settings.

> First, select the principal clause, which in this case is the highest node in the tree. Then press the Wizard button (or hit <F4>). The result is in Figure 145.

We must now decide on the number of levels of analysis to include in our FTF. This is controlled by the 'Prune tree' option in the Wizard. Figure 146 illustrates a number of FTFs that result from applying different degrees of pruning. The default, 1 (upper left), will just include the subject, VP and direct

Figure 145: The FTF Creation Wizard (initial settings, single selection).

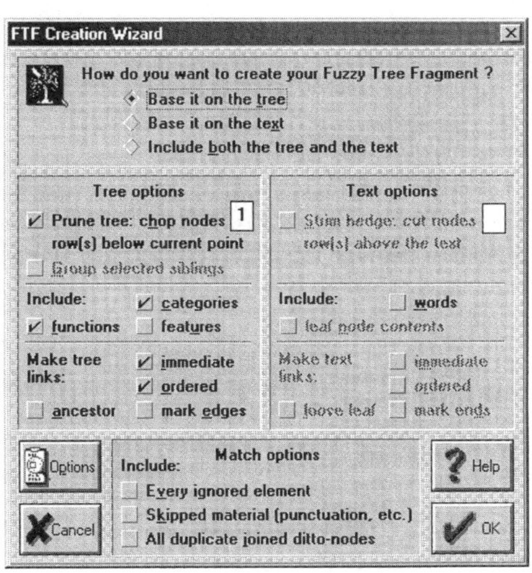

Figure 146: Applying the Wizard to the top of the tree in Figure 144 with different levels of pruning ('Prune tree' is set from 1 to 3).

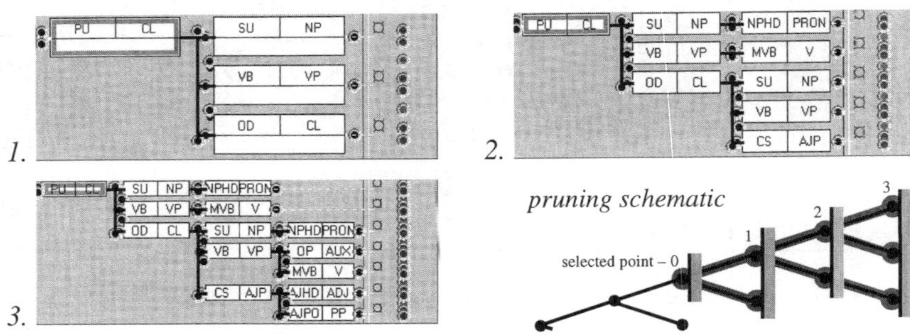

object nodes.[15] Setting 'Prune tree' to 2 will include the tag nodes for *I* and *wish* and the subject, verb phrase and subject complement nodes under the clause (upper right of Figure 146).

If 'Prune tree' is set to 3 (as in the lower part of the Figure) the next level is included. This level also includes the nodes which tag *I* and *could* as well as more analysis of the subject complement. As we are not particularly interested in this branch of the tree, we can stop here.

On the basis that it is easier to remove from than add to the FTF, we will prune the tree to level 3, and then strip all unwanted material out manually.

➢ Set Prune tree to 3, and hit OK. Maximise the FTF window to make editing easier.

We'll first remove the branch containing the subject complement.

➢ Click on the '**`CS,AJP`**' node, and hit <Delete>.

➢ The two children of the excised node, '**`AJHD,ADJ`**' and '**`AJPO,PP`**', move up a level to take the place of the subject complement. One of these nodes will be selected. Select these two children using the 'extend selection' method (see Section 5.10) and hit <Delete> again. Alternatively, delete them separately. When you have finished the FTF should look like Figure 147.

➢ At the moment the top of our fragment will only match parse units. However, we are interested in *any* clausal structure like this, regardless of its position in a tree. Select the parse unit (tip: press <Home> followed by <F2>) and set the function to <none>. The result is a relatively detailed fuzzy tree fragment. Press <F4> to start the search.

---

[15] It *could* also include the final '**`PAUSE`**' node in the tree, which is connected to the parse unit by the link dropping down the left hand side of Figure 144, right. However, the Wizard does not include 'skipped material' such as pauses by default, so it is excluded.

Figure 147: The lower FTF in Figure 146 (prune level 3), after removing the subject complement branch.

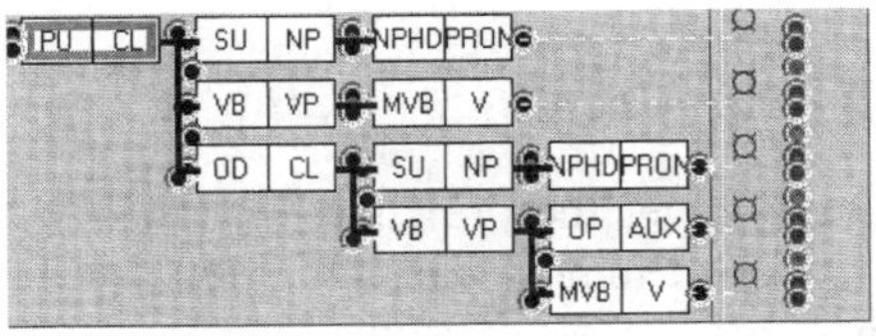

Figure 148: The FTF in Figure 147 after removing content from both verb phrases and allowing any element to be the head of either subject.

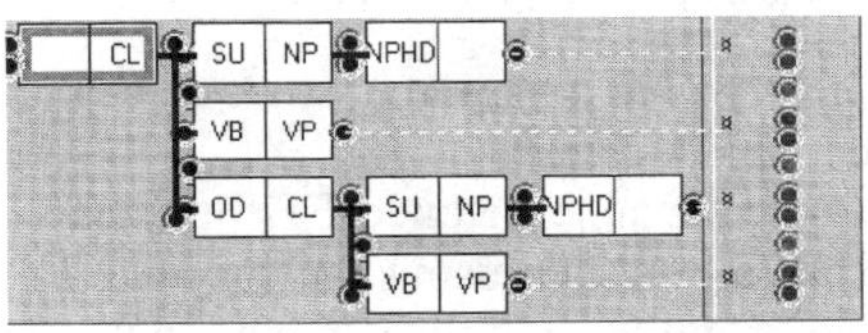

We obtain nearly 1,000 matching cases, including the four *I wish I could* examples in Figure 144.[16] The FTF doesn't match the following case. Why not?

(2) ...on both sides of the Atlantic, *who wish it could* have been different [W2E-007 #43]

On inspection, we can see that the example has an additional auxiliary (*have*) between the operator *could* and the main verb *been*. The simplest weakening of the FTF is to change the **Next child** link between the operator and the main verb to 'After' rather than 'Immediately after'.

> Select the auxiliary operator '**OP,AUX**' node, press down with the right mouse button in the grey space around the node, and choose '**Next: | After**' from the pop-up menu. Alternatively click once with the left mouse button on the **Next child** cool spot. Press <F4> again to see the results.

This FTF is more general than the one in Figure 147, and finds another 250 cases or so. We can continue generalising the FTF by weakening links, removing categories and functions, and removing elements.

Try the following.

> Delete both children under the lower VP (inside the direct object). Press <F4> again.

[16] To check, you may *drag and drop* the text fragment results into the FTF results (see Chapter 6). Minimise the text query results window (entitled '**Query: (wish ? could)**'), and drag it into the FTF results window. This will 'and' the two queries together, giving four matching cases but omitting case (2). To reverse the action, you need to open the Query editor in the combined results window (click on the 'Logical query editor' button, ''), locate the 'query element' in the left hand side logic editor, written '**wish ? could**', and use the mouse to drag the icon out of the window and into the space between the windows.

This obtains around 2,800 cases, *i.e.*, including another 1,600 where either node is absent: the auxiliary, as in (3) below, or, more rarely, the main verb, as in (4).

(3) *I think that* [$_{\mathrm{MVB}}$ *'s*] *fascinating* $_{\text{[S1A-002 \#28]}}$

(4) *but I don't think uhm that anybody else* [$_{\mathrm{OP}}$ *would*] $_{\text{[S1A-015 \#101]}}$

Removing the main verb under the principal verb phrase doesn't make much difference. We can, however, remove the limitation that the subject heads are realised by a pronoun.

- ➢ Go to each noun phrase head node in turn and set the category to <none>. The FTF should now look something like Figure 148. Press <F4>.

The additional 1,800 matches or so are almost all due to non-pronoun heads of the subject in the direct object clause.

We have constructed a quite detailed FTF in stages, starting from a tree fragment snatched from the corpus using the original *FTF Creation Wizard*. However, this method is quite complicated and potentially prone to error. Would not it be better just to indicate those nodes that we would like to include in an FTF, and then ask the Wizard to compose an FTF using these nodes?

ICECUP 3.1 includes a new 'Version II' wizard that works in just this way: composing an FTF from nodes that you marked yourself. With ICECUP 3.1, return to the original text fragment "**wish** ? **could**" query in Figure 144. If you are using ICECUP 3.0 you can skip the next couple of pages.

- ➢ Reopen the third example sentence in the list (S1A-059 #19). Now, with the right mouse button, click on the parse unit node, the subject of that clause and its head, the verb phrase node and the direct object, and then the subject, its head, and lastly, the verb phrase under the clause. Alternatively, select each node and press <Insert> or the 'Select for Wizard' button (Table 36). The result should look like Figure 149.
- ➢ Press <F4> or hit the large Wizard button.

As we have selected some nodes, ICECUP will use the Version II wizard.

- ➢ With the tree options set as in Figure 151 – Function and Category ticked, and 'Make tree links: immediate' set, and all other boxes unticked – hit OK.

Figure 149: Marking nodes in the tree (S1A-059 #19) for inclusion in an FTF.

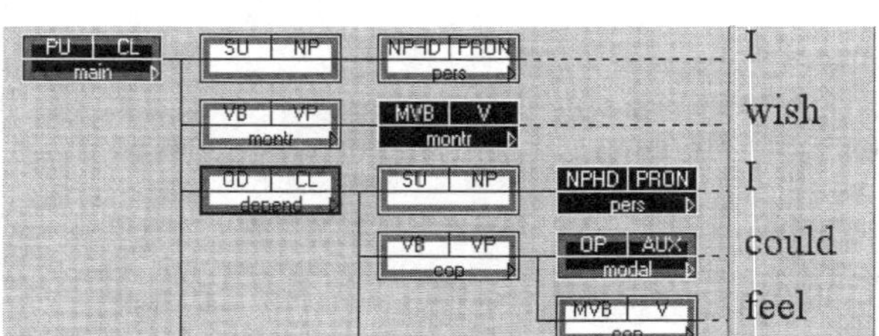

Figure 150: An FTF generated from the selected nodes in Figure 149.

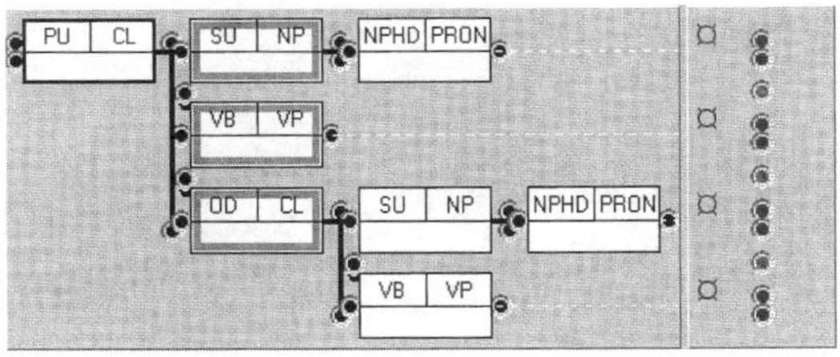

The result will be the FTF in Figure 150. You can easily modify this to match Figure 148 by clearing the function of the parse unit clause and the category of the pronoun NP heads.

The new wizard has another advantage. Nodes can be independently marked for inclusion, regardless of the structure between them. You can ask the wizard to retain the intermediate structure or to remove unmarked nodes and loosen the links between marked ones.

Suppose we repeat the FTF creation process, but this time we will not mark the uppermost verb phrase or direct object nodes.

> Go back to the marked tree window (S1A-059 #19), if it is still open. The tree should look like Figure 149. Unmark the '**VB,VP**' and '**OD,CL**' nodes just under the parse unit by selecting them with the right mouse button again or pressing ''. The result is shown in Figure 152. Alternatively, reopen the third example sentence in the list (Figure 144, left) and mark the nodes from scratch as per Figure 152. Finally, press <F4> to launch the Wizard.

Figure 151: Version II of the Wizard with options set for Figure 150.

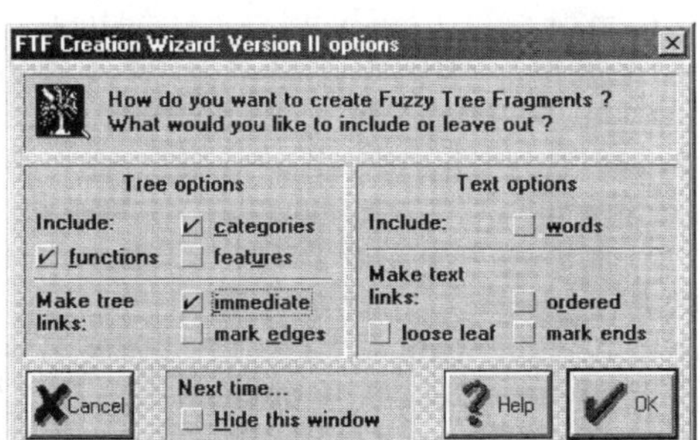

Table 36: Tree view command to select a node for the Version II wizard.

	name	keyboard action	menu command
	Select for Wizard	<Insert>	**Edit | Select Node (for Wizard)**

Figure 152: Marking some of the nodes in Figure 149 for inclusion.

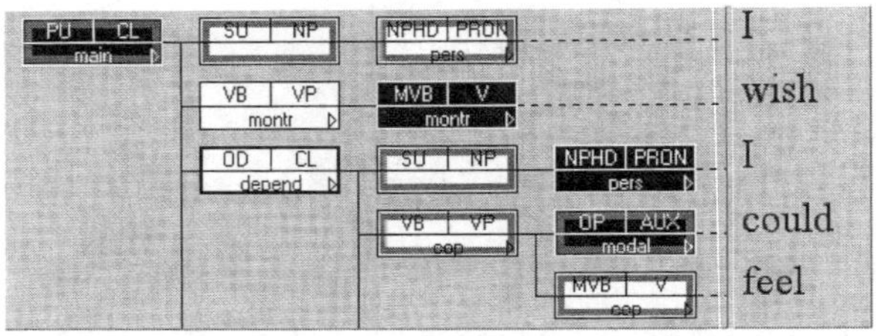

Figure 153: Resulting FTFs, with (left), and without intermediate nodes (right).

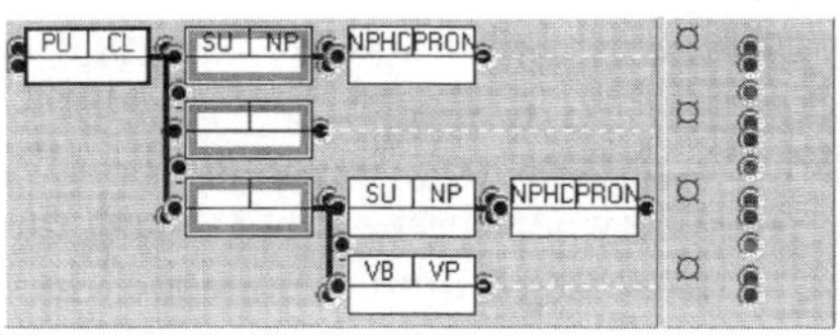

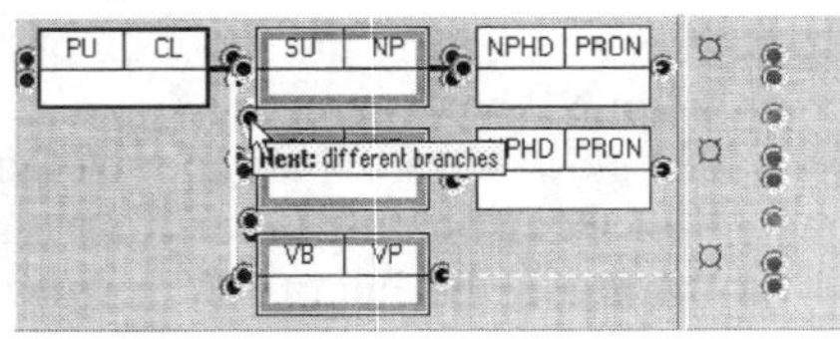

If you kept the Wizard II settings as in Figure 151, the resulting FTF is shown in Figure 153, left. If, on the other hand, you abandon the requirement to incl-ude intermediate nodes ('tree links: immediate' is unchecked), blank intermed-iates are removed and the links between marked nodes are weakened.

In this case you will obtain the FTF in Figure 153, right. The upper VP and the direct object clause node have been excised. The pair of nodes which were under the direct object (the VP and the subject NP) are now linked to the parse unit clause by 'eventual' links. These are linked by an 'immediately after' **Next child** link. On the other hand, the two subject NP nodes in the middle of the figure are kept apart by the presence of the highlighted '**Next:** Different branches' link. The three major sibling nodes are given the FTF focus. As we have mentioned, if you want to make a 'different branches' link order-depend-ent, set the **Next word** link on the right hand side to 'After'.

These wizard tools are extremely effective at composing grammatical FTFs from selected corpus material. This does not mean that such FTFs should not be edited prior to use. Any editing will tend to be to increase the generality of the FTF rather than to make it more specific. Material to be manually excised will typically be some features, where specified, and functions and categories at the extremities of the FTF (*cf.* Figure 148).

As well as creating grammatical FTFs using the Wizard, you can also build *text-oriented* fragments. This also works in ICECUP 3.0. Refer back to Figure 145 (page 169), which shows the initial settings of the original Wizard if a single node in the tree is selected. This wizard is divided into four panels. The uppermost panel contains three alternative choices: to base the FTF on the tree structure below the currently selected point, on the currently dominated text sequence, or on a combination of tree and text. In the example above, we simply skipped this choice and chose the default, to base the FTF on the tree. To end this section we will briefly examine these other two options.

The two middle panels – 'Tree options' and 'Text options' – specify what tree material to include. The availability of these options is dependent on the primary choice in the first panel. The bottom panel's choices specify whether to include ignored, skipped over and compound ('ditto-tagged') material.

The default 'Text' setting will create a multi-word Text fragment for the material under the current node. Note that if you have selected the top of the tree, as we did in Figure 144, you will get the entire sentence. You can easily delete nodes and words manually, however. Suppose we take a simpler example as a starting point, and select the nodes under the principal clause.

- ➢ Return to the original sequence of results. Select the second text unit (S1A-040 #232), and, if necessary, reopen the tree window.
- ➢ Next, select the three nodes – subject NP, VP and direct object clause (Figure 154, upper left) – and press <F4> or hit the 'Wizard' button.
- ➢ Select 'Base it on the text' in the upper panel of the wizard. By default this would construct an FTF containing just the word sequence. To include tags, select 'leaf node contents' and then tick 'category' and 'features'. The result is as shown in Figure 154, lower left.

This option also lets you include more material than would normally be possible in a text fragment. By default, all material more than one node up from the text is simply removed. However, by increasing the 'strim hedge' parameter, you can include structure above the tags.

'Pruning' removes material at a given distance below the current selection, whereas 'strimming' removes material at a specified distance above the

Figure 154: Using the original wizard to select textual material from the second text unit in the sequence of results in Figure 144 (left).

Three nodes selected in the tree

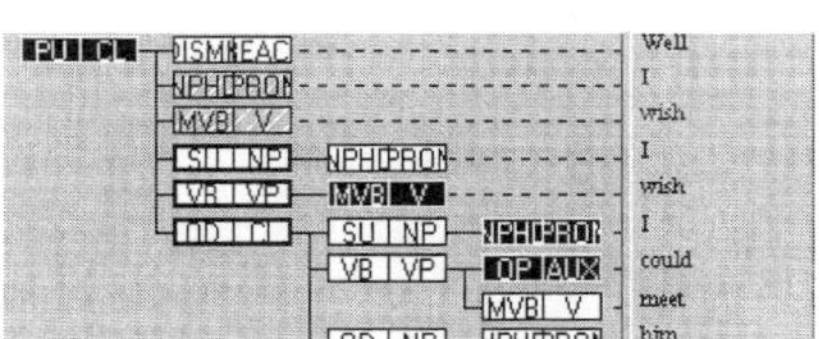

Strimming schematic

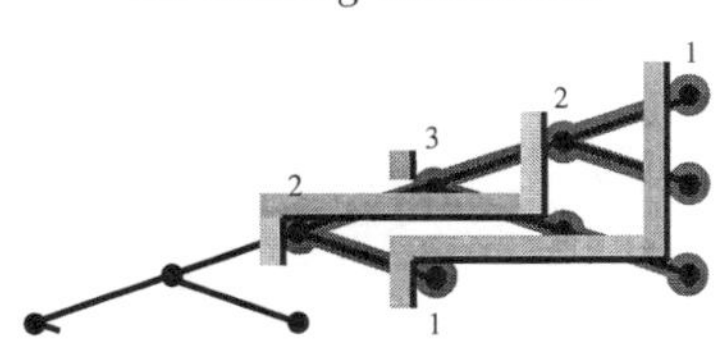

A 'text fragment' with tags (strim = 1)

A combined 'tree plus text' FTF

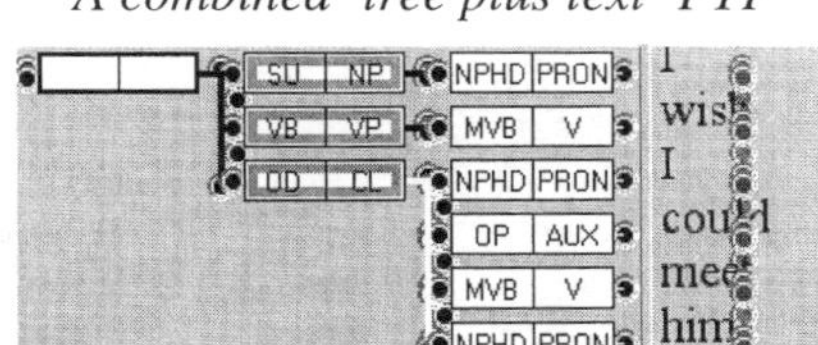

text. A prune depth of 2 means 'include material down to the grandchildren of the current node'; a strim height of 2 asks the wizard to include the parent of the leaf node annotating each word.

The last primary option is to construct an FTF based on both text and tree. While the first option works from the selected node or nodes down, and the second, from the sentence up, the third option combines both approaches by removing nodes that are too far from either the selected node(s) or the text. If a node is removed, the gap is bridged with 'eventual' links. Thus, in Figure 154, bottom right, the tag nodes for *I could meet him* are eventually connected to the direct object because their parent nodes (subject NP, verb phrase and direct object NP, *cf.* Figure 154, top left) have been stripped out.

This last FTF is constructed as follows.

> Locate the tree window. With the same three-node selection as before, press <F4> or Wizard. Select 'include both tree and text'. Set the prune depth to zero. Press OK.

This concludes our discussion of FTFs in ICECUP 3.0. (In Chapter 7 we introduce a number of enhancements to FTFs in ICECUP 3.1.) We have demonstrated how you can construct searches for lexical sequences using the Text fragment query command. Fuzzy Tree Fragments, on the other hand, search the grammatical analysis in the corpus. We have shown how text fragments can be defined in terms of FTFs, and how to construct FTFs from scratch. We have also explained how they match the corpus, what the links and edges mean, and how an FTF can be created from an example tree in the corpus. So far we have concentrated on the process of exploring the corpus, rather than experimenting with it. In the next chapter we discuss how FTFs can be combined with other queries, which is a necessity if we are to carry out research with ICECUP.

6. COMBINING QUERIES

If you have been working through Part 2 you should now be able to perform a variety of different queries. But what if you want to combine queries, *e.g.*, to search for a word in a particular part of the corpus, or compare the use of a particular grammatical construction across the sexes?

6.1 A simple example

A quick way to combine simple searches is to use the "apply to" option, common to all query windows, which is depicted by a 'magnifying glass and arrow' icon near the bottom of the window. This gives you a choice of applying the query to the whole corpus or a part (*e.g.*, the set of results in a browser window or a selected corpus map category). Figure 155 illustrates an (inexact) 'Node' search for '**`CJ,NP`**' being applied to the subtext S1A-002:1.

> Open the corpus map, and select this particular subtext (tip: first expand the map completely with '' or <Ctrl>+'4'). Then open the inexact Node search window (press the main command button or use the menu). Type '**`CJ,NP`**' and you will be given the option of applying the search to this subtext. Click on the small diamond-shaped button ('◈') labelled 'S1A-002:1' to select it.

Figure 155: Applying a node query to a subpart of the corpus.

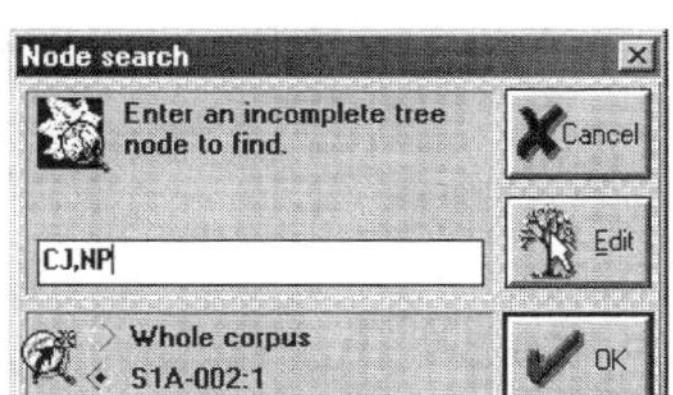

Figure 156: The results of the query in Figure 155.

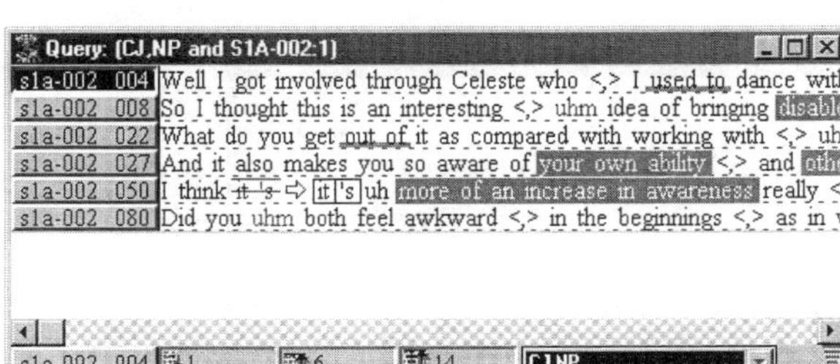

This produces a query results window as usual (Figure 156). The window looks similar to that produced by a standard nodal query, although there are not as many cases. The only hint is the title at the top of the window, which reads: "Query: (CJ,NP and S1A-002:1)". What are the brackets and the "and" for? Why not label this window "CJ,NP applied to S1A-002:1", which might be more intuitive?

Readers familiar with logic may hazard a guess. Behind the scenes, ICECUP uses logic. The expression means, find those text units which contain a '**CJ,NP**' node *and* are in subtext S1A-002:1. Brackets can be used to specify the order in which operators should be applied (see Section 6.3).

Propositional logic represents a state of affairs, rather than an explanation of how that state arose. Expressions like 'applied to' are opaque: they tell us more about what actions were performed rather than what the end result is. In logic, "*A* and *B*" is equivalent to "*B* and *A*". We say that 'and' is reversible. It is more difficult to see that "*A* applied to *B*" is the same as "*B* applied to *A*".

Many people have difficulty with logic, and for good reason. We don't naturally think in logic – on the contrary, logic has to be learned. Logic may often be unnecessarily complicated. Note, however, that we did not define anything formally in logic. We just applied a query to a subtext.

6.2 *Viewing the query expression*

We stated that logic operated 'behind the scenes' in ICECUP. Now, in order to proceed, we must peer behind the scenes ourselves.

In the bottom right corner of the query window, in the status line, you may notice what looks like a faint triangle pointing down (Figure 157). If you move the mouse pointer over this, it becomes an up/down black 'drag cursor'. This is a 'grip' that allows users to split the window horizontally.

> Click down with the left mouse button over the 'south cone' element and drag the mouse up the screen a short distance.

When you release the button, the display should be something like the window on the left of Figure 157. The top part of the window still displays the query

Figure 157: Revealing the query editor.

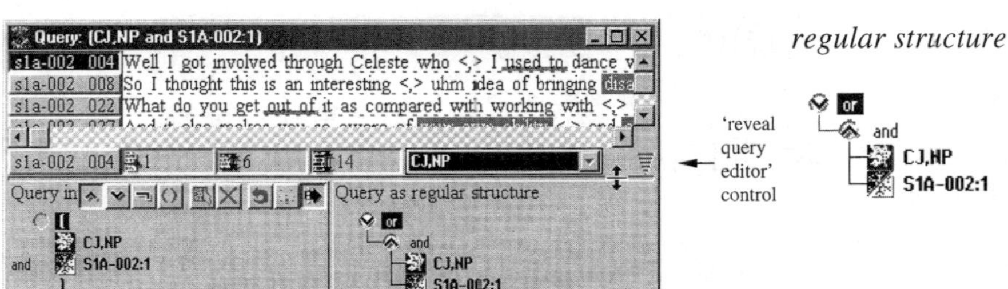

Table 37: ‘Show logical query’ command.

	name	keyboard action	menu command
	Show logical query	(none)	**Edit	Show logical query**

Figure 158: Query editor buttons.

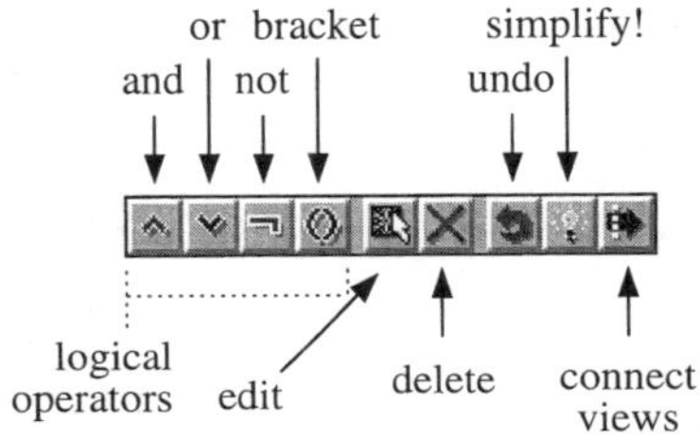

results. The area below the status bar is divided into two equal spaces. On the left is the query editor, which displays the query expressed in logic, with each row being occupied by either a single independent ‘query object’ or a bracket.

On the right is the same query, but this time it has been turned into a kind of ‘regular structure’,[1] looking rather like the corpus map. The regular structure, expanded on the right of the figure, is a “logical picture of the implications of your query”. Both views contain distinct query objects, shown as small labelled icons, with the graphic depicting the kind of query performed. So the *nodal* query is shown as a ‘leaf’ against a coloured background (the matching colour), while the *subtext* element appears as it does in the corpus map.

The editor allows you to manipulate these ‘query objects’ to form any logical expression. If you select the query editor part of the window with the mouse, you can use the cursor keys to select different elements in the query.

You can also reveal the expression with the ‘show logical query’ command (Table 37). The ‘Edit’ (or ‘Logic’ in ICECUP 3.1) menu contains the commands to modify the query, mirroring the buttons in the query editor.

Normally the query editor is hidden when you open a new query window. You can change this behaviour, which is useful if you are combining and adjusting queries a lot. Select ‘Corpus | Viewing options...’ and tick ‘Show query editor on opening viewer’ in the window (see Figure 173, page 188).

As well as the conventional query results button bar, the query editor also contains a set of buttons (Figure 158). These are quite simple. The first four are ‘logical operators’ that alter the logic of the query. We will consider these in the following section. The second pair act on the currently selected query

---

[1] Technical note: the “regular structure” is a *disjunctive normal form* (DJNF), that is, a standardised representation which consists of a set of alternate (ored) “disjuncts”, each of which is a set of co-occurring (anded) signed propositional elements. See Section 6.9.

*Figure 159: Two sets, A and B, and the effect of '**and**' and '**or**' – A* **and** *B, sometimes written 'A ∧ B' (left), A* **or** *B ('A ∨ B', right).*

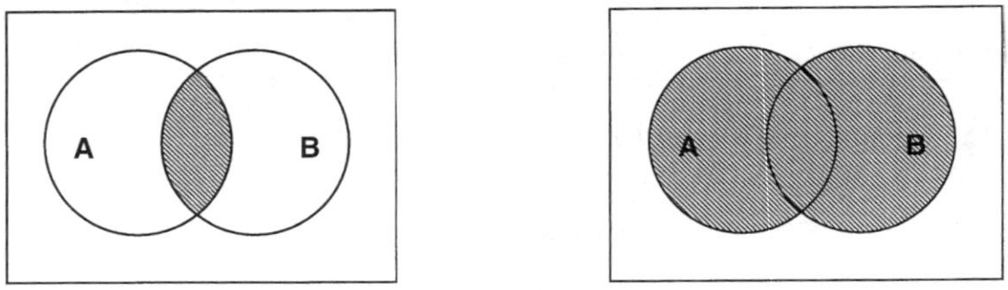

object: 'edit' and 'remove'. The last three perform miscellaneous tasks: 'undo', 'simplify' and 'connect views'.

6.3 Modifying the logic of query combinations

The query editor allows you to directly alter the logic of your query. This sounds intimidating, but is actually very simple in practice.

In this section we will look at the difference between 'and' and 'or'; negating an element, and the entire expression, with 'not'; and the role of brackets to control the scope of these three 'operators'. In the process we will have to examine how the query editor affects the viewed results.

First we will see how the 'and' in our query can be changed to an 'or'.

➢ Click on the query editor view. Select the subtext specification element. In Figure 157, this is labelled "S1A-002:1".

Note that this second element has 'and' written in the margin. This means that it is combined with the first using the logical operator 'and'.

When applied to corpus queries, 'and' calculates the overlap between the two sets (Figure 159, left). In our case, this means where cases of '**CJ,NP**' coincide with subtext S1A-002:1. 'And' is a 'mask' or *exclude* operator.[2]

➢ Now suppose we change the 'and' operator to 'or'. Click on the 'Or together' button

Table 38: 'And' and 'or' commands.

	name	keyboard action	menu command
	'And' together	'A'	**Edit | And together**
	'Or' together	'O'	**Edit | Or together**

[2] Logicians would say that 'and' "conjoins" two elements, or 'propositions', but we have avoided this term because it conflicts with the linguistic meaning of "conjoin".

Figure 160: Connections between the panels of the query window.

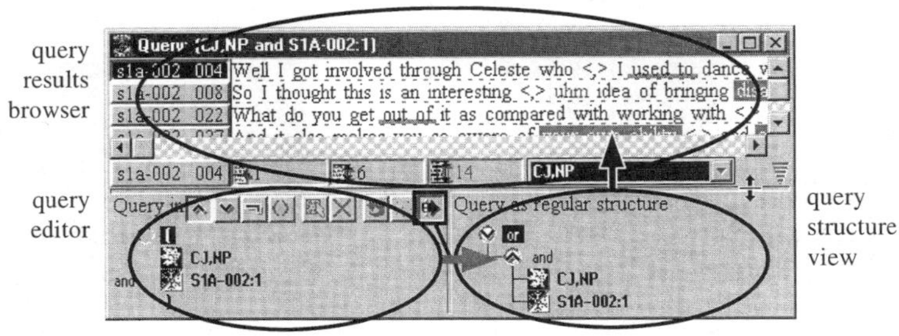

('') or select the subtext element and press the 'O' key.

This produces the set of cases where *either* A *or* B are true (the right hand diagram in Figure 159). The result is a much longer list, containing all the cases of '**CJ,NP**' in the corpus (including those in S1A-002:1), plus the rest of the subtext without the conjoined NP. 'Or', *i.e.*, inclusive-or, is a 'merge' or join operator. We discuss some of the implications of this below.

At the moment we are more concerned with the dynamics of the query editor. Every operation in the query editor has a series of consequences for the rest of the window. The query editor operates dynamically – changing the logic of the query changes the results of the query. You can therefore see the consequences of every edit action immediately. However, since the window has to reload the query results, the process can be slow (particularly if you are currently viewing a lot of results). You can turn this 'propagation' effect off temporarily, which is useful if you want to make a lot of changes.

- The rightmost button in the editor ('') is called 'connect views'. By default, this is on, *i.e.*, pressed down. Release it with a mouse click. Now if you make a change to the editor it will not be propagated through the rest of the window, except to the title.
- By way of illustration, press the 'and together' button (''). Now, reconnect the views with the 'connect views' button. The change you made will be propagated when you reconnect. Press 'or together' ('') again to return the view to Figure 161.

Figure 161: The query editor after combining query objects with 'or'.

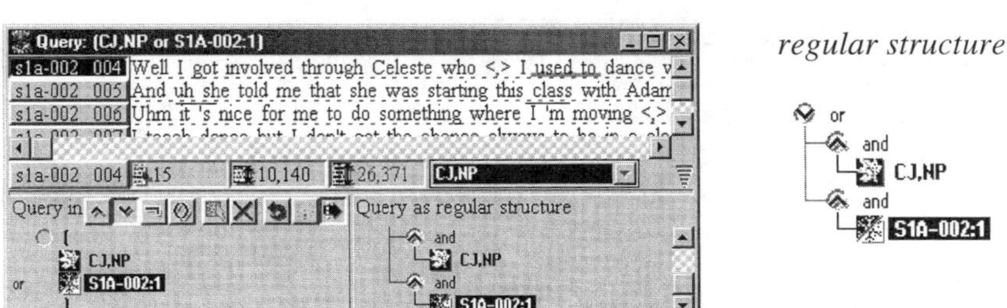

*Figure 162: Applying '**not**': "**not** A" (left), and an example of combining '**not**' with '**and**', "A **and not** B", written A ∧ ¬B (right).*

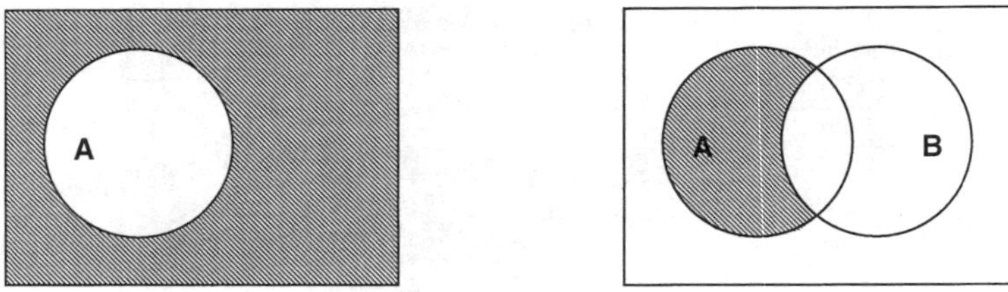

As we have seen, the title always summarises the current query being edited. When the 'connect views' button is down, the other two views are automatically updated (Figure 160), as follows.

1) The translated 'query structure view' on the right changes with every edit action. This panel describes, *as a set of possible alternatives*, how the corpus query results will appear. In the examples we have seen so far, the translation is very simple. In Figure 160, the view states that every line in the results must be a conjoined NP, a unit from the subtext, or both. Compare this to Figure 157, where the two elements are grouped together under the 'and' node in the structure and the cases must coincide.

2) The results browser at the top of the window changes automatically to conform to the query structure. This illustrates the impact of applying this structure to the corpus.

As well as combining queries with 'and' and 'or', you can invert queries with the 'Not element' button. This allows us to retrieve every text unit that *did not* match the element, and omit those that do. We are not usually interested in simple inversion (Figure 162, left), but it is occasionally useful to exclude cases by using a combination of 'not' and 'and' (Figure 162, right).

Try the following.

> Using the same query as before, switch the relationship between the two objects to 'and', using the 'And together' button (remember: the second of the two elements should be selected). Then click on the 'Not element' button.

*Figure 163: Excluding the subtext from the list of '**CJ,NP**' (cf. Figure 157).*

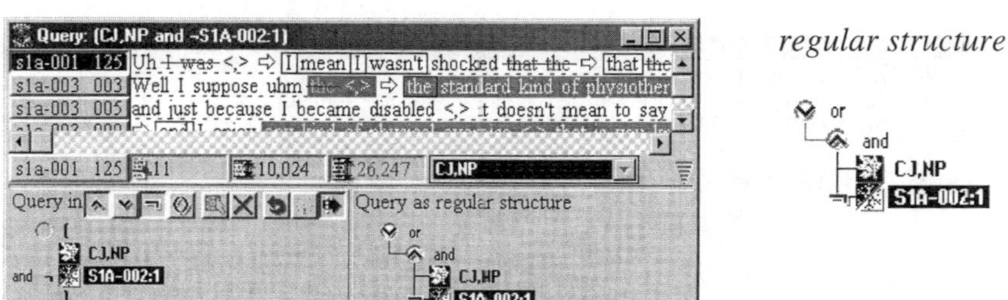

Figure 164: The subtext, excluding text units which contain a conjoined NP.

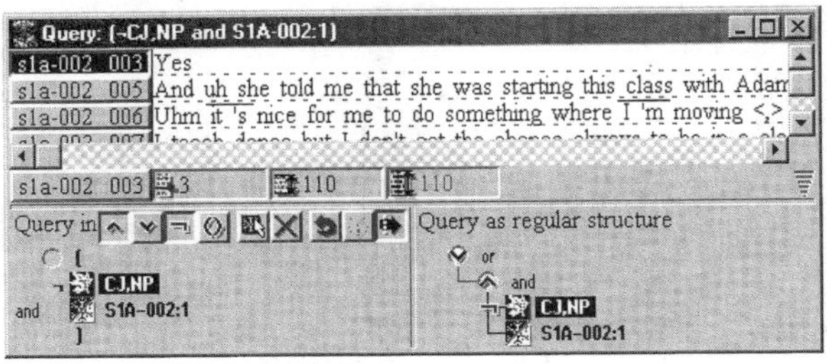

regular structure

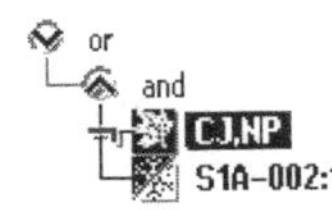

Table 39: The 'Not element' command.

	name	keyboard action	menu command
	Not element	'N'	**Edit | Not element**

'Not' only applies to a single query object, while 'and' and 'or' apply to a pair of objects. Figure 163 illustrates the consequences of negating the subtext query, S1A-002:1. A red *not* symbol ('¬') also appears in the regular structure to indicate that the element is negated.

Instead of negating the subtext, we could negate the little '**CJ,NP**' FTF.

➢ Press the 'Not element' button ('▭') again to remove the 'not' sign from the subtext element. Then select the conjoined NP and apply 'not' to it. The results are illustrated in Figure 164.

What happened? We generated a list of the part of S1A-002:1 that does not contain a match for '**CJ,NP**'.[3] The 'selector' in the status bar has been hidden. We will see what this control does later.

What happens if we invert the entire expression?

➢ Remove the 'not' from '**CJ,NP**' (press '▭' again). Then move the selection to the very first element in the expression – the opening bracket, depicted with a recessed circle icon. Press the 'Not element' button again. Figure 165 shows what happens.

Something rather radical has happened on the right hand side. The expression "not('**CJ,NP**' and S1A-002:1)" has been translated into "(not '**CJ,NP**' or not S1A-002:1)". This particular rule is called De Morgan's Law, and, as you should be able to see from Figure 166, the two expressions are logically equivalent. But why might we want ICECUP to do this?

---

[3] This logic operates on text units, not matching cases within them. Thus "S1A-002:1 ∧ ¬'CJ,NP'" is not the same as "S1A-002:1 ∧ '¬CJ,NP'". You can perform searches like the second one, where logic is employed within nodes of an FTF, in ICECUP 3.1.

Figure 165: After applying 'not' to the bracketted pair of queries.

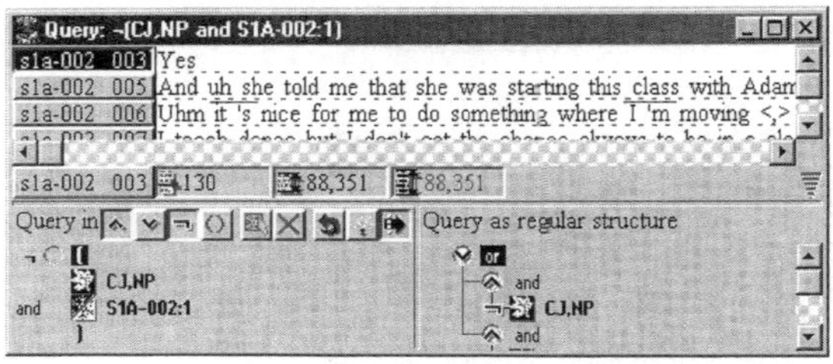

regular structure

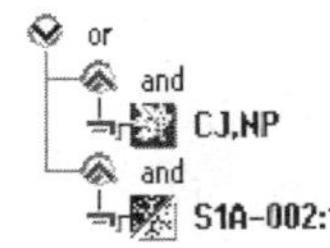

Figure 166: De Morgan's Law: **not** *(A* **and** *B) = (***not** *A* **or not** *B).*

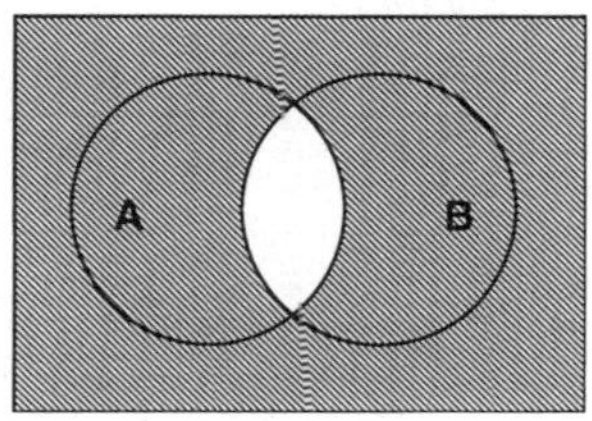

The answer is that *applying this translation ensures that we can identify the independent alternatives*: either a case must belong to "not '**CJ,NP**'" or "not S1A-002:1". However, the resulting expression is not very transparent.

The translation *limits the potential complexity of the result*, but it does not always make it simpler. Suppose you further negate an element, *e.g.*, the conjoined NP. FTF matches are revealed again because the '**CJ,NP**' object is now 'positive' (Figure 167). The new expression is equivalent to "('**CJ,NP**' or not S1A-002:1)". Section 6.10 discusses the translation process in more detail.

Bracketting affects the order in which elements are interpreted. So, "not (A and B)" is different from "not A and B". We may insert brackets around an element using the 'Bracket element' command.

> Press the '…' button with the conjoined NP object selected.

You can insert a series of brackets if you want, although there is usually little

Figure 167: Applying a double negative: in logic, two wrongs do *make a right.*

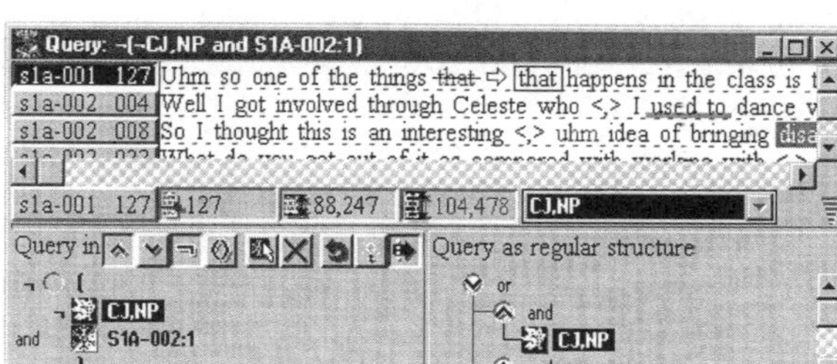

regular structure

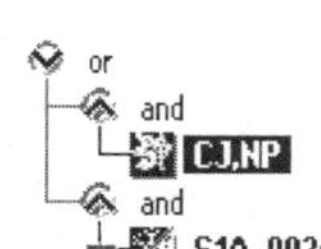

Table 40: Bracket element command.

	name	keyboard action	menu command
	Bracket element	<Insert>	**Edit | Bracket element**

Figure 168: Inserting a bracket around the conjoined NP.

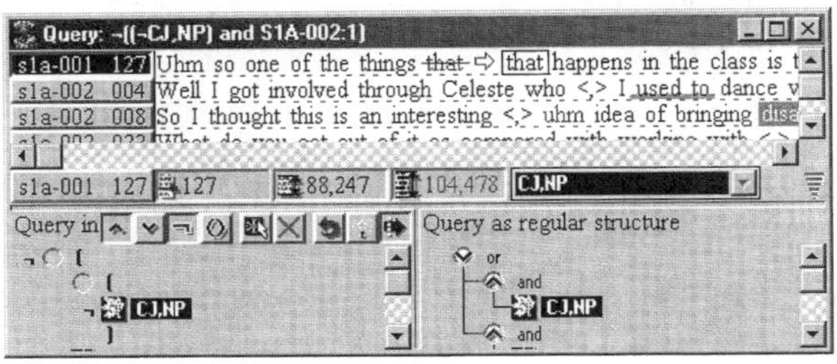

point (Figure 168). The act of inserting a bracket does not change the logic of the expression. "A", "(A)" and "((A))" are all equivalent. Rather, brackets help you ensure that operators are applied in the right order. They are essential for composing complex expressions. You can remove the bracketting that you have inserted by pressing 'undo' (' , or <Alt> and <Backspace> together).

6.4 *Using drag and drop to manipulate query expressions*

ICECUP uses a powerful "drag and drop" system to move 'query objects' around the query editor and between windows. Drag and drop allows you to 'pick up' a query object and move it to another location or another window, or drop it in the space between windows, in which case you gain a new window.

> First, remove any added brackets and negation signs (perform 'undo' a few times if it is easier). The expression should now read "('**CJ,NP**' and S1A-002:1)".

> Next, move the mouse over the '**CJ,NP**' leaf icon in the query editor. Press down with the left mouse button, and drag the cursor away from this point.

*Figure 169: Dragging a copy of the '**CJ,NP**' object in the query editor.*

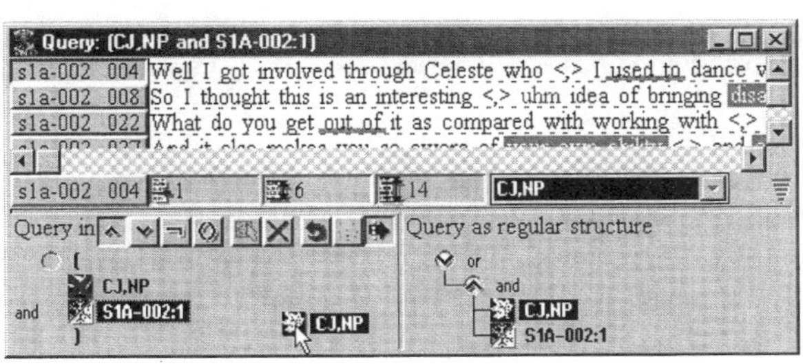

When dragging, take your time: a brief delay is imposed in order to avoid dragging elements by mistake. A red cross is drawn over the original '**CJ,NP**' in the window, meaning that it will be removed when you drop the object.

You can choose to copy, rather than move, the object by pressing the <Ctrl> ('Control') key. If you press <Ctrl> when you drop the element a copy will be placed at the target location. The red cross appears and disappears depending on the status of the <Ctrl> key. The status is used when you release the mouse button and drop the object.

➢ Drag the object over the subtext element. The current selection in the query editor will change as you drag the element over it. This lets you choose where in the expression the element will be dropped. Keeping the mouse inside the query editor and holding <Ctrl> down, release the button when the mouse is over the subtext.

The result should look like Figure 170. You can scroll the query editor window to see the new element. Note that this hasn't caused any change to the query results because in logic, "A and A" is equivalent to "A".

What happens if you...

1) Do the exact same operation as above, but without holding down <Ctrl>?
2) Drag the element to another point within the window but outside the query editor?
3) Drag the element outside the window into the blank space between windows (you may need to reorganise your windows to do this)?
4) Drag the element into another query window?

Make sure you hit 'undo' after each action. The results are as follows.

1) The two objects swap position in the sequence. Note that dropping an element onto a target object places the dragged element *after* the target.
2) The dragged element is 'anded' together with the entire query. If the source object was marked for removal, it is removed before the query is joined. The query is then tidied up by removing single brackets. In this case, if <Ctrl> is not pressed, the result is as point (1) above. Otherwise it reads "(('**CJ,NP**' and S1A-002:1) and '**CJ,NP**')". Both results are logically equivalent to the original, so no changes are propagated.

Figure 170: After dropping the object over the subtext.

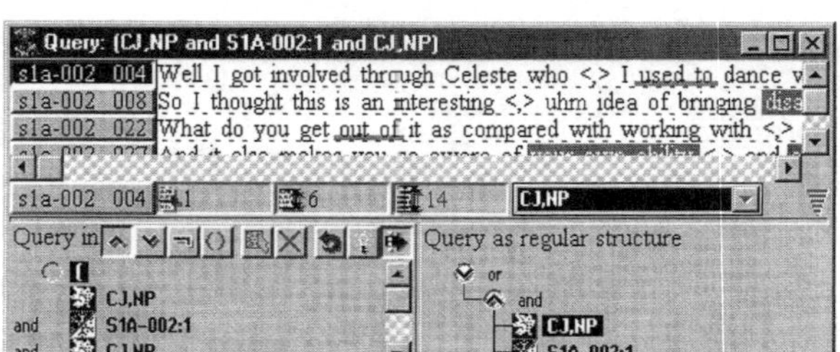

3) The query object opens a new query window containing that object. If it was marked for removal, it is deleted from the source query editor.

4) The query object is introduced into the target query. If you drop it into another open query editor, you can control how it is introduced as before. If you drop the object elsewhere in the window, the query will be introduced by the method summarised in point (2). The source element is deleted as specified.

Point (3) above duplicates the branch of a query. This action can also be performed by the large 'Duplicate' button on the command bar (or <F4>) provided no search is currently being performed in the window.

When the object you have selected is the only element within a pair of brackets, or when it is the only object in the query editor, ICECUP will not remove the from the window. You can still delete a bracketted group or close the window. You can also drag and drop a bracketted group of elements by selecting the initial bracket surrounding them.

➢ Click on the recessed circle icon and drag it as you would any single query object.

A slightly different way of performing drag and drop is to drop a 'minimised' query window into an open browser. However, in this case you cannot control how the query is inserted. Instead, queries are combined with the standard 'and together' join procedure as before. The original window is removed.

➢ Try a simple text search, *e.g.*, for the word *interesting*. Then minimise the window, and drag it into another query window.

This is effectively the inverse action to picking up elements and dropping them in the space between the windows, which causes a window to be created and deletes the original.

A third type of drag and drop works with the corpus map, lexicon or grammaticon (see Chapter 7). This is very similar to dragging elements from a query editor, except that the corpus map may not be modified. After you have become used to using drag and drop, it may feel more natural than the normal 'Browse' method.

Figure 171: Dragging a minimised query window into an open query.

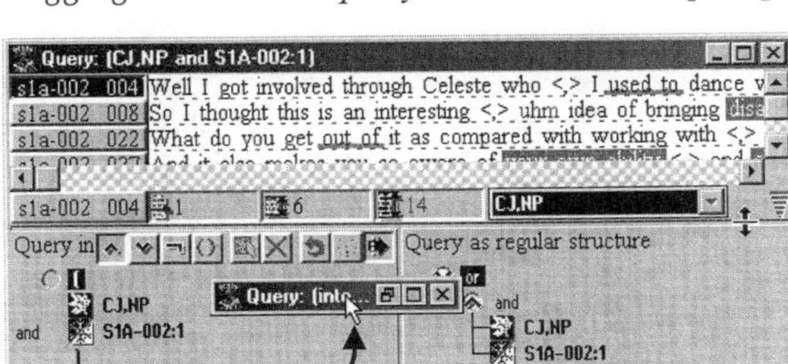

Figure 172: Dragging an element from the corpus map into a query editor.

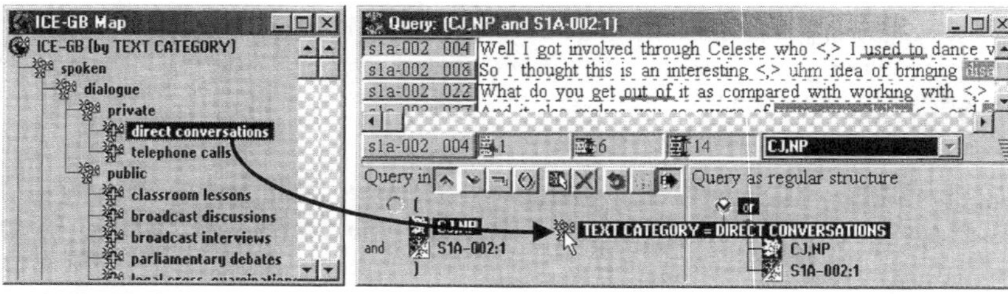

- To use drag and drop with the corpus map, first ensure that it is not in the default 'maximised' view. You will need to be able to drag objects out of the window.
- Click and hold the mouse on an icon in the corpus map, and drag it into another query window (Figure 172) or into the space between windows.

This works as if the corpus map was a query viewer:

1) You can open a new window by dropping the element outside an existing window.
2) You can join the element to the entire expression with 'and' by dropping it in any part of the query window apart from the query editor.
3) You can insert the element at a precise point by dropping it in the query editor.

Drag and drop is a powerful way of combining elements on the desktop. It is quite easy to make a mistake, particularly when dragging a minimised window into an open one. You can recover by dragging the inserted element out of the window. You *can* use the 'undo' operation ('') to reverse the effect of an action on a window, but be careful: undo applies to every window independently. It will not recreate a lost window, just delete the inserted elements.

If you are performing a number of logical operations you can ask ICECUP to automatically open the query editor when a new browser window is opened. Select 'Viewing options' (Figure 173) from the 'Corpus' menu and tick "Show Query editor on opening viewer."

Figure 173: Making the query editor automatically open by default.

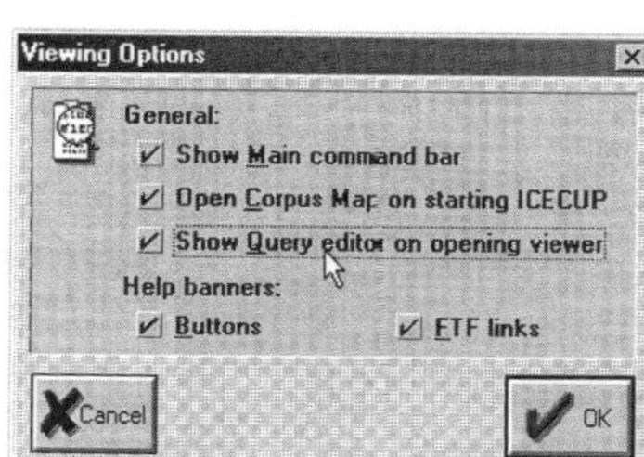

6.5 *Removing parts of the query*

You can remove both single elements and bracketted expressions from a query expression very simply. To remove a single element, just select it and press the <Delete> key or click on the 'Remove branch' button (Table 41). As we mentioned, you are prevented from removing the last element in a query.

To remove a bracketted group of nodes, move to the opening bracket and press <Delete>. 'Undo' ('') will reverse the action.

> Try selecting an element and removing it, and then reversing the action.

This 'remove' command provides a quick way of 'tidying up' unwanted elements in a query. However, it is easy to make mistakes. To preserve the logical integrity of a query, but simplify its structure, use the 'Simplify' command instead (see also Section 6.10).

Table 41: The remove branch command.

	name	keyboard action	menu command
	Remove branch	<Delete>	**Edit | Remove branch**

6.6 *Logic and Fuzzy Tree Fragments*

Fuzzy tree fragment queries, whether simple or complex, are drawn silhouetted against a coloured background, coloured by the *match colour* for the FTF. ICECUP generates a new colour for every new FTF: first dark brown, then blue-green, *etc.* Eventually ICECUP runs out of distinct colours and begins again. It displays every match against the FTF in this match colour. Secondly, the query object may be shown as a 'nodal' leaf (''), a 'text fragment' capital letter T ('') or a general FTF (''), depending on how an FTF was created.

> Suppose we construct a query consisting of two FTFs. Create a window containing '**CJ,NP**' and the single-word Text Fragment query "**interesting**". By now you should be able to obtain a window like Figure 174 without much difficulty.

Figure 174: Two simple FTFs joined by 'and' in a query window.

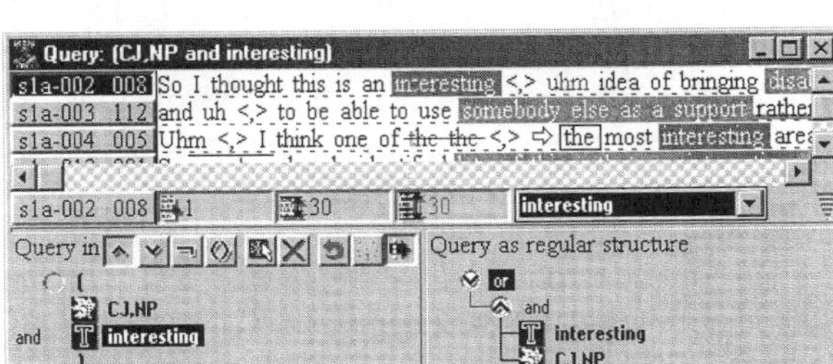

*Figure 175: Concordance view of ('**CJ,NP**' and "**interesting**"), focused on '**CJ,NP**' (left), and "**interesting**" (right).*

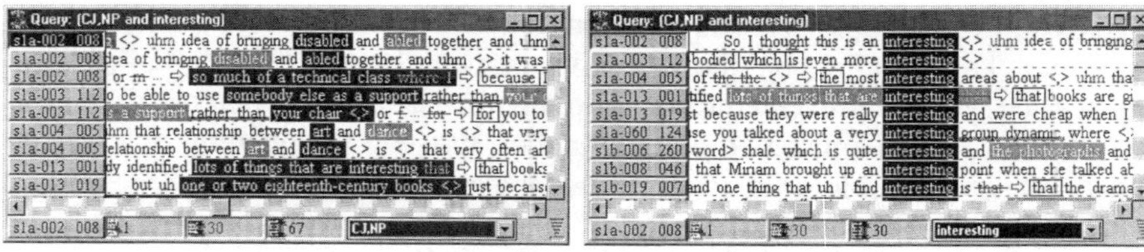

➢ Now, click on the concordance button in the menu bar ('', or <F2>) to switch to one of the concordance views. Reveal the number of hits per text unit by clicking on the 'Number of matches' button ('', or press <Shift> and <F2> together).

➢ Finally, hide the query editor by dragging the division line down or using the menu command 'Edit | Hide logical query'. The window should look like Figure 175, left.

Up to now, we have taken the presence of the pull-down selector in the status bar (see Figure 175) for granted. This selector determines the query element to focus on when displaying the concordance.

Recall that our query is joined together by 'and'. This means that we must have *at least one* match from *both* FTFs in every text unit. Since we can only concordance one of these at a time, we have a choice of focus. This choice is made using the selector.

➢ Click to open this selector and pick "**interesting**". The display will change to suit (Figure 175, right).

Notice that the two lists have different lengths. This is because in ICE-GB there are only 30 cases of *interesting* (in 30 text units) which have a conjoined NP in the same unit. On the other hand, there are 67 conjoined NPs to be found in these 30 text units (Figure 175, left). As a result, changing the choice of focus element may alter the number of cases as well as reorganise the view.

What happens if you concordance two 'ored' FTF elements?

➢ Reveal the query editor, select the "**interesting**" object and press the 'Or together' button (''). Figure 176 (left) shows the result.

The window now shows *two* pull-down selectors, one for each FTF, and a much longer list. If you hide the query editor the window looks like Figure 176, right.

The concordance view focuses on both FTFs together. Recall that the query demands that at least one of the FTFs must appear in the results. Each match, therefore, forms a distinct independent case to be concordanced. Thus text unit S1A-002 #8 includes a number of cases matching the first FTF ('**CJ,NP**'), which appear first, followed by the second FTF ("**interesting**"), which appears next. Note that this ordering takes precedence over the position of these

*Figure 176: Concordance view of (‘**CJ,NP**’ or “**interesting**”) – with the query editor revealed (left), and after it has been hidden again (right).*

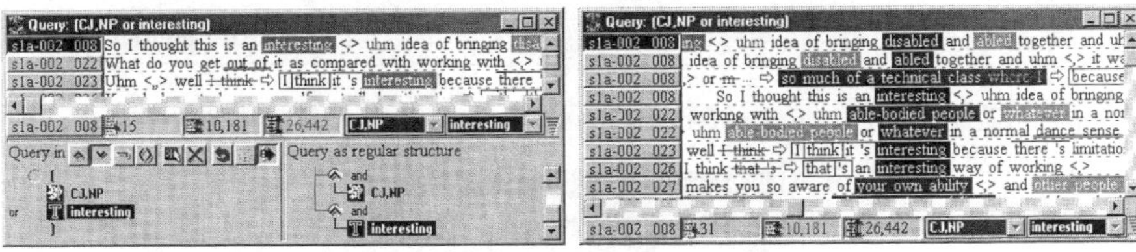

matches in the tree. Unit 8 is followed by unit 22, which only matches the first FTF, and 23, which only matches the second.

You can use drag and drop logic to explore combinations of FTF queries. As we have stressed, this kind of logic operates on *text units*, not FTF cases. If you need to perform experiments with corpora (see Chapters 8 and 9), you must make sure that you count cases correctly.

The FTFs in our example above were arbitrary. In practice, ‘and’ is typically employed to *subdivide* a single FTF and ‘or’ to *join* subcategories together. Since FTFs are essentially conjunctive, it is relatively easy to combine two FTFs with ‘and’. The intersection between ‘**PU,CL**’ and ‘**CL(main)**’ is ‘**PU,CL(main)**’. Likewise, the intersection between a subject clause and a clause in the first position of a set of child nodes is a subject clause in the first position. However, it is rather more difficult to introduce ‘or’ and ‘not’ into nodes, and this is not supported in ICECUP 3.0. However, ICECUP 3.1 (see Chapter 7) does allow you to specify the following:

- A node that is *either* a subject *or* a clause (written ‘**(SU, or ,CL)**’).
- A noun phrase head that is *not* a pronoun (‘**NPHD,{~PRON}**’).
- A node that is *either* a pronoun *or* a noun (‘**,{PRON,N}**’ or ‘**(,PRON or ,N)**’).
- An intensifying *or* exclusive adverb (‘**ADV(inten,excl)**’). (This is equivalent to ‘**(,ADV(inten) or ,ADV(excl))**’ because ‘**inten**’ and ‘**excl**’ are both members of the same set and only make sense as a disjunction.)

6.7 *Editing query elements*

You can adjust the contents of a query object without modifying the rest of the expression. To edit a query object, such as a text fragment query or FTF, you can either double-click with the left mouse button on the element in the query editor, or press the ‘Edit element’ button in the query editor.[4]

---

[4] Hint: you can use this command to resample a random selection from the corpus by editing a ‘random sample’ element.

Table 42: Edit element command.

	name	keyboard action	menu command
	Edit element	(none)	**Edit | Edit element**

Figure 177: Editing a query element using the inexact 'Node' window.

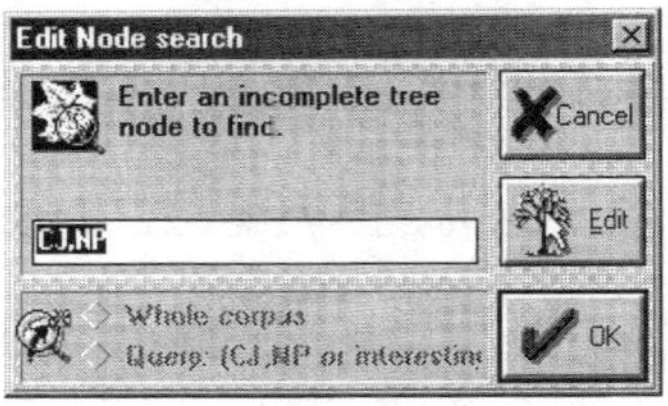

➢ Reopen the query editor with the 'show logical query' button. Now double-click on the label of the '**CJ,NP**' element, or move the current position over it and click on the 'Edit element' ('') button.

The dialog box that appears lets you edit the existing element or cancel without making any changes. You cannot change the basic query *type*, *e.g.*, an FTF into a variable query. The 'apply to' option (see Section 6.1) is disabled.

Query elements are created by simple query windows (Chapter 3), the corpus map, lexicon, grammaticon and the FTF editor. ICECUP also inserts *text* ('') and *subtext* ('') elements, equivalent to those in the corpus map, when you perform a 'browse text/context' command (see Section 4.9). (In addition, ICECUP 3.1 creates a user-definable *selection list* element, '', described in Section 4.12, but these are edited by selecting text units). As a consequence, the process of modifying an existing query depends on the element. Essentially, there are three different ways to modify individual query elements in ICECUP.

1) **The 'query window' method**. This is used for *Variable*, *Exact* and *inexact Node*, *Markup*, *Random sample* and *Text fragment* queries and is straightforward, as we have seen. FTF-based queries (*Node*, *Text fragment*) may be converted into general FTFs by pressing 'Edit'. This invokes the 'FTF editor' method (2).

2) **The 'FTF editor' method** is described below. This is used for general FTFs and simple FTF-based queries that have been converted into FTFs as above.

3) **The 'corpus map' method**, new to ICECUP 3.1, works for *Corpus Map*, *Grammaticon* and *Lexicon* entries. In ICECUP 3.0, corpus map elements are treated as *Variable* queries, and are altered by method (1) above.

To see how the FTF editor method works, suppose we want to edit the existing conjoined NP element as an FTF and extend it.

➢ Double-click on the '**CJ,NP**' icon or press '' ('Edit element'). Then press 'Edit' in the 'node' query dialog window to create a new FTF.

Figure 178: Inspecting a link: the 'first child' status of the node.

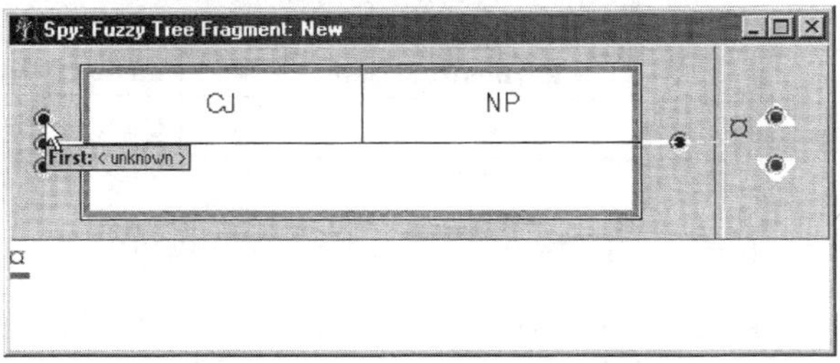

Let us suppose that we are only interested in conjoined noun phrases in initial position. We perform this very simple adjustment by changing the **First child** status of the node (see Figure 178) to 'Yes' by clicking on the cool spot with the mouse (twice with the left button or once with the right).

Note also that the title bar of the FTF starts with "Spy:". This means that the FTF is connected to the query viewer, like the spy tree windows. If we close the FTF, ICECUP will ask us if we wish to update the results.

Alternatively, we can update the results ourselves, without closing the FTF. Simply press <F4> or the 'Update!' button to update the query results. The 'Update!' button replaces 'Start!' in the command bar.[5]

The difference between 'Update!' and 'Start!' is that when you press the button, the edited FTF is sent to an existing query window to replace a previous FTF element, rather than being used to create a new window. In effect, this is what 'OK' does in the 'query window' method.

Due to the additional 'edge' setting, the search has to be recalculated in the background, so the entire list doesn't appear immediately. As usual, starting this search stops any other background search that may be running.

As we have commented, the process works by employing an implicit link between the editor window and the viewer showing the results. If you wish, you can 'disconnect' this link by separating the FTF editor from the text viewer. You do this by selecting 'Disconnect query' in the FTF editor (Table 43). You can then start a search in a new window as before.

Finally, a warning is due. When switching between two connected editors, it is easy to get confused between the effect of the 'undo' button in the FTF editor and the equivalent button in the query editor. Note the following.

- 'Undo' in the query editor after an 'Update!' command will revert to the situation prior to the update.
- 'Undo' in the FTF editor will reverse the previous editor action.

---

[5] If you were to reselect 'Edit element', you would be presented with this FTF editor window, not the original dialog box. The FTF editor and the query browser are now linked.

Table 43: FTF editor command to break the link between the editor and the query results viewer, preventing future updates.

	name	keyboard action	menu command
	Disconnect query	<F3>	**Query | Disconnect query**

6.8 Modifying the focus of an FTF during browsing

If you use 'Edit element' to modify a general Fuzzy Tree Fragment, the FTF will open in a new window. Typically, when you update the query browser, you cause ICECUP to start a new search.

The exception is when you modify the FTF focus, which we first discussed in Section 5.10. The FTF focus determines the material that should be highlighted in the query browser, and how concordance is determined, but it doesn't alter the actual content of the search. We can change the FTF focus in a spy window and press 'Update!' to set it in the connected browser, without having to restart the search or open a new window.

To demonstrate this, we will use the example FTF we constructed in Chapter 5 (see Figure 180, upper right, for a recap). If you worked through the previous chapter you should be able to reconstruct this fairly quickly. The element between the subject NP node and the word *I* is blank, a single child, and intimately connected to the lexical item and the NP node.

- ➢ Press 'Start!' to initiate the FTF search. Then press <F2> a couple of times to concordance the display centrally, and open the query editor. The window should look like the one in the upper left corner of Figure 180.
- ➢ With the query element revealed, you can now edit the element. This opens a second FTF editor, connected to the query window and marked with "Spy:" in the title (Figure 180, upper right).
- ➢ Now to change the FTF focus, and thus the concordance display. In the FTF editor, you move to the node (or nodes) you wish to concordance, hit 'mark FTF focus' (' '), and then 'Update!' to transfer the changes.
- ➢ Move the focus to the subject NP node (Figure 180, lower left) and press 'Update!' again. The results are shown in Figure 180, lower right.

We can continue to adjust the FTF focus, or modify the search, while the spy window is open. The important point to remember is that you have to press 'Update!' to bring the query window into line with the FTF in the editor.[6]

---

[6] When an FTF editor is connected to the query window, its query object (the FTF) is visualised in the query editor. We could have chosen to automatically update the query from the FTF editor, just as the tree viewer is maintained by the current selection in the results

Figure 179: Summary: three connected windows and the query editor.

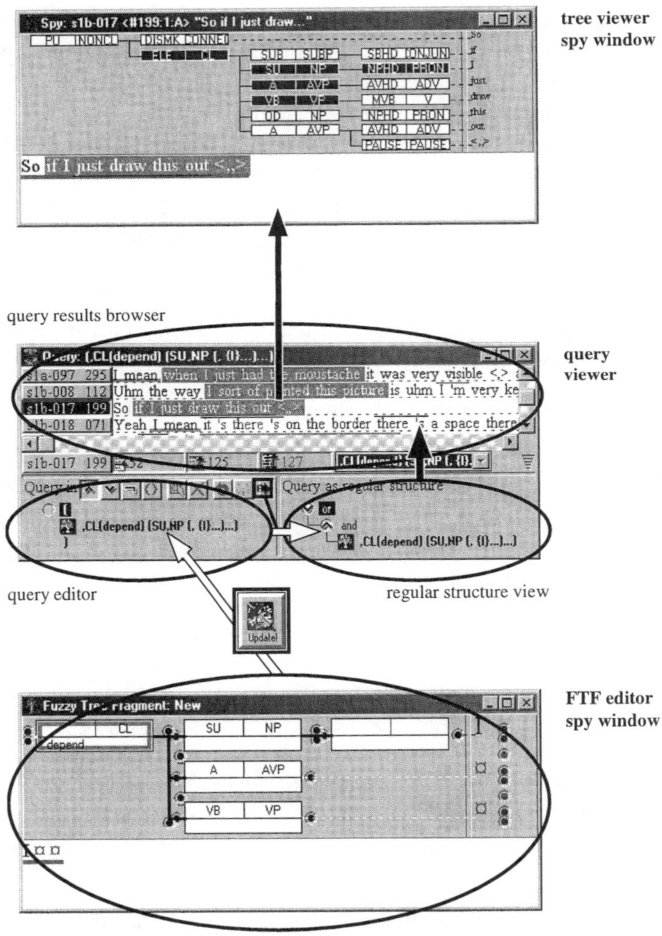

This 'update' process is the first link in a chain of connections that may connect an FTF editor, through the results browsing window, to a single view of the results of a query. This chain is illustrated in Figure 179. The connection between these three windows is an extension of the connection between the three panels of the query window (see Figure 160, page 181).

browser. However, this would mean that every adjustment to the FTF could cause a background search to restart with consequences for ease of editing, *etc.*

6.9 *Background FTF searches and the query editor*

Fuzzy Tree Fragment searches are often performed as *background* searches (see Section 3.9), that is, they take some time to process and operate in the background. This places a number of constraints on how you work with the query window, and the query editor especially.

In the query editor, incomplete queries are indicated by a ‘broken’ element icon (either ‘’ or ‘’). They are also indicated in the status line by the progress gauge in the pull-down selector. This guage shows the proportion of the candidate set processed (*e.g.*, ‘this was’). Finally, the title of the window also states whether the search is progressing or is stopped but incomplete.

What happens if you perform a background search for an FTF *when it is not the only element* in a query? This could happen in a number of ways.

1) A non-trivial text fragment search is applied to another set of results.
2) A new element is dropped into the window receiving the results of a search.
3) The logic of a query expression containing a sought after element is modified during the search process. For example, suppose a sought for query element is negated.
4) An unfinished query is combined with an interrupted query, and then ‘Continue’ is pressed to resume the background search process.

Note that a background search is *a complete search of the entire corpus* to establish a definitive set of results. This definitive set may then be combined, using logic, with other query results.

Figure 180: Adjusting the FTF focus while browsing – a centred concordance (upper left), the spy window after ‘Edit element’ (lower right), changing the FTF focus (lower left), and the original browser after ‘Update!’ (lower right).

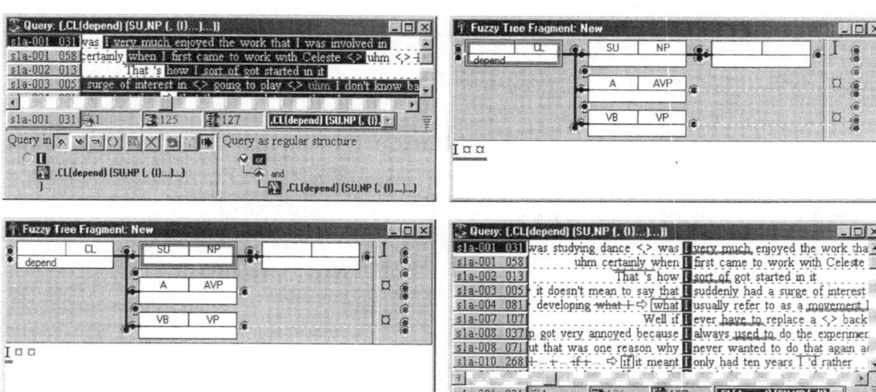

During search, however, only the results of the query being searched are shown in the browser. This is indicated by the title bar, which might read something like: 'Query: (*x* and *y*) – searching: (*x*)'. When the search stops, whether complete or incomplete, the matching set is combined to generate a new set of results. While we may edit the query in the query editor during search as normal (with a few restrictions), we cannot see the result of this editing until the search stops. During search the 'connect views' button ('▶') is up (off), and disabled (Figure 181, upper right).

Let us take the simplest example, that of negation. Try the following.

➢ Start a 'text fragment' search for "**that was**". When the query window appears, open the query editor (upper left, Figure 181), select the query element, and press 'not' ('¬' or 'N'). If you have a fast computer, do this quickly!

Notice that nothing has happened to the regular structure in the right hand panel, or to the content of the browser. However, the title of the window now reads 'Query: (¬that was) – searching: (that was)', indicating the distinction between what your overall query *is*, and what ICECUP is currently *searching for* (Figure 181, upper right). You may continue to browse trees in the corpus or perform a concordance display on the results.

➢ If you press <Esc> or <F4> to stop the search process, the views are reconnected, and the negated query is shown in the regular structure. This re-synchronisation means that the browser results now reflect this overall query. The title now reads 'Query: (¬that was) – search incomplete' (Figure 181, lower left).

Figure 181: Negating a query during search – the initial query (upper left), negating it (upper right), stopping the search (lower left), the final set of results (lower right).

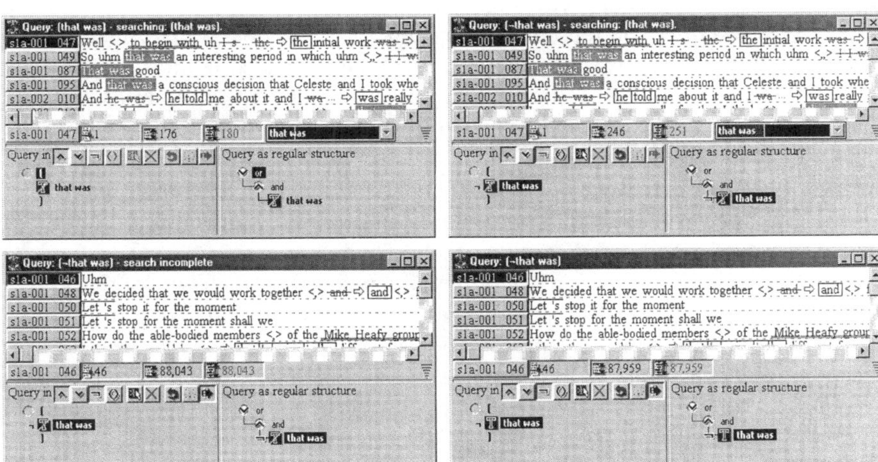

➢ If you continue the background search, and let it run to completion, the complete negated query will be presented (illustrated in the lower right of Figure 181).

The list of results is now shorter than when the search was incomplete, because more cases have been found and eliminated.

Ensuring that background searches are completed makes manipulating the query easy. Once a query has been performed, ICECUP remembers it, until you close all the windows that refer to it. This has a number of implications.

- We can duplicate the query without having to redo the background search. This introduces a further "side-effect". For example, try duplicating an incomplete query object (use drag and drop, not <F4>). 'Continue' the search in this new window. When the search stops again, the original window will be updated as well.
- We can delete the query in the query editor and then undo the deletion ('undo' refers to the query) and the results of the background search reappears.
- We can save the results of a background search with the FTF that generated it, either by pressing 'Save' from an FTF editor window, or from the query results window (tick the 'cache background searches' option).

Note that if you have more than one incomplete query in a query results window, only one may be processed at one time. After the first query finishes, restart the second with 'Continue' (<F4>).

6.10 Simplifying the query

If you edit a complicated logical query, adding and removing elements, you may find that it appears to diverge from its structural counterpart on the right hand side. In Section 6.3 we saw that an expression of the form "not(not A and B)" became something like "(A or not B)". To the uninitiated this is disconcerting even if it is "truth-preserving".

The 'Simplify' button applies the same set of logical transformations, or 'axioms', to the query as are applied to create this logical structure.

Pressing 'Simplify' removes unnecessary brackets from queries. It turns "not(not(X))" into "X". It applies a host of rules to the query in order to turn it into a logical equivalent of the regular structure. Understanding how 'simplify' works, therefore, is really a question of understanding this regular structure.

The 'regular structure' is a standard ('normalised') logical representation. It consists of a set of 'ored' groups, each of which consist of a set of 'anded' elements, each of *which* can be optionally negated (*i.e.*, have 'not', or '¬', applied to them). Figure 182 illustrates examples of this regular structure.

In logic, this kind of representation is called a *disjunctive normal form*, meaning that the primary division is between "disjuncts", *i.e.*, 'or' operators. We have drawn it as a two-level tree-like structure. The first division is

Table 44: The Simplify! command in the logical query editor.

	name	keyboard action	menu command
	Simplify!		**Edit	Simplify!**

Figure 182: Combinations of 'and', 'or' and 'not' in the regular structure.

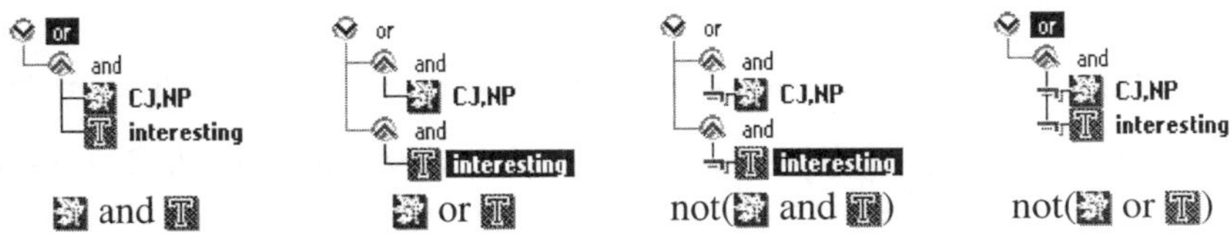

between alternatives, drawn with grey lines. The secondary division, representing co-occurring elements, is drawn with black ones.

The representation identifies *sets of alternative situations* which, when taken together, correspond to the set of query results. In the leftmost case in Figure 182 there is only a single acceptable situation, *i.e.*, where both elements are present in the same text unit. In the second example, there are two independent situations – where either element is present. The pair of examples on the right of Figure 182 show the result of applying De Morgan's Law (see below) to negative expressions. We demonstrated the power of this in 6.5, when we discussed how Fuzzy Tree Fragments could be combined with logic.

In order to translate the logical expression in the query editor into this standardised form, we require a number of 'translation rules', or *axioms*. Most of these are simple and obvious. They correspond to the kind of rule that you learn in algebra, like "$a + a = 2a$", except that in logic, instead of using '×', '÷', '+' and '-' we employ 'and', 'or' and 'not'. For example, "¬(¬A) = A" is equivalent to the rule "-(-a) = a". The translation process consists of detecting where these rules apply, and then applying them with the aim of simplifying the expression, and converting it into disjunctive normal form.

Although most of these rules are intuitive, a couple of them are a little more complex and give non-intuitive results because they do *not* make the query shorter. The first of these is De Morgan's Law, which we saw in action in Section 6.3. This can be written as

¬(A **and** B **and**...) ⇒ (¬A **or** ¬B **or**...), or

¬(A **or** B **or**...) ⇒ (¬A **and** ¬B **and**...). **De Morgan's Law**

Note that 'A' and 'B' here could be a single element or a further logical expression. The rule states that we can dispense with an initial 'not' outside a pair of brackets on the condition that we negate every element within the set of brackets, and change every 'and' to 'or', and vice-versa. Why do we do this?

The rule is necessary in order to dispense with all '¬' signs at every point *apart from in front of every individual element.*

The other major translation rule is the 'cross product' rule. This is necessary in order to determine sets of 'or' alternatives from a set of expressions joined by 'and'. It is the equivalent rule to the algebraic conversion '$A \times (B+C) \Rightarrow (A\times B) + (A\times C)$'. The conversion is necessary to ensure that 'or' takes precedence over 'and'.

A **and** (C **or** D **or**...) ⇒ (A **and** C) **or** (A **and** D) **or** ... **Cross product**

Figure 183 shows one example of the effect of the cross product rule. However, it gets more verbose as the number of disjuncts increase. ICECUP has to list every combination of all elements on one side of the 'and' *with every element on the other side*.

With two elements on either side of the 'and', the expansion becomes:

(A **or** B) **and** (C **or** D) ⇒ (A **and** C) **or** (A **and** D) **or** (B **and** C) **or** (B **and** D)

The 'Simplify' ('') command does not, therefore, always reduce the size of your query. Rather, it brings it into line with the regular expression.

The logical system performs a final important function. It detects when all, or part, of your expression, is redundant. This can happen in two ways.

1) **It is always true**. The expression is what we call a 'tautology'. If you write an expression such as "A or ¬A", it will always be true, irrespective of what A is.
2) **It is always false**. The expression is a 'contradiction'. "A and ¬A" will always be false, regardless of the value of A.

If one part of your expression is redundant, then this may also have the effect of making the rest of your combined query redundant as well. Anything that is 'ored' with a tautology, *e.g.*, "(X *or* A *or* ¬A)", and anything 'anded' with a contradiction, *e.g.*, "(Y *and* B *and* ¬B) will also be redundant.

If one of your query elements does not appear *at all* on the right hand side, it will be because ICECUP has detected that it is redundant. The regular structure is a logical picture of the implications of your query. It gives you a chance to remove unnecessary elements or correct mistakes in your expression.

ICECUP employs two special symbols, 'True' and 'False', which

Figure 183: A simple cross product derived from (or) and .

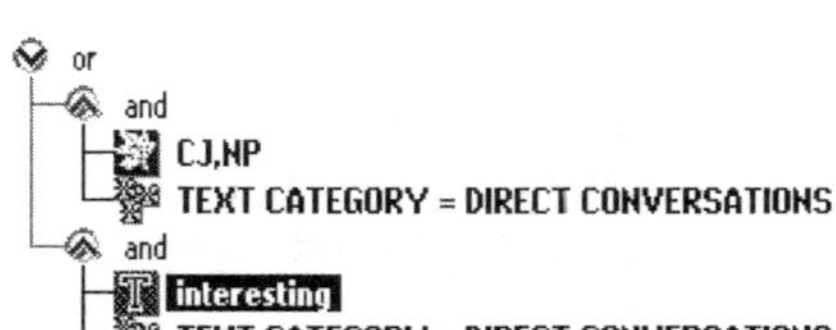

Figure 184: A contradiction (left), a tautology (right), and the results of simplifying a tautology (below).

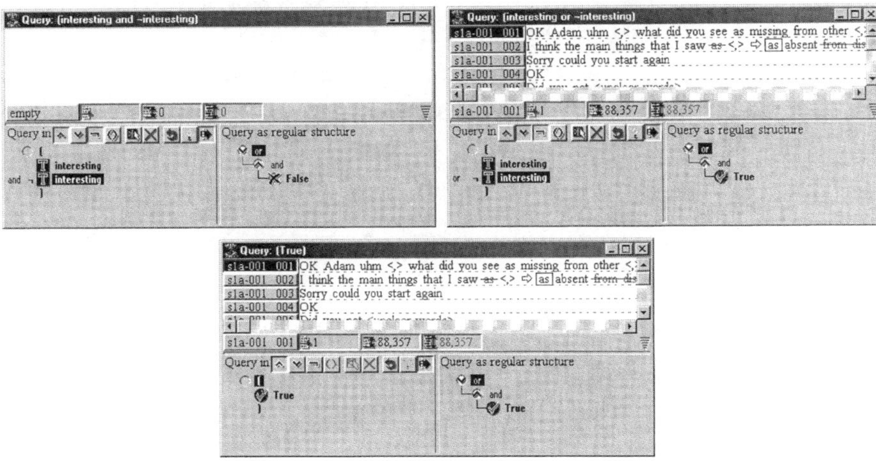

produce <everything> and <nothing> respectively from the corpus. If the entire query reduces to a contradiction, then 'False' is generated and an empty list is displayed. Likewise, if it reduces to a tautology, then 'True' is produced and the entire corpus is shown. Try the following.

- Perform a simple query, and open the query editor in the window. Then make a copy of the element using drag and drop (you won't need to worry about holding the <Ctrl> key down, because it is a lone element). Now press 'not' ('¬') to negate the second element. You should get the empty 'False' value as shown in Figure 184, left.
- If you now press 'Or together' ('∨') to 'or' the two elements, you will get the tautology in Figure 184 (right). If you simplify this list with '', you will obtain the simple value 'True' (Figure 184, below). Although you have now lost your original query element, you can press 'undo' to recover it.

Finally, in some circumstances it is not desirable to eliminate all logical redundancy. These circumstances are when removing a query would eliminate a visible FTF object, and therefore remove the matched range.

Consider the 'browse context and query' command in ICECUP 3.1, which you can perform when browsing query results. This lets you see a match in the context of a text/subtext. It creates a logical expression of the form in Figure 185, *e.g.*, "((S1A-002:1 and "**interesting**") or S1A-002:1)".

In propositional logic, this expression is equivalent to the subtext alone (S1A-002:1), but this would remove the FTF and thus the match. ICECUP 3.1 employs a subtly modified version of the simplification rule which retains FTFs and selection lists where they would otherwise be redundant and therefore eliminated.

Figure 185: Browsing a text including a source query, in ICECUP 3.1.

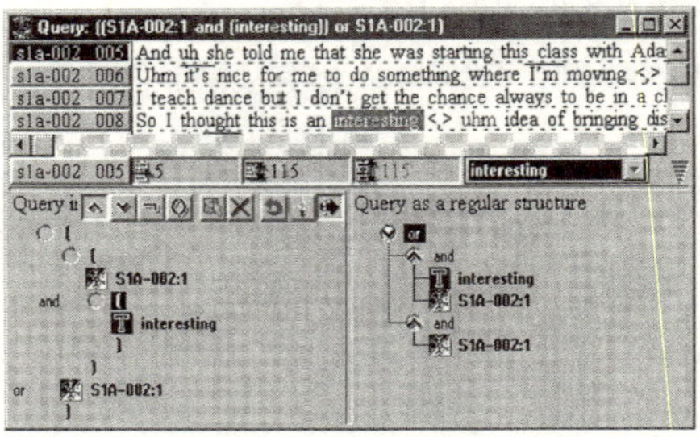

7. ADVANCED FACILITIES IN ICECUP 3.1

ICECUP, in its widely-used 3.0 version, has proved to be popular and powerful. It was released in September 1998 with ICE-GB on CD and, with a sample corpus, over the internet. With a parsed corpus, Fuzzy Tree Fragments, grammatical concordancing and drag and drop logic, users had to cope both with the detail of the grammar and a new way of working with the corpus. Hence this book.

ICECUP 3.1 is an evolutionary advance on ICECUP 3.0. Although there are changes between versions of the software, the underlying principles of the program remain. Facilities are extended rather than curtailed. As a result, users will have no problems switching to the new platform.

As we commented, parsed corpora of any size are a recent phenomenon. Their existence challenges previous research methods and provokes new kinds of research questions. We will look at this in some detail in Chapter 9. ICECUP 3.1 provides a number of enhancements to support researchers, including two new corpus overviews, automatic generation of tables of freq-uencies and more expressive FTF queries. At the time of writing (December 2001) the software was awaiting finishing touches prior to its release. Some facilities may vary slightly between this description and the final version.

7.1 Introducing ICECUP 3.1

After it was released, users of ICECUP were asked for their opinions and suggestions. The most common request was to incorporate more familiar lexical facilities in the new version. We therefore decided to bridge the gap between lexical and parsed corpora by providing integrated support for lexical studies via a *Lexicon* and *lexical wild cards*. These are tightly integrated, so the Lexicon behaves like the Corpus Map (see Section 4.2), providing an overview of simple lexical queries, *i.e.*, one-word FTFs or FTFs composed of a word and a tag node. Lexical wild cards are introduced into FTFs.

Some researchers may be primarily concerned with lexical variation and how it relates to the grammar while others may be more interested in listening to phonetic variation. ICECUP 3.1 includes the playback of recorded speech from CD. In the future, ICECUP could be extended to allow other (*e.g.*, prosodic) annotations in a corpus to be represented and searched.

Teachers wishing to find a small number of examples to illustrate a grammatical point or test a class, desire straightforward and rapid access to examples and a clear display. Researchers, on the other hand, are more interested in exploring the permutations of the grammar, possibly by perform-ing a number of related queries (see Part 3). One kind of user requires an easy and clear user interface; the other, greater computational support in searching and visualising the results of searches.

ICECUP straddles these groups of users. It is a general-purpose tool. Of course, to some degree, both sets of requirements, ease of access and computational support, overlap. It bears repeating: experimentalists must be able to ground their generalisations in real examples (see Chapter 9). Likewise, the grammar is best learned through application.

ICECUP 3.1 includes a number of general enhancements, of which most are of greater interest to researchers than teachers. The principal ones are described in subsequent sections in this chapter and are the following.

- A *lexicon* and a *grammaticon* generated from, and cross-referencing, the corpus (see Sections 7.2 and 7.3).
- *Statistical tables* are introduced into the corpus map, lexicon and grammaticon (Section 7.4). These permit the collection of statistics and the rapid performance of simple experiments.
- Lexical queries are extended by the possibility of using *wild cards* and *logical expressions* (see 7.5).
- Queries involving FTF nodes are also extended to permit the user to specify *logic within a sector* (function or category) or *feature class*, logical *combinations of node patterns*, and a number of other improvements (see 7.6).

A number of further improvements are summarised earlier in the book.

- Extensions to *grammatical concordancing* (see Section 4.8).
- Simultaneous *playback of recorded speech* (with sound CD; see 4.11).
- User defined *selection lists* (see 4.12).

We have also taken the opportunity to improve the user interface to enhance the

Figure 186: Scrolling (left) and zooming (right) the tree viewer with the mouse. The main panel will slide in any direction and may be scaled independently in both the horizontal and the vertical.

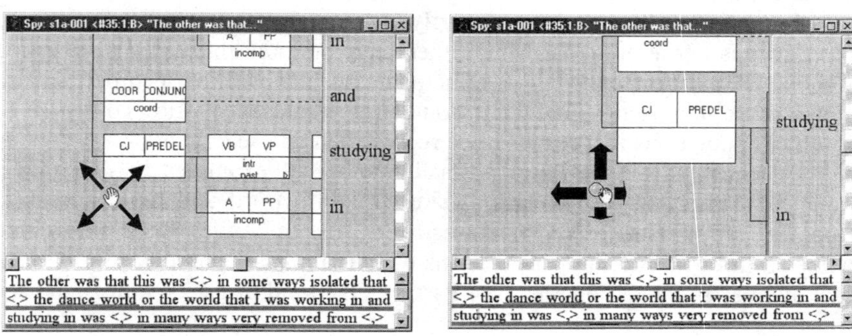

Table 45: Scrolling and zooming with the mouse in ICECUP 3.1.

View	Where to click	Notes
FTF editor and tree viewer		
Tree view (Figure 186)	2D (tree): In the background area between nodes.	The panel will not scroll if the entire tree is visible in the window, but you can zoom in and then scroll. Autoscale is switched off by either operation.
	1D (text): In the area between words.	Vertical and horizontal zooms are independent. (Press <Shift> to perform rubber-banding multiple selection – see Section 5.10.)
Query results window		
Text view	2D: In the sentence. 1D: In the margin.	Horizontal drag will not work if word-wrapping is on or visible sentences are too short.
		Zooming is by font size, and is not smooth.
		Clicking down also selects the current sentence.
Query editor	1D: In the view.	Vertical scroll only, with no zoom.
Corpus map, lexicon and grammaticon		
Map structure and table	2D: In the table, when revealed.	Vertical scrolling is per line, and is not smooth. Horizontal scrolling in the table is smooth.
	1D: In the structure view.	Clicking in the table or on an element label selects it. Zooming is not available.

browsing of the corpus. For example, you can now ask ICECUP to display sentences in the results viewer so that long sentences are split into several lines. You can also scroll and zoom all of the viewers in Table 45 by using simple mouse actions. The idea is that you can drag a panel up, down, left or right with the mouse. Figure 186 illustrates scrolling and zooming in the tree viewer. You can scroll the view vertically if you click and drag within the text portion of the view on the right hand side.

- You *scroll* all the viewers by clicking down with the mouse and dragging the pointer in the direction you want to scroll. Some may be scrolled in every direction (2D) while others can move only up and down or left and right (1D).
- You *zoom* by pressing the <Ctrl> key down and then drag. The rule here is: dragging up or to the left zooms *in*, dragging towards the bottom or right zooms *out*.

  The tree viewer may be scaled independently in the vertical and horizontal axes, as shown in Figure 186, right.

As we mentioned, a significant amount of development in ICECUP 3.1 has gone into the so-called *corpus overviews*: the corpus map, lexicon and grammaticon, which we describe below. One such enhancement is that you can now *track* elements in an overview to see how they are instanciated in the corpus. This means connecting the overview – *e.g.*, the lexicon – to a text viewer displaying examples of the lexicon query, so that when the selection changes in the lexicon, the query is updated in the viewer.

Table 46: Connection controls.

	name	keyboard action	menu command
	Autoconnect	(none)	**View | Autoconnect**
	Disconnect query	<Shift>+<F4>	**View | Disconnect from query**

There are two ways of doing this. One method is to switch on the 'autoconnect' ('') option (see Table 46). This automatically links every new 'Browse' operation to the overview. The second method connects an existing query element to the overview from which it was created.

> Hit <F4> in the corpus map, lexicon or grammaticon to browse an element.

> In the query window, open the 'logical query editor' (see Chapter 6) to locate and edit the element. Then hit the 'Edit element' ('') button in the query editor (Section 6.7). This establishes a link to the original overview and opens the overview window.[1]

Either way, if you move the selection in the overview now, the query results will update dynamically, allowing you to compare the impact of different queries. You can break the link from either end: either select 'break connection' ('') in the overview window or double-click on the 'chain' link in the logical query editor. The process is similar to that for the FTF editor (see Section 6.7) except that the window is automatically updated.

7.2 The Lexicon

ICE-GB contains over a million words of English, consisting of a little under forty-six thousand *lexically distinct* word tokens. If we distinguish between words with different word class *tags* (categories and features) this figure rises to about sixty-three thousand. The *lexicon* organises and displays all the lexically distinct words in the corpus plus their grammatical subcategorisations.

> To open the lexicon, press the large 'lexicon' button or select 'Corpus | Lexicon' in the menus.

The lexicon is an overview like the corpus map (see Section 4.2) and the view can be organised as a tree of query elements (Figure 187, left). In the corpus map, these 'query elements' consist of a sociolinguistic variable and its values, and texts, subtexts and speakers under these values. At any point the currently selected query can be viewed via the large top-right Browse button, hitting <F4>, or by employing drag and drop (see Chapter 6).

---

[1] Hint: to keep things clear when tracking, concordance the display or select word wrapping in the text viewer (Section 4.6). Also, try tiling vertically, using '**Window | Tile vertical**'.

Figure 187: An example Lexicon view: looking at "work".

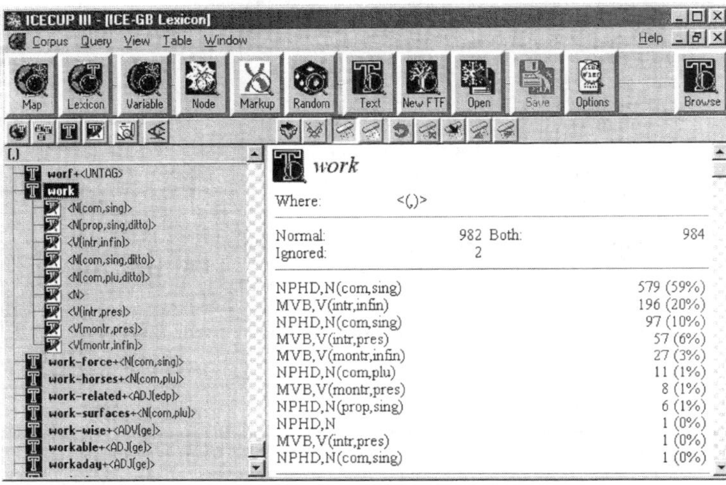

While the corpus map is composed of portions of the corpus text subdivided sociolinguistically, the lexicon is composed of single-word FTFs (*e.g.*, "**work**") and tagged-word FTFs ("**work**+<V(intr, infin)>"). Both the lexicon and *grammaticon* (see below) are wholly generated from ICE-GB. As we have seen, they cross-reference the corpus so that at any point you can locate the set of cases summarised by any node in the tree (and we can track through the tree).

As in any dictionary, a lexically distinct element can be found with different word classes. So *work* can be subdivided into verb and noun uses, listing the features in each case (Figure 187). However, unlike a dictionary, word *senses* are not included in the lexicon because they are not represented in the corpus annotation. Nor does the lexicon include relationships between word *forms* (*e.g.*, *work* and *worked*).[2]

If the word is part of a ditto-tagged compound (Section 5.13), for example, *dance work* or *work surfaces*, the word will be included with the tag for the compound (*e.g.*, in the case of *work surfaces*, as "**work**+<N(com,plu,ditto)>"). If it is hyphenated, as in *work-surfaces*, it will be included in this literal form. By default, the lexicon contains statistics on the frequency of the word in the corpus, with columns for 'normal', 'ignored', and 'both'. All lexical variants, including spelling mistakes, are represented (misspellings should be marked as 'ignored').

---

[2] This would entail the merging of the lexicon with an electronic dictionary or lexical database which would have to be compiled separately for every variety of English.

Figure 188: Lexicon buttons and the Find field.

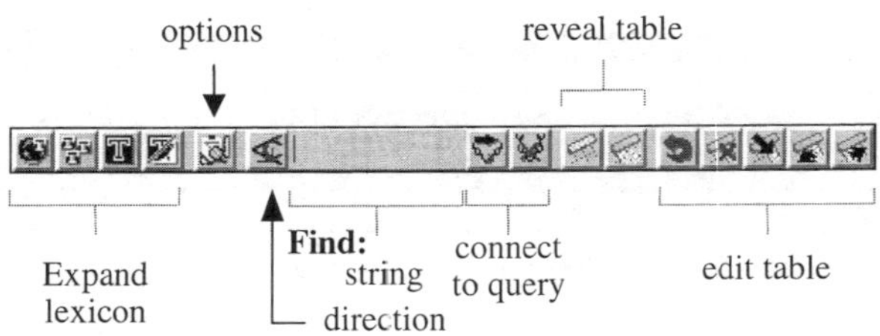

Table 47: Expansion and contraction commands for corpus map (M), lexicon (L) and grammaticon (G, see Section 7.3).

M	L	G	name	keyboard action	menu command
			Collapse tree	<Ctrl>+'0'	**View I Collapse tree**
			Expand values	<Ctrl>+'1'	**View I Expand values**
			Expand texts, *etc.*	<Ctrl>+'2'	**View I Expand texts** *etc.*
			Expand subtexts, *etc.*	<Ctrl>+'3'	**View I Expand subtexts** *etc.*
			Expand all	<Ctrl>+'4'	**View I Expand all**

As we mentioned at the outset, the lexicon contains many thousands of distinct items. The tool must therefore let the user explore the data effectively. Lexicon commands are summarised by the button bar in Figure 188.

- **Expand and contract lexicon structure.** As with the corpus map, these expand or collapse the tree to different extents (top, groups, words and tags; Table 47).
- **Options button.** Lets you restructure the lexicon view using a window (Figure 189).
- **Find commands.** This consists of a direction switch and a string. Hitting <Return> finds the next matching element.
- **Connect and track commands.** These are 'autoconnect' and 'disconnect from query' (see Table 46, Section 7.1).
- **Reveal and edit table commands.** See Section 7.4.

The 'lexicon options' button ('') opens a window (Figure 189), allowing users to restructure the lexicon. You can specify the structure by the following:

1. **Where to start:** you can determine a subset of the lexicon that you wish to explore by specifying a tagged-word FTF. By default, this FTF is simply *any node with any word.* You can be extremely specific, *e.g.*, the category is a verb and the word must start with *work* ("**work***+<V>") or very general, *e.g.*, omit all ditto-tagged elements ("<¬ditto>"). Note that ICECUP 3.1 allows logic ('¬') and wild card ('*') components to be included in the FTF (see Sections 7.5 and 7.6).
2. **How to split:** you may specify subdivisions of the lexicon. This is an extension of the first principle. We choose a sequence of criteria, a *path*, that specifies how the tree is

Figure 189: Lexicon options. The grammaticon options are very similar.

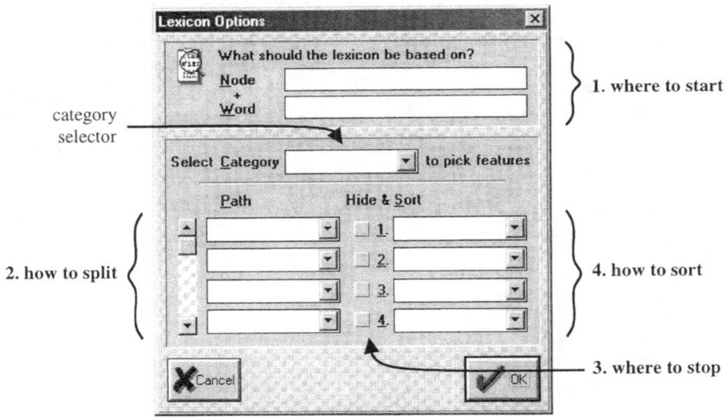

split into groups. For example, we could subdivide the lexicon first by category and then by function; or by initial letter, by category, and by the first feature, *etc*. The following criteria may be used.

a) **Lexical.** 1st, 2nd, 3rd... letter; last, last but 1, last letter but 2...; word length.

b) **Grammatical.** Function, category; features *if category is specified.*[3]

3. **Where to stop:** you can hide and combine elements. For example, in the lexicon we are often not interested in distinguishing between the different grammatical roles that words play, so we may hide *functions* in the tags. In this case the fact that the verbal examples of *work* are main verbs and that the noun examples are heads is omitted. Removing restrictions can also cause elements to be combined (*e.g.*, if 'ditto' is hidden, "<N(com,sing)>" and "<N(com,sing,ditto)>" will be merged).

4. **How to sort:** lastly, we can choose to specify the order in which tags are listed.

These commands are supplemented with the Find facility indicated in Figure 188. The user types a word or tag into the command bar and then presses <return> or <F3> to locate the next instance of the element. Pressing <F3> repeats the search.

7.3 The Grammaticon

If the lexicon lets you browse lexical items and their grammatical realisation, what does the grammaticon do?

---

[3] The choice of category at any point determines the set of features which are applicable to a node. This means that it is not meaningful to structure the lexicon (by subdividing, sorting, or hiding) according to a particular feature unless the category was previously determined. Secondly, we may permit different structures within different category branches.

Figure 190: A grammaticon view subdivided by function, and by category.

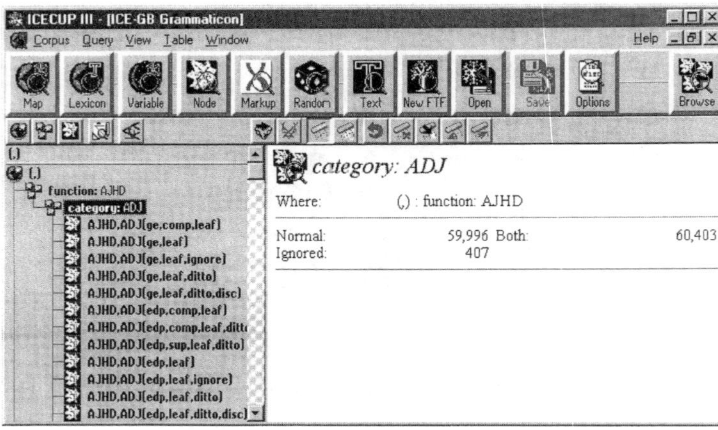

ICE-GB is a parsed corpus. Moreover, it is parsed with a detailed multi-featured phrase structure grammar so that for each word in the corpus, there are approximately two nodes. The grammaticon lets you explore the set of around eight thousand seven hundred *differently annotated nodes* in the corpus. Some of these nodes (with the optional pseudo-feature 'leaf') are tag nodes, and may be further explored using the lexicon. The remainder comprise the bulk of the clause and phrase analysis of the corpus. Each element in the grammaticon is equivalent to a single-node FTF.

- To open the grammaticon, simply select 'Corpus | Grammaticon' from the menu.

The grammaticon tree is very simply split into three levels (top, groups and nodes) as shown in Figure 190. Grammaticon commands mirror their lexicon equivalents, and the buttons are very similar (see Table 47). The user can choose how to structure the grammaticon using an 'options' window, although naturally, lexical restrictions cannot be employed in either the root specification or the path. Organising a list of elements into a tree is particularly effective when their meaning is relatively unfamiliar. Whereas the lexicon may be browsed as an unstructured list, it is more common to structure the grammaticon with a path, *e.g.*, the function followed by the category, as shown in Figure 190.

One point that becomes apparent as you browse a structured grammaticon tree is that *not every legal permutation is present*. For example, according to the grammar, adjective phrase head (AJHD) may feasibly co-occur with adjective (ADJ), conjoin (CJ) or disparate (DISP). However, in ICE-GB, only adjectives are ever found as heads of adjective phrases.

Figure 190 lists all distinct node patterns under a path of <function, category>. However, many features and pseudo-features may not be particularly interesting (*e.g.*, in Figure 190 ignored, dittoed and discontinuous nodes are all distinguished from one another). It is a good idea to selectively ignore certain features and thereby simplify the tree. You can do this with the 'grammaticon options' window.

7.4 Statistical tables

As well as a tree structure, all of the overview windows in ICECUP 3.1 support the visualisation and adaptation of a *table of frequencies*. In ICECUP 3.0, the corpus map displays statistical information on the number of subtexts, speakers, words, *etc.* at the current point in the map. In version 3.1, this data may be presented in the columns of a *table*.

➢ Open the corpus map and select 'Show columns' ('' or '**Table | Show Columns**'). Alternatively, place the mouse pointer over the left-hand edge of the panel and pull it rightwards. This will expose part of the table, with a scroll bar.

➢ Expand the corpus map incrementally by clicking on the 'plus signs' in the hierarchy.

The table will look like Figure 191. To help you read it, note first that the way the tree hierarchy is displayed means that in each case, *totals are at the top*. White dashed lines subdivide parent elements from their children. Group (variable and value) data are emboldened, while data for texts, subtexts, *etc.*, are listed in a plain face. The table grows with the corpus map tree. As a result, you can open branches of the tree (double-click on the icon or hit <Ctrl> and cursor-right) which appear to be interesting and close others which are less so.

Of course, the statistics presented here are general baseline frequencies: the number of words in a text category, for example. For experimentalists, they are not particularly interesting in and of themselves.

The last set of buttons in the button bar (see Figure 188) are dedicated to managing tables. Table 48, overleaf, lists these commands. The first pair are simple switches which reveal or hide the headings or columns of the table. The remaining buttons let you edit the table in conjunction with drag and drop.

Figure 191: The default table in the corpus map: from 'texts' to 'words'.

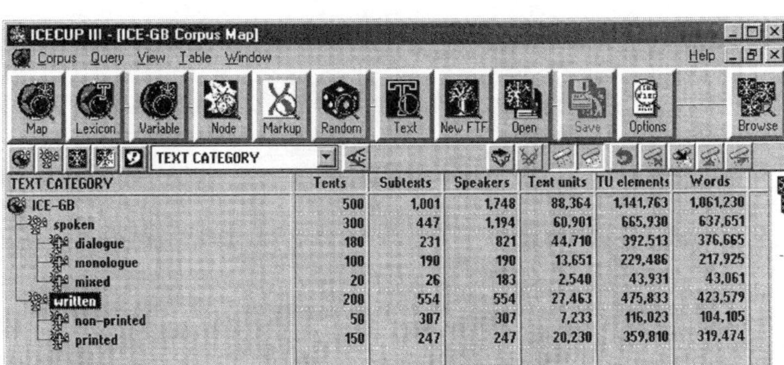

TEXT CATEGORY	Texts	Subtexts	Speakers	Text units	TU elements	Words
ICE-GB	500	1,001	1,748	88,364	1,141,763	1,061,230
spoken	300	447	1,194	60,901	665,930	637,651
dialogue	180	231	821	44,710	392,513	376,665
monologue	100	190	190	13,651	229,486	217,925
mixed	20	26	183	2,540	43,931	43,061
written	200	554	554	27,463	475,833	423,579
non-printed	50	307	307	7,233	116,023	104,105
printed	150	247	247	20,230	359,810	319,474

Table 48: Reveal and edit table commands.

	name	keyboard action	menu command
	Show heading	(none)	**Table | Show Heading**
	Show columns	(none)	**Table | Show Columns**
	Undo	<Alt>+<Backspace>	**Table | Undo**
	Delete column	<Delete>	**Table | Delete Column**
	Insert column	<Insert>	**Table | Insert Column**
	Shift column left	<Shift>+'←'	**Table | Shift Column Left**
	Shift column right	<Shift>+'→'	**Table | Shift Column Right**

The idea is very simple. *If you drag a query into the table it creates a column.* ICECUP calculates the *intersection frequency* for each row in the table. This is the number of cases in the overlap between the cases for the row element and those matching the column element, for each cell in the table.

- Open a *Text fragment* query and type a word, *e.g.*, "**work**".
- Next, drag the query into the table. You can do this using one of two methods. You can drag the minimised window into the corpus map. Alternatively, for greater control, you can open the query editor and drag the *query element* from the query window to the corpus map and then drop the element over the table.

You should gain an additional column in the table, listing the number of occurrences of the word *work* in each subcategory of **text category**. This method is certainly a lot easier than performing each search manually!

Raw frequencies do not reveal much, as each category contains a different number of words. The most basic comparison is to compare the frequency of the word *work* with the number of words in each text.

- If the two columns ('Words' and '(work)') are not adjacent, shift one of them towards the other by using either the 'Shift column left' ('') or 'Shift column right' ('')

Figure 192: Inserting a new 'statistics' column into the table.

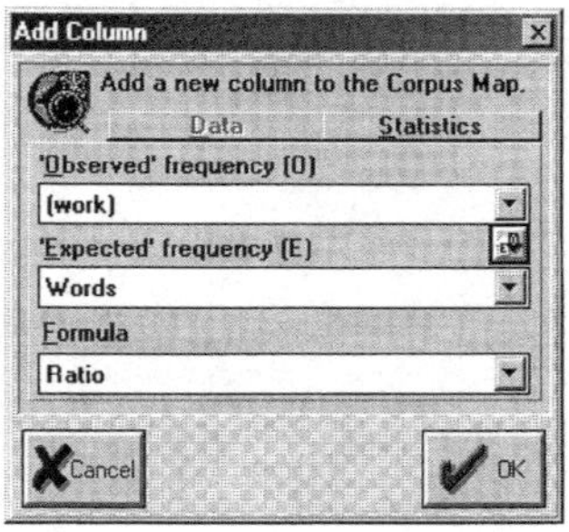

command. (You may also remove irrelevant columns with the 'Delete column' command, '', see Table 48.)

- Next we want to compare the columns. To do this we need to add a new column to put the results in. Press 'Insert column' (''). The result is the window in Figure 192.

In this window there are three selectors. The first two are pull-downs which select two columns of data. The third specifies one of a list of pre-defined formulae, including 'ratio' and 'significant result' (the result of carrying out a significance test).

- Select '(work)' in the 'observed' selector and 'Words' in the 'expected' selector. Select 'ratio' in the last. This calculates the ratio *observed:expected*, *i.e.*, the proportion of times the word 'work' appears compared to the total number of words in each category. Select 'OK'.
- Press 'Insert column' again, but this time select 'significant result' and then 'OK'.
- Open the corpus map to all subcategories by hitting 'Expand to values' ('') in the button bar. Now browse the expanded table.

The result will be two new columns. The first contains the ratio, to three decimal places, of the word 'work' to the number of words, for each row in the table. The average is 0.001 with a small amount of variation on either side.

The second column, which consists mostly of 'non-significant' indicators ("ns"), indicates the result of computing a *log-likelihood test* (a kind of chi-square) *across the children* of each node. If **spoken** is significant at the 0.05 level it means that the number of instances of *work* compared to the number of words fluctuated significantly across the text categories **dialogue**, **monologue** and **mixed** (the children of **spoken**).[4] However, in this example, the most likely interpretation is simply a variation across texts.[5]

Dynamic tables have two principal advantages over a manual experimental procedure (see Part 3): they are quick and easy. The statistical calculation is performed automatically, painlessly, and – if defined correctly – error-free. Drag and drop intersections are onerous by comparison. However, we should point out certain drawbacks.

- **Flexibility.** This method is less flexible than drag and drop. You cannot combine or restructure sociolinguistic variables.

---

[4] Throughout, the log-likelihood calculation and the number of degrees of freedom is calculated automatically and compared with the critical value. The result is simply reported as 'ns' or, if significant, the error level of the test (*e.g.*, '0.05' means 'significant with an error of 1 in 20'). To quote *log-likelihood values* or *degrees of freedom*, insert further columns.

[5] A more realistic example might be the "what/which N" case study described in Section 8.4. In this case we need to add three columns to the corpus map. We perform FTF queries for "what N", "which N" and "{what, which} N" as described, and then drag the results into the table. We then compare *a particular grammatical choice* (*e.g.*, "what N") with *the possibility that the choice could be made in the first place* ("{what, which} N"). See the next Part.

- **Grammatical limitations.** You cannot study the interaction of one grammatical variable on another (see Section 9.7) using this method. You may add a sociolinguistic query to the lexicon or grammaticon or an FTF query to the corpus map. If you drag an FTF into the lexicon or grammaticon, ICECUP cannot know how the two FTFs (the one that you dragged in and the query for the row in the table) are related within the sentence. It can only measure *the number of times both elements appear in the same sentence*, not whether the two are structurally related.[6]
- **Annotation imperfections.** Any 'computational' approach that draws the researcher's attention away from individual sentences towards frequency statistics risks letting the researcher take the annotation for granted. We can expect some errors, and they may well be concentrated in certain problematic areas. Simply relying on the results of queries is not sufficient. You should always double-check your cases in the corpus before introducing a column into a table.

In summary, dynamic statistical tables in the corpus map and other overviews are an effective way of automatically computing *contingency tables* using index intersection. Rapid calculation means that we can look at far more possibilities than would otherwise be possible. Expanding or contracting a hierarchy is useful if the distinction at a given point is linguistically meaningful.

Using this method we can set up multiple experiments into two-variable interactions where at least one of the variables is sociolinguistic. As we shall see in Part 3, however, this is a small subset of the possible experimental questions that the corpus is capable of addressing.

7.5 Lexical wild cards

In ICECUP 3.0 you can introduce a lexical item into the 'text unit element' position in an FTF, which is by default unspecified (shown as '¤'). Searches for sequences of lexical items are constructed by constructing a text-oriented FTF. You may enter a word, a number, a symbol or a non lexical item (a pause or laughter). And the lexical items may match by taking the case or accent of a letter in the query into consideration, or not. Chapter 3.3 discusses this kind of search at some length.

Often, however, you do not wish to specify the lexical item with this degree of preciseness. ICECUP 3.1 enhances FTFs by allowing you to introduce a lexical *wild card* into the 'text unit element' position.

A wild card is *an imprecise definition of a lexical item*, such as "**l***", which means 'any word beginning with *l*', or "**???ing**", which would match any six-letter word ending in *-ing*. Case and accent sensitivity settings are still applied to the pattern, so, for example, "**A***" with case sensitivity **on** would match *Asterix* but not *asterisk*. The structure of lexical wild cards is quite complex.

[6] If you want to study the interaction between two grammatical FTFs you must use the method described in Section 9.7. Further considerations, *e.g.*, exploring multiple variables and dealing with case intersection, are worthy of future research (see Chapter 10).

Table 49: Two kinds of flexibility: the four basic components of a wild card.

	description	examples	matches
*	Any number of characters, zero or more	**a*** ***ing** **b*ing**	A word starting with "a"; one ending with "ing"; one starting with "b" and ending with "ing".
?	Any single character	**a???** **b?c?u?e**	A four-letter word starting with "a"; a seven-letter word with "b", "c", "u", and "e" in odd positions.
^	Escape. The next character is either: 1: a member of a set	**b^vd** **be^c^v**	A three letter word "b", vowel, "d"; "be" followed by a consonant and then a vowel. See Table 50.
	2: literal	**^? ^* ^{ ^- ^& ^^**	A literal question mark, *etc.*
{ }	User set. See Table 51.	**w{0123}** **t{a-c}**	"w" followed by 0,1,2, or 3; "t" followed by "a", "b", or "c".

There are four basic optional components ('*****', '**?**', '**^**' and '**{ }**') which have precise meanings and can replace any character in an exact text sequence.

Finally, you can employ *logic* to combine wild card patterns, which is necessary if you want to list irregular verbs, for example.

Like Fuzzy Tree Fragments (which are a kind of 'wild card for grammar', Chapter 3.4), lexical wild cards can be imprecise in two ways: in terms of *the relationship between elements* (characters), and in terms of *the specification of the elements themselves*.

The first two components in Table 49, *asterisk* ('*****', sometimes called the "Kleene star") and *query* ('**?**'), stand for any number of characters and a single character respectively. The second pair of components are *escape* ('**^**') and *user set*, which is indicated by a pair of curly brackets, thus: '**{}**'. Escape lets you specify that a character belongs to one of a predefined set. These sets are listed in Table 50. For example, '**^v**' means 'any vowel', '**^+**' means 'any mathematical symbol', and so on.[7]

To match a character against one of a number of characters where the set has not been predefined, you can specify it yourself using the 'user set' format summarised in Table 51 on page 217. This method also lets you match *a string of characters* against a set. A user set can contain three basic types of element.

- **Lists and ranges.** The *list* "**{abcde}**" means any character from 'a' to 'e'. In this case, you could simply write a *range* of characters using a hyphen, thus: "**{a-e}**".[8]
- **Logical combinations.** You can specify the set using a simple reduced logical form. Use a comma to separate *or*ed alternatives, as in "**{z-,-a}**" (every character before and

[7] You can also use the escape symbol to introduce any special character, *e.g.*, the question mark, as a literal. If you want to specify that you want to match the question mark, you precede it with the escape character: '**^?**'.

[8] You can place one set within another, *e.g.*, "**{y^v}**" matches the letter 'y' or any vowel.

Table 50: Predefined sets of characters (see also Appendix 6).

symbol	description[9]	explanation
^@	non-alphabetic	Any character not present in the English alphabet.
^!	symbol	Any of the following:
^>	arrow	←, ↑, →, ↓, *etc.*
^.	punctuation	Any punctuation symbol, including comma, query, *etc.*
^(	bracket	Any bracket.
^[	left bracket	Any left bracket.
^]	right bracket	Any right bracket.
^"	quote	Any quote.
^`	left quote	Any left quote.
^'	right quote	Any right quote.
^+	maths	+, -, /, >, », *etc.*
^|	mark	†, ‡, ●, ■, *etc.*
^$	money	Currency symbols.
^<	corporate	©, ™, *etc.*
^%	fraction	¼, ½, ¾, *etc.*
^_	dash	-, –, —, ~, *etc.*
^/	hyphen	- or /.
^#	digit	0 to 9.
^L, ^l	Letter, letter	Any letter, including greek. Case and accent sensitive.
^A, ^a	alphabetic	Any letter from the Western alphabet.
^V, ^v	vowel	a, e, i, o, u.
^C, ^c	consonant	Any English consonant (defined as '**{^A~^V}**').
^N, ^n	accent	Accented letter, with the following specifics:
^T, ^t	tilde	Any letter with a tilde on top (ã, ñ, *etc.*).
^E, ^e	acute	Similarly: é, í, ú, *etc.*
^R, ^r	grave	à, è, ò, *etc.*
^L, ^l	ligature	æ, œ, *etc.*
^S, ^s	cedille	ç or Ç.
^U, ^u	umlaut	ü, ë, ï, *etc.*
^F, ^f	circumflex	â, î, *etc.*
^G, ^g	greek	Any letter from the Greek alphabet.

including 'a', and after and including 'z'), and tilde ('~') to *negate*. The latter is interpreted to mean 'and not' or "except", so "**{a-z~def}**" means any character from 'a' to 'z' except 'd', 'e', or 'f'.

- **Multiples.** Finally, if you want to specify that *a number* of characters match the set, you can end the set definition with a query and asterisk, so "**{abcde??}**" means two characters matching this set, while "**{^v*}**" equates to zero or more vowels.

Of course, in ICECUP 3.1, lexical wild cards are one aspect of Fuzzy Tree Fragments. This means, for example, that you can search for all deverbal '*-ing* nouns', such as *feeling* and *beginning*:

➢ Perform a Text fragment query for "***ing+<N>**" and browse the results.

---

[9] For compatibility with ICECUP 3.0, you can also employ the ampersand notation with the 'description' column (*e.g.*, '**&accent;**'), instead of the equivalent wild card symbol ('**^n**').

Table 51: Parts of a user set specification.

	description	examples	explanation
	List	{abcde} {y^v}	Any character in the list.
-	Range	{a-z} {-z} {a-}	Any character in the range.
,	Alternate elements	{abc,d-f} {z-,-a}	'Or'. Use the comma to separate.
~	Except	{~def} {a-z~def} {^c~y} {~{^c~a-g}}	'(And) not'. Initially means "everything except".[10]
? *	Wild sequence	{abcde??} {a-k*} {^v*}	The set matches multiple characters.

We can also edit a wild card specification when editing a Fuzzy Tree Fragment by modifying the specification of the word part.

Although this wild card system is quite flexible, there are, of course, limits. You might need to list a set of alternatives. You might also wish to define a general form using a wild card, and then discount certain exceptions. We can solve this problem by using a simple *logical combination* of wild cards.

1) "**[am is are]**" matches *am*, *is* and *are*.

2) "**[*ing & ~being & ~becoming]**" matches any word ending in *-ing*, except *being* and *becoming*.

We place the entire expression within square brackets ('[ ]'), use ampersand ('**&**') for logical 'and' and tilde ('~') for 'not'. These are straightforward to type, unlike the formal symbols ('¬', '∧', '∨'). If no '&' sign is found between elements, then they are assumed to be ored together.

7.6 Extensions to Fuzzy Tree Fragment nodes

As well as extending the representation of text unit elements in FTFs in ICECUP 3.1, you can specify FTF nodes in a much more flexible way.

1. **'Exact matching' is performed using an FTF.** An FTF node can be specified to match exactly.

2. **Features are extended.** The absence of a feature in a feature class may be specified, and pseudo-features (*i.e.*, the structural markers 'ignored', 'superseding', 'ditto-tagged' and 'discontinuous') are also brought into the query.

3. **Simple logic within sectors is provided.** Sectors of an FTF may be specified by using a simple 'signed set' representation.[11] Using this notation one can state that the

[10] The order of elements matters. The sequence "**{~^c,abc}**" (everything except a consonant, or 'a', 'b' or 'c') is different from "**{abc~^c}**" ('a', 'b' or 'c', but not a consonant, which reduces to 'a'). Negation continues until a comma, asterisk or query, or the bracket is closed. Finally, commas have precedence over, and reset, negation, so "**{~a-z~{0-9}}**" ≠ "**{~0-9,~a-z}**".

Two kinds of logic

To see the difference between a logic of text units and a logic of cases, perform the following simple experiment (use any version of ICECUP). Review Chapter 6 if the actions are unclear.

- Open a Node query, type '**CL**' (clause) and hit the OK button. Repeat, and apply '**PU**' (parse unit) to the first query using drag and drop (see Section 6.4). This should create the combined query '**(PU, and ,CL)**', with around 63,700 cases.
- Now type '**PU,CL**'. This returns over 62,600 cases.

Why is there a difference? One query finds all text units containing both a parse unit and a clause, the other, those text units where the parse unit *is* a clause. If you subtract '**PU,CL**' from the compound query, the result will be a series of more than 1,000 sentence fragments where the parse unit is not a clause, but where there is a clause in the text unit.

- Drop '**PU,CL**' into the compound query. Open the query editor in the compound query window, select '**PU,CL**' and click 'Not element' (''). Close the query editor again.

Applying logic within a node guarantees that the resulting expression will apply to the same tree fragment in each text unit. In summary, if you combine two FTFs with logic and require that the logical expression is applied to the same case, you must create a single merged FTF.

There is one exception that proves the rule. You may *add* the results of two independent queries together (using 'or'), provided that the queries are *mutually exclusive*, *i.e.*, you can guarantee that they cannot apply to the same case.

For example, a parse unit cannot be simultaneously a clause and a nonclause, so the combined query ('**PU,{CL,NONCL}**') is equivalent to the disjunction of the two separate queries ('**PU,CL**' ∨ '**PU,NONCL**'). However, if the two queries are not mutually exclusive, cases which match both queries will be counted twice rather than once.

If you want to calculate the intersection between two FTF queries *you must create a single combined FTF*. (This is how we investigate interactions between two grammatical variables in Section 9.7.) Thus the intersection between a clause acting as a parse unit ('**PU,CL**') and a main clause ('**CL(main)**'), is a parse unit clause marked as 'main' ('**PU,CL(main)**'). The process of defining a single combined FTF is simplified greatly by the introduction of logical expressions into a node.

category is one of a number of alternatives, or that the function is absent from a list of functions. This is a convenient shorthand that often avoids the complexity of full logic and multiple node patterns (point 4; Section 7.6.4).

4. **General logical combinations of nodes is supported.** Propositional logic may be used to combine different node patterns. This allows distinct alternative nodes to be considered, *e.g.*, 'this node is a transitive clause acting as a subject *or* it is an NP in subject position'.

ICECUP 3.0 employs logic in combining queries. using the 'drag and drop' method described in Chapter 6. However, this kind of logic operates on *text units* rather than grammatical *cases*. This is often OK for exploring the corpus,

[11] A 'signed set' is, simply, a set of alternatives – '{*a*, *b*,...}' – with the option of negating the entire set: '¬{*a*, *b*,...}'. Any set can be expressed as a series of 'ored' terms: '*a* ∨ *b* ∨...'.

*Figure 193: Two examples of employing logic within sectors: a simple function and positive set '**NPHD, {PRON,N}**' (left), an example with a negated set '**, {~NUM, ~N}**' (right).*

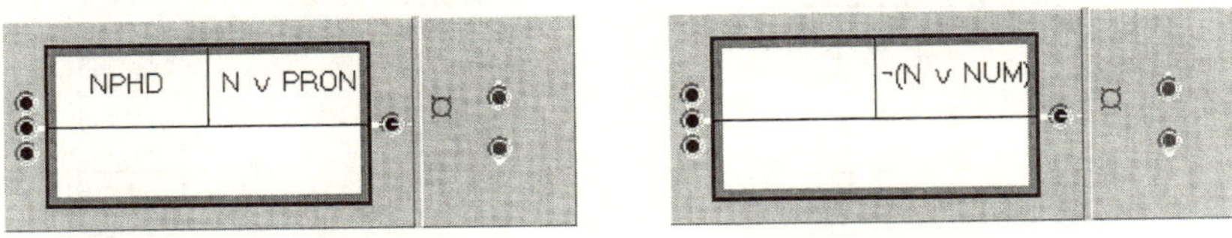

but can cause problems when we perform experiments with the corpus (see Chapter 9). To see the difference between these two levels of logic, see the box above. (You may also wish to look at Section 6.6, which discusses the concordancing of two FTF queries combined with logic.)

In ICECUP 3.1, you can introduce logical operations into FTF nodes at two levels: at the level of *sectors and feature classes*, and at the level of *entire node patterns*.

1. **Function and category sectors, and feature classes**. In order to introduce logic into the function sector of FTFs, we need only specify a particular set of possible functions, and state whether the function is, or is not, a member of it. A similar approach is possible for categories, as well as for features within feature classes.

   a) **Sectors.** Consider the statement that the category is either a noun or pronoun, which in set notation we may write as '$C \in$ {**N**, **PRON**}'. This is visualised in the FTF using the logical notation '**N** ∨ **PRON**' within the category sector (Figure 193, left). Similarly, to state that the category is neither a noun or numeral, you might write '$C \notin$ {**N**, **NUM**}', which is displayed as '¬[**N** ∨ **NUM**]' in the category sector (Figure 193, right). This is a straightforward extension of the way that a single category or function is depicted.

   b) **Feature classes.** In ICECUP 3.0 you can specify one feature from any class. If there are two or more features they must all be present. In ICECUP 3.1, we permit features and unmarked feature classes to be specified independently as present or absent. Two features belonging to the *same* class are assumed to be *disjunctive* ('ored': f_1 or f_2). We discuss this in more detail below.

2. **Entire node patterns.** You can use propositional logic to combine different node patterns. For example, you can state that a particular node is either a *main clause* or not a *subject*, typing "**CL(main) or ~SU**" into the Node window. This kind of expression is interpreted and displayed in a logical form within the node itself as '**(,CL(main) ∨ ¬SU,)**'. The comma explicitly distinguishes the function from the category. If the element is to the left of the principal comma, it is a function; if it is to the right, it is a category. This clarifies the display especially for labels such as **PAUSE** and **PUNC** which can be either function or category. Finally, node patterns may also include logical expressions in their sectors, *e.g.*, '**(SU, ∧ ,[CL ∨ NP])**'.

You may create single node FTFs by typing logical expressions directly into the Nodal query window (Figure 194).

Figure 194: Typing queries into the Nodal query window: an exact match example (left), a logical expression (right).

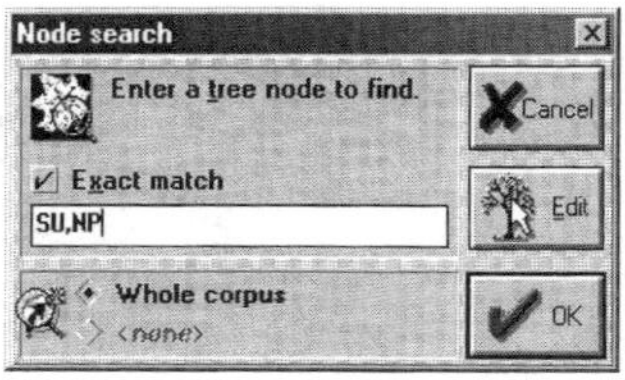

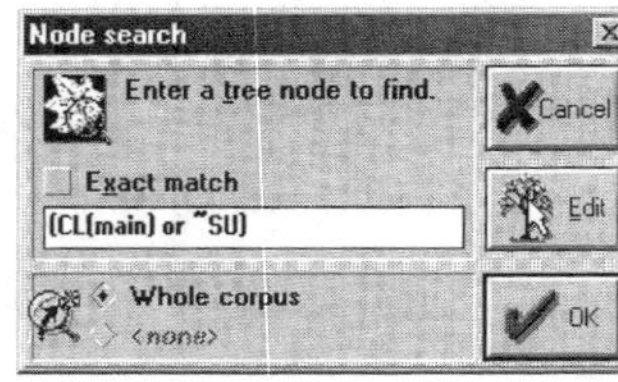

As a guide, note the following.

1. An *exact match* is indicated by a preceding equals sign ('**=**'), *e.g.*, "**=SU,NP**".
2. An exclamation mark before a term in the set of features indicates that it is a feature class that is unspecified. Thus, "**NP(!defunc)**" means an NP which does not have a feature in the detatched function class. You can also write "**!CAT**" for a node with a blank category.
3. A swung dash ('**~**') is used for *not*, thus: "**~SU**".
4. A simple *signed set* notation, employing curly brackets and negation symbols, is used to define function and category sectors. Thus, "**{~PU}**" is a node that is not a parsing unit and "**{PRON,N}**" is a node that is either a pronoun or noun. ICECUP recognises '**PU**' as a function and '**PRON**' as a category; so it can infer whether a set is composed of functions or categories. To be precise, you can add a comma into the string, *e.g.*, "**{~PU},**". Negated sets are written by negating all the terms, *e.g.*, "**{~PRON,~N}**" means 'neither a pronoun nor a noun'.
5. Features and feature classes are simply listed within brackets and may be signed with *not*. It is then up to ICECUP to interpret the list.[12] Features in the same class are interpreted disjunctively (f_1 or f_2) while features in different classes are interpreted as in ICECUP 3.0, *i.e.*, they must be true together (conjunctively: f_1 and f_2).
6. Propositional logic between patterns is introduced using round brackets and negation signs: '**and**'/'**&**' for "and", and '**or**', or a gap, for "or". ICECUP will bracket strings like "**CL(main) ~SU**" and infer an 'or' between the terms: "**(CL(main) or ~SU)**" (Figure 194, right). You can use curly (set) brackets to establish what the negation sign applies to. Thus "**~A,CL**" is interpreted as 'anything apart from an adverbial clause' rather than "a clause that is not adverbial" ("**{~A},CL**").

---

[12] The set of possible features and classes are defined separately for each category. In ICE, some features can be in different classes or in classes with different members (Section 2.4). This means that the list may be interpreted differently according to the category. For example, if the category of a node is **auxiliary**, the features **(¬let, semi, ¬semip)** are in the same class (see Subsection 2.2.4) and this class is interpreted as "not let, or semi and not semip" (*i.e.*, neither let nor semip). If the category is **verb phrase**, the same feature labels are in different classes (they are independent), so the series is interpreted as "not let *and* semi *and* not semip". In practice, you can edit the FTF, let ICECUP simplify the expression by splitting it up into different categories (see box on page 228), and then edit the new logical expression.

*Figure 195: FTFs with exact matching '**=SU,NP**' (left), and matching an NP with no 'detached function' feature: '**NP(!defunc)**' (right).*

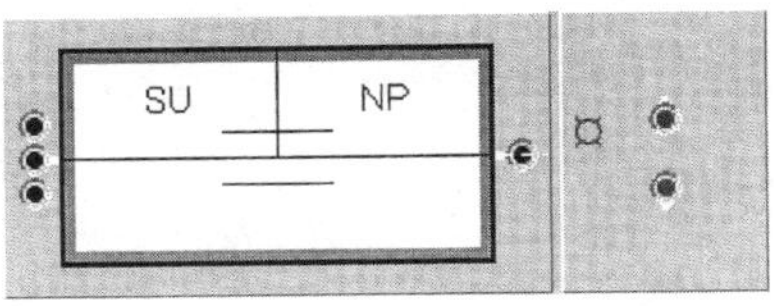

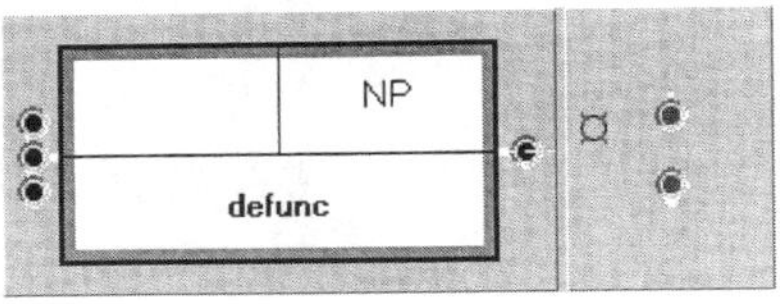

7.6.1 *Performing exact matching in FTFs*

In ICECUP 3.0 you can look for a specific node pattern using the Exact Nodal search (Section 3.6). However, this query is not integrated into FTFs, so ICECUP cannot concordance the results, and the node cannot be combined with other restrictions, *e.g.*, by relating it to other nodes in a query.

In ICECUP 3.1, performing 'Query | Exact Nodal...' takes you to the general Nodal window where the 'Exact match' option is already ticked.

➢ Go to Query | Exact Nodal... and type "**SU,NP**" (subject NP). The window should look like Figure 194, left. Hit the Edit button.

The resulting FTF should look like Figure 195, left. The pair of horizontal bars (an 'equals sign') indicate that this node must match exactly. If written out explicitly, ICECUP precedes the node with an equals sign ('**=SU,NP**'). Pressing <F4> will perform a search for the FTF. You can also type '**=SU,NP**' into the Node query window instead of ticking 'Exact match'.

To specify a node as 'exact' in the FTF editor, you use the pop-up menus for either function or category. In ICECUP 3.1 these menus contain additional commands: 'Tidy functions/categories', 'Exact match', 'Specific function/category' and 'Negate function/category'. We discuss the other commands below.

➢ Open the Feature menu (press down with the right mouse button over the Feature sector) and click on the ticked 'Exact match' menu item to remove it.

7.6.2 *Specifying missing features and pseudo-features*

In Version 3.0 of ICECUP you can specify *only one feature* from a feature class, and you cannot search directly for cases where no feature in a particular feature class is specified. Often the unmarked case is simply the general one.

The ability to specify that a feature class is unmarked can be useful, particularly in research. We demonstrate this in Section 9.7.

ICECUP 3.1 extends the representation of features in the following ways.

1. **You can specify that no feature in a particular feature class is present**, *e.g.*, to specify an adverb which has not been given an adverb type, you write '**ADV(!adv)**'. An absent feature may be due to an unresolvable ambiguity, an annotation error, or it

Figure 196: Selecting features from the feature pop-up menu in ICECUP 3.1.

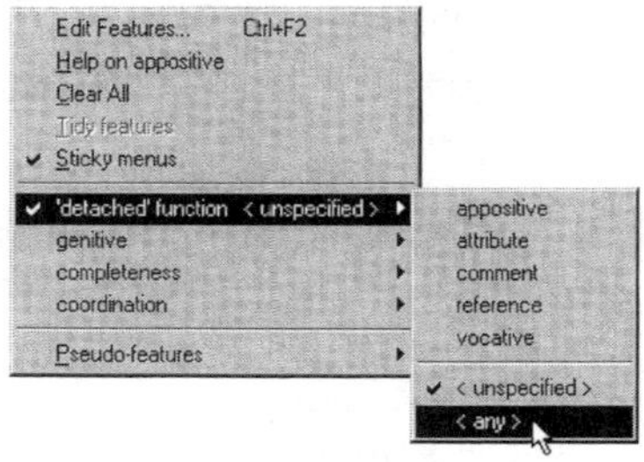

may simply be the default condition. The label is preceded by an exclamation mark ('**!adv**') to state that the element refers to a feature class.[13] Class labels are shown emboldened in the FTF editor (Figure 195, right).

2. **You can employ logic in each feature class.** This lets you state that at least one of the features in a set is present, or that none of the features listed is present, *e.g.*, '**ADV(inten,excl)**' means 'an intensifying *or* exclusive adverb'.

3. **The presence or absence of various structural 'pseudo-features' can be specified.** These include flags for the node being 'ignored' and 'ditto-tagged'.

We will describe each of these possibilities in turn.

➢ Hit Node and type '**NP(!defunc)**' and select the 'Edit' button. This creates an NP where the detached function feature is unmarked, shown in Figure 195, right.

In the FTF editor, you can edit the class with the feature pop-up menu. Locate the feature class submenu and '<unspecified>' within it. Figure 196 illustrates the principle. Features may be *specified independently* and *negated.* You state that a feature is absent or present, while deferring the interpretation of ambiguous feature classes until you either perform a search of the corpus or a "simplify" operation, which we discuss in the next section.

➢ Select the feature name or '<unspecified>' once to add it.

➢ Select the feature (or '<unspecified>') twice to negate it.

➢ Select '<any>' to clear all restrictions on the feature class.[14]

➢ Select 'Clear all' to clear all features.

This is a bit more complex than in ICECUP 3.0, where you could only select one of a set of features. This additional complexity makes the process of editing

---

[13] Some features and classes have the same label. The *class* '**!coordn**' means that no coordination feature is specified. On the other hand, '**coordn**' specifies the *feature* 'coordination'.
[14] We refer to '<none>' (*i.e.*, no specified element) more correctly as '<any>' (any element). A feature class, function or category may also be left blank, *i.e.*, '<unspecified>'.

features slower but lets you assemble feature sets belonging to the same class. We return to this below.

You can also specify a small number of 'pseudo-features' from the feature menu. In ICECUP 3.1, these are 'ignore', 'supersede', 'ditto' and 'discontinuous'. While features are essentially refinements of the *category* of the node, a pseudo-feature is a kind of *structural marker* that is independent of the category. For example, 'ignore' does not relate to the category of a node, but the interpretation of that part of the tree – namely, that it should be ignored by a reader wishing to ascertain the author's intended sentence.

Since pseudo-features guide the interpretation of the tree structure, their limitations between pseudo-features are also structural. Dittoed nodes must be leaf nodes. 'Discontinuous' is a subtype of 'ditto' marker, so if 'disc' is marked, so must 'ditto'. Only non-ignored nodes may be marked as 'superseding'.

To add a pseudo-feature, use the submenu at the bottom of the feature menu (see Figure 196).

7.6.3 Specifying sets of functions, categories and features

The most important enhancement to FTF nodes in ICECUP 3.1 is the ability to introduce logical expressions within *sectors* (*e.g.*, to state that the category is a noun or pronoun) and *node patterns* (*e.g.*, to state that either the category is a noun or the function is an NP head). As we have seen, for sectors, we employ *set notation* (the function, say, is a member of a particular set defined in the FTF) plus *negation* (it is not present in the specific set).

We can enter a formal expression directly to specify a single-node FTF. Figures 197 shows a couple of examples.

In order to build or modify structured FTFs we use the FTF editor. In ICECUP 3.1 the first difference that you will notice is that you now obtain a complete list of all permissible functions, categories or features from the pop-up menus if the node is unspecified (Figures 198 and 200). This means that you do not have to use the "Edit Node..." command to set the function and category: it is quicker and easier to do it directly. However, the menus are rather large!

As well as listing functions, categories, or feature classes and features, these pop-ups gain a number of new options and commands. We need two new commands in order to create signed sets. The first of these, **Specific**, states that we are adding or removing elements from a set, rather than the conventional

Figure 197: Specifying signed sets in an FTF node using the Node query. These obtain the FTFs in Figure 193.

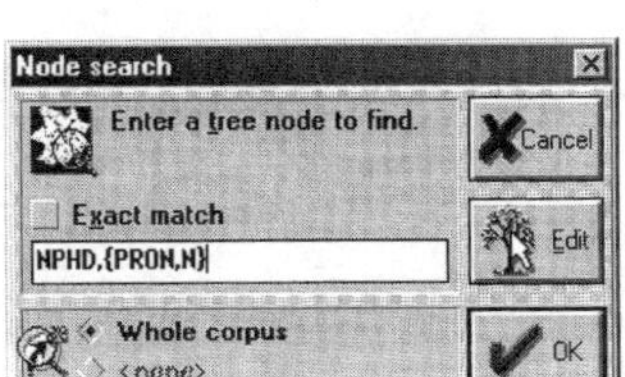

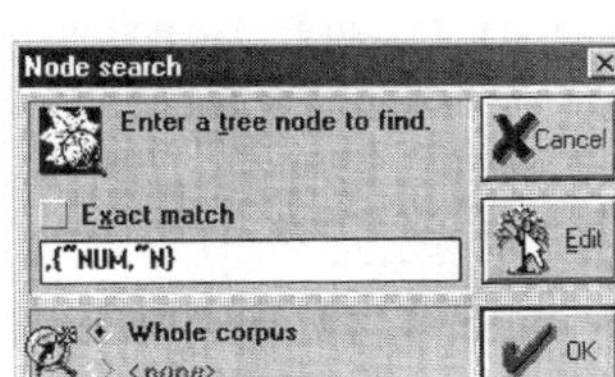

Figure 198: New pop-up menus for function (left) and category (right) if the category and function is undefined.

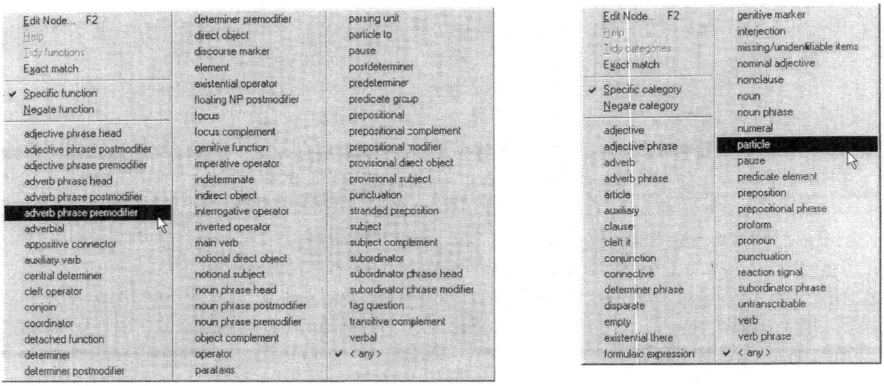

behaviour of replacing one single element with another. The second simply states that the set is negative or positive. The function and category menus now include the following.

- **Tidy** functions/categories (shown disabled in Figure 198).
- **Exact match** (see Subsection 7.6.1).
- **Specific** function/category. You turn 'specific' off to define a set.
- **Negate** function/category. When marked, it states that the function or category is *not* the specified element or in the set.

The 'Exact match' option indicates that the node must match the pattern shown exactly, *i.e.*, that every omitted feature is in fact absent in the corpus node. We have seen what this does already. The real meat of the extensions are in the **Specific**, **Negate** and **Tidy** commands.

If Specific is set, selecting a function replaces the currently selected one (as in ICECUP 3.0). Unless you have already specified a set (*e.g.*, by typing '**{PU, OD}**' in the Edit Node window and pressing Edit), Specific will be *on* by default. To create a list of acceptable functions, for example, you first remove this restriction and then select each individual function in turn (the menus are 'sticky' to assist with this). Try the following.

- ➢ Open a new FTF window in ICECUP 3.1.
- ➢ Place the mouse pointer over the top-left function sector and press down the right mouse button to get the pop-up menu.
- ➢ Select 'parsing unit' from the menu followed by 'direct object'. Selecting the second will overwrite the first because 'Specific function' is on by default. Or is indicated using the standard '∨' signs.

> Uncheck 'Specific function' by selecting it. Now reselect 'parsing unit'. Click outside the menu to make it go away.

The FTF should now show '**PU** ∨ **OD**' in the function sector. Next, we'll assert a similar set in the category sector.

> Select 'Specific category' to switch off the restriction.

> Next, select 'noun phrase', 'nonclause' and 'clause'. The result is shown in the left of Figure 199. During the selection process the parse unit element (PU) will turn red to show that it is inconsistent when the category is specified as an NP.

Recall that in ICECUP 3.0, when you change the function or category of a node, the corresponding set of co-occurring categories or functions will also change (see Section 5.7). These 'complementary sets' are used to construct menus and the options listed in the Edit Node window. If the function and category are incompatible, an error will be indicated.

What happens in ICECUP 3.1, if it lets us specify functions and categories with *signed sets*? Note that two implications follow from this.

1. The *open set* of all possible compatible partners of a source set consists of the union ('or') of all partners of the *positive* interpretation of the source set (*i.e.*, all those that are not in a negated set).
2. The *closed set* of all *entirely compatible* partners of a source set is the intersection ('and') of all partners of the positive interpretation of the source set.

These principles are used to create the two menus. Each menu lists all compatible partners of the corresponding sector (principle 1). As a result ICECUP can have a pop-up menu with a long list of functions (up to 61 in ICE).

Those partners that are inconsistent with *some* members of the source set (*i.e.*, they are excluded by principle 2) are marked with a small centred dot ('•'). You can select these, but some combinations cannot appear. This is intended to guide users to a pair of compatible function-category set descriptions.

Naturally, using this method it is entirely possible to create inconsistent or partially redundant descriptions, as we saw in our worked example. In ICECUP 3.0 the FTF editor shows a compatibility error as a red line between the function and category sectors. Now, however, *parts* of either expression may be in error because they are completely incompatible with the contents of

Figure 199: Logic in sectors: a disjunctive set (left), with negation (right).

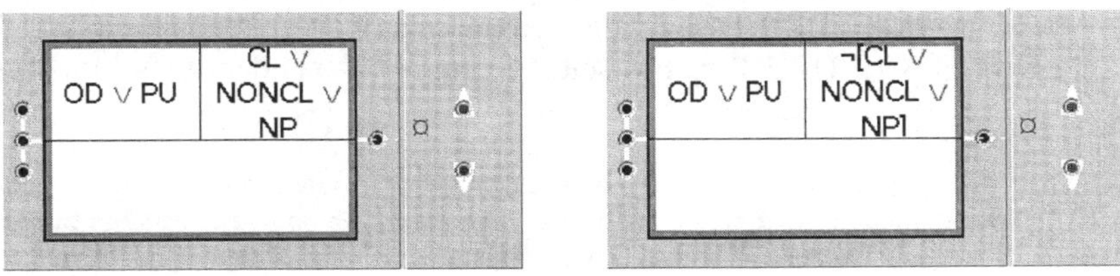

Figure 200: Specifying features. If both the function and the category are undefined the number of permissible features is very large, and three levels of pop-up menu are required (right).

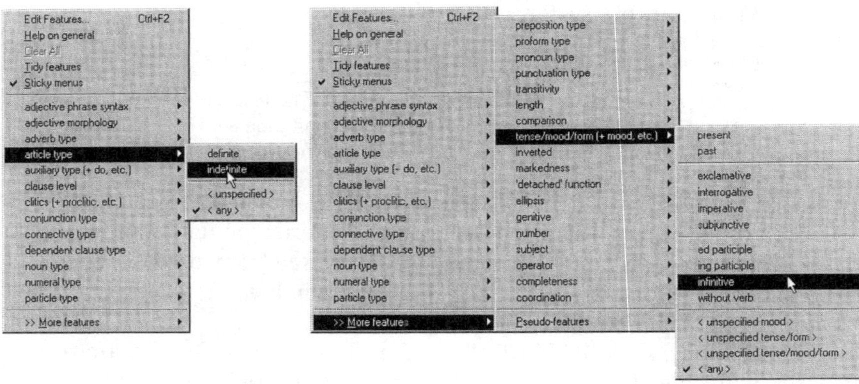

the complementary sector. These elements are absent from the relevant menu (as in ICECUP 3.0) and if present in the FTF editor, will be coloured red. The **Tidy** command removes all such redundant elements.

If **Negate** is indicated for a sector, the FTF insists that in a matching node in the corpus, none of the specified contents of the sector must be present. Every currently selected element in the sector will be negated, so '**OD** ∨ **PU**' becomes '**¬[OD** ∨ **PU]**'. Negation places a not ('¬') sign before the expression and introduces brackets if more than one element is negated. The menu replaces crosses ('✘') for tick marks ('✓'). By using this pair of commands with the selection procedure we can create a signed set of functions or categories.

➢ In the Category menu, select 'Negate category' (Figure 199, right). Select 'Negate' again to switch it back.

As we have seen (page 222), features are added to the node by using the feature menu in a similar way, although negation is handled by selecting the same feature twice. Pseudo-features are also added using the Feature menu.

The set of permissible features and classes depends on the possible category of the node.[15] Now that a category may be defined by a signed set, the set of acceptable features can be very large, as shown by Figure 200. As in version 3.0, each feature class defines a submenu consisting of its permissible features. We also gain an additional '<unspecified>' element in the submenu.

Whereas in ICECUP 3.0 only one feature in any given feature class could be specified, in ICECUP 3.1 we can select features independently and interpret

---

[15] ICECUP 3.1 also takes the function into account, so it can limit available features indirectly. For example, if the function is given as 'main verb', the only permissible category is 'verb', whether specified or not, and so available features are limited to features of verbs.

them together at search time. As before, the feature 'general' can be selected under either 'adverb type' or 'connective type'. ICECUP resolves ambiguities when the search begins. As a corollary, we can display overlapping feature classes (*e.g.*, 'tense/form' and 'mood') together in the same submenu.

As with functions, those features that are not compatible with the current signed set of categories are shown in red, and will be absent from the menu. As in ICECUP 3.0, features which are incompatible with the category are shown in red. Some features are incompatible with one another because they do not belong to any shared category (*e.g.*, no node can be both 'general' and 'incomplete'), so no node in the corpus can match both of them. In the FTF these features are marked with a red dotted underline.

If you want to specify that a particular feature class is unmarked, locate the '<unspecified>' or '<unspecified class>' element in the feature menu for the particular class. As we have seen, these elements are displayed in bold to distinguish between, for example, *without operator* ('-op') and the absence of a feature in the feature class 'operator' (**'-op'**).

In summary, ICECUP 3.1 permits the user to define a set of acceptable values in a sector or feature class. Ambiguities that may arise are due to feature re-use: the fact that the same feature label may be used to mean something different in a different category. With complex patterns, and, in particular, if a node has more than one potential category, it can be a good idea to ask ICECUP to spell out the logical implications of the pattern (see the box on page 228). This process is performed anyway prior to searching. As usual, you can then edit the result.

To simplify our current example (see Figure 199), do the following.

> First, hit the <Tab> key or go to 'Edit | Edit Node Formula | Edit logic'. This displays the node as a formula (Figure 201, left).

Figure 201: Two example simplifications, one where the category set is positive (top) and one, negative (bottom).

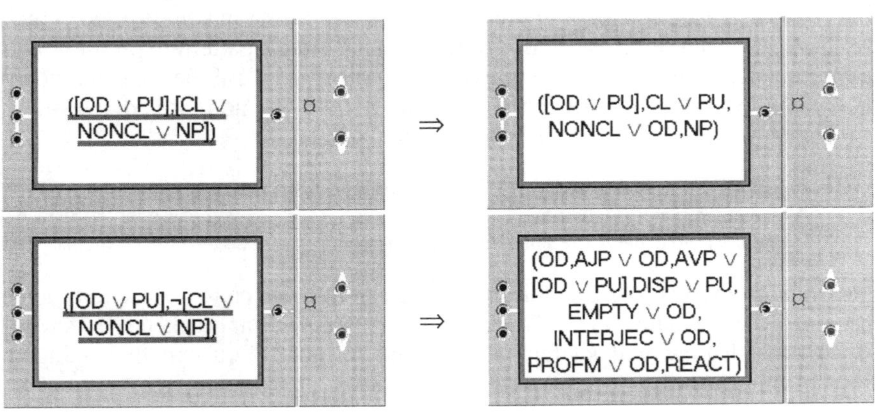

Translating and simplifying nodes

ICECUP 3.1 includes a 'translate and simplify' procedure which 'spells out' the implications of a complex expression by translating it into a logical series of simpler expressions. The idea is that these simpler expressions are easier (and faster) to look up in the precalculated indices, but are also easier to comprehend. This process does three things.

1. It expands *category sets* into a set of alternative ('ored') nodes where the *category* is known, then it expands the feature list to find compatible categories. Thus the expression "**NPHD,{PRON,N}**" becomes "**(NPHD,PRON or NPHD,N)**". If no category or feature is given, then only the function is specified. (This is because the category is key to the meaning of features.)
2. It employs many of the standard simplification axioms used by *drag and drop logic* (see Section 6.10) to simplify the expression as much as possible.
3. It employs additional axioms exploiting function-category compatibility constraints. This process can establish, for example, that the intersection of two sets, one of functions and one of categories, '**{PU,OD},{CL,NONCL,NP}**', is equivalent to '**({OD,PU},CL or PU,NONCL or OD,NP)**'. A nonclause cannot be a direct object, nor an NP a parsing unit.

For example, translating and simplifying **(inter) or ({CL,NONCL,NP} or {PU,OD})** becomes **({OD,PU}, or ,CL or ,NONCL or ,NP or ,PREP(inter) or ,PRON(inter))**

> Then, press down with the right mouse button outside the formula. You will then get the 'Edit Node Formula' as a pop-up menu and may select 'Simplify'. The result is shown in Figure 201, right.

If you forgot to un-negate the category you will obtain the expression at the bottom of Figure 201. Note that you get a pattern for every distinct possible category. Both of these expressions are *longer* but consist of less complex patterns. You can now examine and edit the results before starting the search.

7.6.4 Specifying a logical formula

There are at least three ways of creating a logical formula in a node. One, which we have just seen, is to ask ICECUP to expand a single-pattern expression into a formula consisting of nodal expressions. Another is to use the 'inexact Node' query window. If the expression contains more than one node it is displayed as a formula in preference to the familiar 'sector' display.

> Open the Node query window, type '**(NPHD and (PRON or N))**' and press Edit. You can leave out the first and last brackets and the 'or', so you can type '**NPHD and (PRON N)**' to achieve the same result. Do include a space between the elements.

The third method is to create a logical expression from scratch. An empty node becomes the formula '**(,)**', *i.e.*, an empty node within brackets. If you hit <Tab> the display will switch to show the formula. You can then edit the expression.

Figure 202: Selecting elements of a simple node and a formula consisting of three node patterns.

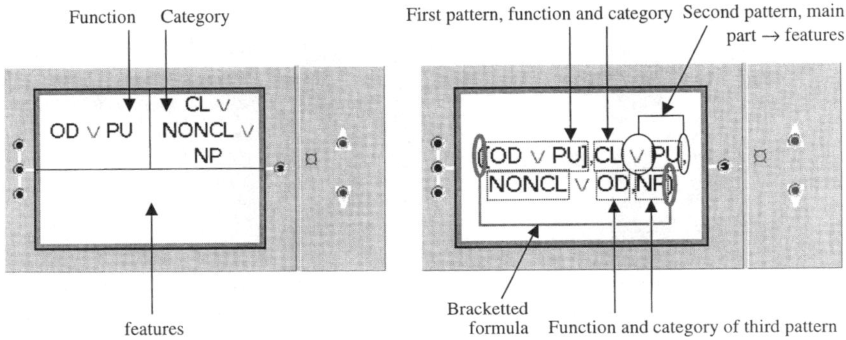

The node looks a bit different in the formula display (see Figure 202 overleaf). The sectors have disappeared. Instead different parts of the formula become 'live'. By clicking on different parts of the formula, you can specify the function, category or features, and edit the formula. Since we have an expression composed of a number of distinct parts, you can now select *part* of the expression. The selected part is given a broad pale underline.

You can use cursor keys to move through this expression. Pressing the right cursor key will move through the sequence by selecting bracketted expressions before their subexpressions (Table 52). You can also press <Insert> to add brackets, <Delete> to remove elements, and <Ctrl>+<Insert> to add a new pattern node.

This process lets you change the currently-selected subexpression and add or remove elements. You can also use the mouse to change the selection, and, through pop-up menus, to assign functions, categories and features to any one of the subexpressions.

Note that previously the FTF editor only allowed you to edit one node pattern within a node at a time. To edit a formula we must be able to say change

Table 52: Keyboard commands to edit an expression in a node mirror those to edit the entire fuzzy tree fragment. <Tab> switches mode.

key	Action
'←'	Previous child (left), then parent (+<Ctrl> = previous child only)
'→'	Next child below, then right (+<Ctrl> = next child right only)
'↑'	Parent (bracketting expression)
'↓'	First child within brackets

key	Action
<Home>	Entire expression.
<End>	Deselect entire expression.
<Page Up>	First leaf.
<Page Down>	Last leaf.

Figure 203: The Edit Node Formula pop-up menu (left) and using this to specify the category (right).

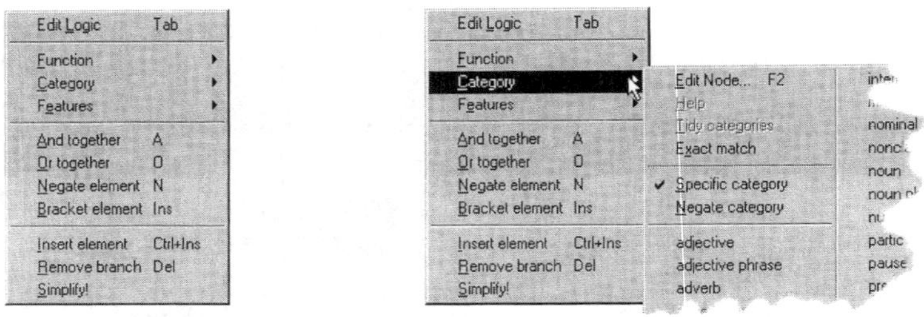

that function or add a feature to *this* element. Different subareas of a simple three-pattern expression are shown in Figure 202. Moreover (if enabled, see 'Corpus | Viewing options...'), the pop-up help will change as the mouse moves over these different elements.

You can select parts of the expression with the mouse as follows.

- Clicking with the left mouse button on either the opening or closing bracket of an expression will select the expression within the brackets. A broad pale underline will be drawn under the selected elements.
- Clicking on any part of a node pattern (function, comma, category and optionally, features) selects that pattern. Clicking on any preceding logical operator *e.g.*, the '∨' (or) operators in Figure 202, also causes that pattern to be selected.
- Clicking elsewhere removes the selection.

If you want to change, say, the function of the third node pattern in the FTF in Figure 202, right, you click on the function element, in this case the individual '**OD**', with the right mouse button. You can then change the direct object to any other compatible function. How do you specify a sector of an element if the sector is empty to begin with, *i.e.*, how do you select a non-existent sector?

- ➢ Open an empty formula expression by performing a New FTF and then hit the <Tab> key. Place the mouse pointer over the comma in the middle of the expression and press down with the right mouse button. You should get the pop-up menu in Figure 203, left.
- ➢ Drag the mouse down until 'Category' is selected. This opens the category pop-up as a submenu (see Figure 203, right).
- ➢ Now drag the mouse to the right and select a category, *e.g.*, noun phrase.

The remaining parts of the menu are very similar to those used in drag and drop logic (Chapter 6). You can *negate* an element, specify that the element is 'ored' or 'anded' with the previous one, or insert brackets around an element. As we have seen, you can also insert or delete an element at any point.

Pressing <Tab> or selecting 'Edit Logic' in the pop-up will deselect the current selected pattern. You can then navigate and edit the FTF as usual. When you are finished, you can hit <F4> to start the search as usual.

This concludes our discussion of ICECUP 3.1. Up-to-date information and support is available on-line at the Survey of English Usage website. In the next part of the book we consider how ICECUP and ICE-GB may be used to address research questions.

PART 3:
Performing research with the corpus

8. CASE STUDIES USING ICE-GB

The previous chapter described the ICECUP software at some length. Here we illustrate some of the ways in which ICE-GB can be used to explore a range of lexical and grammatical issues. The six case studies presented are not intended as full-scale explorations of their topics. Instead, they have been selected to illustrate the various kinds of information that the corpus contains, and how ICECUP may be used to retrieve and explore this information. For one of these – case study 4 – we discuss how a statistical method can be used to allow evidence from the corpus to be generalised to statements about contemporary British English.

The first two case studies are lexical. They demonstrate how to search for words, and how we can examine words in context using ICECUP. The other case studies are progressively more complicated, and address a range of issues in clause structure and phrase structure.[1]

8.1 Case study 1: Pretty *much an adverb*

Dictionaries almost invariably define the word *pretty* primarily in terms of its adjectival uses. Thus, *Collins English Dictionary* (3rd edition, 1991) states:

> **pretty** adj., -tier, -tiest. **1**. pleasing or appealing in a delicate or graceful way.
> **2**. dainty, neat or charming.

The entry goes on to define eight other adjectival meanings, including some archaic ones, before coming to:

> *~adv*. **10**. *Informal.* fairly or moderately, somewhat. **11**. *Informal.* quite or very.

In fact, if corpus evidence is to be believed, *pretty* is far more commonly used as an adverb than as an adjective. Here we will use ICE-GB to determine the exact proportions.

> Click on the 'Text' button and type "**pretty**" in the dialog box that opens (Figure 204 – see also Chapter 5 for more information). Do not type a space after "**pretty**".

---

[1] In the following case studies, we will search the principal material in the corpus (*i.e.*, excluding the 'ignored' material), perform case- and accent-independent comparisons and employ the 'skip over' option. These settings may be modified from the 'Search Options' window (select the menu item 'Query | Search options...' or hit the 'Options' command button – see Section 3.13). If these settings are not assigned, you may obtain slightly different results to those quoted here.

Figure 204: Entering '"pretty" as an adverb' into a text fragment search.

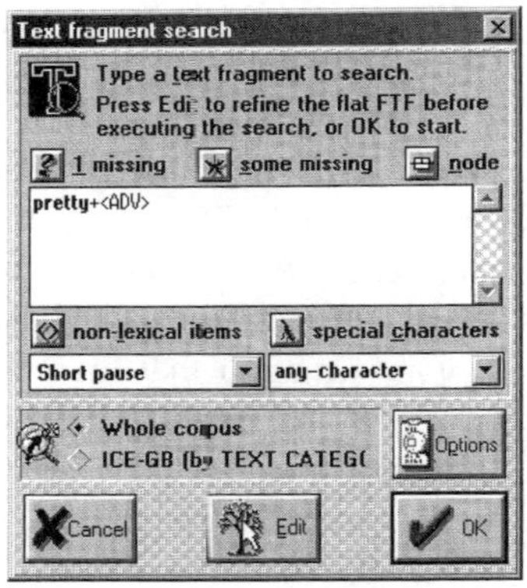

> Select the 'node' button in the box ('', or press <Alt> and 'N' together) and type "ADV" (adverb) between the brackets. Your query should now look like Figure 204.

> Hit <Enter> or select the 'OK' button to launch the search.

This search retrieves 112 instances. To find out the number of times it appears as an adjective, simply change "ADV" to "ADJ" (adjective) in the dialogue box. To ensure that we compare all forms, we should also search for *prettier* and *prettiest*. The results of these searches are shown in Table 53.

With just 20 instances, adjectival *pretty* is rare in ICE-GB. In contrast, adverbial *pretty* is used much more frequently, and, as we'll see, it exhibits a range of meanings, and can occur in a wide range of syntactic environments.

We can inspect the set of results generated by adverbial *pretty*. Open the window and scroll down to examine them.

Like other intensifiers, *pretty* most commonly modifies an adjective.

I'm *pretty* sure it is [S1A-029 #35]

And uh was the pool *pretty* busy [S1B-066 #90]

The engine's *pretty* good [S2A-055 #67]

Table 53: How often "pretty" is used in ICE-GB.

part of speech	lexical item	frequency
adverb	*pretty*	112
adjective	*pretty*	19
	prettier	0
	prettiest	1

Less commonly, it modifies another adverb.

> I think they did *pretty* well... [S1A-095 #94]
>
> ... they would have come up with that *pretty* quickly [S1A-058 #91]
>
> Now I shall summarize the evidence I hope *pretty* briefly [S2A-061 #32]

In each case, *pretty* may be replaced by *fairly* or *very*, as the dictionary definition suggests. The corpus contains just one example of *pretty* premodifying a determiner:

> While some but as yet *pretty* few women are at last achieving promotion to senior rank <,> senior black officers are rare indeed <,> [S2B-037 #64]

Here, the semantic equivalent would again seem to be *very* or *quite*.

Pretty sometimes occurs with *well* in pre-adjective position:

> ...it would have been *pretty well* impossible to get in... [W1B-007 #53]

This is an interesting construction, since the status of *well* is unclear. In the most likely interpretation, *well* postmodifies *pretty*, since it may be omitted (*pretty impossible*). *Well impossible* seems unacceptable, although in current British English, *well* is increasingly being used in constructions like this, as in the following.

> *Well* nice [S1A-071 #333]

The corpus contains just one example of this type, though there is some anecdotal evidence that it is gaining acceptability. Notice, however, that *very well nice* or *pretty well nice* remain unacceptable.

In the following example, neither *pretty* nor *well* may be omitted:

> ...those percentages were *pretty well* reversed [S2A-037 #19]
> (*cf.* ?those percentages were pretty reversed / ?those percentages were well reversed)

Similarly, in the following, *pretty* forms a close syntactic link with *well,* to premodify a noun phrase:

> ...and foretells of 100,000 dead (*pretty well* the size of the BEF then being mobilised). [W2A-009 #10]

Again, neither part can be omitted (**pretty the size*/**well the size*), and indeed it is difficult to think of any other adverb that could replace *pretty* in this construction (**quite/very well the size*).

Semantically, *pretty well* seems to be equivalent to *more or less*, or *almost.* The same is true of some uses of *pretty much.*

> all my friends were trying to have sex with <,> pretty <,> *pretty much* anybody they they <,> wanted to <,> [S1A-072 #187]
>
> And it's been *pretty much* at the same temperature for a long time [S2A-043 #40]
>
> And of course the weather can do *pretty much* what it wants and you'll still be mobile [S2A-055 #137]

In some cases, we have to see a sentence in context in order to make an interpretation. To view context, press down with the right mouse button over the sentence and select either 'Browse Text' or 'Browse Context' from the menu. A new window shows the sentence in the context of the whole text.

In the following examples, the context shows that *pretty much* is used in a response to another speaker, and means something like *more or less* or *that is approximately correct*:

> **Speaker A:** When you switched to the emphasis being on Architecture <,,> did you initially think that you wanted to go into that as a career or were you doing it just as a degree because you enjoyed the subject
> **Speaker B:** *Pretty much* yeah I've got to admit [S1A-034 #93-94]

In our final example, the context is less clear, though it does seem to illustrate *pretty much* as equivalent to *very much*, rather than to *more or less*:

> **Speaker A:** But you said you're not familiar with it in practice <,> because you're not working as a counsellor <,>
> **Speaker B:** Oh well we didn't have enough practice I don't think on our course <,>
> Uhm <,> but the reality of it was I could do I mean you know I think I <,>
> I could do the counselling that I had to do there <,>
> Probably
> I mean I was I was *pretty much* advanced on the delegates [S1A-060 #64]

Despite its semantic and syntactic versatility, the adverb *pretty* is not established in formal, written English. The vast majority of instances in ICE-GB occur in the spoken component, and particularly in dialogues. We can see this by scrolling through the concordance lines in ICECUP. Textcodes beginning with 'S' (shown on the left of the screen) denote spoken sources, while those beginning with 'W' denote written sources. Only 13 instances of *pretty* as an adverb occur in written texts, and of these, 8 are non-printed sources (the W1B texts), and two are from dialogue in fiction (the W2F texts).

This leaves just three instances in formal, printed English. It is likely that its rarity in formal writing explains the status accorded to adverb *pretty* by lexicographers.

8.2 *Case Study 2: Exploring the lexeme* book *with the lexicon*

The previous case study illustrated the simplest approach to searching for lexical items in ICECUP. We will now describe a second method, using the lexicon facility in ICECUP 3.1 (see Section 7.2). The lexicon provides a 'lexical overview' of lexical items and word class tags, and is therefore appropriate for certain types of research. It looks rather like the corpus map, but contains POS-classified lexical items rather than texts and speakers.

In this example, we will use the lexicon to determine whether the lexeme *book* occurs more frequently as a noun or as a verb in ICE-GB.

- Select the leftmost menu item in ICECUP, 'Corpus'. Choose 'Lexicon' from this menu. Open the lexicon options by pressing <Ctrl> and 'L' together (or hitting ''). In the first Path box, select '1st letter' and hit OK. Then press the control key (<Ctrl>) and '1' together or hit ''.
- You should now see a list of letters of the alphabet. Next, we have to open up the list of all lexical items that start with the letter *B*. Press the key 'B', to move to the B-group element. This is labelled 'B'. Then hit <Ctrl> and the right cursor key ('→'), which opens the branch. Alternatively, 'double-click' with the mouse on the icon.
- The tree expands to display all the lexical items in ICE-GB starting with 'B', in alphabetical order. Now, scroll down until you find the item *book*. (The list is a long one, so you may wish to jump entire pages at a time.)
- Many of the lexical items have only one grammatical tag in ICE-GB, so they are listed with this tag. However, when you reach the lexical item *book*, you will note that no tag is given and the icon is marked with a yellow 'plus'. When you expand the element, you should see a display like that shown in Figure 205.

Figure 205: The lexicon list with the item "book" expanded (left); the categorial instantiations of "book" with their percentages (right).

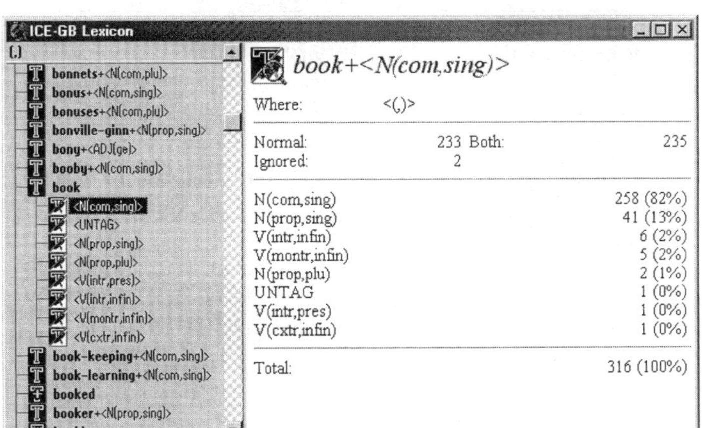

ICECUP's lexicon shows that *book* occurs a total of 315 times in ICE-GB, with a total of 8 different word class tags. On the right-hand side of the screen (Figure 205), the lexicon lists the frequency and the percentages of the instances of each tag. Thus we see that 258, or 82%, of all instances of *book* are common singular nouns.

➢ To retrieve these from the corpus, select '<N(com,sing)>' in the lexicon tree on the left of the screen and press <F4> or the large 'Browse' button. A new text browser window appears, showing all these instances of *book*.

In the same way, we can examine *book* as a proper noun.

➢ Highlight '<N(prop,sing)>' on the left and click on 'Browse' again.

This shows that all of these instances occur as part of a compound, *e.g.*, *Book of Revelations*, *Book of Malachi*. (Note: all items appear in lower case in the lexicon, regardless of their case in the corpus).

Table 54: The forms and uses of "book" in ICE-GB, as displayed by the lexicon.[2]

book		*books*	
N(com,sing)	258 (82%)	N(com,plu)	190 (95%)
N(prop,sing)	41 (13%)	N(prop,plu)	8 (4%)
V(intr,infin)	6 (2%)	N(prop,sing)	1 (1%)
V(montr,infin)	5 (2%)		
N(prop,plu)	2 (1%)		
UNTAG	1 (0%)		
V(cxtr,infin)	1 (0%)		
V(intr,pres)	1 (0%)		
booked		*booking*	
V(montr,edp)	12 (55%)	N(com,sing)	4 (40%)
V(montr,past)	5 (23%)	V(montr,ingp)	3 (30%)
V(intr,edp)	4 (18%)	N(com,plu)	2 (20%)
ADJ(edp)	1 (5%)	UNTAG	1 (10%)

Table 55: Overall figures for "book" as a noun and as a verb.

Noun	499 (93%)
Verb	37 (6%)
Other	3 (1%)
Total	539 (100%)

[2] See Chapter 2 for a detailed explanation of these word class tags and features.

ICE-GB has not been lemmatized, so all forms of the lexeme *book* (*book*, *books*, *booked*, *booking*) are listed separately. Consulting each form in turn in the lexicon, we get the results in Table 54.

Overall, the lexeme *book* appears in a total of 13 different grammatical guises in the corpus. Collating the data from Table 54, we calculate the overall figures for the various nominal and verbal uses, and display these in Table 55.

The results show that *book* rarely occurs as a verb. As a monotransitive verb it occurs just 22 times. When we examine these occurrences in the corpus (again, click on 'Browse' to view them), we find that they generally fall within a fairly narrow semantic range, namely travel and holidays (*book a flight*, *book a room*, *etc*.).

How does using the lexicon differ from the 'Text fragment' search, as described in the previous case study? The lexicon allows the user immediate access to grammatical information about lexical items, such as word class membership, transitivity, number, *etc*. You can browse the lexical items (so you can check to see if all forms are present in the corpus), and you can restrict the set of lexical items to, say, just the nouns or verbs. The lexicon also offers statistical assessments of forms.

Note, however, that the lexicon supports single lexical items only. If you wish to search for longer strings, including phrases and discontinuous strings, you must use the 'Text fragment' search. Also, if you simply want to perform a quick search for a single word, the 'Text' search is fast and effective.

8.3 Case Study 3: Transitivity and clause type

This case study aims to investigate the syntactic positions that dependent complex transitive clauses can occur in. Complex transitive clauses are clauses which contain a direct object ('**OD**') followed by what Quirk *et al*. (1985) call an object complement ('**CO**'), as in the following.

(1) I consider [$_{\text{OD}}$ my teachers][$_{\text{CO}}$ fools]

In ICE-GB, all units have been assigned grammatical functions. In addition, all clauses have been marked for transitivity. ICE-GB uses the following transitivity features (for examples, see Subsection 2.2.20 on verbs).

- intransitive
- transitive
- monotransitive
- ditransitive
- complex transitive
- dimonotransitive
- copular

Most of these features are familiar, though one or two require some further comments. We use the label 'transitive' in a specialised sense to apply to clauses where the transitivity of the main verb is unclear. An example would be the verb *believe* in sentence (2) below.

(2) I *believe* our teachers to be fools.

Sentences like this have generated an enormous amount of attention over the last three decades, and receive different treatments in different frameworks. In descriptive frameworks the postverbal NP is usually treated as a direct object, followed by a nonfinite subjectless clause functioning as object complement. In early theoretical approaches (*e.g.* Postal 1974) the postverbal NP was sometimes regarded as a 'raised object', positioned in the subject position of the lower clause at Deep Structure, and then subsequently raised to the object position of the higher clause.

In more recent theoretical frameworks the NP *teachers* is the subject of the subordinate clause *our teachers to be fools*. In ICE-GB, in order not to prejudge the issue, the label 'transitive' is used in a specialised sense for clauses containing 'raised objects'. Monotransitive verbs and clauses are then simply verbs and clauses that contain only a postverbal direct object.

Dimonotransitive verbs (and clauses) are verbs that take only an indirect object, as in the sentence below:

(3) She was in tears after I had *told* her.

In such cases the direct object is contextually recoverable.

Transitivity features percolate up to the verb phrase that contains the verb in question, as well as to the containing clause, as the following tree diagram from the corpus shows.

We now wish to focus on complex transitive patterns to see if they can occur in dependent clauses functioning as subjects, as direct objects, and as adverbials. This question is of interest because it investigates whether there is a relationship between the grammatical function of a clause and its transitivity.

Figure 206: A tree diagram showing a complex transitive verb (S1A-002 #35).

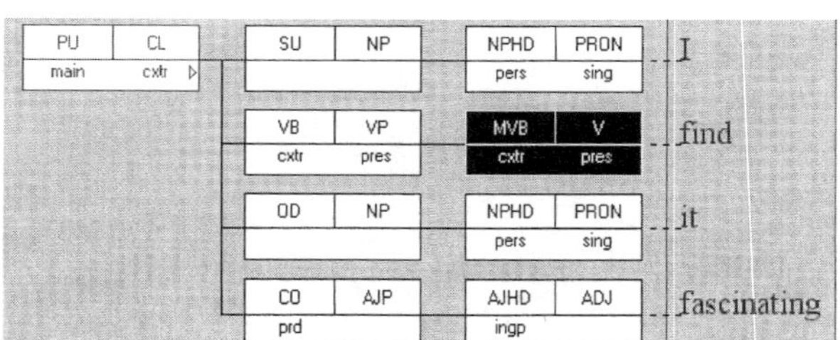

Figure 207: FTFs showing complex transitive clauses functioning as adverbial (left), subject (right) and direct object (lower).

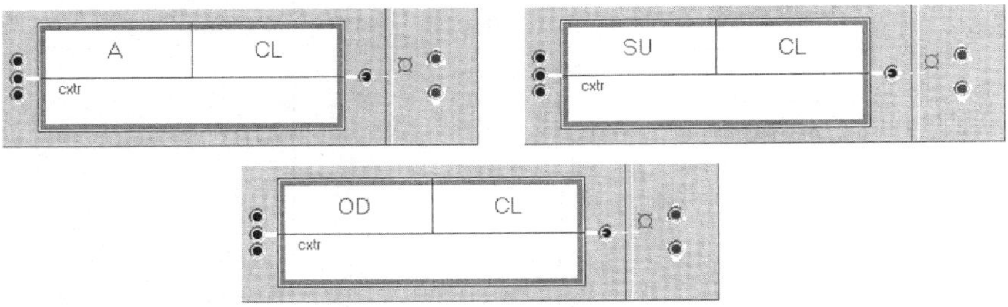

This kind of pattern is very difficult to find in an unparsed corpus. By contrast, the task is straightforward for ICECUP on ICE-GB. We simply construct single-node Fuzzy Tree Fragments (see Chapter 3) like those in Figure 207, to find the constructions we're interested in.

In Figure 207 we have specified three separate FTFs, which ICECUP will use to find matching nodes of the trees in the corpus. The node is divided into three sectors (see Section 2.1). These are specified for function (top left sector), form (top right), and features (bottom). Any one of these sectors may be left unspecified, allowing a researcher to be more or less specific. For example, we may wish to look for all clauses (with *any* function) containing a complex transitive verb. In that case we would simply leave the top left sector empty.

There is a quick way of constructing such simple (single-node) FTFs. This is to use the (inexact) 'Node' search (Section 3.6).

- ➢ Press the big 'Node' button on the command bar. Type "**`OD,CL(cxtr)`**" (Figure 208).
- ➢ Hit 'Edit' to edit the FTF as shown in Figure 207. You can then change the function in the usual way (press down with the right mouse button over the function sector and select from the list of compatible functions).

The FTFs in Figure 207 yield the results listed in the first line of Table 56. For comparison we have added the data for the number of clauses marked for the other types of transitivity.

Figure 208: Specifying an FTF node using the Node search window.

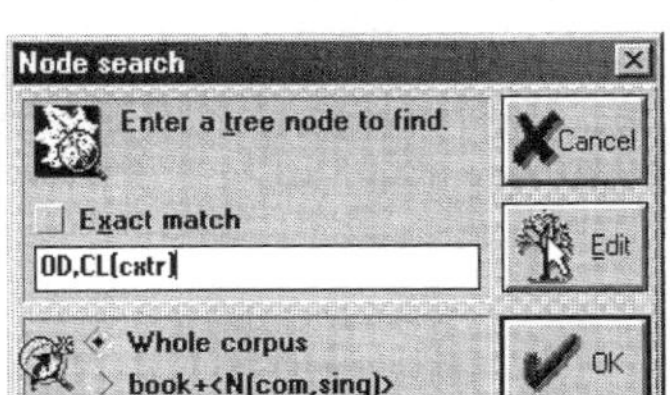

Table 56: Frequencies of adverbial, subject and direct object clauses in ICE-GB, according to their transitivity properties.

	`A,CL`	`SU,CL`	`OD,CL`	TOTAL
complex transitive	460	38	338	**836**
ditransitive	173	13	155	**341**
monotransitive	7,268	535	5,094	**12,897**
dimonotransitive	32	0	16	**48**
transitive	311	9	203	**523**
intransitive	4,369	159	2,552	**7,080**
copular	2,534	97	3,174	**5,805**
TOTAL	**15,147**	**851**	**11,532**	**27,530**

The numbers in Table 56 themselves mean very little, but they can be the starting point for interesting qualitative research questions. These questions include the following.

- Why are clauses functioning as subjects so limited in their distribution?
- Why are ditransitive and transitive verbs so rare in subject clauses?

Of course, some of these questions have already been studied (*cf. e.g.*, Mair 1990), while others have not. Although this is not the place to cover research questions in any detail, we can explore some possible avenues of investigation in order to answer one of the questions posed above.

Suppose that we examine the examples of subject clauses containing a transitive verb. The results found by ICECUP, together with their sentence identifiers, can be saved to a file (refer to subsection 6.13). All nine instances are listed below, with the clauses containing transitive verbs highlighted.

(4) Uhm <,> *what I found happening* <,> *over the period of study* was that <,> I began to bring those two areas together so that <,> uhm the work that I was doing in the in the fine art part of the course was beginning to spill over <,> both in terms of <,> choreography and also in terms of <,> art work <,> in relation <,> to people moving <,> [S1A-004 #4]

(5) so *what I want you to be stuck on* is F X equals X cubed [S1B-013 #59]

(6) and *what I'd like people to do* is uh give brief <,> summaries to the group about the contents of their essays [S1B-016 #3]

(7) *What I would urge him though to do* is not unless the press report is incorrect start contacting in particular the French to urge support for their attitudes in agriculture because I don't think that's going down very well in Wales [S1B-056 #74]

(8) *What I was asking you to deal with* is the situation where <,,> in relation to that one per cent or three per cent or whatever it is <,,> [S1B-062 #130]

(9) *Letting me lie my head down for a few days in your Penthouse* was great. [W1B-001 #109:3]

(10) *What many felt to be Serbia's dominant position* had to be diminished, and satisfaction given to the differences that existed in these regions. [W2B-007 #66]

(11) The ministry felt that *to allow ex-servicemen, as many of the unemployed and destitute were, to enter the workhouses* would fuel public discontent. [W2B-019 #56]

(12) *Watching Patriot missiles rush into the night sky* to explode and destroy the Iraqi Scuds was like taking part in a brilliant computer game. [W2E-007 #5]

One plausible reason why transitive subject clauses are so rare is that their syntax is rather complex and 'top heavy': the 'regular' transitive pattern is Subject+Verb+NP+infinitive. As a result of this it is likely that sentences involving the transitive complementation pattern in subject position are difficult to process mentally, and are therefore avoided. Speakers and writers are likely to prefer to extrapose subject clauses, as the examples below show:

(13) Letting me lie my head down for a few days in your Penthouse was great (=(9))
\> It was great letting me lie my head down for a few days in your Penthouse

(14) The ministry felt that *to allow ex-servicemen, as many of the unemployed and destitute were, to enter the workhouses* would fuel public discontent (=(11))
\> The ministry felt that it would fuel public discontent *to allow ex-servicemen, as many of the unemployed and destitute were, to enter the workhouses*

However, notice that six of the examples in (4)-(12) involve fronting of one of the arguments (the *wh*-phrase). The fact that these examples occur, despite their sentence-initial heaviness can be explained by the fact that the *wh*-clauses cannot be extraposed:

(15) *so what I want you to be stuck on* is F X equals X cubed (=(5))
\> *so it is F X equals X cubed *what I want you to be stuck on*

(16) *What many felt to be Serbia's dominant position* had to be diminished (=(10))
\> *It had to be diminished *what many felt to be Serbia's dominant position*

Figure 209: A tree showing a direct object clause with a complex transitive verb (S1A-023 #25).

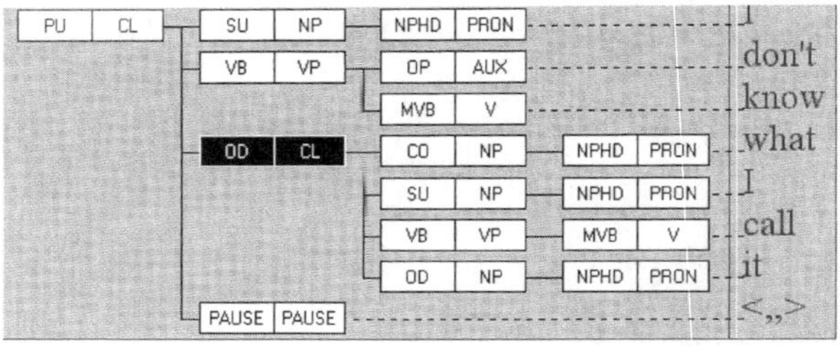

In conclusion, as an initial hypothesis we can explain the scarcity of transitive clauses in subject position by the fact that they are top-heavy, a situation which is compounded by the fact that their syntax is complex, which leads to processing difficulties for speakers and hearers.

Finally, note that you can inspect trees while browsing the corpus. In addition, ICECUP offers the FTF Creation Wizard facility (Section 5.14) to help researchers construct FTFs from corpus trees. Let's assume that while browsing, you find a tree like the one in Figure 209. Suppose you want to construct an FTF for the pattern defined by clause node and the four nodes 'below' it (*i.e.*, object complement NP+subject NP+verb phrase+direct object NP).

> In the tree window, press <F4> or click on the 'Wizard' button. Press 'OK' without setting any switches (by default, the Wizard will include just these nodes and will disregard features).

The FTF can be modified in the usual way (see Chapter 5). For example you can explicitly add the complex transitive feature to the clause, remove function and category terms, nodes, and alter links and edges. It can then be deployed in order to find other trees containing this pattern.

8.4 *Case Study 4: What size feet have you got?* wh-*determiners in noun phrases*[3]

English noun phrases allow the element *what* to function as a determiner, as in the title above (*what size feet*). English also allows *which* to occupy this position: *which size feet*. How can we use ICECUP to find the data which will allow us to study the factors that influence the choice of wh-elements in structures like this?

[3] An expanded version of this case study appeared as Aarts, *et al.* (2002).

*Figure 210: Constructing a text fragment query for "***what** *<N>".*

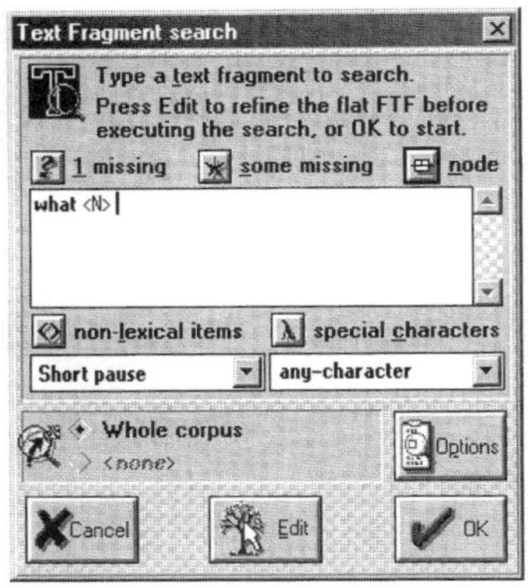

The simplest way to search for such structures is to construct a *Text fragment* query (Chapter 5), as shown in Figure 210. We used this method in the first case study (Section 8.1).

- ➢ Click on the 'Text' button and type "what" in the dialog box that opens (Figure 210). Type a space after "what".
- ➢ Select the 'node' button in the box ('', or press <Alt> and 'N' together). You can then enter, between the angled brackets, a tag label. Type "N" (noun) between the brackets. The query should now read "**what** <N>" like Figure 210. Do not type the angled brackets yourself, as this will not work.
- ➢ Hit <Enter> or select 'OK' to launch the search.

This particular query will find all instances in the corpus where *what* is immediately followed by a noun. By changing "**what** <N>" to "**which** <N>" we find the alternative pattern. Once you've constructed the query click on 'OK' to start the search.

Of course, if we use the search query shown in Figure 210, we risk missing a number of interesting examples, namely those where there is some lexical material between the *wh*-determiner and the head noun, as in the noun phrase *what exact size feet*. How do we make sure that we don't miss anything?

ICECUP's *Text fragment* system lets us allow for 'missing' or unspecified elements. Section 5.3 describes this in detail. The commands for these are labelled '1 missing' and 'some missing' in the text fragment window.

- The '1 missing' command, '' (<Alt>+'1'), introduces a non-bold question mark ('?') into the text fragment. This indicates that there must be exactly one lexical item between anything before, and anything after, the '?'. (Note that the search options apply, so, for example, pauses may not be counted.)

*Figure 211: Text fragment queries: “***what** *? <N>”, left, and “***what** ** <N>”, right.*

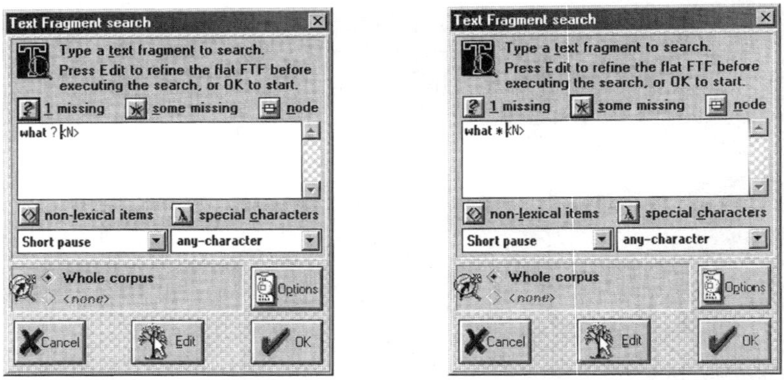

- The ‘some missing’ command, ‘’ (<Alt>+’S’), inserts a non-bold asterisk (‘*’) into the text fragment. This element stands for *any number* of lexical items, including zero, between prior and posterior material.

To see how this works, re-enter “**what** <N>” into the window again, but don’t press <Enter> to start the search immediately.

➢ Next, position the cursor between “**what**” and the “<N>”. Click on the buttons for ‘1 missing’ or ‘some missing’. In the first case (Figure 211, left), select ‘1 missing’.

➢ Now press ‘OK’.

This search yields 397 instances. Now let’s see how many hits we get when we specify that there is any number of missing elements between “**what**” and “<N>”. The query is illustrated on the right of Figure 211.

This new search yields 6,247 examples, rather more than we obtained with a simple search for “**what** <N>” or “**what** ? <N>”! In fact, the high number suggests that the query was too general, and the search may therefore have found us irrelevant examples. A quick look at the results for both searches shows that this is indeed the case. Some of the unwanted material is shown in (1) and (2) below.

(1) *What was Easter* like? [S1A-021 #252]
Now *what is evidence*? [S2A-061 #14]
...we can also question the truth of *what the author* says. [W1A-018 #108]
What has Margaret Thatcher done to the lot of them? [W2C-008 #103]

(2) *What is the time*? [S1A-007 #197]
What about tying that scarf round the middle of it? [S1A-007 #300]
What is essential to this mechanism is for the animal to feel... [W1A-017 #090]
What I am sensing is my own dread, she told herself. [W2F-020 #043]

*Figure 212: A detailed FTF to search for "***what** *<N>" in the same phrase.*

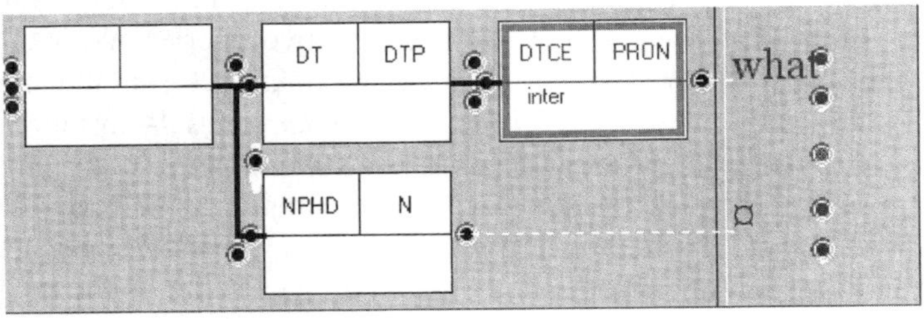

In each of these cases we have the element *what* followed by a noun, though separated by one (1) or more elements (2). In none of these cases does the *wh*-element function as a determiner, which is the pattern that we are interested in. How can we be more precise?

We can construct a Fuzzy Tree Fragment which allows us to specify that the elements that occur between *what* and the head noun should belong to the same (noun phrase) element. Review Chapter 5 for instructions on how to create FTFs. Note, in particular, that we can select an example tree from the results of a text fragment search, and then employ the FTF Creation Wizard to form an FTF from the relevant nodes.

Figure 212 represents a well-defined – although quite detailed – Fuzzy Tree Fragment for the phenomenon that we are interested in. This time, in order to define our query, we will rely on the grammatical analysis in the corpus rather than the sequential order of lexical items.

Notice the white unidirectional arrow between the determiner phrase and noun phrase head nodes. This arrow indicates that the head follows the determiner in the grammatical analysis, although not necessarily immediately (they share a parent node). The other lines are black, which means that there is a direct (immediate) relationship between parent and child nodes. Finally, we specify that *what* is an interrogative pronoun.

So what results do we obtain? Running the FTF search in Figure 212 yields 220 instances which occur predominantly in spoken English (at a ratio of almost 4:1). To calculate the number that are spoken, we must add the sociolinguistic variable query "text category = spoken" into the results (refer to Chapter 6 on combining queries). To recap:

- From the query results window, press the 'Variable' button in the command bar (or select 'Query | Variable...' from the menu. By default you can see the text category variable. Select "spoken" in the value window.
- We now apply the results to the query we have previously calculated. Click on the radio button ('◈') in the lower "apply to:" panel (the one with the magnifying glass and arrow) to select 'Query: ...' instead of 'Whole corpus'.

An alternative way to combine queries is to use 'drag and drop', as we do in the following case study (Section 8.5). The net result is the same with either approach: the overlap (intersection) between the two queries. We can do the same for the written material (or just subtract the spoken set from the total).

Substituting the word *what* for the word *which* yields 44 instances, 31 of which are spoken. This dataset can be used as a starting point to investigate the differences between the two patterns, which for simplicity we will refer to as '*what* N' and '*which* N'. Preliminary results given in Table 57 suggest that the former might be more informal than the latter, at least as far as the medium in which they occur is concerned.

We can determine the significance of these values using the chi-square test. Chi-square, written χ^2, compares the results across each category, called *the observed distribution*, **O**, against the results that would be found if the data was distributed evenly (called the *expected distribution*, **E**). For an explanation of the contingency table and the chi-square statistic, refer to Chapter 9.

To find out if there is any significant variation going on at all we compare the slightly skewed observed results with an averaged expected distribution. The observed distribution is, therefore (reading left-to-right and top-down), {175, 45, 31, 13}. Appropriately scaled, the expected distribution is thus **E** = {171.67, 48.33, 34.33, 9.67}, and the value of χ^2 is 1.765, which is non-significant with a 0.05 margin of error. We cannot reject the 'null hypothesis' (see Chapter 9) that any perceived variation is just due to chance.

This does *not* rule out the possibility that variation within subcategories of the spoken or written parts could not be significant, although, because the numbers are quite small we should be wary of the possibility that any detected variation, in, say, subcategories of the spoken component is not due to repeated use by a few speakers in a small number of texts. We discuss this problem in more detail in Chapter 9 (see, in particular, Section 9.6(d)). In case of doubt, it is a good idea to check the distribution of cases across texts.

A related idea would be to modify the experimental hypothesis and subdivide the corpus according to a different definition of 'formality' than simply 'spoken vs. written'.

Nor does this conclusion mean that if we had more data our results would not be significant. It means that we cannot make any predictions from our data. We can still look at the examples in the corpus and their distribution. We can

Table 57: A contingency table for the results (see Section 9.3).

	spoken	**written**	**TOTAL**
'*what* N'	175	45	**220**
'*which* N'	31	13	**44**
TOTAL	**206**	**58**	**264**

measure the size of *indicative* variation within the sample, using *relative swing* (see Section 9.5). Such variation simply indicates differences which may not be significant but may be worthy of repeated experiments.

In any case, we would need to look at the examples to try to suggest *why* 'what N' constructions might be preferred in one category over another. We have to consider what alternative constructions could be used and explore the interaction between different grammatical variables. This whole question is discussed in Chapter 9.

We do not have space to discuss the factors that influence the choice between *what* and *which* as determiners any further here. Please refer to Aarts *et al.* (2002) for discussion.

8.5 Case Study 5: Active and passive clauses

It is almost axiomatic that the use of the passive is characteristic of 'scientific' writing. Crystal (1997: 385) suggests that the passive is probably the best-known grammatical feature of the language of science, while Quirk, *et al.* (1985: 166) relate its use to the "impersonality" and "objectivity" of that genre. Corpus-based studies have generally supported these views. Francis and Kucera (1982: 554) examined the Brown Corpus of American English, and found that in informational writing (news reports, academic writing, *etc.*) 14.6% of all clauses are passive, compared with only 4.2% in novels and stories. Svartvik (1966) examined passives in the SEU Corpus of British English, and found the highest frequency in scientific prose.

Using ICE-GB, we can examine the distribution of passives across text categories. All passive clauses in the corpus have been assigned a feature label passive ('**`pass`**'). Active clauses are not explicitly marked: all clauses without the '**`pass`**' feature are by default active.

Let's begin by finding out what percentage of clauses are passive in the following six written categories:

- social letters
- business letters
- academic writing
- non-academic writing
- press reports
- fiction

To do this, we need to obtain, first the total number of clauses, and second, the number of passive clauses, in each of these categories.

*Figure 213: An FTF that searches for clauses ('**CL**').*

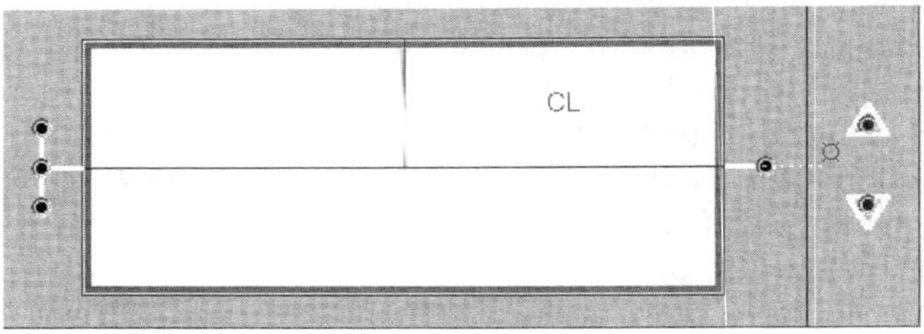

The procedure is as follows.

- Click on 'New FTF' on the button bar. In the blank FTF that appears, right-click in the upper right (category), and select clause ('**CL**') from the list of categories. The FTF should now appear as shown in Figure 213.
- Click on 'Start' to launch the search. The search retrieves all clauses in the whole corpus, and displays them in a new window. The frequency (145,479) is displayed at the bottom of the screen.

We now want to restrict these results to each of our text categories in turn. We begin with social letters.

- Open the corpus map and select the 'expand all categories' button ('').
- Using the mouse, select the icon next to 'social letters' in the corpus map. If you hold down the left mouse button over the icon the label should expand to read 'TEXT CATEGORY = SOCIAL LETTERS' and a copy of the element should 'detach' from the corpus map tree.
- Now, holding the mouse button down, drag the element across the screen, and drop it into the results window showing the clauses.[4]

The results window is automatically updated. It should now display only those clauses occurring in social letters, together with their frequency: 5,085.

Next, we will retrieve all the passive clauses in the category of social letters. To do this, we will repeat the entire process for passive clauses.

- Return to the FTF editor window and perform a right-click with the mouse in the lower (features) sector of the FTF. Select "voice" from the menu list that appears. This inserts the feature label '**pass**' (passive) into the FTF, which should now appear as shown in Figure 214.

Work your way through the remainder of the procedure, using the results of the search performed by the new ('passive clause') FTF. This yields a frequency count of, for example, 181 passive clauses in the social letters.

[4] For a more detailed explanation of the 'drag and drop logic' system, see Chapter 6.

Figure 214: An FTF used to search for passive clauses.

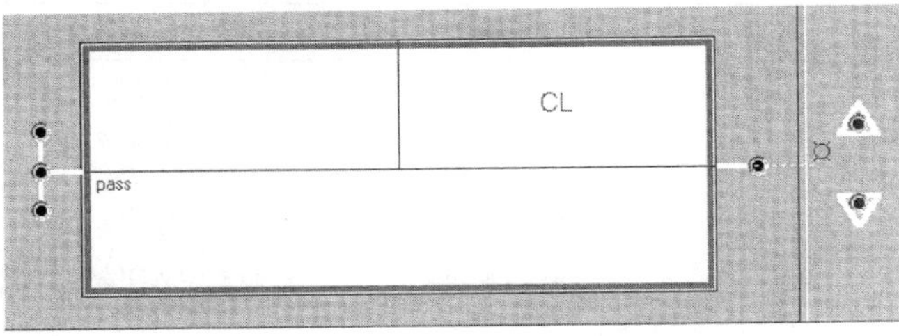

Table 58: Actives and passives in six text categories.

	Active	Passive	Total
Social letters	4,877 (96.4%)	181 (3.6%)	5,085
Business letters	3,463 (87.7%)	484 (12.3%)	3,947
Academic writing	7,206 (78.0%)	2,043 (22.0%)	9,249
Non-academic writing	8,858 (83.0%)	1,810 (17.0%)	10,668
Press reports	4,716 (86.7%)	727 (13.3%)	5,443
Fiction	6,832 (94.2%)	421 (5.8%)	7,253

Using the same method we obtain the frequencies of all clauses, and then of passive clauses, in our other categories. The active clauses, which are unmarked, are obtained by subtracting the passives from the total. The results are shown in Table 58.

The results confirm previous studies. Passives are proportionally most common in the informational categories, academic writing, non-academic writing, and press reports.

Suppose we now look more closely at academic writing, which exhibits the highest proportion of passives. This category is further subdivided into:

- humanities
- social science
- natural science
- technology

To obtain frequencies for these subcategories, we repeat the procedure, selecting different subcategories from the corpus map. Table 59 shows the results.

This seems to bear out the view that the passive is characteristic of scientific writing. Not only is passivization most common in scientific texts, it appears to play a greater role the more 'technical' the writing becomes.

It would be interesting to see if the same pattern is observed in the category of non-academic writing, since this consists of four parallel subcat-

Table 59: Actives and passives in subcategories of academic writing.

	Active	Passive	Total
humanities	1,956 (83.4%)	391 (16.6%)	2,347
social science	1,914 (81.5%)	435 (18.5%)	2,349
natural science	1,638 (75.3%)	539 (24.7%)	2,177
technology	1,698 (71.5%)	678 (28.5%)	2,376
TOTAL	7,206 (78.0%)	2,043 (22.0%)	9,249

Table 60: Actives and passives in subcategories of non-academic writing.

	Active	Passive	Total
humanities	2,316 (84.7%)	419 (15.3%)	2,735
social science	2,347 (86.2%)	375 (13.8%)	2,722
natural science	2,156 (84.7%)	389 (15.3%)	2,545
technology	2,039 (76.5%)	627 (23.5%)	2,666
TOTAL	8,858 (83.0%)	1,810 (17.0%)	10,668

egories. To do this, we again repeat the procedure, this time selecting the four subcategories of non-academic writing. The results are shown in Table 60.

In this case the pattern is not so clear, although once again 'technology' displays the greatest proportion of passives. It is initially surprising to find the same proportion of passives in natural science as in humanities. Clearly, much depends on what we mean by 'scientific' writing in the context of non-academic ('popular') texts. Overall, our results seem to suggest that, strictly speaking, passives are characteristic of 'technological' writing, and of 'scientific' writing specifically when it is produced in an academic context.

8.6 *Case Study 6: The positions of* if*-clauses*

Adverbial clauses vary to some extent in their position relative to the host clause (Quirk *et al.* 1985: 8.14ff). The two most prominent positions are:

1. Clause-initial – before all obligatory clause elements:

   (1) *If it's a really nice day* we could walk [S1A-006 #301]

2. Clause-final – after all obligatory clause elements:

   (1a) We could walk *if it's a really nice day*

Table 61: Initial and final positions of semantic types of adverbial clauses (after Greenbaum and Nelson 1995a).

Semantic Type	Initial Position	Final Position	Total
Condition	184 (64.8%)	100 (35.2%)	284
Concession	24 (45.3%)	29 (54.7%)	53
Time	113 (38.8%)	178 (61.2%)	291
Reason	24 (8.4%)	263 (91.6%)	287
Manner	8 (6.1%)	123 (93.9%)	131
Purpose	6 (3.6%)	161 (96.4%)	167
Result	0 (0%)	41 (100%)	41

An earlier study by Greenbaum and Nelson (1995a) examined the positions of semantic types of adverbial clauses in a subcorpus of ICE-GB. The subcorpus consisted of just 42 texts (89,051 words) selected from three spoken categories (conversations, broadcast discussions, unscripted monologues) and three written categories (academic writing, non-academic writing, social letters). We annotated the subcorpus manually for adverbial clause semantic type and position, since at that time ICE-GB had not been parsed.

Our investigation showed that the final position is the unmarked (*i.e.*, usual) position for all the semantic types, with the exception of conditional (*if*-) clauses, which preferred the initial position. The figures from our original investigation are reproduced in Table 61. It is also worth noting that initial position was preferred in all six of the text categories that we looked at.

The aim of this case study is to test our original conclusion about the positions of *if*-clauses, this time using the whole of the ICE-GB corpus (1,061,264 words in 25 text categories) as our dataset.

The search requires two separate FTFs, one to retrieve *if*-clauses in initial position, and another to retrieve *if*-clauses in final position.

We begin by creating an FTF to retrieve *if*-clauses in initial position.

- Select 'New FTF' on the command bar. An empty FTF window will appear.
- Click on '[icon]' ('Insert Node After') twice to insert two additional nodes below the

Figure 215: Three-node FTF after introducing labels and the word "if".

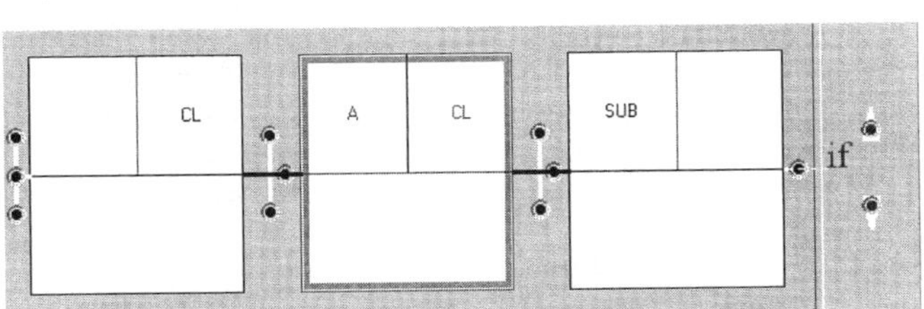

Figure 216: Using 'cool spots' and links between a child and its parent.

*Three links: **Parent**, **First** and **Last child*** — *Specifying that the child is in the **First** position* — *Specifying that the child is in the **Last** position*

current one (Figure 215).

We now have an FTF consisting of three unlabelled nodes. The first node (on the left) will represent the host clause. The second will represent the *if*-clause, while the third will represent the subordinator *if*.

- With the mouse, do a 'right click' over an upper sector on the first (left) node and select 'Edit Node...' from the menu. Alternatively move to this node and press <F2> or the button ''. Select clause ('**CL**') from the pull-down 'current category' list on the right. Hit 'OK'.
- Repeat on the middle node but this time select 'current function' as adverbial ('**A**') and 'category' as clause ('**CL**'). Hit 'OK'.
- Finally, select the third node and specify that this has function subordinator ('**SUB**') using the dialog box.

We must now specify that we want the subordinator to contain at least the word *if* (this allows for *if*, *even if*, *only if*, *etc.*).

- Double-click on the '¤' (unspecified word) symbol on the right of the FTF, or select the last node and press the 'Edit word(s)' button (''). Type the word "**if**" in the dialog box that appears and press 'OK'. The resulting FTF is given in Figure 215.

We now must specify the positional relationship between the first two nodes, namely, that the adverbial clause ('**A,CL**') must be the first constituent of the host clause (*i.e.*, it must be in clause-initial position).

The relationship between any two nodes is indicated by colour-coded lines (black, white or absent: see Section 5.12). Each link is controlled by a "cool spot", as shown in Figure 216.

- In the area between the first two nodes (*i.e.*, the first clause and the adverbial clause), place the mouse over the uppermost spot. Click down with the mouse on the spot (see Section 5.8) until the pop-up banner reads "**First:** yes", as in the middle of Figure 216. The white line will disappear (no line means no prior child node). This setting insists that the adverbial (*if*-) clause must match the first constituent of the host clause.

The modified FTF is shown in Figure 217 overleaf.

Figure 217: FTF to retrieve if-*clauses in initial position.*

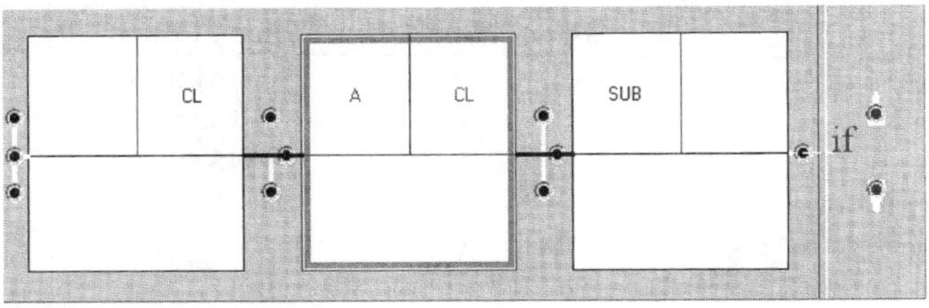

Table 62: Initial and final if-*clauses in the whole corpus.*

Initial Position	Final Position	Total
955 (57.7%)	700 (42.3%)	1,655

➢ Click on 'Start!' to launch the search. The results are displayed in a new window as they are found, and the frequency is shown on the bottom of this window.

The next step is to retrieve *if*-clauses in final position. The FTF requires only a simple modification. In this case, we must specify that the adverbial *if*-clause must be the last, rather than the first, constituent of the host clause.

➢ Click once on the upper 'cool spot' with the left mouse button. The banner should now read "**First:** unknown" and the link should be white again. Now click on the lower spot until it reads "**Last:** yes" and the lower link disappears, as in Figure 216, right.

➢ Click on 'Start!' to launch the search. The results are displayed in a new window.

The results of both searches are summarised in Table 62.

In general terms, these results confirm our original finding, namely, that initial position is the unmarked position for *if*-clauses. However, the difference is not nearly as great as our original study of just six text categories would lead us to expect (see Table 61).

ICE-GB contains a total of 25 major text categories (see Appendix 1). Using ICECUP, once we have performed the search, we can easily obtain data for each of these categories separately. The procedure involves dragging the relevant categories from the Corpus Map, and dropping them in turn into the two windows containing the *if*-clauses. The method is as described in Section 8.3. Results are given in Table 63.

At this level of detail, of course, the figures become very small in many categories, but they do indicate a very different picture than the one suggested by the global results, both in the original study (Table 61) and Table 62.

In particular, Table 63 suggests that Greenbaum and Nelson's conclusion only holds for writing. Without exception, the written categories prefer the initial position for *if*-clauses.

Table 63: Initial and final if-*clauses in spoken and written text categories.*

Text Category	Initial Position	Final Position	Total
Conversations	111 (35.1%)	205 (64.9%)	316
Telephone calls	3 (15.0%)	17 (85.0%)	20
Class lessons	43 (50.0%)	43 (50.0%)	86
Broadcast discussions	32 (47.0%)	36 (53.0%)	68
Broadcast interviews	18 (50.0%)	18 (50.0%)	36
Parliamentary debates	17 (68.0%)	8 (32.0%)	25
Legal cross-examinations	19 (54.3%)	16 (45.7%)	35
Business transactions	18 (48.6%)	19 (51.4%)	37
Spontaneous commentaries	3 (15.0%)	17 (85.0%)	20
Unscripted speeches	38 (43.2%)	50 (56.8%)	88
Demonstrations	28 (59.6%)	19 (40.4%)	47
Legal presentations	15 (65.2%)	8 (34.8%)	23
News broadcasts	27 (51.9%)	25 (48.1%)	52
Broadcast talks	22 (47.8%)	24 (52.2%)	46
Non-broadcast talks	11 (64.7%)	6 (35.3%)	17
SPOKEN	**405 (44.2%)**	**511 (55.8%)**	916

Text Category	Initial Position	Final Position	Total
Student essays	8 (80.0%)	2 (20.0%)	10
Examination scripts	15 (83.3%)	3 (16.7%)	18
Social letters	33 (68.7%)	15 (31.3%)	48
Business letters	53 (73.6%)	19 (26.4%)	72
Academic writing	63 (74.1%)	22 (25.9%)	85
Non-academic writing	67 (68.4%)	31 (31.6%)	98
Press reportage	35 (61.4%)	22 (38.6%)	57
Instructional writing	211 (84.4%)	39 (15.6%)	250
Press editorials	29 (69.0%)	13 (31.0%)	42
Creative writing	36 (61.0%)	23 (39.0%)	59
WRITTEN	**550 (74.4%)**	**189 (25.6%)**	739

In the spoken data as a whole, the final position is preferred, though there is considerable internal variation. It is worth noting, perhaps, that the more ‘formal’ spoken categories – parliamentary debates, legal presentations and non-broadcast (scripted) speeches – show a marked preference for the initial position.

9. PRINCIPLES OF EXPERIMENTAL DESIGN WITH A PARSED CORPUS

We follow our case studies by examining the design of experiments in the light of a parsed corpus. So far we have looked at a small number of current research questions in linguistics and demonstrated how ICE-GB and ICECUP may be used to address them. However, we have not really considered the question of experimental design. What is an experiment? What makes a 'good' experiment? How should researchers employ grammatical queries to carry out experiments on a parsed corpus? And what kind of experiments are possible with ICE-GB?

As the preceding case studies should make clear, these questions are perfectly valid. Provided that the corpus is collected systematically, and annotated consistently and in good faith, there is no particular reason why an experimental approach should not be applied to a corpus, even a parsed one.

These questions are also very important. It is one thing to find examples of a particular construction in a corpus, quite another to make any general claims about the presence of such constructions in contemporary British English or in English in general. Individual examples merely indicate the existence of possible phenomena, they do not explain *why* they appear. The latter requires both a well-defined experimental method and a clear theoretical defence.

ICECUP 3.1 includes some enhancements for supporting experimental research.[1] The examples given here work equally well with ICECUP 3.0.

Good experimental design is not a question of software – or mathematics. Rather, we would like to make the central point that all researchers should be able to organise their experimental approach and defend their conclusions. The purpose of this chapter is to address these issues.

We start with some introductory comments about experimental design. We summarise the general method and common pitfalls you should be aware of if you define experiments which examine if a sociolinguistic variable predicts a grammatical one. We end with the more complicated problem of investigating the interaction between two grammatical aspects of a single phenomenon.

Many of these issues are central to the investigation of *any* corpus, including plain text and tagged corpora. The problem simply becomes more acute with a parsed corpus like ICE-GB and rapid retrieval software like

---

[1] It supports the construction of simple tables using the corpus map, lexicon and grammaticon (see Chapter 7.4). However it does not support the construction of general contingency tables and the automatic collection of frequency statistics. You will have to perform the process of extracting data from the corpus by hand. We believe that automating many of the procedures described here (see Chapter 10) would be highly advantageous, but that is another matter.

ICECUP. However, some issues, such as dealing with the overlap of one case with another, specifically arise due to the structure of parsed corpora.

9.1 What is a scientific experiment?

The answer is that it is a test of a hypothesis. A *hypothesis* is a statement that may be believed to be true but is not verified, such as

1. Smoking is good for you.
2. Dropped objects accelerate toward the ground at 9.8 metres per second squared.
3. The element *'s* is a clitic rather than a word.
4. The word "whom" is used less in speech than writing.
5. The degree of preference for "whom" rather than "who" differs in contemporary spoken and written British English.

In each case, the problem for the researcher is to devise an experiment that allows us to decide whether evidence in the real world supports or contradicts the hypothesis. Compare Examples 4 and 5 above. If a statement is very general

a) it is hard to collect evidence to test the hypothesis and
b) the evidence might support a variety of other explanations.

So we need to "pin down" a general hypothesis to a series of more specific *experimental hypotheses*, which are more easily testable. The art of experimental design is to collect data appropriate to the research hypothesis.

In brief, a simple experiment consists of

a) a *dependent variable*, which may or may not depend on
b) an *independent variable*, which varies over the normal course of events.[2]

Thus in Example 5, the independent variable might be 'text category' (spoken or written), and the dependent variable, the number of times "whom" is used where applicable, that is, *when either "who" or "whom" could be uttered.*

A statistical test lets us measure the strength of the correlation between the dependent and independent variables.

- If the measure is small, the variables are probably independent from one another.
- If it is large enough, it means that the variables correlate, *i.e.*, they change together.

---

[2] As a convenient shorthand, we will also refer to the independent variable as the "**IV**" and the dependent variable as the "**DV**". It is possible to have experiments with more than one **IV** or outcome but these are actually carried out as a series of simpler experiments (see 9.8.2).

Does a significant result mean that we have *proved* our hypothesis? No. Something else may be going on. A correlation is not a cause.

- For example, taken across a population, height (A) and educational attainment level (B) may correlate. But growing taller does not increase one's thirst for knowledge, nor one's ability to pass exams. The reverse may be true, *i.e.*, that knowledge tends to improve diet and general well-being.

- Another possibility is that other *root* causes (*e.g.* distribution of wealth, C), might be said to contribute *instrumentally* to both height and education simultaneously. (Thus, one technique is to eliminate any such possible cause by repeating the experiment with a sample of people of very similar wealth. However, the result would only apply to the population from which the sample was taken. This is one kind of *reductionism*.)

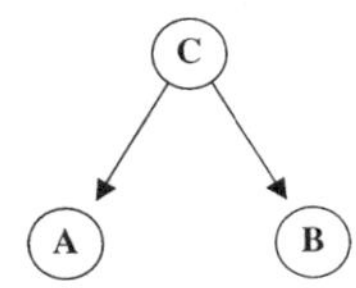

In our case, we must use a linguistic argument to try to establish a connection between any two correlating variables.

What about the converse? Does a non-significant result *disprove* the hypothesis? If a test does not find sufficient variation, we say that *we cannot reject the null hypothesis*.[3] This does not mean that the original hypothesis is wrong, rather that the data does not let us give up on the default assumption that nothing is going on. Experiments allow us to advance a position. If independent pieces of evidence point to the same general conclusion, we may be on the right track.

9.2 What is an experimental hypothesis?

An experiment consists of at least two variables: a dependent and an independent variable. The *experimental hypothesis*, which is really a summary of the experimental design, is couched in terms of these variables.

Suppose we return to Example 5. Our dependent variable is the usage of "whom" versus the usage of "who", our independent variable is the text category. Suppose that we take data from ICE-GB, although we could equally take data from other corpora containing spoken or written samples. Note also that the size of the two samples need not be equal as long as you work with relative frequencies (see below).

Our experimental hypothesis is a more specific version than our previous one, *i.e.*,

6) the word "whom" over "who" varies in usage between spoken and written British English *sampled in a directly comparable way to ICE-GB categories.*

---

[3] The conventional (Popperian) language used to describe an experiment is couched in double negatives. The "null hypothesis" is the opposite of the hypothesis that we are interested in.

Figure 218: Absolute and relative frequencies: assessments of risk

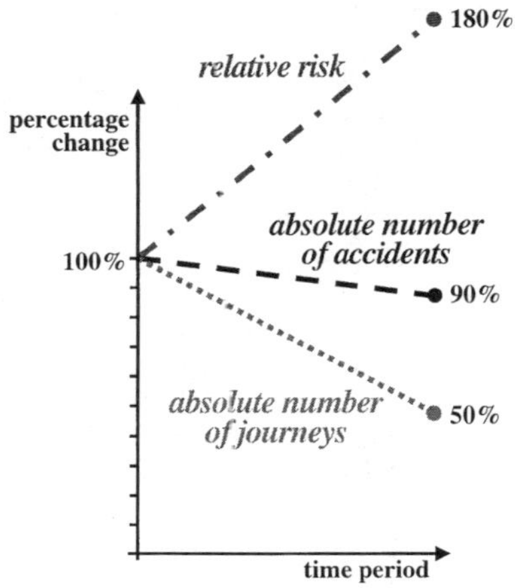

Note that we are not interested in the *absolute frequency* of "who" or "whom", *e.g.*, the number of cases per 1,000 words. Rather, we examine the *relative frequency* of "whom" when the choice arises. An example will hopefully make this clearer.

> Suppose someone tells you that train journeys are becoming safer. Between 1990 and 2000, they say, the number of accidents on the railways fell by ten percent. But what if the number of journeys halved over the same time period? Should you believe their argument? The relative risk of injury (assessed, in this instance, *per journey*, but you could also consider *per distance travelled* instead) has increased (by 90/50 × 100% = 180%, see Figure 218), not fallen.

- An **absolute frequency** tells you how frequent a word is in the corpus. But the reason that a word is there in the first place might depend on many factors that are irrelevant to the experimental hypothesis.
- Using **relative frequencies** focuses in on variation *where there is a choice*. The bad news is that you may need to check the examples in the corpus to see if there really is a choice in each case. You cannot absolutely rely on the annotation. In many circumstances you will have to investigate example cases in their context.

In order to use relative frequencies, therefore, you must be able to identify at what points in the corpus the choice occurs. If you are looking at phenomena that are explicitly represented by the grammar, there are two ways of doing this with ICECUP. You can group together all possible responses to the choice, using several Fuzzy Tree Fragments, or define a single FTF that encapsulates the choice itself. The former means working 'bottom-up', the latter, 'top-down' (see Section 9.6.1).

If you have a large number of cases and the parse decision is relatively uncontroversial, you may rely on the parsing, with one proviso: *that there is not*

Figure 219: The methodological continuum in corpus linguistics

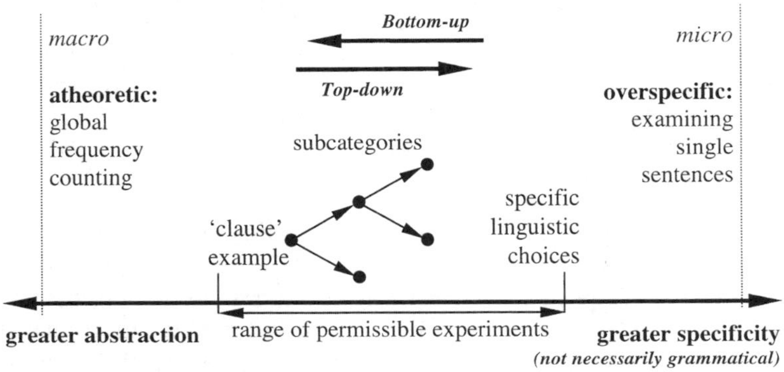

a systematic bias in the annotation (*i.e.*, either the corpus has been hand-corrected as per ICE-GB, or uncertain choices have been resolved at random). *Annotation errors that are systematic are a bias, those that are random are noise.* As a golden rule, you should always publish your results with a clear description of your method, and list your FTFs so that other researchers can attempt to reproduce your experiments.

As a result, one of the common criticisms of data driven corpus linguistics – that it consists of atheoretical frequency counting – 'number crunching' – is removed. Focusing on an individual choice tends to reduce the possibility that detected variation is due to sampling, because any such sampling bias will affect the probability of the *choice* to a greater extent than the probability of one decision over another. You should always aim for a representative sample as far as possible, however.

Our methodological position is summarised by Figure 219. Valid experiments are more general than single examples, while being more context-specific than summary statistics. Since an independent variable defines a set of sub-contexts (each value is a sub-context), we can potentially identify factors that contribute towards a particular outcome.

The upper bound of an acceptable method is illustrated by the clause experiment described in Section 9.8.1. In this experiment, cases (clauses) occur in a *variety* of distinct linguistic contexts, where the factors affecting the correlation of the two variables (mood and transitivity) will also vary according to context. Such an experiment is really too general to form any definite conclusions on its own. The lower limit of our approach is where we have *a single linguistic choice* and *sufficient data to permit a statistical test*. We will see this kind of experiment later. Note that when we refer to the specificity of the linguistic context, this may be semantic and pragmatic as well as grammatical.

In this book we are concerned with a particular parsed corpus, ICE-GB. Parse analysis can be exploited in experiments in two important ways.

- It is easier to be more precise when establishing the grammatical typology of a lexical item, saying "retrieve this item in this grammatical context". We can also *vary the preciseness* of our definitions by adding or removing features, edges, links, *etc*.
- It is possible to precisely relate two items grammatically, *e.g.*, "*the* and *man* are both part of the same noun phrase".

Here we should deal with a major objection to our line of reasoning. This is the claim that an experiment must necessarily be in the context of a particular set of assumptions, *i.e.*, a specific grammar. However, this does not rule out the possibility of scientific experiments. Rather, it means that we must qualify our results – "NP, according to *this* grammar", *etc*. In a parallel-parsed corpus one could in principle study the interaction between two different sets of analyses.

We use ICECUP's *Fuzzy Tree Fragments* (see Chapter 5) to establish the relationship between two or more elements. We can study the interaction between grammatical terms, a process discussed in some detail at the end of this chapter. We turn first to a slightly simpler problem: how to determine if a *sociolinguistic* variable affects a grammatical one.

9.3 The basic approach: constructing a contingency table

In order to evaluate a hypothesis we perform a series of searches in the corpus and construct a table, called a contingency table, which summarises the data. An outline is given below. The table helps us to collect and organise our data in order to perform a χ^2 (chi-square) significance test.

We confine ourselves first to investigations where the independent variable is sociolinguistic. In our example, we are interested in finding out whether a sociolinguistic variable (**text category**) affects the grammatical 'choice' of using "whom" rather than "who".

*Table 64: A general contingency table (**DV** × **IV**) with two or more columns and rows. Each total sums the preceding row or column, and '$a \wedge x$' means the intersection of '**IV** = a' with '**DV** = x'.*

		dependent variable (grammatical choice)			
		DV = x	**DV** = y	...	**TOTAL**
independent variable (sociolinguistic context)	**IV** = a	$a \wedge x$	$a \wedge y$		$a \wedge (x \vee y \vee ...)$
	IV = b	$b \wedge x$	$b \wedge y$		$b \wedge (x \vee y \vee ...)$
	...				
	TOTAL	$(a \vee b \vee ...) \wedge x$	$(a \vee b \vee ...) \wedge y$		$(a \vee b \vee ...) \wedge (x \vee y \vee ...)$

We will first outline the basic approach. An experiment tests the hypothesis that "**the IV affects the DV**" (the independent variable affects the dependent one – see section 9.1).

1. We construct a *contingency table* as per Table 64, completing the shaded cells by searching the corpus. Using ICECUP, we perform a series of FTF queries, one for each grammatical outcome (**DV** = *x*, *y*,...). We then calculate the overlap, or 'intersection', between each of the FTF queries and each value of the sociolinguistic variable (**IV** = *a*, *b*,...). In ICECUP, you can employ drag and drop logic to compute the intersection (see Chapter 6).
2. We want to find out whether the independent variable affects the value of the dependent variable, *i.e.*, the choice of the grammatical construction. To do this we contrast the distribution of each grammatical choice with the distribution that would be expected if it were unaffected by the **IV**. These distributions are shown in Table 65.
3. We can set up a simple chi-square test for a particular outcome **DV** = *x*. If this chi-square is significant it would mean that the value of the independent variable appears to affect a linguistic preference for outcome *x*. (Strictly: the null hypothesis, that there is no variation, is not supported.) The chi-square compares an *observed distribution,* **O**, for **DV** = *x* with an *expected distribution,* **E**, *based on the total* (**DV** = <any>). This ensures that the expected distribution is proportional to the likelihood of the choice occurring in the first place.
4. Before performing the test, the expected distribution must be *scaled* so that it sums to the same as the observed distribution. To calculate the scale factor, divide the column totals by one another, so that SF = TOTAL(**O**)/TOTAL(**E**). We then scale the expected column by multiplying its values by SF.

We can perform the chi-square for any other choice: **DV** = *y*, *etc*., and for the entire table. All observed distributions are compared against all expected distributions in a single chi-square.

Suppose our **IV** is **spoken** or **written**, *i.e.*, the simplest subdivision of **text category**, and we are interested in a grammatical choice: *who* vs. *whom*. Table 66 is a simple 2×2 contingency table, *i.e.*, both variables have two possibilities. By performing the necessary searches we obtain the four central figures, then sum the rows and columns. We then apply this data to a χ^2 test. We'll demonstrate the idea with some invented numbers for clarity (Table 67). We now return to our research question. Is *whom* preferred more in writing?

Table 65: Observed and expected distributions for ***DV*** *= x in Table 64.*

		dependent variable (grammatical choice)		
		DV = *x*	**DV** = *y*	**TOTAL**
independent variable (sociolinguistic context)	**IV** = *a*	$a \wedge x$	$a \wedge y$	$a \wedge (x \vee y \vee ...)$
	IV = *b*	$b \wedge x$	$b \wedge y$	$b \wedge (x \vee y \vee ...)$
		observed		***expected***

Table 66: Constructing a table for our example experiment

		dependent variable (use of "whom" over "who")		
		DV = *who*	**DV** = *whom*	**TOTAL**
independent variable (text category)	**IV** = *spoken*	*who* in *spoken*	*whom* in *spoken*	*who+whom* in *spoken*
	IV = *written*	*who* in *written*	*whom* in *written*	*who+whom* in *written*
	TOTAL	*who* in *written+spoken*	*whom* in *written+spoken*	*who+whom* in *written+spoken*

Table 67: A simple (invented) example of a contingency table

		dependent variable (use of "whom" over "who")		
		who	*whom*	**TOTAL**
independent variable (text category)	*spoken*	**150**	**50**	**200**
	written	**60**	**40**	**100**
	TOTAL	**210**	**90**	**300**

Superficially, it looks as though there is a preference. According to the table there are 50 cases of *whom* in the spoken sample, compared to 40 in the written subcorpus. There are rather more uses of *either* "who" or "whom" in the spoken data.

The statistical test takes this variation into account. It compares the difference between the observed distribution, **O**, and the expected distribution, **E**. The formula for chi-square is

$$\text{chi-square } \chi^2 = \sum \frac{(o-e)^2}{e} \text{ where } o \in \mathbf{O} \text{ and } e \in \mathbf{E}.$$

We then choose a *critical value* which must be surpassed by the evaluated χ^2. Appendix 8 has a table of critical values for χ^2. There are two cells in the distribution, so the number of degrees of freedom, $df = r\text{-}1 = 1$. By convention, we can accept an error of 1 in 20 (0.05). The following shows the working.

Q1. Is a preference for *whom* significantly affected by the **text category**?

Observed **O** = {50, 40}, scale factor SF = 90/300 = 0.3,
expected **E** = {200 × 0.3, 100 × 0.3} = {60, 30}.
Chi-square $\chi^2 = \Sigma(o\text{-}e)^2/e = 10^2/60 + 10^2/30 =$ **5.000**.
Chi-square critical value ($df = 1$, error level $p = 0.05$) = crit(1, 0.05) = 3.841.
Since χ^2 > critical value, the result is significant and the null hypothesis, *i.e.*, that *whom* does not correlate with variation of **text category**, is rejected.

A. Yes. In the next section we discuss what this might mean.

Q2. Is a choice of *who* over whom affected by the **text category**?

Observed **O** = {150, 60}, scale factor SF = 210/300 = 0.7,
expected **E** = {200 × 0.7, 100 × 0.7} = {140, 70}.
Chi-square $\chi^2 = \Sigma(o\text{-}e)^2/e = 10^2/140 + 10^2/70 =$ **2.142** < crit(1, 0.05) = 3.841.
Since χ^2 < critical value, the null hypothesis, *i.e.*, that the choice of *who* does not correlate with variation of **text category**, cannot be rejected.

A. No. The values in the expected distribution are higher. As a proportion of the expected distribution, the deviation is smaller and the chi-square argues that it could be explained by chance. *The variation in the choice of a relatively infrequent item, like* whom, *is more important than the variation in the choice of a more common one.*

Q3. Is the *entire grammatical choice* (*who* or *whom*, but not specifying which one) significantly affected by the **text category**?[4]

Observed **O** = {150, 60, 50, 40},
expected **E** = {140, 70, 60, 30}.
Chi-square $\chi^2 = \Sigma(o\text{-}e)^2/e = 10^2/140 + 10^2/70 + 10^2/60 + 10^2/30 =$ **7.142** > 3.841.
Since χ^2 > critical value, the null hypothesis, *i.e.*, that the grammatical choice does not correlate with variation of **text category**, is also rejected.

A. Yes. We would expect this from the fact that at least one separate outcome is significant. This kind of test is weaker than the first two: there is a significant overall variation but we cannot say *where* it is.

Finally, let us consider what it would mean if the *dependent* variable is socio-linguistic, *e.g.*, can we predict the text category from lexical or grammatical aspects of a text? This approach is used in stylistic author-attribution research.

Q4. Can we predict that a text is, say, **written**, by whether an author chose *who* over *whom*? **Text category = written** is the **DV** and the linguistic choice is the **IV**. We contrast the observed "written" row in Table 67, with an expected "total" (*i.e.*, all of ICE-GB) row, scaled appropriately.

Observed **O** = {60, 40}, scale factor SF = 100/300 = 0.6667,
expected **E** = {70, 30}.
Chi-square $\chi^2 = \Sigma(o\text{-}e)^2/e = 10^2/70 + 10^2/30 =$ **4.762** > 3.841.
Since χ^2 > critical value, the null hypothesis, *i.e.*, that writing is not different from other types of utterance in the choice of *who* or *whom*, is rejected.

A. Yes. This suggests that writing is different from the norm in this respect.

---

[4] This is usually how the question is put in books in experimental design. In this case the number of degrees of freedom, $df = (r\text{-}1) \times (c\text{-}1)$, where r is the number of rows and c the number of columns in the table.

9.4 *What might significant results mean?*

A significant result simply means that perceived variation is large enough to not be due to chance. Statistical results indicate a *correlation*, they cannot prove a *cause*. The variation would be reproduced if we were to take similar samples (of text) from the population (of all texts from the same period, authorship, genres, *etc*., and annotated in the same way). It doesn't say *what is going on*. This is the corollary of the argument regarding the difficulty of proving or disproving a hypothesis.

There is another aspect to significance. If the sample size is very large, almost every apparent variation will be significant (*i.e.*, it would exist in the population). The question is then, it may be significant, but how big is the effect? We consider measures of effect size in the next section.

The significant result could be an artifact of the annotation. There are at least three different kinds of problem here.

1. **Circularity.** You may find that in practice you are measuring aspects of the same phenomenon in two different ways (e.g., predicting the transitivity of a verb from the presence of a direct object) in which case it is no wonder the result is significant!
2. **Unrepresentative sampling.** The result might be due to an imprecise FTF definition, incorrect annotation or an inadequate sample in the corpus. Are all your cases really expressing the same linguistic phenomenon? Are there other cases of the phenomenon in the corpus that perhaps should have been included? Another possibility is that cases are not strictly independent. We will return to this question in Section 9.6.4.
3. **Poor experimental design.** Are all possible values of a variable listed? Are some of the outcomes expressing something that is quite linguistically distinct from the others? If so, you might want to restructure the experiment to deal with two distinct subgroups (see 9.6.3).

To determine the answer to these questions, you must *inspect the cases* and *relate the design to a theory*. One possible explanation is that the correlation could be a result of a third factor affecting both the **DV** and the **IV** separately: our old friend the *root cause*.[5]

The central point is this: to ascertain the *reason* for a correlation requires more work. You should inspect the corpus and *argue* your position. Relate your results to those reported in the literature: if they differ, why do they do so? Play 'devil's advocate' and try to argue against your own results. Dig deeper – try looking at subcategories of each FTF, for example – and anticipate objections. The beauty of a public corpus and query system is that, provided you report your experiment clearly, everyone has the opportunity of reproducing your

---

[5] Gould (1984) gives the example of the price of petrol correlating with the age of a petrol pump attendant. Just because the petrol price may rise over time, as the attendant ages, it does not mean that the age of the attendant **causes** the price to rise, or vice-versa!

results (and possibly raising alternative explanations). *The corpus is a focus for discussion, not a substitute for it.*

As well as detecting a significant difference and even explaining it, it is also useful to be able to measure how big an effect is: a small variation can be significant without being very interesting, a larger variation might indicate that there is something more fundamental going on.

9.5 *How can we measure the 'size' of a result?*

Below, we discuss four different ways of measuring the size of an interaction. These are:

1) Relative size (proportion)
2) Relative swing (change in proportion)
3) The contribution of each element pair toward the total chi-square
4) Cramer's phi "measure of association"

We will look at each of these in turn.

9.5.1 Relative size

One useful indication of the size of the effect is simply the proportion of cases in a particular category with a particular outcome, *i.e.*, the sample probability that a specific outcome is chosen (*e.g.*, *who* over *whom*), given a particular value of the independent variable (in the example, **text category**).

In the previous example (see Section 9.3), 150 out of 200 cases (75%) found in the **spoken** category are *who*, falling to 60 out of 100 cases (60%) in the **written**. The relative size equals the probability of a particular value of the dependent variable, *dv*, being chosen if **IV** = *iv*. This may be written as

$$\text{probability } pr(dv \mid iv) = \frac{o(dv,iv)}{\text{TOTAL}(iv)},$$

where $o(dv, iv)$ is the observed value for **DV** = *dv* and **IV** = *iv*. Thus

$$pr(who \mid \textbf{spoken}) = \frac{o(who, \textbf{spoken})}{\text{TOTAL}(\textbf{spoken})} = \frac{150}{200} = 0.75.$$

Probabilities are *normalised frequencies* (they are between 0 and 1 and, for a fully enumerated set of alternatives, must sum to 1). The 'relative size' probability is a *sample probability* of the experiment, that is, it is the probability if the sample were truly representative of the population.

9.5.2 *Relative swing*

We can use relative size to calculate the percentage *swing*, or change in the probability towards, or away from, a particular value of the independent variable depending on the grammatical choice.

In our example, 150 out of 200 instances found in the **spoken** subcorpus were *who* (75%) compared to the remaining 50 cases (25%), where *whom* is used. Suppose that we calculate the swing towards *who* in the **spoken** category. As before, consider the case where *iv* is **spoken** and *dv* is *who*.

The swing is calculated by the difference between this value and the *prior probability* for the text category, *i.e.*, 200 out of a total 300 instances are in the **spoken** category. The prior probability is:

$$\text{prior probability } pr(iv) = \frac{\text{TOTAL}(iv)}{\text{TOTAL}}, \text{ and thus}$$

$$\text{swing}(dv, iv) = pr(dv \mid iv) - pr(iv),$$

where TOTAL is the grand total. This gives us a percentage swing towards **spoken** for *who* as follows:

$$\text{swing}(who, \textbf{spoken}) = pr(who \mid \textbf{spoken}) - pr(\textbf{spoken}) = 0.75\text{-}0.667 = 0.083,$$

which we could write as +8.3%. As before, this makes the naive assumption that the sample is representative of the population.

9.5.3 *Chi-square contribution*

We pointed out that relative size and swing are based on sample frequencies. They do not take into account the margin of error introduced by the fact that we are guessing population variation from a sample. We should take this into account, particularly where the sample is small (at a conservative estimate, where there are less than 20 cases per cell or less than 100 cases in total).

Suppose we consider, not the significance test itself, but the individual contribution made towards the total chi-square *by each value*. We return to our

*Table 68: Calculating χ^2 contributions for **spoken** and **written***

		dependent variable (**choice** = **whom** over **who**)		
		observed **O** 'whom'	*expected* **E** **TOTAL/SF**	**chi-square contribution**
independent variable (**text category**)	**spoken**	50	60	1.667
	written	40	30	3.333
	TOTAL	90	90	**5.000**

invented example to illustrate the point. Recall that chi-square $\chi^2 = \Sigma(o\text{-}e)^2/e$, so

chi-square contribution = $(o\text{-}e)^2/e$,

where $o = o(dv, iv)$ and e = TOTAL(iv)×TOTAL(dv)/TOTAL. If an individual contribution is high, it is either because the expected value is low or the difference between the observed and the expected is reasonably high.

If the independent variable has more than two values, you might like to consider whether the distinction between one specific value and all the others would be significant. You can do this with a simple mini-χ^2: the "x vs. the world" chi-square. This is a 2×2 chi-square which consists of the chi-square contribution for a particular value plus *its complement*, defined as

chi-square contribution complement = $(o\text{-}e)^2/(\text{TOTAL}(iv)\text{-}e)$.

You can compare this mini-χ^2 with a critical value for χ^2 (df = 1) to ascertain whether a value is individually significant. (If the chi-square contribution alone surpasses the critical value, you don't have to work out the complement!)

9.5.4 *Cramer's phi*

The problem with using chi-square as a measure of association is that it is *proportional to the square of the size* of the dataset and *unscaled*. This means that it is difficult to compare values between different samples. "Cramer's phi" (ϕ) corrects for this. This is written

Cramer's $\phi = \sqrt{\chi^2/\text{TOTAL}(iv) \times df}$.

All of these measures may be used in conjunction with significance tests to perform two tasks: first, to measure the size of the overall effect and second, to indicate specific values that you might wish to focus on and further subdivide.

9.6 *Common issues in experimental design*

9.6.1 *Have we specified the null hypothesis incorrectly?*

The null hypothesis is a statement that the variation does not differ from the expected distribution. If the expected distribution is incorrectly specified, the experiment will measure *the wrong thing*, and your claims will not be justified. (This is another way of saying, *get the experimental design right*.)

If you followed the steps in the basic example above, you should have no problem. However, often researchers make the assumption that the expected distribution is just based on the quantity of material in each subcorpus. In a lexical or tagged corpus it can be more difficult to calculate an expected distribution because it might involve listing a large number of possible alternatives.

For example, suppose we compare the frequency of the modal verb *may* in a series of subcorpora, with the quantity of material in each one. Appropriately scaled, this could be quoted as the frequency 'per million words', 'per thousand words', *etc*. However, what if we found that *may* appeared more frequently than expected in, say, formal writing? This does not tell us if either

a) there are more uses of *modals per se* in formal writing, or

b) modal *may* is more frequent **than its alternatives** (*e.g.*, *can*) in formal writing.

Detected variation may be due to the variation in the distribution *of* an entire group (type a), in which case the explanation should really be more general; or due to variation *within* the group (type b), variation that may be hidden if we simply compare the distribution of cases with the overall distribution of words.

This means that we should avoid, whereever possible, using the quantity of material in a corpus to estimate the expected frequency. In grammar, the possibility of a particular linguistic expression is dependent on *whether the expression was feasible in the first place* (see sections 8.4 and 9.1), and this feasibility may also vary with the independent variable.

Instead of using the distribution of corpus material, we base the expected distribution on a 'general case' that identifies when the possibility of variation arises. There are two ways of doing this: working from the top, down, or, as in the previous example, bottom-up.

- **Bottom-up.** List the outcomes that we are interested in and then define the expected distribution by adding together each of these outcomes' distributions. This is what we did in our "who vs. whom" experiment.
- **Top-down.** Define the case first, and then subdivide it fully, listing all possible alternatives. On the next page we illustrate this with some examples exploring grammatical interaction.

In summary, the useful null hypothesis is that the outcome does not vary *when the choice arises in the first place* rather than that it does not vary in proportion to the amount of material in the corpus.

Finally, note that you can, of course, work in both directions within the same experiment. In the following example we define **who** vs. **whom** and work from the bottom-up; then we define a **which/what+N** group and subdivide this (*i.e.*, work top-down).

9.6.2 Are all the relevant values listed together?

When you fail to list all possible outcomes of a particular type, it affects the conclusions that you can draw.

In the worked example we suggested that there were two possible alternative outcomes: *who* and *whom*. The **DV** was defined as one or the other of these. Note that in Table 64 we wrote that the row total was an expression like '$a \wedge (x \vee y \vee ...)$' rather than just '$a$'. This was because there might be other values excluded from '$(x \vee y \vee ...)$'. If we fail to consider all plausible outcomes our results may be too specific to be theoretically interesting (see the discussion on meaning) and are more likely to be due to an artifact of the annotation.

A corrollary of failing to list all relevant alternatives is that some outcomes are more similar to one another than others. For example, *who* or *whom* are more similar to each other than they are to '*which*/*what*+N' constructions (*e.g.*, "*which man*...").

This means prioritising certain distinctions over others. To do this, we *group* alternatives hierarchically to form an outcome *taxonomy* (Figure 220). We may consider two different tables and two different sets of tests:

a) to compare the first two aggregated together versus the third (when do we use *who* or *whom*?), and

b) to focus on the difference between the first two (when do we prefer *who* over *whom*?).

The contingency table should be split into two, as in Table 69. We may then further subdivide the '*which*/*what*+N' constructions (Figure 220: greyed, right).

Figure 220: Elaborating a taxonomy of linguistic decisions

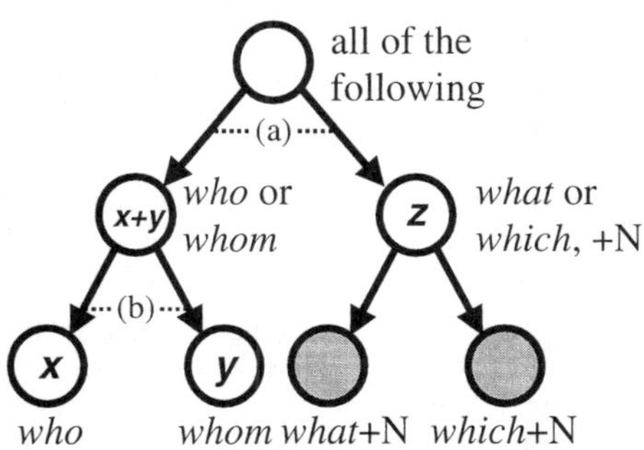

Table 69: Subdividing a contingency table for ***DV*** *= x vs. y vs. z (left), by (a) considering conditions x and y together vs. z, and (b) x vs. y*

	DV			
IV	*x*	*y*	*z*	total
a				
b				
total				

(a)	DV		
IV	*x+y*	*z*	total *x+y+z*
a			
b			
total			
	(b)		

(b)	DV		
IV	*x*	*y*	total *x+y*
a			
b			
total			

9.6.3 Are we really dealing with the same linguistic choice?

Working from the bottom to the top encourages you to think about the specifics of each linguistic choice. Note how we have assumed that *who* and *whom* are interchangeable, *i.e.*, any time a speaker or writer employs one expression the other could equally be substituted. Likewise, in the illustration above, we effectively assumed that in all cases where *who* or *whom* were used, a '*which/what*+N' expression could be substituted, and vice-versa. Sometimes you will need to check sentences in the corpus to be sure.

This is a particular problem if you want to examine a phenomenon that is not represented in a corpus. For example, in ICE-GB, particular sub-types of modals are not labelled. Suppose we wished to contrast deontic (permissive) *may* with deontic *can*, and then compare these with other ways of expressing permission. We don't want deontic *may* to be confused with other types of modal *may*, because these other types do not express the same linguistic choice. The solution is to classify the modals manually first (effectively by performing additional annotation). This is possible in ICECUP 3.1 through the use of 'selection lists' (see Section 4.12).

9.6.4 Have we counted the same thing twice?

A central requirement of a statistical test is that all cases are independent from one another. *You must not count the same thing twice.*

The problem arises because unlike a regular database, 'cases' in a corpus can interact with one another. There are several ways this "bunching" can arise. We list these below, from the most grammatically explicit, including overlapping matches (see Section 5.13) to the most incidental.

1. A match *fully* overlaps another. The only aspect of this matching that can be said to be independent is that different nodes refer to different parts of the same tree. This can only happen if you use *unordered* relationships in FTFs.
2. A match *partially* overlaps another, *i.e.*, part of one FTF coincides with part of another. There are two distinct types of partial overlap: where the overlapping node or nodes in the tree match the same, or different, FTF nodes. The first type can arise with *eventual* relationships, depicted by white arrows and lines, *e.g.*, '**Next child** = After'. The second type can only occur if two different nodes in an FTF could match the same constituent in a tree. We will see an example of this in Section 9.8.4.
3. One match can dominate, or subsume another, *e.g.*, a clause in a clause.
4. A match might be related to another via a simple construction, *e.g.*, co-ordination.
5. The construction may simply be repeated by the same speaker (not necessarily in the same utterance) or by another speaker.

If you are using ICECUP to perform experiments, you can 'thin out' search results by defining a 'random sample' and applying it to each set. However, this

The concept of a 'case' in a grammatical sample

If we want to investigate how two aspects of a grammatical phenomenon interact, we should ensure the following.

- The two variables *must apply to the same phenomenon*. That is, both variables must be based on the same fundamental definition of the case in question. Note that this fundamental definition could be specified as a set of alternative FTFs (as in the optional adverbial clause example in 9.8.3), but these alternatives should form a meaningful group (*e.g.*, identical structure with an optional constituent). We will adopt the convention of specifying the case in the top left of the contingency tables.
- In practice, this means that we *specify FTFs for every cell in the contingency table*, not just for every column. ICECUP's drag and drop logic (see Chapter 6) is inappropriate. We should also avoid ambiguous (unordered or eventual) links.
- *We should enumerate all alternatives of the case.* Where an FTF cannot be used directly (ICECUP 3.0 does not allow a search for unmarked features, for example) we may infer frequencies by subtraction. An example of this is given in Section 9.7.

thins out *sentences*, not cases. If several cases co-exist in the same sentence and the sentence is included, all these cases will be included. Moreover, since this will mean that the total number of cases will fall, the likelihood that an experiment is affected by the inter-dependence of cases will actually increase.

As we discuss at the end of this chapter, we should put this in some kind of numerical context. If you are looking at 30,000 clauses, it is unlikely that a small degree of bunching will affect the significance of the result. If, on the other hand, you are researching a relatively infrequent item (let us say, in double figures) and, when you inspect the cases, you find that many of these are co-ordinated with each other, you should try and eliminate these additional cases, either by limiting the FTF or by subtracting the results of a new FTF that counts the number of additional co-ordinated terms for each outcome.[6]

9.7 Investigating grammatical interactions

Suppose that we are interested in investigating aspects of clause structure and we want to find out *whether one grammatical aspect* (*e.g.*, the 'mood' of the clause) *affects another* (*e.g.*, transitivity).

We construct a contingency table as before. However, instead of performing FTF queries for each grammatical outcome we must define FTFs for

[6] The ideal solution would be for the search software to identify potential problems in the sampling process and discount interacting cases in some way (see Section 10.4). We have been investigating this problem as part of a process called *knowledge discovery in corpora* (Wallis and Nelson, 2001), and we are hopeful that this can be supported in future software. In the meantime, however, you should bear the preceding points in mind.

*Table 70: A simple contingency table (**DV** × **IV**) for an experiment investigating clauses, where transitivity and mood are specified. The double bars suggest the existence of other values of **IV** and **DV**.*

CL where transitivity and mood are specified		dependent variable (transitivity)		
		DV = *m*	**DV** = *d*	**TOTAL**
independent variable (mood)	**IV** = *e*	**CL(exclam, montr)**	**CL(exclam, ditr)**	**CL(exclam, montr** ∨ **ditr** ∨ ...)
	IV = *i*	**CL(inter, montr)**	**CL(inter, ditr)**	**CL(inter, montr** ∨ **ditr** ∨ ...)
	TOTAL	**CL(exclam** ∨ **intr** ∨ ..., **montr)**	**CL(exclam** ∨ **intr** ∨ ..., **montr)**	**CL(exclam** ∨ **intr** ∨ ..., **montr** ∨ **ditr** ∨ ...)

each *combination* of dependent and independent variable (see box above). The expressions that must be retrieved are shaded in Table 70. As before, each total is the sum of all preceding rows or columns.

If you want to ensure that the mood and transitivity variables are fully enumerated, you should also allow for the possibility that they are unspecified in the corpus. In Table 70, the grand total is the set of all clauses *where both transitivity and mood are stated.* This is not always the case, for a number of reasons, not least because many features are optional. We should therefore include an 'unmarked' value (written '**0**' below), for all cases where the feature class has not been specified.

Adding 'unmarked' values increases the amount of noise slightly, because we might expect that doing so increases the proportion of erroneously annotated nodes, but it also makes the results more general and robust. We can now generalise across *all* clauses, rather than just those where both the transitivity and mood are stated.

Note that there is an important difference between the mood and transitivity features. All clauses should be classified by transitivity, so if the feature is absent, the clause is incomplete ('**CL(incomp)**'), verbless ('**CL(-v)**') or in error. Mood, on the other hand, is optional (and its absence is meaningful): if unmarked, it is assumed to be *indicative*.

Naturally, *predicting* when a feature is absent (**DV** = **0**) may not be very useful, except to detect errors. The column will still affect the total and thus the expected distribution. We introduce a new row and column into the table for the 'unmarked' elements and fill the cells. In ICECUP 3.0 we calculate the frequency of an absent feature by subtraction. You compute an FTF for the *total* (*e.g.*, for the first column, simply '**CL(montr)**'), and then subtract the frequencies from this total. ICECUP 3.1 can obtain these values directly. '**CL(!transy)**' stands for a clause without a transitive feature. The white cells in Table 71 contain the result after subtracting all other values from the total.

*Table 71: Calculating a fully enumerated contingency table (**DV** × **IV**).*

CL		dependent variable (transitivity)			
		DV = *m*	DV = *d*	DV = 0	TOTAL
independent variable (mood)	IV = *e*	CL(exclam, montr)	CL(exclam, ditr)	-	CL(exclam)
	IV = *i*	CL(inter, montr)	CL(inter, ditr)	-	CL(inter)
	IV = 0	-	-	-	-
	TOTAL	CL(montr)	CL(intr)	-	CL

*Table 72: Observed and expected distributions for **DV** = m for Table 71.*

CL		dependent variable (transitivity)			
		DV = *m*	DV = *d*	DV = 0	TOTAL
independent variable (mood)	IV = *e*	CL(exclam, montr)	CL(exclam, ditr)		CL(exclam)
	IV = *i*	CL(inter, montr)	CL(inter, ditr)		CL(inter)
	IV = 0				
		observed			*expected*

The grand total is then simply the result of performing a query for 'CL'. If you can write an explicit FTF here, *it defines the case*. Table 71 shows the idea. As before, we set up a simple chi-square test for each outcome of the dependent variable (Table 72). The chi-square compares an *observed distribution* for **DV** = *m* or *d* with an *expected distribution based on the total* (**DV** = <any>). We scale the expected distribution as before and calculate χ^2.

In summary, we define what we mean by a case, either explicitly – "it's a clause" – or implicitly – "here are *x* different types of thing", and collect frequency statistics for each cell in the table. The variable is completely enumerated for the dataset if the total number of cases always adds up to the total for each separate column or row in the table.

9.8 Three studies of interaction in the grammar

9.8.1 Two features within a single constituent

Q. Does mood affect transitivity in clauses?

Our first example is achieved by completing Table 71, obtaining Table 73. Using ICECUP and the complete ICE-GB corpus, we perform queries for each

Table 73: Frequencies of all permutations of transitivity and mood features for a clause

CL	DV (transitivity)								
IV (mood)	`montr`	`ditr`	`dim'tr`	`cxtr`	`trans`	`intr`	`cop`	**0**	TOTAL
`exclam`	6	0	0	0	0	2	14	1	23
`inter`	2,223	74	17	135	91	1,360	1,895	89	5,884
`imp`	1,066	64	25	126	112	700	54	144	2,291
`subjun`	62	2	1	10	3	83	70	1	232
0	58,984	1,606	203	3,826	2,392	30,522	30,096	9,093	136,722
TOTAL	62,341	1,746	246	4,097	2,598	32,667	32,129	9,328	145,152

combination of mood and transitivity, including cases where features are absent. We will assume that the features within one clause are independent from the features within another. Note that the overwhelming majority of clauses are not marked for mood, *i.e.*, they are indicative.

We can now investigate, for example, if mood affects the use of *monotransitive*:

Observed **O** = {6, 2223, 1066, 62, 58984},
scale factor SF = 62341/145152 = 0.429,
expected **E** = {10, 2527, 984, 100, 58720} (approx.).
Chi-square $\chi^2 = \Sigma(o-e)^2/e = 4^2/10 + 304^2/2527 + 82^2/984 + 38^2/100 + 264^2/58720 = 60.631 > \text{crit}(4, 0.05) = 9.488$.
Since χ^2 > critical value, the result is significant and the null hypothesis, *i.e.*, that monotransitive does not correlate with variation of mood, is rejected.

Table 74 summarises the observed and expected distributions and the contribution that each pair of values makes to the overall χ^2. Note that although there are many cases of 'mood = unmarked' (indicative) , this contributes *the least variation* ($264^2/58720 = 1.187$; see also the second test in section 5.3). The

Table 74: Computing χ^2 for mood → monotransitive

CL	DV (transitivity)		
IV (mood)	observed `montr`	expected **TOTAL/SF**	χ^2 contribution $(o-e)^2/e$
`exclam`	6	10	1.600
`inter`	2,223	2,527	36.571
`imp`	1,066	984	6.833
`subjun`	62	100	14.440
0	58,984	58,720	1.187
TOTAL	62,341	62,341	**60.631**

Table 75: Computing χ^2 for mood → ditransitive

CL	DV (transitivity)		
IV (mood)	observed **ditr**	expected **TOTAL/SF**	χ^2 contribution $(e\text{-}o)^2/e$
inter	74	71.0	0.127
imp	64	27.5	48.445
exclam subjun 0	1,608	1,647.5	0.947
TOTAL	1,746	1,746.0	**49.519**

largest contribution to the chi-square are interrogative and subjunctive.

Similarly, to investigate the effect of mood on the ditransitive, from Table 73 we obtain the distribution: observed **O** = {0, 74, 64, 2, 1606}.

However, one of the assumptions of the chi-square test is that it does not include "low-valued cells", usually taken to mean frequencies below 5. We must therefore merge these cells together, producing a combined row '**exclam subjun 0**' containing the sum of their contents. This is the corollary of the ability to group alternatives (see Section 9.5.2).

What should we do with these values? If we simply discount them then this would mean that our results would not apply to cases where the clause was exclamative or subjunctive. It is preferable to merge them with the unmarked value, because "variation of mood" would then mean variation between interrogative, imperative and everything else. The number of degrees of freedom therefore falls to 2.

> Observed **O** = {74, 64, 1608},
> scale factor SF = 1746/145152 = 0.012,
> expected **E** = {71, 27.5, 1647.5} (approx.).
> Chi-square $\chi^2 = 3^2/71 + 36.5^2/27.5 + 39.5^2/1647.5 = 49.519 > \text{crit}(2, 0.05) = 5.991$.
> Since $\chi^2 >$ critical value, the result is significant and the null hypothesis, *i.e.*, that ditransitive does not correlate with variation of mood, is rejected.

The interaction of mood with other transitivity values is left as an exercise for the reader.

9.8.2 *Two features in a structure*

Q. Does the phrasal feature of an adverb affect the marking of the following preposition?

What happens if we want to look at interactions *within a group of related constituents* rather than in a single node? Consider clauses such as those illustrated by the FTF scheme on the left of Figure 221. This contains two adverbial elements: an *adverb phrase* followed by a *prepositional phrase*.

Figure 221: A schematic representation of an FTF with optional elements (left), and, right, a matching case (S1A-009 #19)

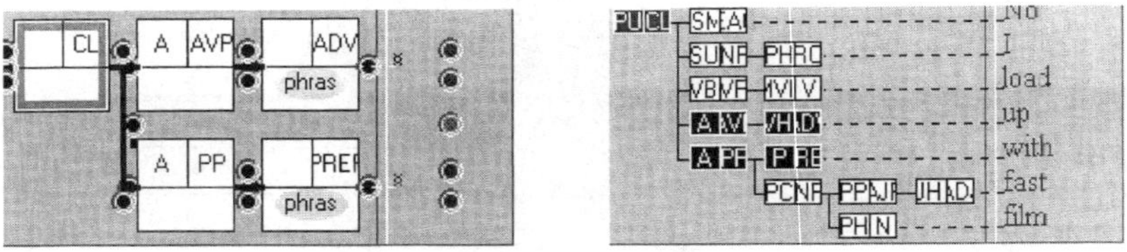

The following matching case is illustrated in Figure 221, right.

No I load [$_{\text{AVP}}$ *up*] [$_{\text{PP}}$ *with fast film*] [S1A-009 #19]

Suppose that we wish to establish if the fact that the adverb in the adverb phrase is or is not marked as phrasal (as in "finding *out*", "moving *on*", *etc.*) affects whether the preposition *in the following prepositional phrase* is also marked as phrasal.

We might write something like the following as a shorthand for an initial hypothesis, the question mark indicating that the feature is optional.

1. **`ADV(?phras) → PREP(?phras)`**

The example in Figure 221 contrasts with cases such as

It's only just come [$_{\text{AVP}}$ *out*] [$_{\text{PP}}$ *in the cinema*] [S1A-006 #60]

where the preposition "in" is general rather than phrasal. We therefore introduce two constituents (one each for the adverb and preposition) into the FTF which optionally bear the required features.

We construct four FTFs with the structure shown in Figure 221, identical in all respects except with a different combination of features. We then complete the table below using the results of these four searches on ICE-GB (shaded cells), subtracting from the total to find cases where the feature is absent. Note that the **IV** and **DV** are both Boolean. The analysis proceeds as before.

Observed **O** = {616, 1428},
scale factor SF = 2044/4170 = 0.490,
expected **E** = {459, 1585} (approx.).
Chi-square $\chi^2 = 157^2/459 + 157^2/1585 = 69.253 > \text{crit}(1, 0.05) = 3.841$.
Since χ^2 > critical value, the result is significant, and the null hypothesis, *i.e.*, the presence of the feature in the adverb does not affect the presence of the phrasal feature in the following prepositional phrase in these structures, is rejected.

Table 76: Completing the contingency table for the example

CL[AVP-ADV PP-PREP]	DV (preposition is phrasal)		
IV (adverb is phrasal)	`PREP(phras)`	`PREP(¬phras)`	TOTAL
ADV(phras)	616	320	936
ADV(¬phras)	1,428	1,806	3,324
TOTAL	2,044	2,126	4,170

The presence of the phrasal feature in the preposition (around half the cases in the corpus) increases to *two thirds* if the adverb contains the phrasal feature. If you wish, you may also perform a second test to check if the *absence* of the phrasal feature in the preposition also varies with the phrasal feature of the preceding adverb (this is almost certain given its relationship with the first test).

Secondly, we can swap the **IV** and **DV** around. Instead of seeing if the presence or absence of the phrasal feature in the adverb affects the presence or absence of the phrasal feature in the following preposition, we could also look at the reverse implication,

2. **`PREP(?phras) → ADV(?phras).`**

The point here is that we should not necessarily limit our investigations to those consistent with word order. The key consideration, as always in designing an experiment, is *what theoretical meaning does it have for linguistics?*

There may be other variables (*e.g.*, the transitivity of the preceding verb) that also predict when the preposition is phrasal. Such variables may predict the outcome *independently*, *e.g.*,

3. **`V(?trans) → PREP(?phras)`**

or *in conjunction* with others, *e.g.*,

4. **`V(?trans) ∧ ADV(phras) → PREP(?phras).`**

The problem with examining the interaction of multiple variables is that it can all get very complicated, produce very large tables, and, if you have to perform the process manually, be rather onerous to complete. However, rather than look at all possible interactions (*e.g.*, between the phrasal feature of the adverb and all types of transitivity), there are some simple ways of progressing.

One method is to base your research on the most previously effective predictor value by using this to specify the FTF that defines your basic case. In Hypothesis 4, above, we suppose that the most effective predictor is where the adverb is marked as phrasal. We then subdivide these cases by the values of the other independent variable (transitivity of an associated verb).

In this situation, if the result is significant, it means that the transitivity affects the likelihood of phrasal prepositions *when the adverb is phrasal*. Moreover, we can expect that certain values of transitivity will *improve on* the default prediction. This approach can be automated by integrating it into an autonomous search algorithm, supporting a process termed *knowledge discovery in corpora* (Wallis and Nelson, 2001).

A brief aside at this point. As we investigate interactions within groups of nodes, we should ensure that the FTF correctly captures the aspect of the annotation we are interested in. There is a certain amount of redundancy in the ICE grammar. In this example, for instance, the phrasal feature of the adverb 'percolates up' to the adverb phrase. We could, therefore, abstract the variable from the feature in the *adverb phrase* rather than the adverb. However, this percolation is a source of potential error, and so it is best to avoid using such features if at all possible. Likewise, in the following example, we pick up the transitivity feature from the verb rather than the verb phrase.

9.8.3 A feature and an optional constituent

Q. Does verb transitivity affect the presence of a following adverbial clause?

In addition to representing aspects of a node (features, function, category), grammatical variables can represent the *presence* of a structural component (such as a node) in the first place. In the following example we consider, does the transitivity of a verb predict whether or not the verb phrase might be followed by an adverbial clause?

The case is defined simply, by all clauses containing a VP (and a main verb). The presence of a following adverbial clause, as in the example below, is detected by optionally extending the FTF (Figure 222, left). A white arrow, meaning that the constituent eventually follows the previous one, is employed between the VP and the adverbial clause.

Doesn't matter [$_{\text{CL}}$ *if it's really crap*] <,> [S1A-006 #197]

If we want to examine each subclass of transitivity separately (the **IV**), we must

Figure 222: A schematic representation of an FTF with optional elements (left), and, right, a matching case (S1A-006 #197)

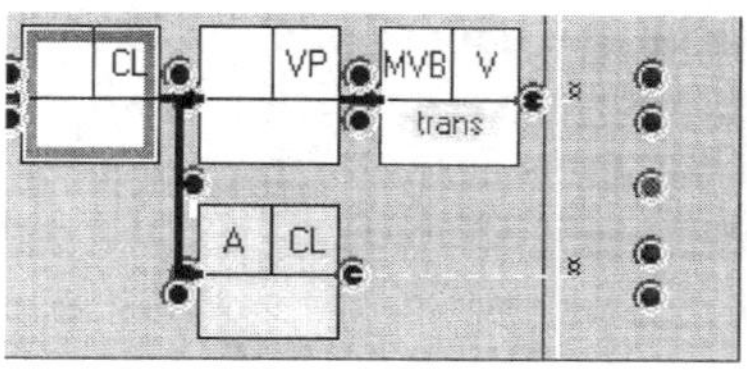

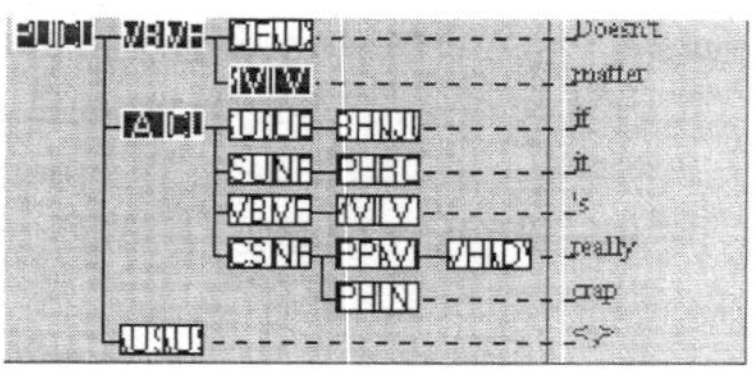

Table 77: The contingency table for the 'optional constituent' example

`CL[VP-V(?trans) ?A,CL]`	**DV** (**adverbial clause present**)		
IV (**transitivity of verb**)	`A,CL`	`¬A,CL`	TOTAL
`intr`	2,766	26,848	29,614
`cop`	2,159	27,371	29,350
`montr`	4,661	54,752	59,413
`cxtr`	285	3,628	3,913
`ditr`	118	1,574	1,692
`*dimontr`	19	241	260
`trans`	130	2,401	2,531
*0	2	46	48
TOTAL	10,140	116,681	126,821

enumerate them in a table and construct FTFs for each one, with and without the adverbial clause. We complete Table 77 by looking up the shaded values and calculating the remainder by subtraction.

The **DV** is Boolean (the presence or absence of a constituent). The analysis for predicting when the adverbial clause is present proceeds as before. Since the unmarked (error, labelled '0') transitivity frequency is low (2), we collapse it into the next lowest cell ('**`dimontr`**'). These are starred in Table 77 and the working below.

Observed **O** = {2766, 2159, 4661, 285, 118, 21*, 130},
scale factor SF = 10140/126821 = 0.080,
expected **E** = {2368, 2347, 4750, 313, 135, 25*, 202} (approx.).
Chi-square $\chi^2 = 398^2/2368 + 188^2/2347 + 89^2/4750 + 28^2/313 + 17^2/135 + 4^2/25 + 72^2/202 = 114.578 > \text{crit}(5, 0.05) = 11.070$.
Since χ^2 > critical value, the result is significant and the null hypothesis, *i.e.*, that the presence of a following adverbial clause within such clauses does not correlate with the transitivity of the preceding verb, is rejected.

The high χ^2 value is mostly due to the large number of applicable cases. The greatest contribution to the overall variation is for intransitive ($398^2/2368 = 66.9$), where the proportion containing an adverbial clause rises from 8 to 9.3%. The next largest contribution is transitive ($72^2/202 = 25.7$), where the proportion containing an adverbial clause *falls* to a mere 2.7% (130 out of 2,531).

9.8.4 Footnote: dealing with overlapping cases

The preceding example can fall victim to two different kinds of overlapping.

- The optional adverbial clause is itself the superordinate clause of another case.
- There is more than one VP or adverbial clause within the same superordinate clause.

The first of these is excluded by the grammar.

Figure 223: Defining FTFs to detect overlapping cases

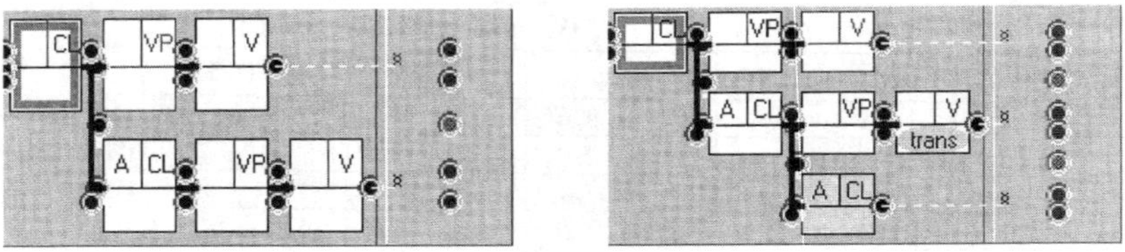

We can construct an FTF to detect both types of overlap. Figure 223, left, depicts an FTF for the first type. This finds 8,993 matches in ICE-GB out of 10,140. Nearly 9 out of 10 adverbial clauses in such structures contain a VP and a verb. This is not altogether surprising! The question is, do these clauses interact with one another, and if so, does this undermine the sampling assumptions of the experiment?

This is not trivial to answer. In a narrow sense, we are obviously referring to two distinct constituents, whereas this compound is recognised by linguists as a "complex clause". When we examine the results of the query, we find that out of the 8,993 cases where the adverbial clause contains a verb, only 472 contain a second adverbial clause. The 8% proportion of cases becomes 4%.

It seems that if the clause we are investigating is itself an adverbial clause within another clause, then it decreases the likelihood that it contains a second adverbial clause. (We can perform an experiment to check this, where the **IV** is the presence of the preceding structure and the **DV** is the presence of the second adverbial clause.)

However, this is not the same thing as saying that if a clause in another clause is adverbial then this will affect our original experiment. We can set up another secondary experiment, subdividing these 8,993 cases (Figure 223, right) to examine the interaction between the transitivity feature of the second verb and the presence of the second adverbial clause. Such an experiment would allow us to generalise about the behaviour of these lower adverbial clauses.

We turn next to the question of sampling. If we argue that cases of adverbial clauses within other cases are *not at all* independent from their parent, the worst case assumption would be that we should *halve* the observed and expected sample before performing the test. As we have seen, for every uppermost case there are 0.9 dependent cases below, and at most 0.04 cases below that. If the strictly independent cases are a little more than 50% of the total then halving the sample seems a reasonable approach.

The original chi-square result therefore simply halves (to 57.289), as do the various χ^2 contributions. Since these are still easily significant, we can be sure that our original result is sound.

The second kind of overlapping is where there is more than one adverbial clause within the same superordinate clause. The adverbial case may be counted twice within the same structure while the more general FTF without the adverbial is only counted once. Searching for structures containing *two* following adverbial clauses yields 327 cases out of 10,140, *i.e.*, around 3% of cases containing one adverbial clause also contain a second, for example,

> Now [$_{\text{VP}}$ *use*] the brake [$_{\text{CL1}}$ *if necessary*] [[$_{\text{CL2}}$ *to stop it*] <,> [S2A-054 #22]

The FTF containing the adverbial clause will match separately for each additional clause. However, these are not really separate cases. We can either

- decrease this number by subtracting the results of each FTF with an additional adverbial clause, saying, in effect, that the 'case' is the overall clause, with the dependent variable being whether or not there is *any* following adverbial clause, or
- increase the total, in which case we are saying that these cases are independent.

Of these strategies, the former is to be preferred. Note, however, that if, instead of simply detecting whether a constituent is present, a variable is specified by part of a constituent (*e.g.*, by a feature), and that constituent can occur more than once, we have a different problem: *if these distinct matches are collapsed to form a single case, which constituent do we choose?* We could construct a further notional outcome value (*e.g.*, 'multiple'), to classify these cases. In our example, the problem could not arise, because grammatical constraints limit VPs to one per clause.

Finally, note that it is always important to put these problems into some kind of numerical context. The second type of overlap only occurs in 3% of cases, so it may be considered within the margins of error. The first kind is not numerically trivial, occurring in around 90% of cases, and therefore should be investigated.

PART 4:
The future of the corpus

10. FUTURE PROSPECTS

10.1 Extending the annotation in the corpus

Future developments in the ICE-GB project are, of course, subject to continued research funding. There are several outstanding issues in the annotation of the corpus which we would like to address, and which we will discuss briefly here.

The first of these are the so-called *'ignored' elements.* Recall that in spoken texts in particular, repetitions, hesitations, and false starts were 'edited out' before parsing, and then loosely re-attached to the trees afterward (see Section 1.6). These elements appear as grayed nodes on the syntactic trees, as shown in Figure 224.

Figure 224: An example of an 'ignored' false start (S1A-036 #57).

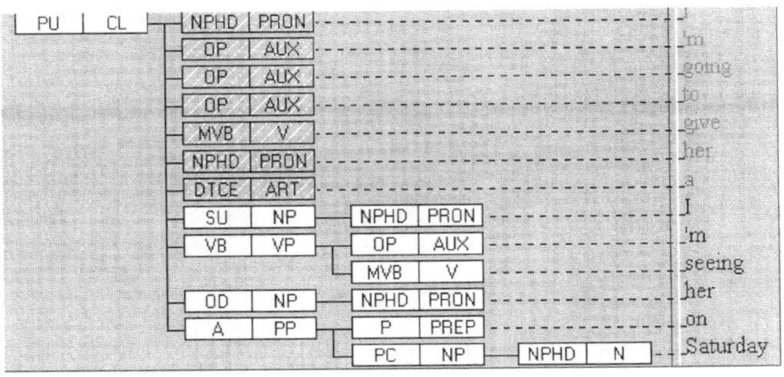

In most cases, these 'ignored' elements have not been internally analysed, as in this example, where it is represented simply as a 'flat' structure. In many cases, however (including the one shown here), it would be possible to analyse them internally, in the same terms as the regular material. This would permit researchers to explore *all* the material in the corpus, and specifically to examine the syntax of nonfluencies in speech.

Similarly, some of the *ditto-tagged elements* (see Section 2.2) could be subjected to further analysis. For example, in order to ease the parsing process, we treated book and song titles as compounds, tagged them as proper nouns, and parsed them as compound noun phrases, as in Figure 225.

Figure 225: Ditto-tagged book title (S1A-011 #123).

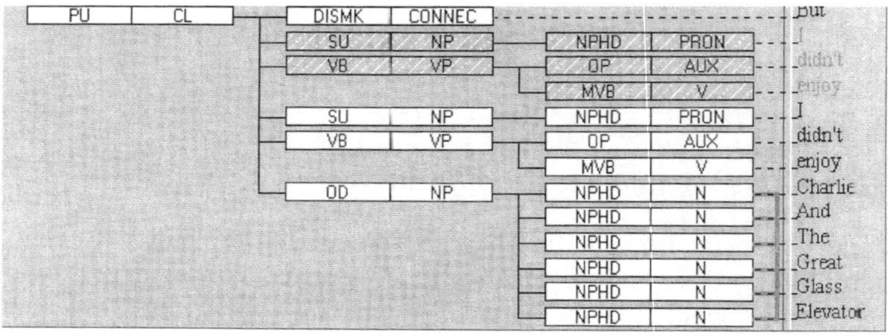

Such strings could, of course, be internally analysed. Following the same principle, we also treated the song title in the following extract as a noun phrase, though it is clearly an imperative clause:

Figure 226: Ditto-tagged song title (W2C-019 #10).

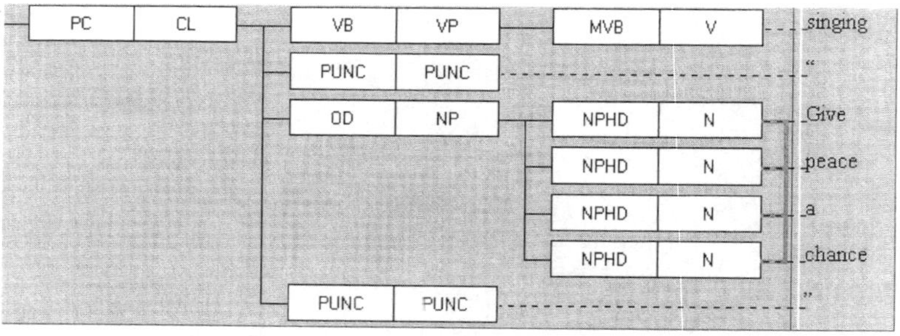

By analysing these items internally, we would introduce more structure to the trees, and hence add more information to the corpus. Naturally, researchers could exploit this additional information using Fuzzy Tree Fragments.

We also envisage several possible extensions to the corpus itself and to the retrieval software, ICECUP. We would like to add more levels of annotation to the corpus in order to enhance its value as a research resource. In particular, we would like to enhance the spoken component of the corpus. For largely practical reasons, the speech recordings were transcribed orthographically (see Section 1.4). Most researchers would agree, however, that this is far from ideal (Knowles 1996). A great deal of valuable, and indeed necessary, information is lost – or at least is not encoded – in a bare orthographic transcription.

A logical extension to the ICE-GB project, therefore, would be to add *prosodic annotation* to at least part of the spoken component. This could be done much more efficiently now than it might have been at the start of the project. The sound recordings have been digitized and aligned with the transcriptions (see Section 1.8), and we may use ICECUP for editing the corpus, so a great deal of computational assistance for the annotation task may be provided. Similarly, we propose to add *pragmatic annotation* (*e.g.*, illocutionary acts, 'turn' taking, and so on) to the conversational data in ICE-GB.

Research based on these enhanced versions of the corpus would make a very valuable contribution to our understanding of the interface between syntax, prosody, and pragmatics.

We note that adding a new layer of annotation to the corpus should be complemented by the addition of a mechanism for *queries* for each new layer. For example, suppose we were to add rising and falling tone prosodic markers to the spoken part of ICE-GB. Unless we can express a query to retrieve all cases of rising tones, say, then these markers cannot be easily employed in research. The research process would require the manual inspection of each sentence, which would vastly limit the possibilities for systematic research.[1]

For every additional layer of annotation, therefore, we should modify ICECUP to, firstly, express individual atomic queries, *e.g.*, 'get me all rising tones', and secondly, link these queries to structured queries (FTFs), so that we can say 'get me all examples of *never* with a falling tone', or 'find me a grammatical pattern like this that has a word in this position with a rising tone'. These annotation levels would be linked through the *sentence text*. We can study parallel analyses of the same text provided that they are related to one another through the words that they annotate.

Once different kinds of annotation are linked together, a researcher can carry out detailed and systematic investigations of how these various levels inter-relate by using the kinds of discovery methods proposed in Section 10.4.

This leads us onto prospects for the ICECUP software, our exploratory and experimental methodology, and the overall perspective in corpus linguistics we suggest in this book.

10.2 Extending the expressivity of Fuzzy Tree Fragments

A more expressive query representation is better able to capture subtle variations between different linguistic cases. ICECUP 3.1 includes a number of important extensions to FTFs. These include specifying a node as an exact match, including pseudo-features such as 'ignore' and 'discontinuous', introducing logic into nodes, and providing logic and wild cards for lexical items. These extensions are described in Chapter 7.

[1] There is a good argument for including certain kinds of annotation, such as the digitised sound recordings, that cannot be (presently) searched. However, the ability to form queries on the annotation provides far greater possibilities for research, as we have seen. See also Chapter 4.4 on the distinction between illustrative and formal annotation.

The main limitation of these extended FTFs is that one cannot combine any two parts of a single FTF with logical operators aside from 'and'. An FTF is a *model*. Every component is held to be true at the same time. For example, in ICECUP 3.1 you can state that an FTF has a node in a child position which is not a clause. However, you cannot state that the FTF *doesn't have a clausal child*, or that it either has a clause in one position *or* an NP in another.

If FTFs were able to do this, they would effectively become a kind of 'tree query logic' (Wallis and Nelson 2000). The idea of an FTF as a simple model would be undermined. Arbitrary logical expressions are difficult to visualise because they contain explicitly absent or alternative structure. It is arguable that this kind of complexity does not necessarily help corpus linguists.

Rather than try to express a variety of outcomes in a single query structure, which may be difficult to visualise, comprehend and communicate, we would suggest that it is preferable to exploit *logical combinations of FTFs*. The key requirement, as we argued in Section 9.6, is to guarantee that such FTFs *refer to the same set of cases in the corpus*. In Section 10.3 we propose a method that ensures this by building on the experimental approach. Hopefully it should be clear from Chapter 9 that an FTF can remain linguistically intuitive, and yet experimentally effective.

If we do not employ logic with FTF links, we may wish to consider possible extensions to the set of permissible links. In this respect we have had few requests for changes from researchers (in contrast, for example, with requests for increased flexibility in defining nodes or wild cards). Our current set of links, summarised in Section 5.12, appears to be sufficient for most purposes. Any limitations can be worked around by using more than one FTF.[2]

For discussion purposes at least, the following are a number of extensions that could be introduced. Here we can distinguish between extensions that are beneficial for *any* grammar, including ICE, and those that have benefits for other analysis schemes. The first three are illustrated in Figure 227.

- **Following ditto links**. ICECUP 3.1 allows you to mark that a node is ditto-tagged using the pseudo-feature 'ditto'. However, you cannot specify that two tag-nodes or words are part of *the same* compound. To do this thoroughly would require the introduction of a new linking relation (say, **Next ditto**, with the same set of options as **Next word**), and two end 'edges' (**First/Last ditto**). To complicate things still further, note that we cannot rely on the word sequence, thanks to the possibility of discontinuous elements. **Next ditto** would be a point-to-point relation (*i.e.*, one where we specify the target as well as the source of the link) which may optionally be applied to leaf nodes.

---

[2] With logical combinations of FTFs, in order to express two alternative structures, you 'or' two FTFs. A query that must not include a particular sub-structure is written by conjoining ('anding') the main FTF with a negated sub-FTF. The principal concern is to ensure that these two FTFs apply to the same set of cases. We propose to do this by using an explicit *experimental design* employing grammatical variables. See Section 10.6 below.

Figure 227: Possible extensions to FTF links.

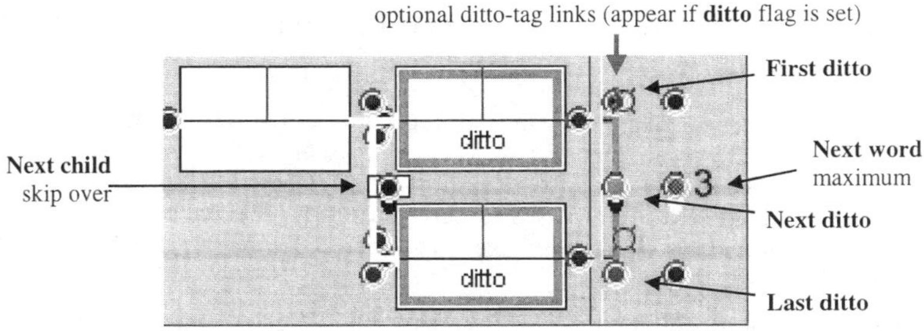

- **Limit conditions (eventual links).** We can express the idea that a node or word is distant from another by *at least n* positions, where *n* is a positive constant. In a wild card, one would write '???*' to mean "at least 3 characters". In FTFs, you can do the same thing by inserting 3 immediately-connected nodes or words, and then add a single eventual link. To *prevent* two nodes or words separated by *more than n* positions being matched, we would have to add an explicit limit, *e.g.*, ' 3 ' (see right of Figure 227). While this kind of extension would certainly be possible, however, we would argue that the richness of the grammatical analysis is more important than any notional 'distance' between elements, a concept more suitable for tagged or plain text corpora where the parse analysis is absent.[3]
- **Skip-over conditions (immediate links)**. Currently, ICECUP has a predefined set of elements that may be skipped over by 'immediate' (**Next word** and **Next child**) links, and the option is globally set (see Chapter 3.13). The reason for this is that the grammar includes elements, such as pauses and punctuation, that can be inserted at any point and can obstruct the matching process. In some circumstances we might wish to specify nodes that can be safely skipped over. One difficulty would be to visualise this. One could depict this as ' ' (Figure 227, middle) but it is not clear which nodes are skipped. This is not insurmountable, but we are moving towards full logic. Arguably, this kind of issue is better dealt with by a set of alternative FTFs.
- **Procedural conditions (eventual links)**. Another kind of extension to links would be to permit certain kinds of *procedural requirement* to select from a number of different matching cases. For example, the *host clause* of a node is the *nearest ancestor clause* above it (Wallis and Nelson 2001). However, this concept is a procedural one, *i.e.*, you perform two operations in a particular order:

  1. find all matching ancestors of *x* marked as clause ('**CL**'),
  2. determine the one that is closest to *x*.

  This is not consistent with the idea of an FTF as a declarative model or a logical construct. Rather, it is better handled when *deciding what to do* with FTF results. We return to this in Section 10.3 below.

A number of extensions would be useful for corpora parsed according to other grammatical frameworks, but are not really beneficial for ICE. Rather than

---

[3] See, *e.g.*, the implications of parsed corpora for experimentation in Chapter 9.

develop a 'universal' specification for parsed corpus queries in isolation, we have found it more productive to concentrate on establishing the practical use of FTF models in corpus research with an existing corpus, and then considering how it can be generalised.

- **Ordered 'Different branches'**. In ICE, links are not allowed to cross one another. This means that we can guarantee that branches are ordered by insisting that the last child of the first branch has a '**Next word** = After' relation with the first child of the second. However, if FTFs are used for any structure where this constraint is broken, such as a dependency grammar, then an ordered 'Different branches' notion is required.
- **Arbitrary point-to-point links.** ICE employs ditto-tagged compounds (see above). Some other parsed corpora follow the University of Pennsylvania Treebank in employing *predicate-argument* relations (Marcus *et al.* 1994) alongside a simplified phrase structure grammar. If ICECUP were extended to support such corpora, FTFs would need to employ arbitrary named links from one node to another.

Many of these developments would be very similar to the extensions necessary to support other layers of analysis in FTFs. Adding point-to-point relations and introducing new groups of relations, such as those for ditto sequences, into FTFs would be necessary in order to relate prosodic and pragmatic structures in the text (Section 10.1 above) to the grammar. The principal difference is that the developments discussed here are extensions to *grammatical node* links rather than linking elements based on parallel analyses of the same text.

10.3 Incorporating experiments in software

ICECUP was designed around a hands on 'exploratory' approach, with the idea that a new user should be able to access corpus examples easily. From the outset we avoided insisting that a researcher must define every aspect of a query before they experiment. As we pointed out in the introduction to Chapter 4, even the most experienced grammarian cannot be expected to learn both the formal definition of a particular grammar *and* how the grammar is realised in the corpus before she begins.

We therefore proposed an 'exploration cycle' supported by software. In this cycle a user forms a query, explores the results, abstracts a new query or modifies the original one, and performs the query again. A query is formed with the corpus map, variable, markup or node queries, text fragments and FTFs. On browsing corpus trees, a user may find an interesting construction and use the Wizard (Section 5.14) to make a new FTF. The process is repeated, with the new FTF as a starting point.

However, while this is highly effective for exploration, it is less effective for experimentation. Large-scale experimentation requires a little more control and support than is provided at present. This is not to say that experiments cannot be performed using ICECUP – as Chapters 8 and 9 illustrate – but it does mean that the user has to be very careful about correctly collecting intersection frequencies and defining a null hypothesis. The more labour intensive the process, the harder, more error-prone and more onerous is the task of repeating it for a variety of different research questions. The question is then, how much software support can we offer to linguists to help them scale up their research?

Central to this question is the formal definition of an experiment, what we referred to in Chapter 9 as *the experimental design*. In order to proceed in this direction, ICECUP must be able to explicitly represent this experimental design. At a minimum this means allowing the researcher to define:

- A **case** that all variables in the experiment are concerned with.
- Two discrete **variables** defined in terms of FTFs.
- The experimental **hypothesis**, *i.e.*, specifying which of the variables (the *dependent variable* or DV) should be evaluated as if it were dependent on the other (the *independent variable*, or IV). (See Section 9.1.)

Together these define a set of cases categorised by an independent and dependent variable. Summary frequencies can be visualised as a *contingency table* and evaluated using the χ^2 statistic, as explained in Chapter 9. This level of automation has the main advantage that frequency collection and statistical evaluation can be performed without further intervention. The experimental hypothesis is explicitly stated and relative frequencies are correctly deployed.

A grammatical case may be defined by a single FTF (working top-down, *e.g.*, the FTF in the top left of Figure 228) or as a set of alternate FTFs which list all possible outcomes of the most specific variable (*i.e.*, working from the bottom, up). Variables would similarly be defined in terms of FTFs and other queries. For our purposes, a variable consists of a discrete (and potentially hierarchical), structure of values, where every value is explicitly defined in terms of a *query*. This parallels the definition of the lexicon and grammaticon discussed in Chapter 7. Once two variables have been defined the experimental hypothesis then simply specifies the direction of the experiment.

To see how this might work, consider the following example. Suppose we are interested in examining facets of noun phrases. The case is an FTF containing a single NP. Figure 228, overleaf, shows a sketch of a variable representing the type of an NP's head.

A variable can be defined *intrinsically* as a structured tree of labelled elements. Ideally, every value should also be defined *extrinsically*. That is, every value in the variable is associated with a query. Variables are assumed to be *mutually exclusive* – an NP head cannot be a pronoun and a noun at the same time – and a parent value is the *union* of its subvalues – an NP with a noun head is a kind of NP. A variable is simply a way of subdividing cases according to a particular classification. In a hierarchical variable the topmost node

Figure 228: Defining a variable for the type of head realising an NP.

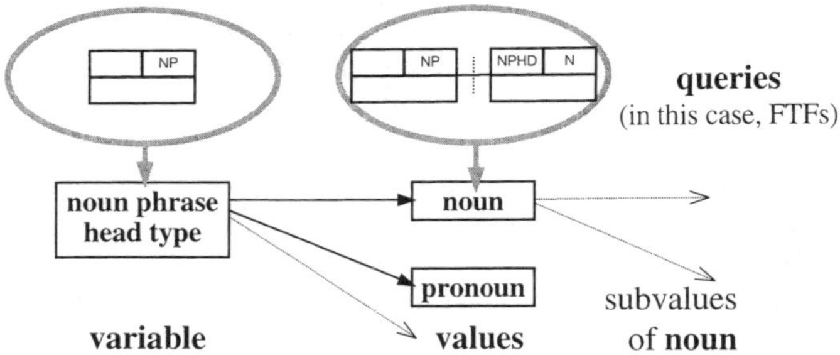

represents the universal set, 'NP head type = <anything>', *i.e.*, we know that the NP has a head but we cannot determine what it is.

There is obviously a strict relationship between the structure of a variable and the queries that realise each value. This means that you can extend the structure from the top down, by specifying, for example, that you wish to subdivide **noun** in Figure 228 by a particular feature class, say, **noun type** = {**proper**, **common**}. Alternatively, you could subdivide the value by a structural consideration, *e.g.*, the presence or absence of a preceding determiner.

Every FTF in the definition must be related to the same case, *i.e.*, at least one node in every FTF must match the same node (the NP in our example) in a corpus tree. We specify this node using the 'focus' property.

An important reason for defining queries for every point in the structure is that the software can work out if the definition is *fully enumerated* (see Box in Section 9.6). When variables have been defined, one can ask the software to evaluate each case in terms of the variable. If any case exists that does not match any leaf definition, the variable cannot be fully enumerated. For example, in Figure 228, if we only defined head types for **noun** and **pronoun**, any NP without a head, or with a head that is a **proform**, **nominal adjective**, *etc.* would fall into a third category we could call **other**.

Conversely, this classificatory process will also identify rare values and low-valued cells (see Section 9.8.3). These cases will be collapsed in any analysis and subdividing them is not useful.

A final advantage of this approach is that we can ask the software to list possible alternatives according to a particular consideration. Suppose we want to subdivide a **nominal adjective** case by lexical item. There is little point in trying to specify such a list in advance. Instead, the software can build a list of types as it extracts and sorts cases: *disabled*, *able-bodied*, *abled*, *own*, *public*,... This would form a broad set of values, each relatively infrequent. These could then be grouped manually, based on a stated criterion, *e.g.*, a semantic distinction, chosen according to the motive of the research.

As we mentioned above, defining an experimental variable as a typological hierarchy of queries is entirely consistent with the corpus map and the lexicon, as well as the grammaticon proposed in the previous section. Cases may not be classified as both **spoken** and **written** ('written to be spoken' texts have to be placed in one or the other group). The word *work* can be classified as a **verb** or a **noun**, but we do not permit them to be both at the same time. A clause is a **subject** or **direct object**, but not both simultaneously.

The main difference between these overviews and experimental variables is that variables are user-defined hierarchies of complex objects grounded in a particular case definition. Indices are not precalculated.

For every case in a tree, the software applies each variable, and the FTFs within the variable definition, to it. The software works downwards from the top of the hierarchy, meaning that first the top-most node in the variable is matched. If successful the siblings are matched; if one of these matches and has children, then these are matched, and so on.

What happens if the case matches more than one sibling, which is possible if sibling FTFs overlap? Recall that we have assumed that values are mutually exclusive, *i.e.*, the same case must match only one value. We can accept the presence of a default, or '**other**' value for those cases that do not match any sibling. There are two choices: *select* or *split the case* between alternatives. The simplest way of selecting between alternative matches is simply to evaluate the siblings in a particular order. This should be avoided, however. Each value should be fully defined in isolation. It is preferable to explicitly represent indeterminacy by allocating a proportion of the case to each value. This fact should be indicated to the researcher, who can then choose to modify the definition of either value in order to make the distinction explicit.

Apart from efficiency, a top-down procedure can select between multiple matches where eventual or unordered FTF relations are specified. Wallis and Nelson (2001) describe how a 'host clause' (the nearest ancestor clause) can be related to the principal case (in this example, a postmodifying clause), and may be discriminated.

A further consideration was mentioned in Chapter 9. This is the problem of *case interdependence*. How do we know, for example, if noun phrases can contain one another, that cases abstracted from NPs in the corpus are independent from one another? The simple answer is, of course, that we don't. Statistical independence can only be strictly guaranteed if cases are randomly sampled from the entire output of the English language of the period we would like to generalise over. Sampling cases more than once from a relatively small number of texts is bound to be problematic. The problem is connected to the frequency of cases. Very common structures, such as NPs, are easily dealt with by working from a randomly sampled subset. Taking, say, 5% of NPs in ICE-GB still leaves us with a sample size of 15,000 – enough to be getting on with! The drawback is that this is very wasteful. It limits the sensitivity and specificity of our experiments.

There are essentially two ways of getting around this problem, or rather, *trading experimental purity for increased sensitivity*. In Section 9.6.4 we suggested assessing the interdependence of cases by looking at examples. Suppose the software measures the overlap of nodes or assesses case *proximity* during the classification process. It then probabilistically *scores* cases. We may say that if two cases are in close proximity (*e.g.*, they overlap or share the same parent) then they should be treated as two aspects of the same case, *i.e.*, assume that each contributes 50% of variation. If they differ in some respect we allocate half a case to one value in a contingency table and half to another. As cases become more distant we may discount them by less than 50%. Note that this approach requires a combinatorial assessment, *i.e.*, if a tree contains 3 cases we assess all three together. It can also be combined with random sampling.

This approach is not foolproof. For example, we have not considered proximity between cases in different text units in the same subtext. We have assumed that proximity itself is a reliable indicator of independence. This kind of approach should therefore be complemented by attacking the problem from another direction. Suppose we contrast our largish sample with a small random sample where very few cases are taken from each subtext. We could do this separately for each variable using χ^2. If our synthetic dataset differs significantly we need to modify our sampling criteria.

The obvious point is that any such process requires significant computation and the incorporation of the experimental process within the software. Note that whereas ICECUP operates by manipulating ordered sets of text units, the implication of this transition to experimentation is that the software must explicitly create and manipulate a new abstract *database table* of cases defined by a case definition and a sampling procedure, and classified by variables. Just as the lexicon cross-references the corpus, each abstract case in this experimental dataset includes a reference back to a single matching case in a corpus text unit. As we point out in Chapter 9, to explain novel experimental results you have to examine the linguistic examples from which they derive.

Incorporating experimentation into software is not the endpoint of supporting research. The next stage is to provide methods for setting up more complex experiments involving multiple independent variables. Instead of performing a single χ^2 test, such a system could actively *search* combinations of variables, evaluating large numbers of related hypotheses statistically, and focusing on the most promising.

10.4 Knowledge discovery in corpora

Wallis and Nelson (2001) describe a perspective that we call *Knowledge Discovery in Corpora* (KDC).[4] In experimentation, the researcher defines a pair of variables, one dependent (the DV) and the other independent (IV), basing these variables around a case definition. In knowledge discovery, this is extended to allow the researcher to specify numerous independent variables. In order to evaluate how these IVs contribute to predicting a dependent variable, we need to consider large numbers of permutations; far more than would be possible by hand. As before, we sample and classify cases in the corpus and form an abstract database table (cases × variables). Every case in this dataset can be cross-referenced to its origin in the corpus.

The problem is then to find the most salient and predictive combinations of independent values that predict particular values of a dependent variable, *i.e.*, to find independent hypothesis *rules* of the form

$$IV_1 = iv_1 \wedge IV_2 = iv_2 \wedge IV_3 = iv_3 \ldots \rightarrow DV = dv,$$

where IV_1, IV_2, IV_3 are independent variables, DV is the dependent variable, and iv_1, iv_2, iv_3 and dv are selected values of these variables.

The advantage of this approach over experimentation is that it allows us to perform many related experiments very quickly and to automatically weigh up competing hypotheses. In the previous section we commented that incorporating experimentation in software would render individual experiments more rapid, less error-prone, and more sensitive. As the cost of performing experiments falls, researchers can afford to be increasingly speculative about the variables that they choose to define and include. Knowledge discovery goes further still by allowing researchers to compare the predictive performance of *many* independent variables, separately and in conjunction. As an approach, it is somewhere between 'black box' computation and classical experimentation. KDC applies computation to theory-directed corpus research with the proviso that the researcher must be able to both direct the process and discover why a particular conclusion was drawn. It is therefore centrally important that the results are simple and understandable to researchers, hence the use of simple independent hypothesis rules.

Wallis and Nelson summarise a 'machine learning' algorithm, UNIT, which performs a search for hypothesis rules by steadily increasing the complexity of the left hand side of the rule and experimentally evaluating each potential hypothesis.

---

[4] Our approach is related to existing work on *knowledge discovery in databases* (Fayyad 1997), but with a number of important differences.

This evaluation means that we retain every rule where the precondition (left hand side):

1. significantly affects the distribution across the dependent variable,
2. predicts the closest matching value of the DV, *dv*, with greater 'effectiveness' (according to a predefined accuracy measure) than its predecessor, and
3. significantly alters the distribution across the DV compared to its predecessor.

This process is deterministic. Unlike many similar algorithms, it rejects hypotheses only for poor quality rather than by competition. As a result, it can be set up to explore all significant independent hypothesis rules using the given variables and dataset. The rules are limited only by the necessity for the precondition to significantly interact with the DV (point 1), and for more complex preconditions to 'significantly improve' their predictive ability (points 2 and 3).

After the dataset has been analysed, the resulting rules must be evaluated. The rules can represent *different alternative explanations* for some of the same phenomena. Because they are independent, hypothesis rules can be removed or adjusted without affecting the way the others are interpreted.[5] The semi-exhaustive nature of the search procedure means that if an expected hypothesis failed to appear we can try to establish why.

Every rule is associated with the set of cases in the dataset that support the rule (*i.e.*, all conditions are true), known as the *true positives*, and those cases that contradict the rule, called the *false positives* (where the precondition is true but the conclusion is false). Unexpected or novel rules can be evaluated concretely by examining the cases in the corpus which gave rise to the rule. Competing explanations may be contrasted by examining the cases that overlap or are distinct, again referring to the corpus where necessary. Moreover, it should be possible to introduce rules anticipated by results in the literature, but not found by the analysis process, and these can be contrasted with respect to cases in the corpus.

At this point it would be possible to remove variables from the abstract dataset or define new ones. For example, if we notice a particular distinction in cases in the corpus that is not expressed as a variable, but appears to coincide with different outcomes of the dependent variable, then we might choose to represent this as a variable and perform the process again.

In Wallis and Nelson (2001) we demonstrated that this process scales up to serious investigations of grammatical variation (in our pilot experiment, 20 variables and 4,000 cases). Our dataset was created from the corpus but was not cross-referenced back to the original set of examples. We had a set of independent tools rather than an integrated research platform. Consequently it was difficult to identify cases in the corpus justifying particular conclusions.

---

[5] Independent rules are much easier to understand than the typical rule *networks* ("decision trees") generated by most machine learning algorithms. See Wallis and Nelson (2001).

Despite this, we were able to demonstrate that the approach was able to perform large-scale experiments and obtain interesting and novel research results. We can say with some confidence that this approach extends the experimental perspective into a highly effective and general method for supporting the investigation of grammar in a parsed corpus. The approach would also be effective for cross-comparing layers of analysis (*e.g.*, trying to predict the presence of a structure in one layer from aspects of a different grammatical analysis) provided that these layers were present in the same corpus and could be queried in an integrated way.

10.5 Aiding the annotation of corpora

Apart from formal research, experimentation and analysis, another application of our software is corpus correction. In fact, ICECUP was used to assemble and correct ICE-GB. Although this function is disabled in the software released with the corpus, ICECUP can in principle edit any tree and sentence in the corpus. In short, it is also *an annotation workbench*. Moreover, in conjunction with a corpus query, such as an FTF, we can change the way that we correct a corpus.

At present, putting a corpus like ICE-GB together involves a series of stages, often involving large numbers of separate files. Different file formats may be required at different stages so that material can be processed by automatic taggers and parsers. Unlike tagging, parsing is particularly problematic. Additional information to help the parser may be required. Parsers may produce ambiguous output (several possible trees for the same sentence), incomplete or wrong analyses, or they may fail altogether. At the end of the process disparate files must be re-integrated into a single corpus and corrected.

Naturally, researchers have been working hard at tackling some of these problems. Famously, the Text Encoding Initiative has defined very detailed standards for corpus encoding (Sperberg-McQueen and Burnard 1994), which could in principle be used by parsers and annotation workbenches. The University of Sheffield General Architecture for Text Engineering (GATE) projects (Cunningham, Humphreys, Wilks and Gaizauskas 1997; see also http://gate.ac.uk/) have developed a 'plug-together' approach to integrating different natural language processing components.

However, the problem remains that the large-scale analysis of genuine natural language will not be possible by an automatic process in the foreseeable future. Human annotators have to work on the results.

The trick is then to maximise their efforts. Here also, there have been a number of approaches. One of the simplest is to allow annotators to use 'macro' operators to insert entire structures into a tree. This facility is provided, for example, by the TOSCA tree editor (see http://lands.let.kun.nl/TSpublic/tosca/treeedit.html). A more sophisticated idea is to integrate the parsing process itself with human decision making, so that the parser offers a researcher a limited number of choices. This approach is employed in Roger Garside's EPICS program (Leech and Garside 1991), and was used to annotate the German NEGRA corpus (Brants, Skut and Uszkoreit 1999).

However, all these approaches perform correction longitudinally: sentence by sentence, text by text. Longitudinal correction has the advantage that correction is performed in context and we know when to stop, *i.e.*, when we hit the end. It has the serious disadvantage that it places a high cognitive burden on correctors (Wallis and Nelson 1997), particularly when applied to a detailed grammar such as ICE. An annotator has to make a series of decisions, each in context, but each typically very different from the previous one. Naturally, mistakes are made and the process is very tiresome. We might say that we have tackled the *correctness problem* (is this sentence analysed correctly?) but not the *consistency problem* (is this sentence analysed consistently with respect to the rest of the corpus?). Reaching the end of the corpus may not represent the endpoint of correction at all.

We therefore introduced a final stage into the building of ICE-GB. We call this *cross-sectional correction* (Wallis 1999; see also Chapter 1). The idea is to use FTFs to search for possible sites of errors, and then to correct them. Correction proceeds on a case-by-case basis, not on a text-by-text one. We have found this to be easier, faster and more consistent than longitudinal correction.

An error-driven approach also promises an efficiency of scale. It seems reasonable to assume that the number of error types will not increase at the same rate as the corpus. In mathematical terms, the problem tends to reduce from an order n process towards order log n. Doubling the size of the corpus, therefore, does not imply doubling the correction effort. Moreover, there is scope for controlled automation across the entire corpus, what we might refer to as 'search and selective replace', once an annotation decision is formalised.

Moreover, grammatical overview facilities such as the lexicon and grammaticon (Sections 7.2 and 7.3) also aid the correction process by revealing certain kinds of improbable annotation, particularly those of low frequency. We have observed how developing ICECUP's querying and browsing capabilities has revealed new sets of error. The correction process will necessarily overlap with external evaluation, experimentation and so forth.

A cross-sectional approach to correction allows for a perspective where new layers of annotation (*e.g.*, prosodic, see Section 10.1 above) may be selectively added onto existing ones in the corpus. FTF searches may be used, although not relied upon exclusively, to aid the annotation task.

One of the themes of our work has been that the relationship between computational processing and human effort is a complex one. As computational resources increase, more corpora are parsed, software becomes more integrated, and new perspectives in annotation become feasible. Thus it becomes possible to train and improve algorithms during the process of corpus annotation itself.

This 'co-evolutionary' perspective is not exactly new, and has underpinned the development of a number of parsing programs (especially in disambiguating parser output). However, in most cases parser development has been seen as primary and corpus annotation as secondary.

In effect, manual cross-sectional correction may be automated (see above) and then integrated into the parser itself. Finally, as more sizeable parsed corpora are built, it becomes desirable to use one corpus to support the correction of another.

10.6 Teaching grammar with corpora

ICE-GB consists entirely of real language, and is thus a wondrous resource for teaching grammar. For many teachers of English language, for whom grammar was a chore at best endured, at worst avoided, a detailed parsed corpus represents a tremendous resource, particularly at a time that grammar is being reintroduced into school and college curricula. This was one of our motivations in freely distributing the sample corpus over the internet.

Scores of teachers, particularly at university level, have used corpora for teaching purposes. In particular, many have used concordancing programs with plain text and tagged corpora for 'data-driven learning' (see http://web.bham.ac.uk/johnstf/timconc.htm; Johns and King 1993). ICECUP offers concordancing by grammatical constituents and structures (see Chapter 4), so this could be seen as a natural extension to this kind of teaching. The introduction of more project-oriented support in general and experimentation in particular could be a boon to student projects.

However, simply providing material and expecting teachers to 'get on with it' is insufficient. For many teaching purposes the corpus is too detailed and intimidating, even if, for example, ICECUP can hide grammatical features in the tree and text views. In addition, the interactive interface can present too many options to a student unfamiliar with basic concepts of grammar.

By contrast, the *Internet Grammar of English* (IGE, see Preface), also developed at the Survey of English Usage, provides a more traditional pedagogical grammar course over the internet. Grammatical concepts are introduced gradually and illustrated by examples. The course is supplemented by interactive exercises and demonstrations.

Most of the examples in IGE originate from ICE-GB, but they are hard-wired. We would suggest that a particularly fruitful enterprise would be to combine a corpus, and a corpus management system based on ICECUP, FTFs, *etc*., with a pedagogical course such as IGE.

The idea is that instead of hard-wiring 'a good example of *x*' into the course, we substitute 'a definition of what a good example of *x* might look like'. The software then performs the query, selects an example, merges it with the page and presents it to the student.

The corpus annotation determines what can be taught. Naturally, we cannot teach the concept of 'a subject', for example, without having explicitly labelled subjects in a corpus.

A central advantage of decoupling fixed examples from course material is that the whole system becomes much more extensible. New course modules may be developed independently from corpus annotation. New corpora could be continually added to a 'super corpus' mounted on a web server. This might include material in other languages, language varieties, contexts and periods. Course material could be translated for second language teaching purposes.

Familiar problems of grammatical and representational consistency arise, but these are not insurmountable. For publishers concerned about protecting copyright, a major advantage of such a system is that only small amounts of material would be distributed to any individual student.

Employing corpora, rather than lists of examples, has other advantages. We could allow teachers to restrict examples by sociolinguistic category, source, *etc*. We can offer students the option of seeing more context at any point, listening to an original speaker or viewing a facsimile page. And we may be able to gradually introduce the idea of a corpus, and empirical research, through the use of increasing numbers of examples and more open-ended questions, ending in independent project work.

REFERENCES

Aarts, Bas, Gerald Nelson, and Sean A. Wallis. 1998. "Using fuzzy tree fragments to explore English grammar". *English Today* 14, 52-56.

—, Gerald Nelson, and Justin Buckley. 1999. "Online resources for grammar teaching and learning: The Internet Grammar of English". In Rebecca S. Wheeler, ed. *Language Alive in the Classroom*. Westport, Connecticut: Praeger, 199-212.

—, Evelien Keizer, Mariangela Spinillo and Sean Wallis. 2002. "Which or what: a study of interrogative determiners in present-day English". In Andrew Wilson, Paul Rayson and Anthony McEnery, eds. *Corpus Linguistics by the Lune: a Festschrift for Geoffrey Leech* (Lodz Studies in Language series). Frankfurt am Main: Peter Lang.

Aston, Guy, and Lou Burnard. 1998. *The BNC Handbook: Exploring the British National Corpus with SARA*. Edinburgh: Edinburgh University Press.

Bauer, Laurie. 1991. "Who speaks New Zealand English?". *ICE Newsletter* 11. London: Survey of English Usage, University College London.

Brants, Thorsten, Wojciech Skut and Hans Uszkoreit. 1999. "Syntactic annotation of a German newspaper corpus". In Anne Abeille, ed. *Journées ATALA sur les corpus annotés pour la syntaxe – Treebanks workshop (Proceedings)*. Paris: ATALA, 69-76.

Capelle, Bert. 2001. "Is *out of* always a preposition?" *Journal of English Linguistics* 29.4, 315-328.

Collins, Peter. 1996. "*Get*-passives in English". *World Englishes* 15, 43-56.

Crystal, David. 1997. *The Cambridge Encyclopedia of Language*. 2nd edn. Cambridge: Cambridge University Press.

Cunningham, Hugh, Kevin Humphreys, Yorick Wilks, and Robert Gaizauskas. 1997. "Software Infrastructure for Natural Language Processing". *Proceedings of Fifth Conference on Applied Natural Language Processing (ANLP-97).*

Denison, David. 2001. "Gradience and linguistic change". In: Laurel Brinton (ed.) *Historical linguistics 1999: selected papers from the 14th International Conference on Historical Linguistics*, Vancouver 9-13 August 1999, 119-144.

Depraetere, Ilse and Susan Reed. 2000. "The present progressive: constraints on its use with numerical object NPs". *English Language and Linguistics* 4.1, 97-114.

Declerck, Renaat and Susan Reed. 2000. "The semantics and pragmatics of *unless*". *English Language and Linguistics* 4.2, 205-241.

Declerck, Renaat and Susan Reed. 2001. *Conditionals: a comprehensive empirical analysis*. Topics in English Linguistics. Berlin and New York: Mouton de Gruyter.

Fang, Alex. 1995. "Distribution of infinitives in contemporary British English: A study based on the British ICE Corpus". *Literary & Linguistic Computing* 10, 247-257.

— 1996. "The Survey Parser: Design and Development". In Greenbaum, ed. 1996a, 142-160.

Fayyad, Usama. 1997. Editorial. *Data Mining and Knowledge Discovery* 1, 5-10.

Francis, W. Nelson, and Kucera, Henry. 1982. *Frequency Analysis of English Usage: Lexicon and Grammar*. Boston: Houghton Mifflin.

Gonzálvez García, Francisco. 1996. *Towards an understanding of the syntax-semanitcs relation in English complex-transitive complementation*, PhD dissertation. University of Bologna – Royal Spanish College.

Gould, Stephen Jay. 1984. *The mismeasure of man*. London: Penguin.

Green, Elizabeth, and Pam Peters. 1991. "The Australian Corpus Project and Australian English". *ICAME Journal* 15, 37-53.

Greenbaum, Sidney. 1988. "A proposal for an international computerized corpus of English". *World Englishes* 7, 315.

— 1991. "The development of the International Corpus of English". In Karin Aijmer and Bengt Altenberg, eds. *English Corpus Linguistics: Studies in honour of Jan Svartvik*. London: Longman, 83-91.

—— 1995. *The ICE Tagset Manual*. London: Survey of English Usage, University College London.

——, ed. 1996a. *Comparing English Worldwide: The International Corpus of English*. Oxford: Clarendon Press.

—— 1996b. *The Oxford English Grammar*. Oxford: Oxfrord University Press

—— and Gerald Nelson. 1995a. "Clause relationships in spoken and written English", *Functions of Language* 2, 1-21.

—— and Gerald Nelson. 1995b. "Nuclear and peripheral clauses in speech and writing". In Gunnel Melchers and Beatrice Warren, eds. *Studies in Anglistics*. Stockholm: Almqvist & Wiksell, 181-190.

—— and Gerald Nelson. 1996. "Positions of adverbial clauses in British English" *World Englishes* 15, 69-82.

—— and Gerald Nelson. 1998. "Elliptical clauses in spoken and written English". In Peter Collins and David Lee, eds. *The Clause in English*. Amsterdam: Benjamin, 111-126.

—— Gerald Nelson and Michael Weitzman. 1996. "Complement clauses in English". In Jenny Thomas and Mick Short, eds. *Using Corpora for Language Research*. London: Longman, 76-91.

—— and Yibin Ni. 1996. "About the ICE Tagset". In Sidney Greenbaum, ed. 1996a, 92-109.

Holmes, Janet. 1995. "The Wellington Corpus of Spoken New Zealand English: A progress report". *New Zealand English Newsletter* 9, 5-8.

Holmes, Janet. 2001. "Ladies and gentlemen: corpus analysis and linguistic sexism". In: Christian Mair and Marianne Hundt (eds.). *Corpus linguistics and linguistic theory*. Amsterdam: Rodopi. 141-156.

Huckvale, Mark and Alex Fang. 1996. "Prosice: A spoken English database for prosodic research". In Sidney Greenbaum, ed. 1996a, 262-280.

Johns, Tim, and Philip King, eds. 1991. *Classroom Concordancing* Birmingham University: English Language Research Journal 4.

Kaltenböck, Gunther. 1998. *Extraposition in English discourse: a corpus study*. PhD thesis, University of Vienna.

Knowles, Gerry. 1996. "The value of prosodic transcriptions". In Gerry Knowles, Anne Wichmann, and Peter Alderson, eds. *Working with Speech: Perspectives on research into the Lancaster/IBM Spoken English Corpus*. London: Longman, 87-105.

Lavelle, Thomas. 2000. *Form, interpretation and constraint: studies of English nominalisations and related constructions*. Phd thesis, published as *Acta Universitatis Stockholmiensis* XCII. Stockholm: Almquist and Wiksell International.

Leech, Geoffrey, 2000. "Diachronic linguistics across a generation gap: from the 1960s to the 1990s". Paper presented at the symposium *Grammar and Lexis* to commemorate the 40th anniversary of the Survey of English Usage.

— and Roger Garside. 1991. "Running a grammar factory: on the compilation of parsed corpora, or 'treebanks' ". In Stig Johansson and Anna-Britta Stenström, eds. *English Computer Corpora: Selected Papers and Research Guide*. Berlin, New York: Mouton de Gruyter, 15-32.

Leitner, Gerhard. 1992. "The International Corpus of English: Corpus design – problems and suggested solutions". In Gerhard Leitner, ed. *New Directions in English Language Corpora: Methodology, Results, Software Developments*. Berlin, New York: Mouton de Gruyter, 33-64.

Ljung, Magnus. 1996. "Non-finite and verbless adverbial clauses in different genres of English". In Carol Percy, Charles F. Meyer and Ian Lancashire, eds. *Synchronic Corpus Linguistics*. Amsterdam: Rodopi, 109-120.

Marcus, Mitchell P., Grace Kim, Mary Ann Marcinkiewicz, Robert MacIntyre, Ann Bies, Mark Ferguson, Karen Katz and Britte Schasberger. 1994. The Penn Treebank: Annotating Predicate Argument Structure. *Proceedings of the Human Language Translation Workshop*. San Francisco: Morgan Kaufmann.
On-line at http://www.ldc.upenn.edu/Catalog/docs/treebank2/arpa94.html

Meunier, Fanny. 2000. *A computer corpus linguistics approach to interlanguage: noun phrase complexity in advanced learner writing*. PhD thesis, University of Louvain-la-Neuve.

Meyer, Charles F. 1994. "Can you see whose speech is overlapping?" *Visible Language* 28, 112-133.

— 1996. "Coordinate structures in English". *World Englishes* 15, 29-41.

Nelson, Gerald. 1993a. *The International Corpus of English: Markup Manual for Written Texts*. London: Survey of English Usage, University College London.

—— 1993b. *The International Corpus of English: Markup Manual for Spoken Texts*. London: Survey of English Usage, University College London.

—— 1996a. "The design of the corpus". In Greenbaum, ed. 1996a, 27-35.

—— 1996b. "Markup systems". In Greenbaum, ed. 1996a, 36-53.

—— 1997a. Cleft constructions in spoken and written English. *Journal of English Linguistics* 25, 340-348.

—— 1997b. A study of the top 100 wordforms in the ICE-GB text categories. *International Journal of Lexicography* 10, 112-134.

—— and Greenbaum, Sidney. 1999. "Elliptical clauses in spoken and written English". In: Peter Collins and David Lee, eds. *The clause in English: in honour of Rodney Huddleston*. Amsterdam: John Benjamins, 111-126.

Oostdijk, Nelleke. 1991. *Corpus Linguistics and the Automatic Analysis of English*. Amsterdam: Rodopi.

Peters, Pam. 1991. "ICE issues in the collecting and transcribing of texts". Unpublished discussion paper.

—— 1996. "Comparative insights into comparison". *World Englishes* 15, 57-67.

Postal, Paul M. 1974. *On Raising*. Cambridge, MA: MIT Press.

Quinn, Akiva, and Nick Porter. 1996. "ICE annotation tools". In Greenbaum, ed. 1996a, 65-78.

Quirk, Randolph, Sidney Greenbaum, Geoffrey Leech and Jan Svartvik. 1985. *A Comprehensive Grammar of the English Language*. London: Longman.

Schmied, Josef. 1990. "Corpus linguistics and non-native varieties of English". *World Englishes* 9, 255-68.

Simkins, N. K. 1994. "An open architecture for language engineering". *Proceedings of the First Language Engineering Convention*, Paris.

Sperberg-McQueen, C.M. and Lou Burnard. 1994. Guidelines for Electronic Text Encoding and Interchange (TEI P3). Association for Computing in Humanities, Association for Computational Linguistics and Association for Literary and Linguistic Computing.
On-line at http://etext.virginia.edu/TEI.html.

Spinillo, Mariangela. 2000. "Determiners: a class to be got rid of?" *Arbeiten aus Anglistik und Amerikanistik*, 25.2, 173-189.

Shastri, S.V. 1988. "The Kolhapur Corpus of Indian English and work done on its basis so far". *ICAME Journal* 12, 15-26.

Svartvik, Jan. 1966. *On Voice in the English Verb*. The Hague/Paris: Mouton de Gruyter.

Taglicht, Joseph. 2001. "Actually, there's more to it than meets the eye". *English Language and Linguistics* 5.1, 1-16.

Wallis, Sean. 1999. "Completing parsed corpora: from correction to evolution". In Anne Abeille, ed. *Journées ATALA sur les corpus annotés pour la syntaxe – Treebanks workshop (Proceedings)*. Paris: ATALA, 7-12.

— and Gerald Nelson. 1997. "Syntactic parsing as a knowledge acquisition problem". In Enric Plaza and Richard Benjamins, eds. *Knowledge Acquisition, Modeling and Management. Proceedings of European Knowledge Acquisition Workshop (EKAW) '97*. Berlin: Springer Verlag, 285-300.

— and Gerald Nelson. 2000. "Exploiting fuzzy tree fragments in parsed corpus linguistics". *Literary and Linguistic Computing* 15, 339-361.

— and Gerald Nelson. 2001. "Knowledge discovery from grammatically analysed corpora". *Data Mining and Knowledge Discovery* 5, 307-340.

Wichmann, Anne. 2001. "Spoken parentheticals". In Karin Aijmer (ed.) *A wealth of English: studies in honour of Göran Kjellmer*. Gothenburg Studies in English 81. Gothenburg: The University of Gothenburg, 177-193.

APPENDIX 1.
ICE TEXT CATEGORIES AND CODES

Numbers in parentheses denote the number of 2,000-word texts in each category.

A1.1 Spoken Categories

Text Categories	Textcodes
SPOKEN (300)	
Dialogue (180)	
Private (100)	
direct conversations (90)	S1A-001 *to* S1A-090
telephone calls (10)	S1A-091 *to* S1A-100
Public (80)	
classroom lessons (20)	S1B-001 *to* S1B-020
broadcast discussions (20)	S1B-021 *to* S1B-040
broadcast interviews (10)	S1B-041 *to* S1B-050
parliamentary debates (10)	S1B-051 *to* S1B-060
legal cross-examinations (10)	S1B-061 *to* S1B-070
business transactions (10)	S1B-071 *to* S1B-080
Monologue (120)	
Unscripted (70)	
spontaneous commentaries (20)	S2A-001 *to* S2A-020
unscripted speeches (30)	S2A-021 *to* S2A-050
demonstrations (10)	S2A-051 *to* S2A-060
legal presentations (10)	S2A-061 *to* S2A-070
Scripted (50)	
broadcast news (20)	S2B-001 *to* S2B-020
broadcast talks (20)	S2B-021 *to* S2B-040
non-broadcast talks (10)	S2B-041 *to* S2B-050

A1.2 Written Categories

Text Categories	Textcodes
WRITTEN (200)	
Non-printed (50)	
students' untimed essays (10)	W1A-001 *to* W1A-010
students' examination scripts (10)	W1A-011 *to* W1A-020
social letters (15)	W1B-001 *to* W1B-015
business letters (15)	W1B-016 *to* W1B-030
Printed (150)	
Informational Writing (100)	
academic (40)	W2A-001 *to* W2A-040
popular (40)	W2B-001 *to* W2B-040
press reports (20)	W2C-001 *to* W2C-020
Instructional Writing (20)	
administrative/regulatory (10)	W2D-001 *to* W2D-010
skills & hobbies (10)	W2D-011 *to* W2D-020
Persuasive Writing (10)	
press editorials (10)	W2E-001 *to* W2E-010
Creative writing (20)	
novels & stories (20)	W2F-001 *to* W2F-020

APPENDIX 2.
SOURCES OF ICE-GB TEXTS

ICE-GB texts are identified using a textcode (*e.g.*, S1A-001, W1A-001. See Appendix 1), which appears in this list in the left-hand column. Many texts are composite, that is, they comprise two or more "subtexts" which have been combined to make a 2,000-word text. The subtext number appears in the second column. A range of numbers in this column, *e.g.*, 1-5, indicates that each subtext in the range is taken from the same source.

The following abbreviations are used.

AUT	Association of University Teachers
BBC	British Broadcasting Company
BMA	British Medical Association
CUP	Cambridge University Press
f	female speaker
GLR	Greater London Radio
HMSO	Her Majesty's Stationery Office
ITV	Independent Television
LAGB	Linguistics Association of Great Britain
LBC	London Broadcasting Company
m	male speaker
RADA	Royal Academy of Dramatic Art
RSA	Royal Society of Arts
SEU	Survey of English Usage
UCL	University College London
UCLU	University College London (Students')Union

A2.1 S1A-001 to S1A-090: Direct conversations

Text	Subtext	Participants, Date [genders]
S1A-001		Instructor and dance student, Middlesex Polytechnic, April '91 [m, f]
S1A-002	1	Instructor and dance students, Middlesex Polytechnic, April '91 [m, 2f]
S1A-002	2	Instructor and dance student, Middlesex Polytechnic, April '91 [m, f]
S1A-003		Instructor and dance student, Middlesex Polytechnic, April '91 [m, f]
S1A-004		Instructors at Middlesex Polytechnic, April '91 [2m]
S1A-005		Student friends, 12-3-91 [2f]
S1A-006		Colleagues, 20-3-91 [m, f]
S1A-007		Family conversation, 8-6-91 [3m, 2f]
S1A-008		Friends, 7-6-91 [m, f]
S1A-009		Mother and son, 2-7-91 [m, f]
S1A-010		Mother and daughter 5-7-91 [2f]
S1A-011	1	Friends, 9-6-91 [m, 2f]
S1A-011	2	Colleagues' conversation, 3-12-91 [2f]
S1A-012		Members of a barbershop quartet, 9-6-91 [4m]
S1A-013		Marketing discussion, April '91 [3m, 2f]
S1A-014		Friends, July, '91 [m, 2f]
S1A-015		Friends, recorded in a pub, 12-6-91 [m, f]
S1A-016		Marketing discussion, April '91 [3m, 2f]
S1A-017		Friends, July '91 [m, 2f]
S1A-018		Friends, 12-4-91 [m, 2f]
S1A-019		College friends, 2-6-91 [2m, 4f]
S1A-020		Friends, August '91 [4m]
S1A-021	1-2	Friends, 3-7-91 [2m, 2f + 3 extra-corpus]
S1A-022		Family conversation, 10-6-91 [m, 3f]
S1A-023		Family conversation, 8-10-91 [m, f]
S1A-024		University professor and PhD student, 7-11-91 [2m]
S1A-025		Brother and sister, March '91 [m, f]
S1A-026		Conversation during singing practice, 9-6-91 [4m]
S1A-027		Friends, 10-11-91 [2m, 2f]
S1A-028		Birthday party conversation, July '91 [2m, 3f]
S1A-029		Programmers' conversation at SEU, 15-11-91 [5m + 1 extra-corpus]
S1A-030		Flatmates' conversation, 21-11-91 [4m]
S1A-031		Friends, 27-11-91 [2f]
S1A-032	1-2	Family conversation, 12-10-91 [2m, 2f]
S1A-033		Careers interview, 4-3-92 [2m]
S1A-034		Careers interview, 5-3-92 [m, f]
S1A-035		Careers interview, 5-3-92 [m, f]
S1A-036		Colleagues, February '91 [2f]
S1A-037		Student friends, May '91 [2f]
S1A-038		Flatmates, October '91 [m, f]
S1A-039		Flatmates, October '91 [2f]
S1A-040		Flatmates, 7-12-91 [m, 4f]
S1A-041		Flatmates, 7-12-91 [2m]
S1A-042		Flatmates, 4-12-91 [3f]
S1A-043		Friends, 21-10-90 [2m]
S1A-044		Friends, 21-10-90 [2m]
S1A-045	1-3	Friends, 23-4-91 [2m]
S1A-046		Family conversation, November '91 [2m, 2f]
S1A-047		Christmas dinner family conversation, 25-12-91 [m, 2f]
S1A-048		Friends, 5-1-92 [3f]
S1A-049		Friends, 12-6-91 [3f]
S1A-050		Counselling interview, 26-2-91 [m, f]
S1A-051	1	Doctor and patient, 12-11-91 [m, f]
S1A-051	2	Doctor and patient, 12-11-91 [2m]

Text	Subtext	Participants, Date [genders]
S1A-051	3	Doctor and patient, 12-11-91 [m, f]
S1A-051	4	Doctor and patient, 12-11-91 [2m]
S1A-052	1-2	Researchers and photographer, June '91 [3m]
S1A-053		Friends, 6-1-92 [2m, f]
S1A-054		Friends, 27-11-91 [2f]
S1A-055		Conversation in canteen, 20-1-92 [2m, 3f]
S1A-056	1-4	Mealtime conversation, 7-2-92 [2m, f + 1 extra-corpus]
S1A-057		Birthday party (family), 8-2-92 [2m, f]
S1A-058	1-2	Family conversation, January '92 [2m, f + 1 extra-corpus]
S1A-058	3	Dinner party conversation, February '92 [m, f]
S1A-059		Counselling interview, February '91 [2m]
S1A-060		Counselling interview, 10-10-90 [m, f]
S1A-061		Colleagues' lunchtime conversation, February '92 [2m]
S1A-062		Counselling interview, February '91 [m, f]
S1A-063		Colleagues' conversation, August '91 [2m, 2f]
S1A-064		Students of speech and drama, November '91 [3f]
S1A-065		Friends, 18-11-91 [2f]
S1A-066		Careers interview, 29-1-92 [m, f]
S1A-067		Friends, 8-11-91 [2f]
S1A-068		Students' Union Office conversation, 6-3-92 [2m, f]
S1A-069	1-2	Students' Union Office conversation, 6-3-92 [m, f]
S1A-070		Students' Union Office conversation, 6-3-92 [2m]
S1A-071		Conversation in a restaurant, March '92 [2m, 2f]
S1A-072		Psychology research interview, April '91 [m, f]
S1A-073		Lunchtime conversation, 10-11-91 [2m, 2f]
S1A-074	1	Conversation in a travel agent's office, 10-12-91 [2m, f]
S1A-074	2	Conversation in a travel agent's office, 10-12-91 [2m]
S1A-074	3	Conversation in a travel agent's office, 10-12-91 [m, 2f]
S1A-074	4	Conversation in a travel agent's office, 10-12-91 [2m, f]
S1A-074	5	Office conversation, 10-2-92 [m, 2f]
S1A-074	6	Office conversation, 10-2-92 [m, f]
S1A-074	7	Office conversation, 10-2-92 [2m, f]
S1A-075		Psychology research interview, April '91 [m, f]
S1A-076		Psychology research interview, April '91 [m, f]
S1A-077		Office conversation, 24-3-92 [2m, 2f]
S1A-078	1	UCLU Rights and Advice Office, 6-3-92 [m, f]
S1A-078	2	UCLU Rights and Advice Office, 6-3-92 [m, 2f]
S1A-078	3	UCLU Rights and Advice Office, 6-3-92 [m, f]
S1A-078	4	UCLU Rights and Advice Office, 6-3-92 [m, 2f]
S1A-079		UCLU Rights and Advice Office, 5-3-92 [m, 2f]
S1A-080		Friends, May '92 [2f]
S1A-081		Family conversation, April '92 [m, f + 1 extra-corpus]
S1A-082		Students of speech and drama, March '92 [m, 2f]
S1A-083		Tennis coaches, April '92 [2f]
S1A-084		Students, March '92 [m, 2f]
S1A-085		Friends, March '92 [m, f]
S1A-086		Friends, April '92 [3f]
S1A-087	1-2	Dentist and patient March '92 [2m]
S1A-088		Dentist and patient, March '92 [2m]
S1A-089	1	Dentist and patient, March '92 [2m]
S1A-089	2-4	Doctor and patient, 12-11-91 [m, f]
S1A-090	1	Students' conversation, March '92 [m, 3f]
S1A-090	2	Students' conversation, March '92 [3f]

A2.2 S1A-091 to S1A-100: Telephone calls

Text	Subtext	Participants, Date [genders]
S1A-091		Friends, August '91 [2f]
S1A-092		Friends, August '91 [m, f]
S1A-093		Sisters, 26-6-91 [2f]
S1A-094		Niece and aunt, 28-7-91 [2f]
S1A-095	1	Brothers, 8-8-91 [2m]
S1A-095	2	Mother and son, 8-8-91 [m, f]
S1A-095	3	Brothers, 8-8-91 [2m]
S1A-095	4	Mother and son, 8-8-91 [m, f]
S1A-096		Friends, February '92 [m, f]
S1A-097		Friends, October '91 [2m]
S1A-098	1	Friends, 4-12-91 [2f]
S1A-098	2	Friends, 4-12-91 [m, f]
S1A-098	3	Friends, 4-12-91 [2f]
S1A-099	1-2	Friends, 20-1-92 [m, f]
S1A-100	1	Secretary and lawyer, October '91 [m, f]
S1A-100	2	Secretaries, October '91 [2f]
S1A-100	3	Friends, 20-1-92 [2m]

A2.3 S1B-001 to S1B-020: Classroom lessons

Text	Subtext	Subject, Year, Date, Institution
S1B-001		Hebrew and Jewish Studies, 3rd year, 16-5-91, UCL
S1B-002		Linguistics, 1st year, 24-10-91, UCL
S1B-003		Psychology, 1st year, 22-10-91, UCL
S1B-004		Community Medicine, 2nd year, 12-3-91, UCL
S1B-005		History, 3rd year, 18-11-91, UCL
S1B-006		Geology, 1st year, 28-10-91, UCL
S1B-007		Geography, 2nd year, 18-11-91, UCL
S1B-008	1-3	Slade School Workshop, 2nd year, 29-11-91, UCL
S1B-009		Anatomy, 2nd year, 22-11-91, UCL
S1B-010		Surgery, 4th year, 19-5-92, UCL
S1B-011		Public Law, 1st year, 14-10-91, UCL
S1B-012		Linguistics supervision with PhD student, 6-12-92, Cambridge
S1B-013		Mathematics, 2nd year, 10-2-92, UCL
S1B-014		History of Art, 1st year, 16-10-91, UCL
S1B-015		Anatomy, 2nd year, 29-11-91, UCL
S1B-016		Psychology, 1st year, 24-10-91, UCL
S1B-017		Archaeology, 3rd year, 20-3-92, UCL
S1B-018		Slade School Workshop, 2nd year, 29-10-91, UCL
S1B-019		Greek and Latin, 1st year, 4-5-92, UCL
S1B-020		Biochemistry, 3rd year, 11-5-92, UCL

A2.4 S1B-021 to S1B-040: Broadcast discussions

Text	Subtext	Programme title, Channel, Date
S1B-021	1	*Sport on Four*, BBC Radio 4, 27-4-91
S1B-021	2	*Andrew Neil on Sunday*, LBC Radio, 21-7-91
S1B-022		*Thames Special: A Question for London*, ITV, 17-6-91
S1B-023		*Richard Baker Compares Notes*, BBC Radio 4, 27-4-91
S1B-024		*Start the Week*, BBC Radio 4, 12-11-90
S1B-025		*Gardeners' Question Time*, BBC Radio 4, 24-2-91
S1B-026		*Midweek With Libby Purves*, BBC Radio 4, 15-5-91

Text	Subtext	Programme title, Channel, Date
S1B-027		*Question Time*, BBC 1 TV, 17-1-91
S1B-028		*The Persistence of Faith*, BBC Radio 4, 27-1-91
S1B-029		*Tea Junction*, BBC Radio 4, 5-4-91
S1B-030		*The Moral Maze*, BBC Radio 4, 27-4-91
S1B-031		*The Moral Maze*, BBC Radio 4, 2-4-91
S1B-032		*Richard Baker Compares Notes*, BBC Radio 4, 9-2-91
S1B-033		*The Scarman Report*, BBC Radio 4, 16-6-91
S1B-034		*Panorama*, BBC 1 TV, 29-4-91
S1B-035		*Any Questions?*, BBC Radio 4, 9-11-90
S1B-036		*Any Questions?*, BBC Radio 4, 2-2-91
S1B-037		*Issues*, BBC Radio 3, 10-11-90
S1B-038		*BBC Radio 4 News* (extended Gulf War edition), 30-1-91
S1B-039		*Andrew Neil on Sunday*, LBC Radio, 13-10-91
S1B-040		*The Wilson Years*, BBC Radio 4, 31-10-90

A2.5 S1B-041 to S1B-050: Broadcast interviews

Text	Subtext	Programme title, Channel, Date
S1B-041		*Mavis Catches up with...Robert Runcie*, ITV, 13-6-91
S1B-042	1	*Aspel and Co.*, ITV, 16-3-91
S1B-042	2	*The Radio 2 Arts Programme*, BBC Radio 2, 9-2-91
S1B-043		*On the Record*, BBC 1 TV, 25-11-90
S1B-044	1-2	*Kaleidoscope*, BBC Radio 4, 21-2-91
S1B-044	3	*Kaleidoscope*, BBC Radio 4, 14-2-91
S1B-045		*Third Ear*, BBC Radio 4, 7-1-91
S1B-046		*Desert Island Discs*, BBC Radio 4, 16-6-91
S1B-047		*The Reith Lecturer*, BBC Radio 4, 7-11-90
S1B-048		*Bookshelf*, BBC Radio 4, 6-1-91
S1B-049		*Tough Cookies*, BBC Radio 4, 1-11-90
S1B-050		*Third Ear*, BBC Radio 4, 11-2-91

A2.6 S1B-051 to S1B-060: Parliamentary debates

Text	Subtext	Debate, Date
S1B-051		Hugo Summerson *et al*, 2-3-90
S1B-052		Public Expenditure Debate, 8-11-90
S1B-053		Margaret Thatcher *et al*, 30-10-90
S1B-054		Overseas Debate, 25-7-90
S1B-055		Employment Debate, 26-6-90
S1B-056		Welsh Debate, 29-10-90
S1B-057		Employment Debate, 11-12-90
S1B-058		Tony Newton *et al*, 26-11-90
S1B-059		Education/Employment Debate, 24-7-90
S1B-060	1	Abortion Debate, 2-4-90
S1B-060	2	Foreign Policy Debate, 16-1-91

A2.7 S1B-061 to S1B-070: Legal cross-examinations

Text	Subtext	Location, Title, Date, Participant roles
S1B-061		Court of Chancery, Hansen Engines *v* Sainsbury, 17-7-90, cross-examination of plaintiff by defence counsel
S1B-062		Queen's Bench, Hawkes *v* Arend, 19-11-90, cross-examination of prosecution witness by plaintiff's counsel and judge
S1B-063		Queen's Bench, Wallings *v* Customs and Excise, 4-10-90, cross-examination of defence witness by plaintiff's counsel and judge
S1B-064		Queen's Bench, Lehrer *v* Lampitt 5-7-90, cross-examination of prosecution witness by defence counsel and judge
S1B-065		Queen's Bench, Lehrer *v* Lampitt, 5-7-90, cross-examination of defence witness by plaintiff's counsel and judge
S1B-066	1	Queen's Bench, Heidi Hoffmann *v* Intasun Holidays, 25-10-90, cross-examination of plaintiff by defence counsel
S1B-066	2	Queen's Bench, Heidi Hoffmann *v* Intasun Holidays, 25-10-90, cross-examination of plaintiff's witness by plaintiff's counsel
S1B-067		Queen's Bench, Heidi Hoffmann *v* Intasun Holidays, 25-10-90, cross-examination of defence witness by plaintiff's counsel and judge
S1B-068	1	Queen's Bench, Tull *v* Olanipekun and other, 25-3-91, cross-examination of police officer by defence counsel and judge
S1B-068	2	Queen's Bench, Tull *v* Olanipekun and other, 25-3-91, cross-examination of expert witness by two defence counsels and judge
S1B-069		County Court, Scott Cooper *v* Manulite, 23-7-90, cross-examination of defence witness by plaintiff's counsel
S1B-070		Queen's Bench, Hawkes *v* Arend, 19-11-90, cross-examination of expert witness by barrister and judge

A2.8 S1B-071 to S1B-080: Business transactions

Text	Subtext	Participants, Date
S1B-071		Architect and 2 clients, 4-6-91
S1B-072		Solicitor and client, 6-6-91
S1B-073		Builder and 2 clients, 24-6-91
S1B-074	1-3	Insurance company and client, 25-3-92
S1B-075		UCL Arts Faculty Meeting, 5-2-91
S1B-076		Business discussion between SEU and CUP, January '91
S1B-077		AUT Meeting, UCL, 16-10-91
S1B-078		UCL Mature Students' Society AGM, 20-2-92
S1B-079		UCLU Social Committee meeting, 6-3-92
S1B-080	1-2	Insurance company and clients, 25-3-92

A2.9 S2A-001 to S2A-020: Spontaneous commentaries

Text	Subtext	Programme title, Channel, Date (Subject)
S2A-001		*Soccer*, BBC Radio 5, 21-5-91
S2A-002		*Sport on Five*, BBC Radio 5, 2-2-91
S2A-003		*Football Extra*, BBC Radio 5, 7-1-91
S2A-004		*Rugby League*, BBC 1 TV, 10-11-90
S2A-005	1-5	*The Grand National*, BBC Radio 5, 6-4-91
S2A-006	1	*The Epsom Derby*, BBC Radio 5, 5-6-91
S2A-006	2-5	*Racing from Newmarket*, Channel 4, 20-6-91
S2A-007	1-13	*Athletics*, ITV, 26-7-91
S2A-008	1	*Snooker*, BBC 1 TV, 11-2-91
S2A-008	2-6	Meeting of John McCarthy with Perez De Cuellar, LBC Radio, 11-8-90

Text	Subtext	Programme title, Channel, Date (Subject)
S2A-008	7	*Athletics*, ITV, 26-7-91
S2A-009		*Champion Sport*, BBC Radio 5, 6-3-91 (Boxing)
S2A-010		*International Soccer Extra*, BBC Radio 5, 23-5-91
S2A-011		*Trooping the Colour*, BBC Radio 4, 15-6-91
S2A-012	1-7	*Sunday Sport*, BBC Radio 5, 19-5-91 (Motor racing)
S2A-013	1-4	*Sunday Sport*, BBC Radio 5, 19-5-91 (Cricket)
S2A-013	5	*Sunday Sport,* BBC Radio 5, 19-5-91 (Motor racing)
S2A-014		*International Soccer Extra*, BBC Radio 5, 23-5-91
S2A-015		*LBC Sport*, LBC Radio, 10-8-91 (Soccer)
S2A-016	1-5	*Tour de France*, Channel 4, 20-6-91
S2A-017		*Capital FM Soccer*, 30-10-91
S2A-018		*LBC Sport*, LBC Radio, 3-8-91 (Soccer)
S2A-019		*The Gulf Ceremony*, BBC Radio 4, 21-6-91
S2A-020	1	*The Maundy Thursday Service at Westminster Abbey*, BBC Radio 4, 28-3-91
S2A-020	2	*National Service of Remembrance and Thanksgiving*, Glasgow Cathedral, BBC Radio 4, 4-5-91

A2.10 S2A-021 to S2A-050: Unscripted speeches

Text	Subtext	Speaker, Title, Organisation, Date
S2A-021		Sir Peter Newsam, 'Teaching the Teachers', Frederick Constable Memorial Lecture, RSA, 22-5-91
S2A-022		Simon James, 'The Ancient Celts Through Caesar's Eyes', British Museum Lecture, 22-12-90
S2A-023		John Banham, 'Getting Britain Moving', RSA Lecture, 29-4-91
S2A-024		Patsy Vanags, 'Greek Temples', British Museum Lecture, 1-5-91
S2A-025		Dr. A. Chandler, 'Earthquakes and Buildings: Shaken and Stirred', UCL Lunchtime Lecture, 14-3-91
S2A-026		David Jeffries, 'Joseph Hekekyan', UCL Lunchtime Lecture, 7-2-91
S2A-027		Prof. Hannah Steinberg, 'An Academic's Path through the Media', UCL Lunchtime Lecture, 5-3-91
S2A-028	1	Wyndham Johnstone, UCL staff training presentation, 10-6-91
S2A-028	2	Mark David Abbott, UCL staff training presentation, 10-6-91
S2A-028	3	Dr. D.M. Roberts, Introduction to Prof. Peter Cook's Inaugural Lecture, UCL, 1-5-91
S2A-029	1	Nicole Gower, UCL staff training presentation, 17-6-91
S2A-029	2	Andy Betts, UCL staff training presentation, 17-6-91
S2A-029	3	Andrew Newton, UCL staff training presentation, 20-6-91
S2A-030		John Local, 'Prosodic Phonology' (lecture), 21-6-91
S2A-031	1	Hilary Steedman, 'Towards a Quality Workforce', RSA Lecture, 23-1-91
S2A-031	2	Sir John Cassells, 'Towards a Quality Workforce', RSA Lecture, 23-1-91
S2A-032		John Hutchins, 'Eurotra and some other Machine Translation Research Systems', King's College London, 25-4-91
S2A-033	1	Katy Ash, UCL staff training presentation, 20-6-91
S2A-033	2	D.R.L. Edwards, UCL staff training presentation, 20-6-91
S2A-033	3	A.N. Lansbury, UCL staff training presentation, 14-6-91
S2A-034	1	Andrew Wood, UCL staff training presentation, 17-6-91
S2A-034	2	Mark Morrissey, UCL staff training presentation, 11-6-91
S2A-034	3	R.Ramsay, UCL staff training presentation, 11-6-91
S2A-034	4	Dr. Jane Stutchfield, UCL staff training presentation, 20-12-91
S2A-035	1	Sharon Spencer, UCL staff training presentation, 12-6-91
S2A-035	2	Lindsay James, UCL staff training presentation, 12-6-91
S2A-035	3	Harriet Lang, UCL staff training presentation, 4-12-91
S2A-036		Dr. M. Weitzmann, Hebrew and Jewish Studies seminar, UCL, 16-5-91
S2A-037		Dr. D.M. Roberts, 'The Relationship between Industrial Innovation and Academic Research', UCL Lunchtime Lecture, 15-10-91
S2A-038		Sir Peter Laslett, 'The Third Age', RSA Lecture, 6-2-91
S2A-039		Andrew Phillips, 'Citizen Who, Citizen How?', RSA Lecture, 27-3-91

Text	Subtext	Speaker, Title, Organisation, Date
S2A-040		Prof. Peter Cook, 'The Ark', Inaugural Lecture, School of Architecture, UCL, 1-5-91
S2A-041		Prof. A.L. Cullen, Barlow Memorial Lecture, UCL, 23-10-91
S2A-042		Prof. Elkins, 'The Immunological Compact Disc', UCL Lunchtime Lecture, 22-10-91
S2A-043		Prof. Rapley, 'Studying Climate Change from Outer Space', UCL Lunchtime Lecture, 12-11-91
S2A-044		Prof. Twining, 'Lawyers' Stories', UCL Lunchtime Lecture, 28-1-91
S2A-045		Gerald Grosvenor, Duke of Westminster, 'Managing a Great Estate', RSA Lecture, 27-11-91
S2A-046	1	Graham Rose, UCL staff training presentation, 12-12-91
S2A-046	2	Andrew Shaw, UCL staff training presentation, 19-12-91
S2A-046	3	Dr. Mark Cope, UCL staff training presentation, 20-12-91
S2A-047		C. Macaskill, UCL staff training presentation, 17-12-91
S2A-048		Dr. Tait, 'Write with your Hand, Read with your Mouth: Scribes and Literacy in Ancient Egypt', UCL Lunchtime Lecture, 24-10-91
S2A-049		Prof. John Burgoyne, 'Creating a Learning Organisation', RSA Lecture, 8-1-92
S2A-050	1-2	Photojournalist's reminiscences, April '91

A2.11 S2A-051 to S2A-060: Demonstrations

Text	Subtext	Speaker, Title, Organisation, Date
S2A-051		Dr. C.A. King, 'Movement in the Microscopical World', UCL Lunchtime Lecture, 28-2-91
S2A-052		George Hart, 'New Kingdom Paintings and Reliefs', British Museum Lecture, 23-4-91
S2A-053		David Delpy, 'Looking into the Brain with Light', UCL Lunchtime Lecture, 21-11-91
S2A-054	1-2	'Pass your Motorbike Test' (commercial video, Duke Video Ltd), 1990
S2A-055	1-3	*Top Gear*, BBC 2 TV, 7-3-91
S2A-056	1-2	Virginia Ball, Demonstration of laryngograph, UCL staff training presentation, 17-12-91
S2A-057	1-2	Prof. Bindman, Demonstration of eighteenth-century caricatures, History of Art Dept, UCL, 16-10-91
S2A-058	1	Dr. Clive Agnew, Demonstration of WordPerfect, Dept of Geography, UCL,18-11-91
S2A-058	2	Dr. Nick Walton, Demonstration of planetary nebulae, UCL staff training presentation, 16-1-92
S2A-058	3	Avril Burt, Demonstration of a wound model, UCL staff training presentation, 16-1-92
S2A-059		Barbara Brend, 'Persian Manuscripts', British Library Gallery talk, 23-11-90
S2A-060		Rowena Loverance, 'The Mosaics of Torcello', British Museum talk, 15-12-90

A2.12 S2A-061 to S2A-070: Legal presentations

Text	Subtext	Location, Title, Date, Participant roles
S2A-061		Queen's Bench, Keays *v* Express Newspapers,11-7-90, judge's summation
S2A-062		Queen's Bench, Ford *v* Kent County Council, 29-6-90, judge's summation
S2A-063		Queen's Bench, Proetta *v* Times Newspapers, 22-6-90, judge's ruling
S2A-064		Slipper *v* BBC, Queen's Bench, 26-6-90, judge's address to prosecution lawyer
S2A-064		Slipper *v* BBC, Queen's Bench, 26-6-90, submission by plaintiff's counsel
S2A-065		Queen's Bench, C L Line Inc *v* J M S Overseas (St Vincent) Ltd, 20-3-91, submission
S2A-066		Queen's Bench, Astor Chemicals *v* GEC Technology, 27-3-91, judgement
S2A-066		Queen's Bench, VHO *v* Coral Sea Enterprises, 21-3-91, judgement
S2A-067		Queen's Bench, Cooke *v* Bournecrete, 21-2-91, judgement
S2A-068		Queen's Bench, Walling *v* Customs and Excise, 4-10-90, submission by plaintiff's counsel
S2A-069		County Court, Bankruptcy Order, 25-7-90, judgement
S2A-070		Queen's bench, 24-10-90, judgement

A2.13 S2B-001 to S2B-020: News broadcasts

Text	Subtext	Programme Title, Date
S2B-001		*Channel 4 News*, 4-2-91
S2B-002		*Channel 4 News*, 11-2-91
S2B-003		*News at Ten*, ITV, 23-11-90
S2B-004		*The Six O'Clock News*, BBC Radio 4, 2-2-91
S2B-005		*The Six O'Clock News*, BBC Radio 4, 9-2-91
S2B-006		*Today*, BBC Radio 4, 7-11-90
S2B-007		*The World at One*, BBC Radio 4, 5-11-90
S2B-008		*BBC Radio 4 News*, 17-1-91
S2B-009		*The World this Weekend*, BBC Radio 4, 25-11-90
S2B-010		*Newsnight*, BBC 2 TV, 15-1-91
S2B-011		*News at Ten*, ITV, 23-11-90
S2B-012		*The PM Programme*, BBC Radio 4, 2-1-91
S2B-013		*Channel 4 News*, 4-2-91
S2B-014		*The World this Weekend*, BBC Radio 4, 24-2-91
S2B-015	1	*Radio Bedfordshire News*, 19-1-91
S2B-015	2	*Radio Oxford News*, 19-1-91
S2B-016	1	*LBC Radio News*, 4-8-91
S2B-016	2	*Capital Radio News*, 25-2-91
S2B-016	3	*Chiltern Radio News*, 13-2-91
S2B-016	4	*GLR Newshour*, 7-11-90
S2B-017		*The World Tonight*, BBC Radio 4, 5-11-90
S2B-018	1	*The Nine O'Clock News*, BBC 1 TV, 28-1-91
S2B-018	2	*The World this Weekend*, BBC Radio 4, 24-11-90
S2B-019		*The World at One*, BBC Radio 4, 1-11-90
S2B-020	1	*News at One*, BBC 1 TV, 22-11-90
S2B-020	2	*Newsview*, BBC 2 TV, 24-11-90

A2.14 S2B-021 to S2B-040: Broadcast talks (scripted)

Text	Subtext	Title, Channel, Date
S2B-021	1-4	Journalists' monologues on presidential wealth, LBC Radio, 7-7-91
S2B-022	1	*The River Thames*, ITV, 21-6-91
S2B-022	2	*Nature*, BBC 2 TV, 5-3-91
S2B-023	1	*Can You Steal It?*, BBC Radio 1, 2-3-91
S2B-023	2	*Spirit Level*, Radio Oxford, 20-1-91
S2B-023	3	*From Our Own Correspondent*, BBC Radio 4, 27-4-91
S2B-024	1	*Viewpoint '91: Poles Apart*, ITV, 30-4-91
S2B-024	2	*40 Minutes*, BBC 2 TV, 8-11-90
S2B-025		*For He is an Englishman*, BBC Radio 4, 5-2-91
S2B-026		*The World of William*, BBC Radio 4, 5-11-90
S2B-027		*Castles Abroad*, ITV, 21-6-91
S2B-028	1	*Lent Observed*, BBC Radio 4, 19-3-91
S2B-028	2	*Lent Observed*, BBC Radio 4, 26-2-91
S2B-029		*The Reith Lecture, No. 2*, BBC Radio 4, 21-11-90
S2B-030	1	*Address to the Nation*, BBC Radio 4, 17-1-91
S2B-030	2	*Address to the Nation*, BBC Radio 4, 18-1-91
S2B-030	3	*Labour Party Political Broadcast*, BBC 1 TV, 13-3-91
S2B-030	4	*Social Democratic Party Political Broadcast*, Channel 4, 13-3-91
S2B-031	1-2	*The BBC Radio 4 Debate: The Police Debate*, 10-2-91
S2B-031	3	*The Week's Good Cause*, BBC Radio 4, 30-3-91
S2B-032	1	*Opinion: King or Country*, BBC Radio 4, 7-11-90
S2B-032	2	*The BBC Radio 4 Debate: The Police Debate*, 10-2-91
S2B-033		*Barry Norman's Film '91*, BBC 1 TV, 12-3-91

Text	Subtext	Title, Channel, Date
S2B-034		*Analysis*, BBC Radio 4, 16-5-91
S2B-035	1-2	*The BBC Radio 4 Debate: The Class Debate*, 24-2-91
S2B-036	1-2	*The BBC Radio 4 Debate: The Class Debate*, 24-2-91
S2B-037		*The Scarman Report*, BBC Radio 4, 16-6-91
S2B-038	1	*Medicine Now*, BBC Radio 4, 12-3-91
S2B-038	2	*Medicine Now*, BBC Radio 4, 19-3-91
S2B-038	3	*The Week's Good Cause*, BBC Radio 4, 17-3-91
S2B-039	1-3	*From Our Own Correspondent*, BBC Radio 4, 2-4-91
S2B-040	1-3	*From Our Own Correspondent*, BBC Radio 4, 27-4-91

A2.15 S2B-041 to S2B-050: Non-broadcast speeches (scripted)

Text	Subtext	Description, Location, Date
S2B-041	1	The Queen's Speech at the Opening of Parliament, 31-10-91
S2B-041	2	Chancellor of the Exchequer, Budget Speech, House of Commons, 19-3-91
S2B-042		Hugh Denman, 'Is Yiddish a Real Language?', UCL Lunchtime Lecture, 12-3-91
S2B-043		Dr. Wendy Charles, 'Anglo-Portuguese Trade in the Fifteenth Century', Royal Historical Society Lecture, UCL, 11-10-91
S2B-044	1	Census Office, 'The Census: It counts because you count', (Public information video)
S2B-044	2	Camden Adult Education Authority, Audio Prospectus, 1990-91
S2B-045		Peter McMaster, 'The Ordnance Survey: 200 years of mapping and on', RSA Lecture, 10-4-91
S2B-046		Prof. Freeman, 'Who owns my cells?', UCL Lunchtime Lecture, 17-10-91
S2B-047		Shirley Williams, RSA Lecture, 28-3-92
S2B-048		Sir Peter Baldwin, 'Transoceanic Commerce', The Thomas Gray Memorial Lecture, RSA, 20-5-91
S2B-049		Prof. Palmer, 'Firthian Prosodic Phonology', LAGB Lecture, 22-6-91
S2B-050		Sir Geoffrey Howe, Resignation Speech, House of Commons, 13-11-90

A2.16 W1A-001 to W1A-010: Untimed student essays

Text	Subtext	Author, Title, Year, Department, Institution, Date
W1A-001		Rodwell, Tom, 'What happened to the British in the 5th and 6th centuries?', 1st year, Dept of History, UCL, 1991
W1A-002		Monks, T.J., 'Discuss the value of Adamnan's Life of Columba for evidence of the structure of society and the nature of politics in seventh-century Ireland and Scotland', 1st year, Dept of History, UCL, 1991
W1A-003		Cunnington, Tara, 'To what extent if any did the Franks 'rule' Brittany in the early Middle Ages?', 1st year, Dept of History, UCL, 1991
W1A-004		Lawrence, Anthony, 'Amnesia: Theory and Research', 3rd year, Dept of Psychology, UCL, 1991
W1A-005		Elkan, David, 'Programs for the Survey of English Usage', B.A. dissertation, Dept of Computer Science, UCL, 1990
W1A-006	1	Reed, Jacqueline, 'Why is the Milankovitch theory currently favoured as an explanation of glacial/interglacial cycles?', 2nd year, Dept of Geography, UCL, 1991
W1A-006	2	Tribe, S., 'Outline the principal problems of presentation and interpretation associated with the depiction of statistical data in the form of choropleth maps', 2nd year, Dept of Geography, UCL, 1991
W1A-007		Beech, Sandra, 'The medical model is alive and well despite numerous criticisms. Discuss', 1st year, Dept of Psychology, UCL, 1991
W1A-008		''Perfect' Man, 'New' Woman and Sacred Art', M.A. dissertation, Dept of the History of Art, UCL, 1991
W1A-009	1	Vale, Barbara, 'Why has intelligence evolved?', 1st year, Dept of Psychology, UCL, 1991
W1A-009	2	Plewes, Anthony, 'To what extent, if at all, can a Pictish identity be established?', 1st year, Dept of History, UCL, 1991
W1A-010		Warner, A., 'Narrative Texts and Intellectual and Cultural Sources', 1st year, Dept of English, UCL, 1991

A2.17 W1A-011 to W1A-020: Student examination scripts

Text	Subtext	Year, Department, Date
W1A-011	1-3	2nd year, Anthropology, 25-5-90
W1A-012	1-3	2nd year, Anthropology, 25-5-90
W1A-013	1-3	2nd year, Geography of Development and Poverty, 1990
W1A-014	1-2	2nd year, Geography of Development and Poverty, 1990
W1A-015	1-4	2nd year, Geography of Development and Poverty, 1990
W1A-016	1-3	3rd year, Psychology, 23-4-90
W1A-017	1-3	3rd year, Psychology, 1990
W1A-018	1-3	1st year, English Literature, May 1991
W1A-019	1-4	3rd year, Post-1945 American and European Art, 19-6-90
W1A-020	1-5	1st year, Structural Geology, 1990

A2.18 W1B-001 to W1B-015: Social letters

Text	Subtext	Author to Recipient(s), Date
W1B-001	1	Sean to Matthew, 1990
W1B-001	2	Sean to Anne-flo, 1990
W1B-001	3	Sean to Darren, 1990
W1B-001	4	Sean to Nordine, 1990
W1B-001	5	Ruthie to Laura, 26-6-91
W1B-002	1	Jane to Emma, April 1991
W1B-002	2	Bryan to Emma and Ginny, 1991
W1B-002	3	Anne Marie to Emma, 1991
W1B-002	4	Nigel to Emma, 1990

Text	Subtext	Author to Recipient(s), Date
W1B-003	1	Isabelle to "Thing", 1991
W1B-003	2	Isabelle to D.B., 1991
W1B-004	1	Ruthie to Laura, 18-4-91
W1B-004	2	Swoo to Laura, 7-7-91
W1B-004	3	Swoo to Laura, 25-7-91
W1B-004	4	Ian to Laura, 26-5-91
W1B-004	5	Ian to Laura, 15-5-91
W1B-005	1	Mary to Laura, 7-5-91
W1B-005	2	Isabelle to David, 5-6-91
W1B-005	3	Joey to Laura, 1991
W1B-005	4	Swoo to Laura, 30-6-91
W1B-005	5	Swoo to Laura, 27-9-91
W1B-006	1	Isabelle to Laura, 14-7-91
W1B-006	2	Isabelle to Laura, 1991
W1B-006	3	Dee to Laura, 1991
W1B-006	4	Ian to Laura, 26-7-91
W1B-006	5	Andy to friend, 1991
W1B-006	6	Ellie to Laura, 21-6-91
W1B-007	1-4	Isabelle to Laura, 1991
W1B-008	1-2	Isabelle to Laura, 1991
W1B-008	3	Sean to Francoise, 1990
W1B-008	4	Sean to Anne Marie, 1990
W1B-008	5	Sean to Lydia and Valeria, 1990
W1B-008	6	Sean to Anne-flo, 1990
W1B-008	7	Peter to Simon, 5-11-90
W1B-009	1	Swoo to Laura, 21-7-91
W1B-009	2	Swoo to Laura, 14-7-91
W1B-009	3	Ruthie to Simon, 2-8-91
W1B-009	4	Jane to Laura, 5-8-91
W1B-009	5	Ellie to Laura, 24-7-91
W1B-010	1	Isabelle to D.B., 20-6-91
W1B-010	2	Jane to F.F., 23-7-91
W1B-010	3	Gill to Laura, 11-8-91
W1B-010	4	Dee to Laura, 5-8-91
W1B-011	1	B.C. to Bea and Dera, 13-7-91
W1B-011	2	B.C. to Mike, 24-8-91
W1B-011	3	Ellie to Laura, 1991
W1B-012	1	B.C. to Mike, 18-8-91
W1B-012	2	B.C. to Mike, 12-8-91
W1B-013	1	B.C. to Mike, 22-8-91
W1B-013	2	B.C. to Rachel, 19-6-91
W1B-013	3	Helen to Laura, 20-8-91
W1B-014	1	June to Yibin, 23-8-91
W1B-014	2	June to Yibin, 12-8-91
W1B-014	3	Alan to Yibin, 25-8-91
W1B-014	4	Tony to Yibin, 28-8-91
W1B-014	5	Nichola to Laura, 7-9-91
W1B-014	6	Karen to Laura, 1991
W1B-014	7	A.A. Leigh to Tony and Joan, 7-12-90
W1B-014	8	A.A. Leigh to Gordon, 14-4-91
W1B-015	1-3	Andy to friend, 1991
W1B-015	4	Andy to cousin, 1991
W1B-015	5	B.C. to boyfriend, 1991

A2.19 W1B-016 to W1B-030: Business letters

Text	Subtext	Author to Recipient(s), Date
W1B-016	1	RNLI to Emma Whitby-Smith, 19-3-91
W1B-016	2	Bank to client, 19-2-91
W1B-016	3	Financial advisors to client, 29-4-91
W1B-016	4	Job applicant to interview board, 31-1-91
W1B-016	5	Linguistics Society to member, 20-6-91
W1B-016	6	Museum to job applicant, 3-7-91
W1B-016	7	BBC to SEU, 3-7-91
W1B-016	8	Client to building contractor, 4-7-91
W1B-016	9	Client to solicitor, 5-11-90
W1B-016	10	Letter from army squadron, 10-8-91
W1B-017	1	Doctor to company, 2-1-91
W1B-017	2	Doctor to colleague, 8-1-91
W1B-017	3	Doctor to colleague, 11-1-91
W1B-017	4	Doctor to architect, 18-1-91
W1B-017	5	Doctor to colleague, 21-1-91
W1B-017	6	Doctor to student, 21-1-91
W1B-017	7	Doctor to colleague, 30-1-91
W1B-017	8	Doctor to patient, 1-2-91
W1B-017	9	Doctor to company, 5-2-91
W1B-017	10	Doctor to student, 20-2-91
W1B-017	11	Doctor to student, 20-2-91
W1B-017	12	Doctor to architect, 7-3-91
W1B-017	13	Doctor to colleague, 14-3-91
W1B-017	14	Doctor to company, 18-3-91
W1B-017	15	Doctor to colleague, 20-3-91
W1B-017	16	Doctor to patient, 5-4-91
W1B-017	17	Doctor to patient, 5-4-91
W1B-017	18	Doctor to colleague, 18-4-91
W1B-017	19	Doctor to colleague, 29-3-91
W1B-017	20	Doctor to company, 7-5-91
W1B-017	21	Doctor to colleague, 8-5-91
W1B-018	1	Doctor to colleague, 15-5-91
W1B-018	2	Doctor to patient, 15-5-91
W1B-018	3	Doctor to colleague, 16-5-91
W1B-018	4	Doctor to colleague, 16-5-91
W1B-018	5	Doctor to colleague, 29-5-91
W1B-018	6	Doctor to colleague, 30-5-91
W1B-018	7	Doctor to student, 4-6-91
W1B-018	8	Doctor to colleague, 7-6-91
W1B-018	9	Doctor to colleagues (circular), 18-7-91
W1B-018	10	Doctor to student, 25-7-91
W1B-018	11	Doctor to student, 26-7-91
W1B-018	12	Doctor to colleague, 26-7-91
W1B-018	13	Doctor to colleague, 26-7-91
W1B-018	14	Doctor to colleague, 26-7-91
W1B-018	15	Doctor to student, 26-7-91
W1B-018	16	Theatre Manager to theatre company, 12-4-91
W1B-018	17	Theatre Manager to company, 11-4-91
W1B-018	18	Theatre Manager to personnel office, UCL, 5-4-91
W1B-018	19	Theatre Deputy Manager to job applicant, 8-3-91
W1B-018	20	Theatre Deputy Manager to company, 8-3-91
W1B-018	21	Theatre accountant to bank, 4-3-91
W1B-019	1	Bookshop Manager to customer, 19-4-91
W1B-019	2	Bookshop Operations Director to customer, 22-4-91

Text	Subtext	Author to Recipient(s), Date
W1B-019	3	Bookshop Sales Manager to company, 9-8-90
W1B-019	4	Bookshop Personnel Officer to job applicant, 25-6-91
W1B-019	5	Bookshop Personnel Office to job applicant, 31-7-91
W1B-019	6	Bookshop Personnel Officer to job applicant, 12-8-91
W1B-019	7	Bookshop Personnel Officer to job applicant, 12-8-91
W1B-019	8	Tourist Authority to client, 12-4-91
W1B-019	9	Tourist Authority to client, 8-2-90
W1B-019	10	Tourist Authority to client, 2-8-91
W1B-019	11	Tourist Authority to client, 30-7-91
W1B-020	1	Client to accountant, 10-7-91
W1B-020	2	Client to security company, 1-2-90
W1B-020	3	Client to insurance company, 28-1-91
W1B-020	4	Client to Electricity Board, 23-1-90
W1B-020	5	Client to solicitor, 25-4-90
W1B-020	6	Letter to Planning Officer, 4-2-90
W1B-020	7	Letter to colleague, 1-5-90
W1B-020	8	Client to solicitor, 3-7-90
W1B-020	9	Letter to neighbour, 3-7-90
W1B-021	1	Theatre Manager to insurance company, 14-2-91
W1B-021	2	Theatre Manager to theatre group, 31-5-91
W1B-021	3	Theatre Administrator to accountant, 30-5-91
W1B-021	4	Theatre Manager to electrical engineer, 31-5-91
W1B-021	5	Theatre Front-of-House Manager to company, 29-5-91
W1B-021	6	Theatre Manager to job applicant, 15-4-91
W1B-021	7	Theatre Manager to Finance Manager, 14-5-91
W1B-021	8	Theatre Manager to Film Institute, 14-5-91
W1B-021	9	Theatre Manager to colleague, 2-5-91
W1B-021	10	Theatre Deputy Manager to whom it may concern, 17-4-91
W1B-021	11	Theatre Technician to RADA, 12-4-91
W1B-022	1	Librarian to publisher, 5-11-90
W1B-022	2	Librarian to publisher, 20-12-90
W1B-022	3	Client to accountant, 12-2-91
W1B-022	4	Client to accountant, 20-6-91
W1B-022	5	Client to accountant, 2-7-91
W1B-022	6	Accountant to client, 15-2-91
W1B-022	7	Accountant to client, 8-3-91
W1B-022	8	Accountant to client, 26-4-91
W1B-022	9	Accountant to client, 8-5-91
W1B-022	10	Accountant to client, 18-6-91
W1B-022	11	Accountant to client, 28-6-91
W1B-022	12	Client to estate agent, 13-3-90
W1B-022	13	Lecturer to employer, 1991
W1B-022	14	Lecturer to college administrator, 1991
W1B-023	1	Accountant to Inspector of Taxes, 20-6-90
W1B-023	2	Accountant to client, 14-12-90
W1B-023	3	Accountant to Inspector of Taxes, 6-2-91
W1B-023	4	Accountant to Inspector of Taxes, 18-3-91
W1B-023	5	Accountant to client, 20-3-91
W1B-023	6	Accountant to Inspector of Taxes, 21-3-91
W1B-023	7	Accountant to client, 4-4-91
W1B-023	8	Accountant to client, 7-5-91
W1B-023	9	Accountant to Inspector of Taxes, 17-6-91
W1B-023	10	Accountant to client, 17-6-91
W1B-023	11	Accountant to client, 17-6-91
W1B-023	12	Accountant to client, 17-6-91
W1B-023	13	Accountant to Inspector of Taxes, 25-6-91
W1B-023	14	Accountant to client, 27-6-91

Text	Subtext	Author to Recipient(s), Date
W1B-023	15	Union President to union member, 19-4-91
W1B-024	1	Union President to union members (circular), 26-1-90
W1B-024	2	Union President to Research Council, 3-2-90
W1B-024	3	Union President to College Finance Office, 19-3-90
W1B-024	4	Union President to College Management, 26-3-90
W1B-024	5	Union President to union members (circular), 21-2-91
W1B-024	6	Union President to Council member, 8-3-91
W1B-024	7	Union President to union member, 13-3-91
W1B-024	8	Union President to union member, 19-4-91
W1B-024	9	Union President to union member, 19-4-91
W1B-025	1	Research Director to colleague, 1991
W1B-025	2	Research Director to colleague, 1991
W1B-025	3	Research Director to publisher, 1991
W1B-025	4	Research Director to publisher, 1991
W1B-025	5	Research Director to publisher, 1991
W1B-025	6	Union President to union members (circular), 29-5-91
W1B-025	7	Union President to union members, 10-6-91
W1B-025	8	Union President to BMA, 24-6-91
W1B-025	9	Letter to Planning Officer, 26-6-91
W1B-026	1	Careers Adviser to company, 24-4-90
W1B-026	2	Careers Adviser to company, 19-6-90
W1B-026	3	Careers Adviser to company, 23-8-90
W1B-026	4	Careers Adviser to company, 13-9-90
W1B-026	5	Careers Adviser to company, 21-9-90
W1B-026	6	Careers Adviser to company, 30-11-90
W1B-026	7	Careers Adviser to company, 12-12-90
W1B-026	8	Careers Adviser to company, 12-12-90
W1B-026	9	Careers Adviser to company, 7-5-91
W1B-026	10	Letter to Local Authority, 15-5-91
W1B-026	11	Client to company, 14-12-90
W1B-026	12	Client to insurance company, 26-8-90
W1B-026	13	Letter to Bowling Club, 18-4-91
W1B-026	14	Letter to Bowling Club, 1-5-91
W1B-026	15	Client to travel agent, 28-1-91
W1B-026	16	Client to bank, 15-4-91
W1B-026	17	Letter to academic society, 14-12-90
W1B-026	18	Client to insurance company, 16-2-91
W1B-026	19	Letter to Bowling Club, 25-4-91
W1B-026	20	Letter to Bowling Club, 7-2-90
W1B-027	1	Letter to colleague, 22-5-90
W1B-027	2	Letter to Criminology Society, 19-1-90
W1B-027	3	Letter to Local Authority, 26-2-90
W1B-027	4	Letter to Chief Planner, 6-7-91
W1B-027	5	Letter to editor, RIPA Report, 5-10-90
W1B-027	6	Client to insurance company, 6-8-90
W1B-027	7	Client to construction company, 25-8-90
W1B-027	8	Client to construction company, 14-2-90
W1B-027	9	Client to decorators, 8-4-91
W1B-027	10	Client to suppliers, 8-1-90
W1B-027	11	Client to hotel, 3-3-91
W1B-027	12	Client to clothing company, 10-2-90
W1B-028	1	Union Officer to UCL Security, 15-7-91
W1B-028	2	Union Officer to UCL Safety Office, 9-5-91
W1B-028	3	Union Officer to cleaning company, 28-5-91
W1B-028	4	Union Officer to cleaning company, 21-6-91
W1B-028	5	Union Officer to flooring company, 6-6-91
W1B-028	6	Union Officer to committee, 26-6-91

Text	Subtext	Author to Recipient(s), Date
W1B-028	7	Union Officer to UCL Security, 27-3-91
W1B-028	8	Union Officer to UCLU Film Society, 15-7-91
W1B-028	9	Union Officer to police, 26-6-91
W1B-028	10	Letter to District Council, 1991
W1B-028	11	Client to bank, 1991
W1B-028	12	Client to insurance company, 1991
W1B-028	13	Letter to Economics Association, 1991
W1B-029	1	Acting Managing Director to Finance Division, 28-6-91
W1B-029	2	Managing Director to academic, 22-5-91
W1B-029	3	Acting Managing Director to colleague, 1-2-91
W1B-029	4	Acting Managing Director to academic, 25-1-91
W1B-029	5	Businessman to patent agent, 18-1-91
W1B-029	6	Theatre Deputy Manager to security officer, 2-4-91
W1B-030	1	Businessman to client, 21-9-90
W1B-030	2	Businessman to client, 11-9-90
W1B-030	3	Businessman to academic, 7-1-91
W1B-030	4	Education Administrator to conference delegate, 21-6-91
W1B-030	5	Conference co-ordinator to delegate, 15-5-91
W1B-030	6	Conference co-ordinator to delegate, 11-5-91
W1B-030	7	Continuing Education Co-ordinator to academic, 31-7-91

A2.20 W2A-001 to W2A-040: Academic writing

Text	Subtext	Reference: Author, Title, Publisher, Date, Pages
W2A-001		Brunt, P.A., *Roman Imperial Themes*, Clarendon Press Oxford, 1990, pp.110-7
W2A-002		Collier, Peter, 'The Unconscious Image' in Peter Collier and Judith Davies (eds), *Modernism and the European Unconscious*, Polity Press, 1990, pp.20-7
W2A-003		Davidson, Graham, *Coleridge's Career*, Macmillan, 1990, pp.1-6
W2A-004		Hill, Leslie, *Beckett's Fiction: In different words*, Cambridge University Press, 1990, pp.1-8
W2A-005		Haldane, John, 'Architecture, Philosophy and the Public World', *The British Journal of Aesthetics*, vol. 30, no. 3, July 1990, pp.4-10
W2A-006		Hutton, Ronald, *The British Republic, 1649-1660*, Macmillan, 1990, pp.25-31
W2A-007		Jackson, Bernard S., 'Narrative Theories and Legal Discourse' in Christopher Nash (ed.), *Narrative in Culture: The Uses of Storytelling in the Sciences, Philosophy, and Literature*, Routledge, 1990, pp.23-31
W2A-008		McKitterick, Rosamond, 'Carolingian uncial: A context for the Lothar Psalter', *The British Library Journal*, vol. 16, no. 1, Spring 1990, pp.1-9
W2A-009		Onions, John, *English Fiction and Drama of the Great War, 1918-39*, Macmillan, 1990, pp.30-37
W2A-010		Vale, Malcolm, *The Angevin Legacy and the Hundred Years War 1250-1340*, Blackwell, 1990, pp.175-82
W2A-011		Campbell, Adrian and Warner, Malcolm, 'Management roles and skills for new technology' in Ray Wild (ed.), *Technology and Management*, Cassell, 1990, pp.111-7
W2A-012		Barker, Eileen, 'New lines in the supra-market: How much can we buy?', in Ian Hamnett (ed.), *Religious Pluralism and Unbelief: Studies Critical and Comparative*, Routledge, 1990, pp.31-7
W2A-013		Mackintosh, Sheila, Means, Robins, and Leather, Philip, *Housing in Later Life: The Housing Finance Implications of an Ageing Society*, SAUS, 1990, pp.109-15
W2A-014		Ferlie, Ewan and Pettigrew, Andrew, 'Coping with change in the NHS: A frontline district's response to AIDS', *Journal of Social Policy*, vol. 19, pt. 2, April 1990, pp.191-8
W2A-015		Davenport, Eileen, Benington, John and Geddes, Mike, 'The future of European motor industry regions: New local authority responses to industrial restructuring', *Local Economy*, vol. 5, no. 2, August 1990, pp.129-37
W2A-016		Shannon, John, Howe, Chris, 'Controlling a growing firm', *International Journal of Project Management*, vol. 8, no. 3, August 1990, pp.163-6

Text	Subtext	Reference: Author, Title, Publisher, Date, Pages
W2A-017		Bloom, William, *Personal Identity, National Identity and International Relations*, Cambridge Universty Press, 1990, pp.128-36
W2A-018		Hutter, Bridget M. and Lloyd-Bostock, Sally, ' The power of accidents: The social and psychological impact of accidents and the enforcement of safety regulations', *British Journal of Criminology*, vol. 30, no. 4, Autumn 1990, pp.409-17
W2A-019		Calvert, Peter and Calvert, Susan, *Latin America in the Twentieth Century*, Macmillan, 1990, pp.186-200
W2A-020		King, Anthony D., *Global Cities: Post-Imperialism and the Internationalization of London*, Routledge, 1990, pp.53-9
W2A-021		Horan, N. J., *Biological Wastewater Treatment Systems: Theory and Operation*, Wiley, 1990, pp.107-21
W2A-022		Little, Colin, *The Terrestrial Invasion: An Ecophysiological Approach to the Origins of Land Animals*, Cambridge University Press, 1990, pp.86-95
W2A-023		Tucker, Maurice E. and Wright, V. Paul, *Carbonate Sedimentology*, Blackwell, 1990, pp.28-34
W2A-024		Waterlow, J.C.,'Mechanisms of adaptation to low energy intakes', in G.A. Harrison and J.C. Waterlow (eds), *Diet and Disease in Traditional and Developing Societies*, Cambridge University Press, 1990, pp. 5-14
W2A-025		Hart, J.W., *Plant Tropisms and other Growth Movements*, Unwin Hyman, 1990, pp.23-32
W2A-026		Smith, P.J., 'Nerve injury and repair', in F.D. Burke, D.A. McGrouther and P.J. Smith, *Principles of Hand Surgery*, Longman, 1990, pp.143-53
W2A-027		Dockray, G.J., 'Peptide neurotransmitters', in W. Winlow (ed), *Neuronal Communications*, Manchester University Press, 1990, pp. 118-25
W2A-028		Jennings, D.M., Ford-Lloyd, B.V. and Butler, G.M., 'Morphological analysis of spores from different *Allium* rust populations', *Mycological Research*, vol. 94, pt. 1, January 1990, pp.83-8
W2A-029		Kilsby, C.G., 'A study of aerosol properties and solar radiation during a straw-burning episode using aircraft and satellite measurements', *Quarterly Journal of the Royal Meteorological Society*, vol. 116, no. 495, July 1990 pt. B, pp. 1173-85
W2A-030		Park, Chris, 'Trans-frontier pollution: some geographical issues', *Geography*, vol. 76, no. 330, January, 1991, pp.26-32
W2A-031		Roberts, D. and Roberts, A.M., 'Blind shaft drilling at Betws Colliery', *The Mining Engineer*, vol. 149, no. 345, June 1990, pp.463-6
W2A-032		Nightingale, C. and Hutchinson, R.A., 'Artificial neural nets and their application to image processing', *British Telecom Journal*, vol. 8, no.3, July 1990, pp.81-5
W2A-033		Frost, A.R, 'Robotic milking: A review', *Robotica*, vol. 8, 1990, pp.311-4
W2A-034		Neale, Ron, 'Technology focus: A reflow model for the anti-fuse', *Electronic Engineering*, vol 63, no. 772, April 1991, pp.31-40
W2A-035		Campbell, J.A., 'Three novelties of AI: theories, programs and rational reconstructions', in Derek Partridge and Yorick Wilks (eds), *The Foundations of Artificial Intelligence: A sourcebook*, Cambridge University Press, 1990, pp.237-43
W2A-036		McNab, A., Dunlop, Iain, 'AI techniques applied to the classification of welding defects from automated NDT data', *British Journal of Non-Destructive Testing*, vol. 33, no. 1, January 1991, pp. 11-16
W2A-037		Drury, S.A., *A Guide to Remote Sensing: Interpreting Images of the Earth*, Oxford University Press, 1990, pp.22-43
W2A-038		Knowles, Dick, 'Mapping a Mascot 3 design into Occam', *Software Engineering Journal*, vol. 5, no. 4, July 1990, pp.207-13
W2A-039		Burcher, R.K., 'The prediction of the manoeuvring characteristics of vessels', *Philosophical Transactions of the Royal Society*, vol. 334, no. 1634, 13 February 1991, pp.79-88
W2A-040		Lord, C.J.R., 'Brayebrook Observatory, part 1', *Journal of the British Astronomical Association*, vol. 101, no. 1, February 1991, pp.42-45

A2.21 W2B-001 to W2B-040: Popular writing

Text	Subtext	Reference: Author, Title, Publisher, Date, Pages
W2B-001		Worsnip, Glyn, *Up the Down Escalator*, Michael Joseph, 1990, pp.127-35
W2B-002	1	Bailey, Martin, *Young Vincent: The Story of Van Gogh's Years in England*, W.H. Allen, 1990, pp.26-32
W2B-002	2	Thomson, Richard, *Camille Pissarro: Impressionism, Landscape and Rural Labour*, Herbert Press, 1990, pp.19-24
W2B-003		Johnson, Paul, *Cathedrals of England, Scotland and Wales*, Weidenfeld and Nicolson, 1990, pp.48-52
W2B-004		Stark, Graham, *Remembering Peter Sellars*, Robson Books, 1990, pp.183-93
W2B-005		McCormick, Donald and Fletcher, Katy, *Spy Fiction: A Connoisseur's Guide*, Facts on File, 1990, pp.111-7
W2B-006		Ackroyd, Peter, *Dickens*, Sinclair-Stevenson, 1990, pp.83-8
W2B-007		Sword, Keith, *The Times Guide to Eastern Europe: The Changing Face of the Warsaw Pact*, Times Books, 1990, pp. 144-50
W2B-008		Greenfield, Edward, Layton, Robert and March, Ivan, *The Penguin Guide to Compact Discs*, Penguin, 1990, pp.412-7
W2B-009		Breen, Jennifer, *In Her Own Write: Twentieth-century Women's Fiction*, Macmillan, 1990, pp.88-103
W2B-010		Rees, Nigel, *Dictionary of Popular Phrases*, Bloomsbury, 1990, pp.142-54
W2B-011		Nugent, Nicholas, *Rajiv Gandhi: Son of a Dynasty*, BBC Books, 1990, pp. 54-60
W2B-012		Lord Young, *The Enterprise years: A Businessman in the Cabinet*, Headline, 1990, pp.49-55
W2B-013		Icke, David, *It Doesn't Have To Be Like This: Green Politics Explained*, Merlin Press, 1990, pp.46-54
W2B-014		Jones, Terry, 'Credit for Mrs Thatcher', in Ben Pimlott, Anthony Wright and Tony Flower, *The Alternative: Politics for a Change*, W.H. Allen, 1990, pp.189-93
W2B-015		Watkins, Alan, *A Slight Case of Libel: Meacher v Trelford and Others*, Duckworth, 1990, pp.15-23
W2B-016		Thompson, Peter, *Sharing the Success: The Story of NFC*, Collins, 1990, pp.37-45
W2B-017		Johnson, Paul, *Child Abuse: Understanding the Problem*, Crowood Press, 1990, pp.11-19
W2B-018		McGraw, Eric, *Population: The Human Race*, Bishopsgate Press, 1990, pp.12-26
W2B-019		Holman, Bob, *Good Old George: The Life of George Lansbury*, Lion Publishing, 1990, pp.100-7
W2B-020		Poulter, Sebastian, *Asian Traditions and English Law: A Handbook*, Trentham Books, 1990, pp.129-35
W2B-021		Nichols, John, *The Mighty Rainforest*, David and Charles, 1990, pp.56-65
W2B-022		Nicol, Rosemary, *Everything You Need To Know About Osteoporosis*, Sheldon Press, 1990, pp.68-75
W2B-023		Lever, Ruth, *A Guide to Common Illnesses*, Penguin Books, 1990, pp.167-76
W2B-024		Haines, Andrew, 'The implications for health', in Jeremy Leggett (ed.), *Global Warming: The Greenpeace Report*, Oxford University Press, 1990, pp.149-57
W2B-025		Gribbin, John, *Hothouse Earth: The Greenhouse Effect and Gaia*, Bantam Press, 1990, pp.154-64
W2B-026		Giles, Bill, *The Story of Weather*, HMSO, 1990, pp.30-42
W2B-027		Mabey, David, Gear, Alan and Gear, Jackie, *Thorson's Organic Consumer Guide: Food You Can Trust*, Thorsons Publishing Group, 1990, pp.29-35
W2B-028		Sparks, John, *Parrots: A Natural History*, David and Charles, 1990, pp.157-68
W2B-029		Dipper, Francis, 'Earth, air, fire, water, oil and war', *BBC Wildlife*, vol. 9, no. 3, March 1991, pp.191-3
W2B-030		Griggs, Pat, *Views of Kew*, Royal Botanic Gardens, Kew and Channel Four Television, 1990, pp.14-21
W2B-031	1	Trask, Simon, 'JD800', *Music Technology*, June 1991, pp.26-32
W2B-031	2	Goodyer, Tom, 'Spirit studio', *Music Technology*, June 1991, pp.50-4
W2B-032		Denison, A.C., 'Is anybody there?', *Practical Electronics*, June 1991, pp.16-20

Text	Subtext	Reference: Author, Title, Publisher, Date, Pages
W2B-033		Royall, David and Hughes, Mike, *Computerisation in Business*, Pitman Publishing, 1990, pp.95-102
W2B-034		Poole, Ian, 'The history of television', *Practical Electronics*, June 1991, pp. 21-4
W2B-035		Ashford, David and Collins, Patrick, *Your Spaceflight Manual: How You Could Be A Tourist In Space Within Twenty Years*, Headline Publishing, 1990, pp.33-44
W2B-036	1	Morse, Ken, 'From little acorns...', *Personal Computer World*, February 1991, pp.237-8
W2B-036	2	Bancroft, Ralph, 'One of the crowd', *Personal Computer World*, February 1991, pp. 249-50
W2B-037		Robson, Paul, *The World's Most Powerful Cars*, Apple Press, 1990, pp.1-3
W2B-038		Fox, Barry, 'Digital compact cassette: the whole story', *Hi-Fi News and Record Review*, March 1991, pp.41- 7
W2B-039		Southgate, T.N., *Communication: Equipment for Disabled People*, Oxfordshire Health Authority, 1990, pp.27-37
W2B-040		Colloms, Martin, 'Transports: The best on test', *Hi-Fi News and Record Review*, March 1991, pp.69-71

A2.22 W2C-001 to W2C-020: Newspaper reports

Text	Subtext	Reference: Author, Title, Newspaper, Date, Pages
W2C-001	1	Brown, Colin and Judy Jones, 'Ministers knew of MoD intervention in Wallace affair', *The Independent*, 1-11-90, p.2
W2C-001	2	Cusick, James, 'Lockerbie lawyers say timing of TV report 'suspicious'', *The Independent*, 1-11-90, p.3
W2C-001	3	Mills, Heather, 'Home Office ready to consider code on rights of prisoners', *The Independent*, 1-11-90, p.8
W2C-001	4	Hughes, Colin, 'Pay-offs for dockworkers '400% above original cost'', *The Independent*, 1-11-90, p.5
W2C-001	5	Anon, 'Detective 'set up man accused of blackmail'', *The Independent*, 1-11-90, p.5
W2C-002	1	Hogg, Andrew, 'The children who know only war and starvation', *Sunday Times*, 28-20-90, p.21
W2C-002	2	Lees, Caroline, 'Heads challenge McGregor on curriculum', *Sunday Times*, 28-10-90, p.3
W2C-003	1	Young, Hugo, 'When Tory jaw-jaw turns to war-war', *The Guardian*, 6-11-90, p.20
W2C-003	2	Dixon, Norman F., 'Will the trigger pull the finger in the Gulf?', *The Guardian*, 6-11-90, p.21
W2C-004	1	Barden, Leonard, 'Karpov slips up', *The Guardian*, 1-11-90, p.16
W2C-004	2	Lacey, David, 'United expose Liverpool rearguard', *The Guardian*, 1-11-90, p.16
W2C-004	3	Bierley, Stephen, 'Magpies make a big issue of 18m', *The Guardian*, 1-11-90, p.16
W2C-004	4	Bateman, Cynthia, 'Soccer', *The Guardian*, 1-11-90, p.16
W2C-005	1	Cowe, Roger, 'Yorkshire banks on homely service as it treks south', *The Guardian*, 6-11-90, p.14
W2C-005	2	Stoddart, Robin, 'Interest rate hopes lift the market', *The Guardian*, 6-11-90, p.14
W2C-005	3	Milner, Mark, 'Bank governor puts regulation at forefront of debate', *The Guardian*, 6-11-90, p.14
W2C-006	1	Wintour, Patrick, 'Brittan offers new European option', *The Guardian*, 5-11-90, p.1
W2C-006	2	Dyer, Clare, 'Empty chairs prevent replay of Bar victories', *The Guardian*, 5-11-90, p.2
W2C-006	3	White, Michael, 'PM plans counter-attack in Queen's Speech debate', *The Guardian*, 5-11-90, p.1
W2C-006	4	Brindle, David, 'Boost for hospital building fund', *The Guardian*, 5-11-90, p.1
W2C-007	1	Anon., 'Steel: the cold economic truth', *The Times*, 11-11-90
W2C-007	2	Anon.,'Justice for criminals', *The Times*, 10-11-90
W2C-007	3	Anon.,'Blood in the oil', *The Times*, 13-11-90
W2C-008	1	Anon.,'Well met in Moscow', *The Times*, 12-11-90
W2C-008	2	Anon.,'The son rises', *The Times*, 12-11-90
W2C-008	3	Anon.,'Chancellor buys votes', *The Times*, 9-11-90
W2C-008	4	Anon.,'Testing the UN', *The Times*, 9-11-90
W2C-009	1	Morris, Nigel, 'Subsidy cut spells woe', *Wembley Observer*, 27-12-90, p.1
W2C-009	2	Morris, Nigel, 'Centre gets a last chance', *Wembley Observer*, 27-12-90, p.2

Text	Subtext	Reference: Author, Title, Newspaper, Date, Pages
W2C-009	3	Morris, Nigel, 'Taxpayers' card 'bribe'', *Wembley Observer*, 27-12-90, p.3
W2C-009	4	Anon, 'Weather aborts poll tax march', *Wembley Observer*, 27-12-90, p.3
W2C-009	5	Anon, 'Still barred from committee service', *Wembley Observer*, 27-11-90, p.3
W2C-009	6	Porter, Toby, 'Ambulance service in crisis: claim', *Wembley Observer*, 27-11-90, p.5
W2C-009	7	White, Marcia, 'Streets sweep nets 68 truants', *Wembley Observer*, 27-11-90, p.7
W2C-010	1	Scobie, William, 'Secret army's war on the Left', *The Observer*, 18-11-90, p.11
W2C-010	2	Flint, Julie, 'Lebanon sets its hopes on the Second Republic', *The Observer*, 18-11-90, p.16
W2C-011	1	Court Reporter, 'Killer used knife like a bayonet, court told', *Willesden and Brent Chronicle*, 8-11-90, p.1
W2C-011	2	Conroy, Will, 'Police smash drugs ring', *Willesden and Brent Chronicle*, 8-11-90, p.5
W2C-011	3	Walsh, Jennie, 'Residents win first stage of battle to halt development', *Willesden and Brent Chronicle*, 8-11-90, p.10
W2C-011	4	Court reporter, 'Judge sends armed robber to secure special hospital', *Willesden and Brent Chronicle*, 8-11-90, p.13
W2C-012	1	Beugge, Charlotte, 'Home thoughts on insurance for going abroad', *Daily Telegraph*, 19-1-91, p.19
W2C-012	2	Hughes, Duncan, 'Wartime investments', *Daily Telegraph*, 19-1-91, p.19
W2C-012	3	Whetnall, Norman, 'Shares end in state of uneasy calm', *Daily Telegraph*, 19-1-91, p. 21
W2C-012	4	Cowie, Ian, 'Reality as euphoria starts to evaporate', *Daily Telegraph*, 19-1-91, p.23
W2C-012	5	Rankine, Kate, 'Tace chief agrees to quit in March', *Daily Telegraph*, 19-1-91, p.23
W2C-013	1	Osborne, Peter, 'Dealers batten down the hatches', *Evening Standard*, 16-1-91, p.23
W2C-013	2	Smith, Paul, 'Dealing slump puts jobs in firing line', *Evening Standard*, 16-1-91, p.25
W2C-013	3	McCrystal, Amanda, 'Europe dodges the credit rating knife', *Evening Standard*, 16-1-91, p.25
W2C-013	4	Hamilton, Kirstie, 'Murdoch faces new debt crisis', *Evening Standard*, 16-1-91, p.26
W2C-013	5	Blackstone, Tim, 'First Leisure in the money', *Evening Standard*, 16-1-91, pp.26-7
W2C-014	1	Hart, Michael, 'Salako expects to finish the job', *Evening Standard*, 22-1-91, p.50
W2C-014	2	Stammers, Steve, 'Clark finds small consolation', *Evening Standard*, 22-1-91, p.50
W2C-014	3	Thicknesse, John, 'Gooch's timely win', *Evening Standard*, 22-1-91, p.51
W2C-014	4	Blackman, Peter, 'Graf meets her match', *Evening Standard*, 22-1-91, p.51
W2C-014	5	Jones, Chris, 'Ryan in the clear over Buckton injury', *Evening Standard*, 22-1-91, p.51
W2C-014	6	Allen, Neil, ''Famous Five' go off to form their own club', *Evening Standard*, 22-1-91, p.51
W2C-015	1	McKenzie, Eric, 'Steel plant union leader vows to fight on', *The Scotsman*, 25-2-91, p.6
W2C-015	2	Scott, David, 'Council house mortgage plan seen as threat to rural areas', *The Scotsman*, 25-2-91, p.6
W2C-015	3	Wilson, Sarah, 'Region acts over racial fostering problem', *The Scotsman*, 25-2-91, p.7
W2C-015	4	Kennedy, Linda, 'Rat clearance plan to lure puffins back to island', *The Scotsman*, 25-2-91, p.7
W2C-015	5	Chisholm, William, 'Tenants launch campaign to block homes sell-off', *The Scotsman*, 25-2-91, p.7
W2C-016	1	Houlder, Vanessa, 'L&M turns 134m of debt into equity', *Financial Times*, 25-2-91, p.19
W2C-016	2	Lascelles, David, 'Banks hope to net a saving', *Financial Times*, 25-2-91, p.19
W2C-016	3	Rawstorne, Philip, 'Reduced importance of the brewer's pub tie', *Financial Times*, 25-2-91, p.20
W2C-017	1	Payton, Richard, 'Youngsters find it tough to buy home', *Western Mail*, 2-3-91, p.4
W2C-017	2	Anon., 'Car hit couple on country road', *Western Mail*, 2-3-91, p.4
W2C-017	3	Betts, Clive, 'Joint bid may force out HTV', *Western Mail*, 2-3-91, p.5
W2C-017	4	Anon., 'Traffic plan for town opposed', *Western Mail*, 2-3-91, p.7
W2C-017	5	Anon.,'Top scientist will launch county's space age project', *Western Mail*, 2-3-91, p.7
W2C-018	1	McGregor, Stephen, 'Decisions, decisions: Major faced with double dilemma after poll disaster', *Glasgow Herald*, 9-3-91, p.1
W2C-018	2	Clark, William, MacDonald, George, 'No Tory seat is safe, says Hattersley', *Glasgow Herald*, 9-3-91, p.7
W2C-018	3	Horsburgh, Frances, 'More interest kindled in plan to assist tenants buying home', *Glasgow Herald*, 9-3-91, p.3

Text	Subtext	Reference: Author, Title, Newspaper, Date, Pages
W2C-019	1	Anon., 'Street fights injure eight in Belgrade', *Yorkshire Post*, 12-3-91, p.5
W2C-019	2	Anon., 'Yeltsin under fresh attack by hardliners', *Yorkshire Post*, 12-3-91, p.5
W2C-019	3	Anon.,'Crackdown in troubled townships', *Yorkshire Post*, 12-3-91, p.5
W2C-019	4	Anon.,'Mandela witness 'in dream world'', *Yorkshire Post*, 12-3-91, p.5.
W2C-019	5	Braude, Jonathan, 'Boatpeople talks planned', *Yorkshire Post*, 12-3-91, p.5
W2C-019	6	Anon.,'Wife's nose for trouble', *Yorkshire Post*, 12-3-91, p.5
W2C-019	7	Anon.,'Flat deaths tragedy', *Yorkshire Post*, 12-3-91, p.5
W2C-020	1	Deans, John, 'Council tax will still punish the big spenders', *Daily Mail*, 22-4-91, pp.1-2
W2C-020	2	Harris, Paul, 'Charles looks to happy days at Happylands', *Daily Mail*, 22-4-91, p.3
W2C-020	3	Anon.,''Graffiti art' student joined gang of spray can raiders', *Daily Mail*, 22-4-91, p.5
W2C-020	4	Rose, Peter, 'Jogger mystery after 'perfect son' murder', *Daily Mail*, 22-4-91, p.5
W2C-020	5	Anon.,'Laureate too ill for royal poem', *Daily Mail*, 22-4-91, p.2
W2C-020	6	Anon.,'Major belt for Owen', *Daily Mail*, 22-4-91, p.2
W2C-020	7	Anon.,'Travel in London dearest in Europe', *Daily Mail*, 22-4-91, p.2

A2.23 W2D-001 to W2D-010: Administrative/regulatory writing

Text	Subtext	Reference: Institutional author, Title, Publisher, Date, Pages
W2D-001		Department of Social Security, *NHS Sight Tests and Vouchers for Glasses*, HMSO, April 1990, pp.4-11
W2D-002		Department of Social Security, *Unemployment Benefit*, HMSO, April 1990, pp.11-6
W2D-003		Department of Education and Science and The Welsh Office, *Grants to Students: A Brief Guide 1990-1*, HMSO, August 1990, pp.2-11
W2D-004		Department of Social Security, *National Insurance for Employees*, HMSO, April 1990, pp.2-7
W2D-005		Department of Social Security, *A Guide to Family Credit*, HMSO, April 1990, p. 4-19
W2D-006	1	British Library Board, *Regulations for the Use of the Reading Rooms*, July 1990
W2D-006	2	University College London Library, *Access and Borrowing Rights for Members of UCL within other Libraries of the University of London*, 1990
W2D-007		London School of Economics and Political Science, *Calendar 1990-91*, 1990, pp.184-99
W2D-008		University of London, 'Regulations on University Titles', *University of London Calendar 1990-1*, 1990, pp.331-41
W2D-009		Department of Transport, *Travel Safely by Public Transport*, HMSO, April 1991, pp. 2-11
W2D-010		Driver and Vehicle Licensing Agency, *Registering and Licensing your Motor Vehicle*, HMSO, January 1990

A2.24 W2D-011 to W2D-020: Skills and hobbies

Text	Subtext	Reference: Author, Title, Publisher, Date, Pages
W2D-011		Branwell, Nick, *How Does Your Garden Grow?: A Guide to Choosing Environmentally Safe Products*, Thorsons Publishing Group, 1990, pp.59-63
W2D-012		Collard, George, *Do-it-yourself Home Surveying: A Practical Guide to House Inspection and the Detection of Defects*, David and Charles, 1990, pp.104-17
W2D-013		Rich, Sue, *Know about Tennis*, AA Publishing, 1990, pp.26-42
W2D-014		Cheshire, David, *The Complete Book of Video*, Dorling Kindersley, 1990, pp. 22-7
W2D-015		Hughes, Charles, *The Winning Formula*, The Football Association and Collins Publishing, 1990, pp.108-12
W2D-016		Pipes, Alan, *Drawing for 3-Dimensional Design: Concepts, Illustration, Presentation*, Thames and Hudson, 1990, pp.28-36
W2D-017		Batten, David, *An Introduction to River Fishing*, Crowood Press, 1990, pp.37-42
W2D-018		Carroll, Ivor, *Autodata Car Manual: Peugeot 309 1986-90*, Autodata Limited, 1990, pp.29-42
W2D-019		Jackson, Paul, *Classic Origami*, Apple Press, 1990, pp.31-63
W2D-020		Barry, Michael, *The Crafty Food Processor Cook Book*, Jarrold Publishing, 1990, pp.72-86

A2.25 W2E-001 to W2E-010: Press editorials

Text	Subtext	Title, Publisher, Date, Pages
W2E-001	1	'The purpose of the war', *Evening Standard*, 28-1-91, p.7
W2E-001	2	'Belittling Europe', *Evening Standard*, 31-10-90, p.7
W2E-001	3	'Challenge to tyranny', *Evening Standard*, 16-1-91, p.7
W2E-001	4	'A doomed dictator', *Evening Standard*, 22-1-91, p.7
W2E-002	1	'Britain at war', *Sunday Times*, 28-10-90, p.5
W2E-002	2	'The duty of the banks', *Sunday Times*, 28-10-90, p.5
W2E-003	1	'Unity: who can provide it?', *The Guardian*, 5-11-90, p.22
W2E-003	2	'The best big bang', *The Guardian*, 5-11-90, p.22
W2E-003	3	'More to share than the burden', *The Guardian*, 29-1-91, p.18
W2E-004	1	'Heseltine's misguided detractors', *The Independent*, 15-11-90, p.26
W2E-004	2	'Bush needs public support', *The Independent*, 15-11-90, p.26
W2E-004	3	'A certain election loser', *The Independent*, 1-11-90, p.26
W2E-004	4	'Dishonesty at the top', *The Independent*, 1-11-90, p.26
W2E-005	1	'The voice of authority', *Daily Telegraph*, 17-1-91, p.16
W2E-005	2	'Socialist folly', *Daily Telegraph*, 17-1-91, p.16
W2E-005	3	'The epitaph of Sir Geoffrey Howe', *Daily Telegraph*, 14-11-90, p.20
W2E-005	4	'Allied advantage', *Daily Telegraph*, 19-1-91, p.12
W2E-006	1	'Voters make all kinds of marks', *The Scotsman*, 9-3-91, p.10
W2E-006	2	'Galleries in the dark', *The Scotsman*, 9-3-91, p.10
W2E-006	3	'Paper warriors', *The Scotsman*, 9-3-91, p.10
W2E-006	4	'The final test of Allied aims', *The Scotsman*, 25-2-91, p.8
W2E-006	5	'Fighting recession', *The Scotsman*, 25-2-91, p.8
W2E-007	1	'Keeping cool while the war hots up', *The Observer*, 27-1-91, p.20
W2E-007	2	'A stark choice that can't be avoided', *The Observer*, 13-1-91, p.14
W2E-007	3	'Putting justice to rights', *The Observer*, 17-3-91, p.20
W2E-008	1	'United in disarray', *Yorkshire Post*, 12-3-91, p.10
W2E-008	2	'Unhappy landings', *Yorkshire Post*, 12-3-91, p.10
W2E-008	3	'No concessions', *Yorkshire Post*, 9-4-91, p.10
W2E-008	4	'While Europe waits', *Yorkshire Post*, 9-4-91, p.10
W2E-009	1	'Now let Irish government act', *Daily Mail*, 26-10-90, p.8
W2E-009	2	'Exporters love EC', *Daily Mail*, 26-10-90, p.8
W2E-009	3	'Embarrassing', *Daily Mail*, 26-10-90, p.8
W2E-009	4	'Those who don't ask don't get', *Daily Mail*, 30-1-91, p.6
W2E-009	5	'A better way of taxing', *Daily Mail*, 22-4-91, p.6
W2E-009	6	'Storming home', *Daily Mail*, 22-4-91, p.6
W2E-009	7	'Simple truth', *Daily Mail*, 22-4-91, p.6
W2E-009	8	'Mr Heseltine spells it out', *Daily Mail*, 24-4-91, p.6
W2E-009	9	'Sanctions must go', *Daily Mail*, 24-4-91, p.6
W2E-010	1	'A president adrift', *Sunday Times*, 21-10-90, p.7
W2E-010	2	'Over to Major', *Sunday Times*, 19-5-91, p.5

A2.26 W2F-001 to W2F-020: Fiction

Text	Subtext	Reference: Author, Title, Publisher, Date, Pages
W2F-001		Enters, Ian, *Up to Scratch*, Weidenfeld and Nicolson, 1990, pp.80-6
W2F-002		Harris, Steve, *Adventureland*, Headline Publishing, 1990, pp. 308-16
W2F-003		Robertson, Denise, *Remember the Moment*, Constable, 1990, pp.182-94
W2F-004		Puckett, Andrew, *Terminus*, Collins, 1990, pp.34-41
W2F-005		Lees-Milne, James, *The Fool of Love*, Robinson Publishing, 1990, pp.86-93
W2F-006		Babson, Marian, *Past Regret*, Collins, 1990, pp.40-6
W2F-007		Thompson, E.V., *Lottie Trago*, Macmillan, 1990, pp.12-9
W2F-008		Sayer, Paul, *Howling at the Moon*, Constable, 1990, pp.142-9
W2F-009		Priest, Christopher, *The Quiet Woman*, Bloomsbury, 1990, pp.8-13
W2F-010		Frame, Ronald, *Bluette*, Hodder and Stoughton, 1990, pp.244-51

Text	Subtext	Reference: Author, Title, Publisher, Date, Pages
W2F-011		Caudwell, Sarah, 'An acquaintance with Mr Collins' in *A Suit of Diamonds*, Collins, 1990, pp.47-60
W2F-012		Dobbs, Michael, *Wall Games*, Collins, 1990, pp.258-65
W2F-013		Owens, Agnes, 'Patience' in Alison Fell (ed.), *The Seven Cardinal Virtues*, Serpent's Tail, 1990, pp.135-42
W2F-014		Symons, Julian, *Death's Darkest Face*, Macmillan, 1990, pp.199-209
W2F-015		Napier, Mary, *Powers of Darkness*, Bodley Head, 1990, pp.215-28
W2F-016		Clay, Rosamund, *Only Angels Forget*, Virago Press, 1990, pp.98-106
W2F-017		Lambton, Anthony, 'Pig' in *Pig and other stories*, Constable, 1990, pp.127-40
W2F-018		Wesley, Mary, *A Sensible Life*, Bantam Press, 1990, pp.355-64
W2F-019		Melville, Anne, 'Portrait of a woman' in *Snapshots*, Severn House, 1990, pp.1-10
W2F-020		Kershaw, Valerie, *Rockabye*, Bantam Press, 1990, pp.154-61

APPENDIX 3.
BIBLIOGRAPHICAL AND BIOGRAPHICAL VARIABLES

Variable	Description	Values
Text Category	The text category to which the text belongs in the corpus as a whole	For a complete list of the ICE-GB text categories, see Appendix 1
Speaker Age	Age of speaker or author.	18-25; 26-45; 46-65; 66+
Speaker Gender	Gender of speaker or author	m, f, <co-authored>
Speaker Education	'Secondary' denotes the educational level of speakers and authors who have completed secondary schooling, but have *not* completed a tertiary course. University undergraduates, therefore, are described as having *secondary* education.	secondary; university
Speaker Role	The communicative role of a speaker.	interviewer, chairman, teacher, etc
TV or radio	Broadcasting medium.	tv; radio
Scope	The scope of a newspaper.	local; London; regional; national
Frequency	The frequency of publication of a newspaper.	daily; weekly
Circulation	The approximate circulation figure, at the time of publication of the text, of a newspaper.	50,000; 260,000; 300,000; 400,000; 700,000; 1m; 1.2m; 1.4m; 2m

APPENDIX 4.
STRUCTURAL MARKUP SYMBOLS

The following table describes the structural markup symbols in ICE-GB, visible in the query browser (text viewer) or tree viewer windows. The symbols themselves are not displayed by default in ICECUP. Instead, the software displays the marked lexical items in a number of ways. These are described in the right-hand column. To display the symbols themselves in any text, press '' on ICECUP's button bar.

Markup Symbol	Meaning	Display in ICECUP
<bold>...</bold>	boldface print	bold text
<it>...</it>	italics	italic text
<ul>...</ul>	underlining	underlined text
<p>...</p>	paragraph boundary	indent and blue arrow, optional blue dashed divider
<h>...</h>	heading	black bold sans-serif
<sb>...</sb>	subscript	subscript
<sp>...</sp>	superscript	superscript
<fnr>...</fnr>	reference to a footnote	superscript text with underline
<footnote>...</footnote>	footnote	blue text
<smallcaps>...</smallcaps>	small capitals	small capitals
<w>...</w>	orthographic word	black overline
<?>...</?>	uncertain transcription	blue underlined text
<unclear>...</unclear>	unclear word(s)	blue underline
<quote>...</quote>	quotation	black bold italic
<foreign>...</foreign>	foreign, non-naturalised word	blue italic
<@>...</@>	changed name or word to preserve anonymity	green text
<del>...</del>	text deleted by the author (in handwritten texts)	diagonal black line through text
<->...</->	text deleted by the annotator	horizontal red line through text
<+>...</+>	text added by the annotator	red arrow and red box
<=>...</=>	self-correction by speaker	red arrow and black box
<{*n*>...</{*n*> and <[*n*>...</[*n*> (*n* is an optional number code)	overlapping string set and overlapping string	variously coloured background
<I>...</I>	subtext boundary	optional red (subtext) or black (text) divider
<&>...</&>	editorial comment	not shown in default view
<O>...</O>	untranscribed material, *e.g.*, graphs, photos, coughs	not shown in default view
<X>...</X>	extra-corpus text	not shown in default view
<$A>, <$B>, *etc.*	speaker identification	optionally shown in the left margin
<sent>	sentence marker	not shown in default view
<#1:2:A>, *etc.*	text unit number	shown in the left margin

APPENDIX 5.
A QUICK REFERENCE GUIDE TO THE ICE GRAMMAR

Function, category, and word class labels are listed in upper case, and are described in Section 2.2. Feature labels are in lower case, and are described in Section 2.3.

Label	Description
A	Adverbial
add	additive (adverb)
ADJ	Adjective
ADV	Adverb
AJHD	Adjective Phrase Head
AJP	Adjective Phrase
AJPO	Adjective Phrase Postmodifier
AJPR	Adjective Phrase Premodifier
antit	anticipatory *it*
appos	appositive
ART	Article
ass	assertive (pronoun)
attrd	deferred attributive (adjective)
attribute	attribute
attru	attributive
AUX	Auxiliary
AVB	Auxiliary verb
AVHD	Adverb Phrase Head
AVP	Adverb Phrase
AVPO	Adverb Phrase Postmodifier
AVPR	Adverb Phrase Premodifier
card	cardinal (numeral)
cbrack	closing bracket
CF	Focus Complement
CJ	Conjoin
CL	Clause
cleft	cleft construction
CLEFTIT	Cleft *it*
CLOP	Cleft Operator
CO	Object Complement
col	colon

Label	Description
com	common (noun)
comma	comma
comment	comment
comp	comparative (adjective, adverb)
conjoin	conjoin
CONJUNC	Conjunction
CONNEC	Connective
COOR	Coordinator
coord	coordinating (conjunction)
coordn	coordination
cop	copular
cquo	closing quotation mark
CS	Subject Complement
CT	Transitive Complement
cxtr	complex transitive
dash	dash
def	definite (article)
DEFUNC	Detached Function
dem	demonstrative (pronoun)
depend	dependent (clause)
dimontr	dimonotransitive
DISMK	Discourse Marker
DISP	Disparate
ditr	ditransitive
do	auxiliary *do*
DT	Determiner
DTCE	Central Determiner
DTP	Determiner Phrase
DTPE	Predeterminer
DTPO	Determiner Postmodifier

Label	Description
DTPR	Determiner Premodifier
DTPS	Postdeterminer
edp	*-ed* participle
ELE	Element (of a Nonclause)
ellip	ellipsis mark (punctuation)
ellipt	ellipted
EMPTY	Empty
encl	enclitic
excl	exclusive (adverb)
exclam	exclamative
exist	existential (clause)
exm	exclamation mark
EXOP	Existential Operator
EXTHERE	Existential *there*
extod	extraposed direct object
extsu	extraposed subject
FNPPO	Floating Noun Phrase Postmodifier
FOC	Focus
for	particle *for*
frac	fraction (numeral)
FRM	Formulaic Expression
ge	general (adjective, adverb)
GENF	Genitive Function
GENM	Genitive Marker
genv	genitive
hyph	hyphenated (numeral)
imp	imperative
IMPOP	Imperative Operator
incomp	incomplete
indef	indefinite (article)
INDET	Indeterminate
indrel	independent relative (clause)
infin	infinitive
ingp	*-ing* participle
inten	intensifier (adverb)
inter	interrogative
INTERJEC	Interjection
INTOP	Interrogative Operator
intr	intransitive

Label	Description
inv	inverted
INVOP	Inverted Operator
laugh	laughter
let	*let* auxiliary
long	long pause
main	main (clause)
modal	modal auxiliary
montr	monotransitive
mult	multiplier (numeral)
MVB	Main Verb
N	Noun
NADJ	Nominal Adjective
neg	negative (pronoun)
nom	nominal relative (pronoun)
nonass	nonassertive (pronoun)
NONCL	Nonclause
NOOD	Notional Direct Object
NOSU	Notional Subject
NP	Noun Phrase
NPHD	Noun Phrase Head
NPPO	Noun Phrase Postmodifier
NPPR	Noun Phrase Premodifier
NUM	Numeral
obrack	opening bracket
OD	Direct Object
OI	Indirect Object
one	pronoun *one*
OP	Operator
-op	without operator
oquo	opening quotation mark
ord	ordinal (numeral)
other	other punctuation
P	Prepositional (function)
PARA	Parataxis
partic	particularizer (adverb)
pass	passive
past	past (tense)
PAUSE	Pause
PC	Prepositional Complement
per	period (full stop)

Label	Description
perf	perfective auxiliary
pers	personal (pronoun)
phras	phrasal (adverb, preposition)
plu	plural
PMOD	Prepositional Modifier
poss	possessive (pronoun)
PP	Prepositional Phrase
prd	predicative
preco	preposed object complement
precs	preposed subject complement
PREDEL	Predicate Element
PREDGP	Predicate Group
preod	preposed direct object
preoi	preposed indirect object
PREP	Preposition
prepc	preposed prepositional complement
pres	present (tense)
presu	preposed subject
procl	proclitic
PROD	Provisional Direct Object
PROFM	Proform
prog	progressive (auxiliary)
PRON	Pronoun
prop	proper (noun)
PRSU	Provisional Subject
PRTCL	Particle
PS	Stranded Preposition
PU	Parsing Unit
PUNC	Punctuation
pushdn	pushdown
qm	question mark
quant	quantifier (pronoun)
REACT	Reaction Signal
recip	reciprocal (pronoun)
red	reduced (clause)
ref	reflexive (pronoun)
reference	reference
rel	relative (adverb, clause, pronoun)
SBHD	Subordinator Phrase Head

Label	Description
SBMO	Subordinator Phrase Modifier
scol	semi-colon
semi	semi-auxiliary
semip	semi-auxiliary + participle
short	short (pause)
sing	singular
so	proform *so*
SU	Subject
-su	without subject
sub	subordinate (clause)
SUB	Subordinator
subjun	subjunctive
subord	subordinating (conjunction)
SUBP	Subordinator Phrase
sup	superlative (adjective)
TAGQ	Tag Question
TO	Particle *to*
to	particle *to*
trans	transitive
univ	universal (pronoun)
UNTAG	Unassignable Tag
V	Verb
-v	without verb
VB	Verbal (function)
voc	vocative
vocal	vocalising
VP	Verb Phrase
wh-	*wh-* (adverb)
with	particle *with*
zrel	zero relative (clause)
zsub	zero subordinate (clause)
?	Untranscribable

APPENDIX 6.
SPECIAL CHARACTERS USED IN ICE-GB

Accented characters, may be replaced by "&Accent;" in search.†

Agrave	À	à	Icircumflex	Î	î
Aacute	Á	á	Ograve	Ò	ò
Acircumflex	Â	â	Oacute	Ó	ó
Aumlaut	Ä	ä	Ocircumflex	Ô	ô
Angstrom	Å	å	Oumlaut	Ö	ö
AEligature	Æ	æ	OEligature	Œ	œ
Ccedille	Ç	ç	Ugrave	Ù	ù
Egrave	È	è	Uacute	Ú	ú
Eacute	É	é	Ucircumflex	Û	û
Eumlaut	Ë	ë	Uumlaut	Ü	ü
Ecircumflex	Ê	ê	Yacute	Ý	ý
Igrave	Ì	ì	Yumlaut	Ÿ	ÿ
Iacute	Í	í	Ntilde	Ñ	ñ
Iumlaut	Ï	ï			

Greek characters, may be replaced by "&Greek;" in search.†

Alpha	A	α	Nu	N	ν
Beta	B	β	Omicron	O	ο
Chi	X	χ	Pi	Π	π
Delta	Δ	δ	Theta	Θ	θ
Epsilon	E	ε	Rho	P	ρ
Phi	Φ	φ	Sigma	Σ	σ
Gamma	Γ	γ	Tau	T	τ
Eta	H	η	Upsilon	Y	υ
Iota	I	ι	Omega	Ω	ω
Kappa	K	κ	Xi	Ξ	ξ
Lambda	Λ	λ	Psi	Ψ	ψ
Mu	M	μ	Zeta	Z	ζ

Miscellaneous symbols, may be replaced by "&symbol;" or label (last column).

double-arrow	↔	*arrow*	copyright	©	*corporate*
left-arrow	←	*arrow*	registered	®	*corporate*
up-arrow	↑	*arrow*	trade-mark	™	*corporate*
right-arrow	→	*arrow*	dagger	†	*mark*
down-arrow	↓	*arrow*	double-dagger	‡	*mark*
ampersand	&	*punctuation*	quarter	¼	*fraction*
left-cbrack	{	*punctuation, bracket*	half	½	*fraction*
right-cbrack	}	*punctuation, bracket*	three-quarters	¾	*fraction*
lsquo	'	*punctuation, quote*	curved-dash	~	*dash*
rsquo	'	*punctuation, quote*	long-dash	–	*dash*
ldquo	"	*punctuation, quote*	very-long-dash	—	*dash*
rdquo	"	*punctuation, quote*	dot	•	*mark*
degree	°	*maths*	square	□	*mark*
semi	;	*punctuation*	black-square	■	*mark*
caret	¦	*mark*	star	★	*mark*
pound-sign	£	*money*	arrowhead	➢	*mark*
yen-sign	¥	*money*	obelisk	◊	*mark*
smaller-than	‹	*maths*	female	♀	
larger-than	›	*maths*	male	♂	
much-smaller-than	«	*maths*	bullet	●	*mark*
much-larger-than	»	*maths*	dotted-line	·····	*dash*
plus-or-minus	±	*maths*	because	∵	
approximate-sign	≈	*maths*			

† For the first two tables, the case (capitalisation) is specified by the initial letter, *e.g.*, δ = 'δ'. When searching the corpus, the case sensitivity option will affect how they are matched. In ICECUP 3.1, the use of predefined group labels, such as '&greek;', is superseded by the more flexible 'user set' facility, although group labels may still be used for backward compatibility. See also Section 7.5.

INDEX

In the series VARIETIES OF ENGLISH AROUND THE WORLD (VEAW) the following titles have been published thus far:

G1. LANHAM, L.W. & C.A. MacDONALD: *The Standard in South African English and its Social History.* Heidelberg (Groos), 1979.

G2. DAY, R.R (ed.): *Issues in English Creoles: Papers from the 1975 Hawaii Conference.* Heidelberg (Groos), 1980.

G3. VIERECK, Wolfgang, Edgar SCHNEIDER & Manfred GÖRLACH (comps): *A Bibliography of Writings on Varieties of English, 1965-1983.* 1984.

G4. VIERECK, Wolfgang (ed.): *Focus on: England and Wales.* 1984.

G5. GÖRLACH, Manfred (ed.): *Focus on: Scotland.* 1985.

G6. PETYT, K.M.: *'Dialect' and 'Accent' in Industrial West Yorkshire.* 1985.

G7. PENFIELD, Joyce & Jack ORNSTEIN-GALICIA: *Chicano English.* 1985.

G8. GÖRLACH, Manfred and John A. HOLM (eds): *Focus on the Caribbean.* 1986.

G9. GÖRLACH, Manfred: *Englishes. Studies in varieties of English 1984-1988.* 1991.

G10. FISCHER, Andreas and Daniel AMMAN: *An Index to Dialect Maps of Great Britain.* 1991.

G11. CLARKE, Sandra (ed.): *Focus on Canada.* 1993.

G12. GLAUSER, Beat, Edgar W. SCHNEIDER and Manfred GÖRLACH: *A New Bibliography of Writings on Varieties of English, 1984-1992/93.* 1993.

G13. GÖRLACH, Manfred: *More Englishes: New studies in varieties of English 1988-1994.* 1995.

G14. McCLURE, J. Derrick: *Scots and its Literature.* 1995.

G15. DE KLERK, Vivian (ed.): *Focus on South Africa.* 1996.

G16. SCHNEIDER, Edgar W. (ed.): *Focus on the USA.* 1996.

G17. PETER PATRICK: *Linguistic Variation in Urban Jamaican Creole. A sociolinguistic study of Kingston, Jamaica.* 1999.

G18. SCHNEIDER, Edgar W. (ed.): *Englishes around the World, Volume 1. General studies, British Isles, North America. Studies in honour of Manfred Görlach.* 1997.

G19. SCHNEIDER, Edgar W. (ed.): *Englishes around the World, Volume 2. Carribbean, Africa, Asia, Australasia. Studies in honour of Manfred Görlach.* 1997.

G20. MACAULAY, Ronald K.S.: *Standards and Variation in Urban Speech: Examples from Lowland Scots.* 1997.

G21. KALLEN, Jeffrey L. (ed.): *Focus on Ireland.* 1997.

G22. GÖRLACH, Manfred: *Even More Englishes.* 1998.

G23. HUNDT, Marianne: *New Zealand English Grammar - Fact or Fiction? A corpus-based study in morphosyntactic variation.* 1998.

G24. HUBER, Magnus: *Ghanaian Pidgin English in its West African Context. A sociohistorical and structural analysis.* 1999.

G25. BELL, Allan and Koenraad KUIPER (eds.): *New Zealand English.* 2000.

G26. BLAIR, David and Peter COLLINS (eds.): *English in Australia.* 2001.

G27. LANEHART, Sonja L. (ed.): *Sociocultural and Historical Contexts of African American English.* 2001.

G28. GÖRLACH, Manfred: *Still More Englishes.* 2002.

G29. NELSON, Gerald, Sean WALLIS and Bas AARTS: *Exploring Natural Language. Working with the British Component of the International Corpus of English.* 2002.

T1. TODD, Loreto: *Cameroon.* Heidelberg (Groos), 1982. Spoken examples on tape (ca. 56 min.)
T2. HOLM, John: *Central American English.* Heidelberg (Groos), 1982. Spoken examples on tape (ca. 92 min.)
T3. MACAFEE, Caroline: *Glasgow.* 1983. Spoken examples on tape (ca. 60 min.)
T4. PLATT, John, Heidi WEBER & Mian Lian HO: *Singapore and Malaysia.* 1983.
T5. WAKELIN, Martyn F.: *The Southwest of England.* 1986. Spoken examples on tape (ca. 60 min.)
T6. WINER, Lise: *Trinidad and Tobago.* 1993. Spoken examples on tape.
T7. MEHROTRA, Raja Ram: *Indian English. Texts and Interpretation.* 1998.
T8. MCCLURE, J. Derrick: *Doric. The dialect of North-East Scotland.* n.y.p.